MODERN FICTION

A Study of Values

MODERN FICTION

A Study of Values

BY

HERBERT J. MULLER, Ph.D.

ASSISTANT PROFESSOR OF ENGLISH
IN PURDUE UNIVERSITY

This enlightenment it is now ours to carry on, undisturbed by the fact that there has been "a great revolution" and then "a great reaction" against it; yes, that both still exist, being as they are but little waves compared with the real and great flood on which we float and wish to float.

NIETZSCHE

FUNK & WAGNALLS COMPANY
NEW YORK AND LONDON

[Printed in the United States of America]
First published—October, 1937

TO

BESS C. MULLER

WHOSE BELIEF IN THIS WORK WAS
A CONSTANT SOURCE OF ENCOURAGEMENT

ACKNOWLEDGMENT

"One does not expect novel cards when playing so traditional a game," I. A. Richards says of criticism; "it is the hand which matters." I could not hope to acknowledge all the sources of my hand, partly because they are so numerous, partly because I am no doubt unconscious of some of them. In my text I have tried, however, to give credit wherever it was due; and I wish here to acknowledge especial indebtedness to Richards' own *Principles of Literary Criticism,* to Kenneth Burke's *Permanence and Change,* to Edmund Wilson's *Axel's Castle,* and to Professor Joseph Warren Beach's *The Twentieth Century Novel.* These men have not only given me many specific ideas, but helped to shape my whole intention.

Finally, I wish to acknowledge the courtesy of the editors of the *Saturday Review of Literature* and the *South Atlantic Quarterly,* in whose pages some of the material in this book has appeared.

CONTENTS

FOREWORD

The stream of prose fiction is today almost as broad as the stream of life itself; and sometimes it seems even muddier. A really comprehensive study of this fiction would fill a five-foot shelf. To cut my work down to a handier size, I have accordingly in the first place given little attention to matters of technique, making only a passing bow to writers like Henry James who have brewed genteel little tempests in exquisite teapots. These matters can never, of course, be entirely ignored; it is the baldest truism that substance and method or form are vitally related and in the greatest works of art inseparable. Yet technique remains a means to an end, and unless it is dictated by this end it becomes simply trickery. At any rate the most sophisticated like the simplest reader instinctively seeks in the novel, not primarily a lovely form or a rare essence, but some solid comment upon life, implicit in a representation or explicit in an edifying message. Hence my concern is the familiar one: the novelist's vision of life, the spirit animating both the selection and the shaping of his materials.

More particularly, however, I am concerned with the relation of modern fiction to the fundamental problem that underlies all the immediate issues of this age and gives it its peculiar form and pressure. This problem is the widespread, often feverish pursuit of meanings and values, motivated by the need to reorganize and harmonize men's responses to the flood of undigested knowledge and to the radically altered conditions of life—the need to adjust men's consciousness to the world at once unimaginably old and disconcertingly new in which they find themselves. It is in short the search for salvation that has been carried on in all ages, but never amid more profound uncertainty and confusion and vexation of spirit than in this one. Even the most carefree of the great entertainers who once romped through the green pastures of the novel—Fielding, Scott, Dickens—were indeed much more than entertainers: all offered a more or less serious "criticism of life." But there is no mistaking the solemnity, the often oppressive self-consciousness, with which many of the moderns go about this business of criticism. What many readers look for in their novels is not an aspect of reality but a mode of conduct, not a vision of life but a way of living. The whole contemporary significance of D. H. Lawrence, Proust, Gide, Mann, Hemingway, and more recently the proletarian writers can be understood only in this light: that they have suggested a means of salvation or at least a route to refuge.

As so often we hear, we are living from hand to mouth in a devaluated world. We have thrown overboard the old faiths and have yet to replace them. We are children of chaos, our spiritual home a crazy shack with wolves breeding at the door. We are everywhere assailed by flux and doubt; we are nowhere at rest. It is an all too familiar tune, sung with many melancholy variations, often keyed to a hysterically high pitch. Yet on these notes I have perforce begun, for they sound the essential problem that confronts the serious artist today. What I have tried to do is clearly to define this problem, then to examine its more significant signs in the work of representative novelists, and finally to appraise the contributions of these novelists. Although I have not judged their work merely on its usefulness as a program, I have studied them in relation to this central dilemma, in the conviction that literature plays an important part in all processes of orientation.

In this view I can give some modest appearance of logic and design to a work admittedly not exhaustive. First, it is not purely arbitrary to label "modern" the fiction of, roughly, the last sixty years. These years have been marked conspicuously by ferment and decay, by departure from venerable traditions in all spheres of activity, by the rapid growth of the "modern spirit" that is cried up and down from every rostrum throughout the land. No other period, I believe, has talked so insistently, so self-consciously, so often neurotically of things "modern"; and upon this, at least, all the prophets of its literature are agreed: it represents a new era. Hence the novelists I have singled out for special attention are those who are in my view the most representative of a changing order, not necessarily the most likely to endure. I have not treated all the distinguished work of this period—I could not pretend to have read it; all I have attempted to cover adequately is the more significant developments, the possible portents.

Work that has remained close to old traditions I have indeed solidly represented, if only to oppose the arrogance of the more extravagant modernists who talk as if old ways of writing had lost their magic and were impossible to enlightened novelists today. The most profoundly exciting and brilliantly successful innovations have not destroyed the validity of *Vanity Fair,* or in recent times of *The Forsyte Saga,* and I see no reason to suppose that men will not indefinitely repeat such performances. Yet simply because the merits of such work are so solid and so obvious, they call for less discussion. One may rightly have raptures over *Growth of the Soil, My Antonia, Kristin Lavransdatter;* none presents a real problem to the critic of the modern novel. Similarly I have not given Russian fiction the attention that its sheer greatness would deserve, for it was an indigenous growth that flourished independently and defies classification in either time or kind. *War and Peace* is perhaps the greatest novel ever written, but it has awed rather than influenced other novelists; *The Brothers Karamazov* is an overwhelming experience, but when the reader collects himself to analyze it, he finds that the methods and insights which undoubtedly have influenced subsequent novelists are in Dostoyevsky subordinated to a simple religious and peculiarly Russian view of life. In short, I have concentrated on the writers who have been the focus of controversy—those who consciously or unconsciously have adjusted their art to a changing order, faced in new directions, suggested new patterns of experience, or, generally, become in any important sense prophets or pioneers.

In my analysis of the work of these writers I have attempted, naturally, to be precise and never merely emotional or lyrical. The whole vocabulary of criticism has in recent years been reinterpreted by psychology. Emotion, pleasure, memory, imagination, attitude, meaning—these and many other ancient counters have been rubbed off and given a new "meaning," more exact no doubt, ultimately more useful, but still strange and difficult. The critic walks uneasily abroad, fearful that at any moment his shiniest coin may be declared counterfeit by the professional psychologist, and that though he fondly regards himself as a merciless analyst, he may be displayed as a mere evangelist. I. A. Richards in particular has made him nervous in his use of Ideal, Profound, Ultimate, Essential, Eternal, and other sonorous adjectives appropriate to the state induced by great art—a state of so intense satisfaction that we feel that we are seeing into the heart of things, confronting absolute Truth. Plainly, we are confronting no such thing; the important references of literature are never verifiable or exact. Nevertheless I have not refrained from the use of the traditional symbols. The novel is typically a representation of human experience, whether literal or ideal, and therefore inevitably a comment upon life. It contributes to our understanding of our fellow men, it influences our dealings with reality; that we cannot measure or prove its effects is simply a comment upon the state of knowledge, and no reason for giving up the effort to communicate them. Culture, for example, is an actuality, a definite value, that is nevertheless impossible of full and exact definition. Hence I should assert only that I am aware of these important linguistic distinctions, that I have kept an eye on the point where language ceases to be referential and becomes primarily emotive, and that I have tried not to substitute fine noises for ideas but to give as cool, precise meaning as possible to the cloudy symbols it is almost impossible not to use.

Finally, I have tried also to maintain a becoming humility. The student of a past age can afford to be oracular. With relative ease he can chart his literature and boldly mark out its direction, for he knows its destination: the eighteenth century goes straight to the nineteenth. Now, we are no doubt going somewhere too, and apparently at a furious pace, but nobody knows where. The critic of modern fiction cannot work along straight lines and refer to fixed points. He cannot be sure which of the swirling currents about him is leading to the future. And he has always to make the effort, however futile, to escape the "climate of opinion" in which he lives—the insidious influence of current attitudes that made so great a critic as Lessing speak highly of what now seems so ludicrous a performance as Lillo's *The London Merchant,* and that constantly makes the sublime and self-evident truth of one age appear grotesque error to the next. In appreciating the real value to his own age of some contemporary work, the critic is prone to see immortal essences and eternal truths when there is only a satisfying adjustment to current needs. If he is to be more than a reporter, he must finally commit himself and judge; but he can yield more safely to the seductiveness of the downright statement if he carries with him his historical sense.

Although the categorical attitude and the sensational statement are popular in this age of uncertainty, this vogue is itself, paradoxically, symptomatic of the disintegration, the breakdown of normal lines of communication, that constitutes its central problem. In a welter of contradictory principles it is natural to seize upon some one as a rock to stand on, and then simply as a matter of self-preservation to defend it against all comers; in a universal uproar one naturally shouts, not only to be heard, but to drown out one's own doubts and misgivings. He who brandishes some half-truth can not merely write a vigorous and striking book (like Max Eastman's *The Literary Mind* or John Strachey's *The Coming Struggle for Power*) and incidentally have the pleasure of whacking the champions of other half-truths; he can set certain valuable ideas in a clearer light. Yet it seems to me more desirable, even at the risk of appearing flabby and joining the depressing company of on-the-other-hand thinkers, to make an effort to maintain a large and catholic view, to weigh conscientiously the various programs and reconcile what is valuable in them, to recognize that in the end one's preferences are more or less arbitrary and one's final explanations metaphorical. This is perhaps a bad disposition in the world of practical affairs, where one has to contend with monstrous realities, like Fascism, that cannot be dispelled by the loftiest thinking. But in the world of literary criticism I see no Cause that needs dying for right now.

H. J. M.

Part One

THE PROBLEM: ANATOMY

I

INTRODUCTION TO THE MODERN SPIRIT

I

THE most fashionable literary issue of the moment is the Marxist approach. Even as oversimplified by the noisier partizans, this is an important issue; in a broader and calmer view it takes one back to first principles of criticism, for it involves not merely the artist's attitude toward capitalism, his classification as proletarian sheep or bourgeois goat, but the whole problem of his relation and his responsibility to his society. Yet a comprehensive study of modern literature must set out from a different port and at once steer into still deeper, more troubled waters. The economic structure of our civilization does not adequately explain the work of Thomas Hardy, Joseph Conrad, D. H. Lawrence, James Joyce, Thomas Mann, or many even of the younger novelists who anticipate its collapse. Underlying their work is a problem of which the economic turmoil is but one facet—a problem that has been raised by forces operating long before the "class struggle" became acute, and that will remain to be faced in either a capitalistic hell or a proletarian paradise. This problem is in its largest aspect the decay of faith and the confusion of tongues: the loss of certitude in the high matters of religion and ethics, the widespread disagreement about first principles in life as in literature, the need for transvaluation in all spheres of thought. It is the problem of how to live and what to live for once a livelihood has been assured.

One must begin, in short, with the large and troublesome matter of the "modern spirit." On all sides one hears that never was an age more harassed and perplexed, more restless and queasy, than ours. On all sides one is met by a feverish quest of salvation—

salvation, curiously enough, of a soul of whose existence we profess to be skeptical. We are, it appears, a rootless generation. We have torn down the old signposts and now wander in a trackless waste. We remain ethical animals, but we can find no authority and no adequate symbols for such values as we wish to cling to. And so we become distrustful of our aims, wearied of our efforts, sickened of our rewards. Those simple souls who continue to live contentedly by the old faiths have to their unhappy fellows the ludicrous appearance, in Havelock Ellis's phrase, of being suspended from hooks that no longer exist.

There are, to be sure, voices crying in the wilderness—an embarrassing multitude of them. One can still hear a rather shrill insistence that God is in His heaven, can still be offered a share in a happy conviction of Progress. The more authoritative prophets, however, are generally less helpful. Thus Professor A. N. Whitehead and other distinguished scientists have fashioned a God for themselves out of mathematical symbols and formulas; but He is a special, very abstract God, useful only in the higher realms of scientific speculation. Scarcely less difficult of worship, if less unintelligible, is the shadowy deity of the Rev. Harry Emerson Fosdick and other liberal clergymen; moreover, they are far more cogent when arguing the desirability of belief than when demonstrating its logical necessity. Such a demonstration T. S. Eliot indeed appears to consider vulgar, for he contents himself with merely repeating that humanism is inadequate without religion; and although he is most supercilious toward these modernistic deities, he is almost as supercilious toward his own God—and certainly extravagantly cool in his regard of the folly and evil of a world trying the experiment of getting along without Him. "The experiment will fail," he assures us; "but we must be very patient in awaiting its collapse."

Impatient, however, continue most of our spiritual doctors, notably Walter Lippmann in *A Preface to Morals* and Irwin Edman in *The Contemporary and His Soul*. Yet, although both brilliantly diagnose the contemporary malady, they fail equally in effecting a cure. Lippmann proposes a synthetic and curiously unsatisfying faith of disinterestedness, and then ends on a high lyrical note that the ordinary reader finds difficult to sustain; Edman's therapeutic program is so vague and half-hearted as to warrant the modesty with which he offers it. In *The Modern Temper,* on the other hand, Joseph Wood Krutch simply throws up his hands; he concludes by offering us only the chill comfort that although ours is a lost cause in this universe, we are yet not sorry to be human, and "should rather die as men than live as animals." But perhaps most sobering is the confession of despair in the closing lines of *Too True to Be Good,* one of the late plays of Bernard Shaw. If this hitherto so breezy physician surrenders the case, it would seem that there is nothing to do but put our ears to the ground and listen for the crack of doom.

In the last few years there have indeed been less worried speculation over and less tinkering with the modern soul, but chiefly because of the pressure of more tangible fears and woes. The depression came upon us; Hitler stepped out of a comic opera and became an ominous reality; and we now gaze at the spectacle of nations busily preparing for a war that may destroy our civilization. In the face of such immediate dangers, fret over one's soul becomes a luxury to be indulged only in boom times. Yet these new specters are only the latest shapes of the same underlying confusion and uncertainty. The restless seeker of faith becomes the uneasy liberal oppressed by a feeling of futility.

Now, much nonsense is written about the "modern spirit"—as it has been in every age. Man thinks too readily that his situation is altogether unlike that of his ancestors, and that his predicaments like his achievements are altogether novel and peculiar. Yet there is no blinking the very real problem that confronts the enlightened contemporary, the very difficult if not unprecedented adjustment that his enlightenment has made necessary. Within the last century there has occurred in man's conception of himself and the universe the most radical change in the history of civilization. The foundations of the thought of ages have crumbled.

The nature and genesis of this revolution in thought have been so thoroughly discussed that I need not labor the point. The hero

—or the villain—of the piece is plainly science, with its fantastic accumulation of -ologies and -onomies:

> Greek endings with the little passing bell
> That signifies some faith's about to die.

Science is today not merely a department of knowledge; it orders the whole pattern of our thought. The man on the street regards it with the simple awe with which the savage regards magic—the wonders it works are even plainer to the naked eye. The intellectual accepts its premises so utterly that any criticism of these premises he at once brands as "unscientific" and therefore necessarily unsound. Yet its rationale is often antagonistic to our deepest sentiments, to the symbols of our oldest experience. Most obviously, science has introduced new knowledge that has undermined certain faiths, corroded the feeling of the transcendent significance of human destiny. More significantly, it has introduced new modes of thought and new conditions of living, weakening the habit of faith and breaking up the settled ways of life in which faith can most easily take root. It has shaken and confused *mores* that only a few decades ago the daring William Graham Sumner considered impervious to any but the most gradual and unconscious change. It has disrupted the whole system of natural pieties that gave the lives of our ancestors dignity, coherence, and purpose.

The necessity of wholesale readjustment is indeed nothing new in human history. It is impertinent or naïve to accept new meanings as invincible, new attitudes as permanent; men have a way of upsetting the most self-evident truths of their predecessors, and they have also a way of twisting the most stubborn fact to suit their needs. Their most astounding discoveries or illusions have not altered their basic physiological and psychological processes. Yet the terms of their present problem are more drastic than ever before. Men are scrapping hitherto unquestioned first principles, the rationalizations of human desire at the heart of all the great religions and philosophies. In the past, moreover, it was relatively easy to correct or overthrow a system of ideas grown inadequate or uncongenial; all these systems were largely speculative and had no indisputable sanction. But the system set up by science cannot so readily be manipulated, for it is supported by a large body of incontrovertible fact as well as by a series of triumphs more dazzling than those provided by any other wonder-working scheme of thought. One may distrust the rationale of science; one cannot play fast and loose with it.

2

In a world where everything is questioned and nothing agreed upon, the position of the artist is clearly a difficult one. It might seem that his subject matter, reality, is still all about him; but as Jacob Wassermann remarked, "Reality in the artist's sense is always something created, it does not exist *a priori.*" More important, the essential scheme of his reality was in the past ordinarily created for him. To demand of the artist that he do his own thinking is not good; the more of it he undertakes, the more of his potential force he is likely to dissipate. However unflattering this assumption, and however unfair to those, like Goethe, who were capable of powerful, sustained, and original thought, the fact is that the premises of almost all the great imaginative creations of the past were ready-made. Artists might build upon a specific philosophical system, such as St. Thomas Aquinas provided for Dante and Bolingbroke for Pope; more frequently—and happily—they simply drew, like the Pericleans and the Elizabethans, from the current of accepted ideas about them, building perhaps unconsciously upon a world view shaped by perhaps forgotten thinkers. In either event their genius is revealed in the eloquence of their expression, the grandeur of the imaginative worlds they erected on whatever first principles, not in the originality or even the clarity or "truth" of these principles; and their imaginations worked more powerfully because unhampered by the need of first working out these principles for themselves.

This at least is clear: in the past his society supplied the artist with both values and symbols that passed current everywhere. There was by no means, of course, a complete agreement or a perfect community of effort. Schools flourished and passed away; reputations rose and fell. The eighteenth-century classicists deposed the "barbarous" Elizabethans and were in turn overthrown by the early nineteenth-century romantics. Yet both movements represented a return to some tradition. All fashions were rooted in well-established first principles, and clustered about a more or less continuous line of development. Choices were relatively limited, differences of opinion concerned means rather than ends. The eighteenth-century dramatist could make Shakespeare acceptable simply by lopping off a few barbarisms; Dryden started to modernize *Paradise Lost* simply by rewriting it in heroic couplets. In short, the artist selected, rearranged, modified, innovated, but he could do this the more comfortably and effectively because he worked within an accepted framework and was relatively untroubled by questions of ultimate meaning or value. If he had not squarely behind him the authority of a long and honorable tradition, at least his references were clear and his point of departure fixed; and if the great artist was often in advance of his age, he was also in the line of it and leading it where it was going. Only an occasional genius, like William Blake, stood outside and produced an isolated achievement.

Today, however, the responsible artist stands alone in a shifting world with the winds of a hundred doctrines howling about him. There is no firmly established school to nurture him. There are only dozens of inchoate "movements" whose principles, even if clearly articulated, are not deeply rooted or universally accepted; whose obsequies are often performed amid the echoes of their manifestoes. He has in a real sense been cut off from the past. Such traditions as survive are bound up with a civilization radically and irrevocably different from his own. It remains his primary business to find meanings and values, but he can refer to no fixed points and take nothing for granted. He cannot even assume the importance of what he is trying to do. Art itself may seem to him merely a childish compensation for "psychic frustrations."

The result of this chaos is in the first place a problem of style.

Formerly writers addressed a fundamentally homogeneous audience; all the different classes and trades were embraced in a compact, definable culture. In the literature of Periclean Greece, Elizabethan England, France under Louis Quatorze, we find, to be sure, many diversities reflecting individual idiosyncrasies, the contradictions within any society, the perpetual process of action and reaction—and always the presence of eccentrics and originals on the fringe. But we also find a solid core, a dominant tone, a characteristic manner. We continue to find this basic homogeneity in the eighteenth century, as indicated by the conventional labels: the Age of Pope, the Age of Johnson. Since 1800, however, ways of living have become steadily more variegated and incongruities within society steadily more pronounced. That nineteenth-century literature is still relatively susceptible of neat summary and category owes chiefly to the hold of tradition; the ferment was only beginning, artists had but a glimmering awareness of what was happening. In the twentieth century this ferment exploded in a burst of centrifugal activity. We face today an extraordinary diversity and individualization of occupation, interest, purpose, way of life—a diversity less between than within classes. The intellectual as well as the industrial world becomes daily more specialized; new points of view multiply as rapidly as mechanical gadgets; experts propagate like rabbits. "They Don't Speak Our Language" is a theme on which the cartoonist Webster plays endless variations; it is a drearily comic statement of one aspect of the profound dilemma of modern literature.

Consequently, as Kenneth Burke points out in *Permanence and Change,* the one really efficient language today is the jargon of science, which is wholly impersonal and merely conceptual—an endless naming and abstracting that never strives to be suggestive or pleasing. The one really universal language is the neutral language of the newspapers, geared to a low-powered recital of factual information. "Except for the yellow journals and the columnists, the prose has arrived at a common denominator of statement wherein the last traces of stylistic ingratiation are eliminated. . . . Effacement is total." These, obviously, are no mediums for literature. Accordingly we find artists everywhere seeking a new mode of communication, a new set of symbols. Hence the typographical stunts of e e cummings, the new language of James Joyce, the automatic writing of Gertrude Stein—the hundred striking and idiosyncratic styles in poetry, all the isms in painting and the dissonances in music. Hence the many efforts to symbolize the forms of an industrial civilization—the effort of Hart Crane, for instance, to make Brooklyn Bridge do the work once done by skylarks and daffodils and unappreciative mistresses. And hence the "obscurity" of modern poetry that distresses plain readers and professors alike. Inevitably these artists succeed in speaking only to a charmed circle, at times only to themselves. Those who use the language of the past are likely to seem archaic, irrelevant; those who invent a new one naturally seem esoteric and abstruse.

This problem of style, however, is only a reflection of the deeper problem of meanings. There is no generally accepted mode of communication for the simple reason that there are no generally accepted meanings to communicate. "In the profoundest human sense," Burke writes, "one communicates in a *weighted* vocabulary in which the weightings are shared by his group as a whole." The most casual, seemingly neutral conversation is a chain of implied judgments and emotive appeals. The difficulty of the serious writer today is that the group as a whole does not accept his judgments or respond to his appeals. There is no underlying agreement about standards of appraisal, no conventional pattern of response. Hence the significance of Thomas Mann, who concerns himself only incidentally with style as he returns to first principles and sets about painstakingly to reexamine and redefine the whole humanistic tradition.

Now, it is easy for austere or cloistered critics to reproach the artist for surrendering to the confusion about him. He may jump too eagerly on the nearest bandwagon, or into the nearest shell hole; he may be too shiftless to work out a solution, or too timid to announce one. But the literary aristocrats should remember the enormous demands they are making of him. To meet them he must have a breadth of vision that not all the great writers of the past had, and powers of thought greater than those of all but a few. He must have as well an integrity and independence, a sobriety and assurance, a clarity and firmness of purpose, for which his society provides no solid assumptions. His whole case has been admirably stated by Thomas Mann:

> Now, if the life about him, if his own time seem, however outwardly stimulating, to be at bottom empty of such food for his aspirations; if he privately recognizes it to be hopeless, viewless, helpless, opposing only a hollow silence to all the questions man puts, consciously or unconsciously, yet somehow puts, as to the final, absolute, and abstract meaning in all his efforts and activities; then, in such a case, a certain laming of the personality is bound to occur, the more inevitably the more upright the character in question. . . . In an age that affords no satisfying answer to the eternal question of "Why?" "To what end?" a man who is capable of achievement over and above the average and expected modicum must be equipped either with a moral remoteness and single-mindedness which is rare indeed and of heroic mould, or else with an exceptionally robust vitality.*

Far more surprising, then, than the flashiness or flabbiness of some of our talented writers is the hardiness of others, the readiness with which many have accepted the challenge; and far more lamentable is the likely fate of these ambitious souls. They exercise all too freely their limited powers of thought, their natural grace is hid beneath the heavy folds of the mantle of prophecy; and when they do not simply collapse under this heroic harness, the pall of self-consciousness settles on their work. Eugene O'Neill has provided perhaps the most fearful example of what happens when a good emotional poet sets out to be the intellectual leader or spiritual doctor of his age. Deliberately he has dug at the roots of the sickness of today—"the death of an old God and the failure of science and materialism to give any satisfying new one." "Anyone trying to do big work nowadays," he writes, "must have this big subject behind all the little subjects of his plays or novels, or

* Reprinted from *The Magic Mountain,* by permission of and special arrangement with Alfred A. Knopf, Inc., authorized publisher.

he is simply scribbling around the surface of things and has no more real status than a parlor entertainer." But the immediate result of this noble impatience with parlor tricks was *Dynamo,* a grotesque combination of balminess and brassiness, hollowness and hysteria; and even in his more successful plays his messianic zeal periodically lands him in mere bathos.

Where, one might ask, are the critics, to whom the mantle of prophecy is more becoming? The trouble is that too many are wearing it—and the mantle resembles the coat of many colors. None speaks with real authority, and all counsel differently. Every day brings a new and exciting point of view, but what one sees from it is likely to look strangely unlike what one has been seeing. Each shift of interest brings new classifications and alignments in which old friends bob up in queer company; each new slice cuts across all the other slices on the bias, if it touches them at all. In all this swirl and ferment of ideas there is as yet no clear direction or design, and in the ceaseless conflict and confusion the artist in his creative activity gets little clear guidance or firm support. There are, to be sure, intelligent critics: as scrupulously sympathetic as Henry Seidel Canby, as magisterial as Paul Elmer More, as fastidious as T. S. Eliot, as downright as the Marxists; but to call the roll is to muddy the Missouri. One often hears a plaintive call for a literary Mussolini: where are the Sainte-Beuves of yester-year? But it is scarcely surprising that we have today no really great critic, none whose pronouncements command universal attention and respect. When first principles are wholly uncertain, it is almost impossible to have such an arbiter.

Ultimately, then, the modern artist is thrown back upon his own resources. He has at once the privilege and the burden of almost complete freedom in choice of materials and methods. The result has been an immense and daring experimentation that makes this one of the most exciting of literary periods. "Literature," Ludwig Lewisohn announces with gusto, "is no longer an art of fixed forms or contents or appropriate imitation, but an endless, ever-changing scripture and revelation, the scripture and revelation of the life of man." Every day sees another refinement of the technique of communicating experience and intensifying consciousness. Every day another banner is raised, another company goes whooping into battle. New materials are unearthed, new devices tried out, and the old art forms are constantly wrenched into new shapes, freighted with new meanings, shanghaied under new flags. Literature is as fluid and intricate as life itself.

One result, of course, is a hundred shiny fads and cults: shifty subterfuges arising from the natural and laudable desire for solidarity. But after discounting the craze for mere novelty, the tendency toward mere freakishness, all this activity is up to a point most healthy and promising. Certainly it is preferable to complacence and stagnation, and preferable as well to the rigid conventionalism that set too narrow bounds to the genius of Euripides and Corneille and Pope—of the many artists who willingly or no accepted the outworn traditions or followed the formal fashions of their day. For the search for new forms is not the result of mere boredom, nor the energy that activates it merely feverish. It is the very necessary adjustment to new conceptions of reality, the very necessary effort to provide a scheme of orientation. One likes to think that we are sowing the seeds of a splendid new epoch; and one cannot think that all this bold and brilliant experiment will come to nothing. Meanwhile it is at least exhilarating.

Yet it is also confusing and distracting. It leaves in its wake perplexity, restlessness, fatigue. In this rich banquet one yearns at times for a little more plain and solid nourishment—and a more orderly bill of fare. In their endless subtleties and complexities modern writers are likely to lose sight of the timeless patterns of experience, the elemental realities at the center of all lives. Excitedly we adventure into unexplored realms with Lawrence and Joyce and Proust, but ultimately we are likely to find these excursions tiring and a little unsatisfying. With something of relief we return to jog with Fielding and Thackeray through familiar landscapes. Hence the popularity of so old-fashioned a romance as *Anthony Adverse,* of so oppressively wholesome a comedy as

The Good Companions, of such a piece of old lavender sentiment as *Good-bye, Mr. Chips.* Hence the piping voice of Alexander Woollcott now carries even further than the voice of William Lyon Phelps.

Often, moreover, our literature is merely strident and explosive, fragmentary and chaotic. No audacity of innovation or brilliance of technical achievement can conceal the hollowness of some of its products. In the absence of a strong tradition there is more temptation to exploit, more compulsion to vociferate; presently the striking in substance or style becomes an end in itself. Accordingly material is confused with meaning, technique with value, eccentricity with originality. The fascinating work of William Faulkner, for example, lacks a spiritual center. So does the still more fascinating work of James Joyce. In short, we are gloriously free, but as Nietzsche remarked, to be freed of a yoke means little unless one has an intelligible goal; and however compelling the various causes proposed, none enlists more than a minority of writers and readers. Undoubtedly modern literature is going somewhere, but it appears to be going everywhere at once, the more furiously as it becomes more uncertain of its destination. Meanwhile it distracts its followers by showers of gaudy, precocious, and pretentious trifles, like the stories of William Saroyan—trifles solemnly weighed by the O'Briens, enshrined in anthologies, gravely discussed as Portents.

Deliverance from convention inevitably creates more problems than it settles, clears the way for new grievances perhaps more distressing because less comfortably familiar. Thus some of our freed souls appear simply exasperated by the conditions of their freedom, and like D. H. Lawrence or Richard Aldington squander much of their energy in incessant protest, become creatures of obsession. Too many are not merely sensitive but neurotic, not merely troubled but jittery, not somber but morose; they fail to sublimate or symbolize their private aches. Yet even those who have made a more satisfactory adjustment to their age and found more positive meanings still suffer from the want of universally accepted symbols, of the discipline of established forms. Their work is apt to be strained, turgid, hectic; it recalls the extravagance of the Elizabethans, who also enjoyed the boon of freedom from tradition. The undeniable power of Robinson Jeffers and Eugene O'Neill, for instance, occasionally degenerates into mere violence; the symbols they choose are lurid and grotesque. Throughout modern literature one finds too much of intensity without warmth, of strength without assurance, of tumult without depth, at best of depth without breadth. Wholeness and heartiness have departed with the simplicities of the old faiths.

Hence other writers attempt to return to these faiths. T. S. Eliot's effort to exorcise the demons of modernity by pronouncing old formulas (classicist in literature, royalist in politics, Anglo-Catholic in religion) is most famous, but Yeats and Ezra Pound in poetry, Sigrid Undset and of late Willa Cather in the novel, the New Humanists in criticism, have also packed up their mental luggage and taken flight out of the waste land of their society into the past, into romantic legend or classic doctrine, into the arms of the church. *Escape* is a horrid word, and used far too freely as a stick. It is easy to stigmatize as evasion any denial of one's own brand of realism or truth; it is much less easy to define the artist's obligation to the present. All imaginative literature is in one sense an escape—an escape, let us say, from the temporal into the universal, from the particular into the ideal—and to turn one's back upon interests and ideals of which one disapproves is not only natural but sensible. The important question is simply escape *from* what and *into* what. Yet if in this view one cannot condemn out of hand Eliot's preference for the company of the ghosts of the past, nor sneer at all the other expatriates from the modern world, from Henry James down, one must still regard their attitude as more a symptom than a cure; and certainly one cannot regard it as a norm. As it commonly appears today, it is more wishful than vital, more self-hypnotic than procreative. It is a defeatist attitude that may afford a sanctuary for a few unworldly spirits, but it holds no promise for the future. At its most wistful and nostalgic it suggests a deficiency in vitality, and is of more medical than philosophical or literary interest.

No less symptomatic of the spiritual chaos of the modern world, however, is the tendency toward the exclusive cultivation of individuality, the retreat from social ideals or any collective ideology. In *Axel's Castle* Edmund Wilson brilliantly tied together a number of our strangest and greatest artists, and traced their common ancestry back to the Symbolists. Marcel Proust, James Joyce, Gertrude Stein, Paul Valéry, T. S. Eliot (as poet, not as critic)—these and others have like Mallarmé made it their whole studied business "to communicate unique personal feelings." Their way is that of shutting oneself up in a private, shuttered world of one's own, "cultivating one's private fantasies, encouraging one's private manias, ultimately preferring one's absurdest chimeras to the most astonishing realities, ultimately mistaking one's chimeras for reality." In their intense self-consciousness, their societal instinct has atrophied, until they suggest what in his study of the child's moral development Jean Piaget calls the "egocentric stage": the stage in which, when the youngster plays marbles with the other little boys, he has the illusion of following the rules but actually pays no attention to what they are doing, disposes of his marbles according to his own free fancy, and for all practical purposes plays by himself. Although the spiritual children of the Symbolists invent elaborate rules and obviously attempt to communicate experience, their game is not really communal. In varying degrees they virtually ignore the wants and doings of their fellows and are absorbed in their own make-believe.

"Poets talking to themselves," Max Eastman accordingly labels this assorted company. He goes on to explain their practice as a result of the march of science, which has driven literature entirely out of the realm of objective truth; to retain his traditional superiority, the aristocratic man of letters has therefore cultivated the idiosyncratic and finally the unintelligible, retreating to a domain where his authority cannot be challenged. This is a naïve exaggeration of both the achievements of science and the arrogance of literary men—who are commonly all too eager to make use of its tentative findings. Science is indeed largely responsible for Symbolism, but in ways less flattering to itself. It has created a heterogeneous society in which the trunk lines of communication have been cut across at a hundred points and finally become tangled in a maze. Its findings are still fragmentary, confusing, and do not adequately replace the meanings and values it has weakened or destroyed. Its triumphant march falters at the critical moment, it does not itself give satisfying answers to the final questions that men put. And so writers have turned inward to the only reality they can be sure of: their own consciousness. At any rate, the sterility that threatens them threatens also the practitioners of such "pure poetry" as Eastman insists is now the only proper province of art—the relatively frivolous business of vivifying pretty bits of experience. Great art has hitherto been a complete and whole-hearted response, and it has been measured by the richness and fullness of its interpretation of human experience. It has been an expression of the universal, the whole man. And though today everything has become immensely complicated and uncertain, the community of man is still not an ideal but a fact, if at times a depressing one.

3

This is of course a very sketchy picture of the modern literary world. One might point out various rashes on its surface: the weary sophisticates who cultivate the wry laugh or cry into their beer; the "hard-boiled school," the hundred little Hemingways who have caught only the externals of the master's manner and whose strength is so often the strength of cheese; and the faddists generally, who strike poses too numerous and too silly to mention. One might also point out other more serious symptoms. In many ways have promising talents been diverted into some form of futility or absurdity. But it is profitless to follow into the bogs and sands all the muddy streams that stem from the central dilemma. I have attempted only to state in general terms the nature of this dilemma and a few of its more important consequences. In such terms the statement applies, however, to the literature of almost the entire Western world. In a recent symposium, *Tendencies of the Modern Novel,* representatives of various nationalities summarized what was going on in their countries. D. S. Mirsky, speaking for Russia, gave an enthusiastic account of a compact school of writers creating a new and vital national literature, seemingly confident of their destination. All the other spokesmen drew the same familiar picture of uncertainty and confusion. All spoke of a "period of transition," most of them hopefully; but all left open the question of transition to what.

Yet if this is in some respects a depressing picture, it need not follow that the future of literature is a dreary waste. What salvation men may ultimately find is not my present concern—and only he who is very bold will prescribe or prophesy. Meanwhile the simple purposes of mere exposition demand a few splashes of brighter colors. If one can point to ugly, cankerous growths—as at what period could one not?—he can also point to healthy ones. At least part of the significance of the Communistic movement, for example, is that it has distracted many of the intellectuals from their private woes and provided them with a faith in something outside and larger than themselves, a hope for a better world than they now know, a vital subject matter. Dissatisfaction with the present is expressing itself more and more in a resolute striving for the future instead of a wistful hankering for the past. Generally there is for every *Waste Land* a *Chorus for Survival*. Moreover, most even of those of little faith take, one suspects, a less desperate view of their predicament than Krutch and some other students of the modern temper imagine. However grave the practical problems that confront it, the spiritual distresses of this generation suggest a colic rather than a cancer. They are more painful than necessarily fatal, and they have been aggravated by a post-war fever of disillusionment, a malady familiar enough in human history. History gives, indeed, sufficient warrant for viewing this period as a period of transition and not as a prelude to damnation, at worst as a purgatory and not as a hell.

In the realm of literature more specifically, one often hears that the Novel is moribund and Poetry dead and Tragedy dead. These lamentations are again, however, usually the sign of growing pains in a changing world, of minds left tender and exposed by the sloughing off of old beliefs before new ones have hardened into a comfortably tight shell. Men tend naturally to despair as they watch the crumbling of familiar forms, for they tend naturally to hypostatize these forms and mistake them for immortal essences. They tend to assume, for example, that the illusions of the past are inherently poetic, forgetting, as Burke has said, that they are poetic only because poets have built poetry on them. The forms of modern life may indeed be less plastic, and its disruptive forces may finally prove unmanageable; but there is as yet no logical necessity for assuming the worst and calling for sackcloth and ashes. One would suspect those who are conducting the last rites of the arts if only because they make so much clamor over the corpses. Their skepticism is too dogmatic, their despair too contentious. Meanwhile the corpses continue to show many signs of vigorous life.

Yet the grave problems remain. We cannot simply wave away the painful disharmonies of the modern world as mere spasms in the organic evolution of human history, for they are our spasms. We cannot view them loftily as mere illusions of a time order, for we are ourselves of this order and we live in time. At present we are still in the wilderness and groping in a dim light. The business of the remaining chapters will accordingly be to explore this wilderness and investigate the sources of this light, to retrace the steps that got us there and study the proposed ways of getting us out. This business I shall carry on primarily through the medium of prose fiction; yet if an acquaintance with the best that has been thought and said, an habitual association with the Sublime, has a somewhat less immediate bearing upon the exigencies of everyday practical life than students of letters like to think, this is by no means a merely academic approach. Despite the seeming inconsequence or irrelevance of many modern novels, "life" and literature were never more intimately connected than now.

II

PESSIMISM

I

TO the plain reader, any novel that does not end happily is a pessimistic novel. Hence modern fiction is notoriously pessimistic; serious writers are forever reminding the plain reader of the kind of thing that he thinks there is too much of in "real life" and that he wishes to escape in his reading. Yet as so often happens, despite the fuzziness of his thinking, he is right: the view of life reflected in most of the more important novels is pessimistic in the strict sense of the word. This is scarcely strange. Pessimism is the natural consequence and the most obvious sign of the widespread decay of faith. Simply because it raises such important issues, however, one must clear the air of a deal of sentimental or hysterical loose talk that befogs these issues. To listen to many who live in Heartbreak House, one would gather that they were its first tenants, and their gloom an altogether new development in human history. Shades of Ecclesiastes!

Actually, pessimism darkens literature from its beginnings. Some periods, like the eighteenth century, have been superficially given to a formal optimism—an optimism that reached its ultimate lunacy in the statements of Hartley, who declared that "all individuals are actually and always infinitely happy," and of Abraham Tucker, who worked with more scientific exactness and calculated that the sum of our suffering equals "a minute of pain once in every twenty-two years." Other periods, like the Victorian, have attempted to stifle the growing doubts of the perfection of their civilization by a morbid, precocious insistence on the wholesome moral and the happy ending. But the great poets of every age have almost uniformly taken a somber view of human life. Thomas Hardy himself never struck a note of more profound melancholy than that in the famous words of Sophocles: "Not to be born is, past all prizing, best; but, when a man hath seen the light, this is next by far, that with all speed he should go thither, whence he hath come."

Tragedy is a universal literary form simply because of the permanence of the inescapable tragic fact of human life: the eternal seeking and not finding, the eternal gap between aspiration and achievement. Those idealistic philosophers, like Hegel, who announce magisterially that destiny is always rationality, and that tragedy displays the eternal justice of the divine order, are arguing their own principles, not interpreting the actual practice of tragic poets. In the lofty and comfortable seclusion of their philosophical chambers they impose upon life a sublime reasonableness that the mere existence of tragedy refutes. Implicit in its existence is a recognition of an inexplicably harsh destiny. Although the poets do ultimately effect some kind of reconciliation with this destiny, there is even in the peace at the end of their works a residuum of the mysterious, the terrible, the seeming unjust.

As the modern pessimist is thus not a wholly new species on earth, similarly he seldom gives his views the logical and consistent application that might actually revolutionize human behavior. It is easy to exaggerate the influence of intellectual concepts in modern literature and life. Thomas Hardy lived with his gloomy notions to a ripe and apparently serene old age. Krutch announced that ours is a lost cause—and continued to be an assiduous critic of our letters. Their readers make the same discount of abstract theory. Some deal of absurdity clings to all pessimistic philosophers, however unquestionable their sincerity. Perhaps the only really genuine, consistent pessimists were the early Thracians, who, if we can believe Herodotus, greeted the new-born child with lamentations, pointing out the sufferings in store for him, and buried the dead with rejoicings and festivities.

Even in the purely intellectual realm, moreover, one hears curiously discordant notes. These same distracted moderns have given the world the idea of historical evolution, the ideal of Progress, and have been busiest fashioning Utopias. Early peoples put their Utopias behind them; they had rather the notion, still incorporated in orthodox Christianity, of a decline from a primitive state of happiness. Even the highly civilized Greeks did not seriously conceive the progress of mankind toward a higher state. As Irwin Edman has pointed out, to them intelligence was primarily a "faculty of vision"; they did not, like the moderns, cultivate it as an instrument of action, a technique of regeneration. And though in recent years the faith in intelligence has been going the way of older faiths, though hymns of progress have for many ears a sour note, something of the new hope persists. A number of our most distinguished scientists are rediscovering God, pointing out that He appears to be a super-mathematician and scientist whose ways may accordingly be fathomable; and in the political world the Communists, despite their materialistic philosophy, are battling to establish an ideal as profoundly optimistic as man has ever conceived. The very indignation in the social tragedies of confirmed pessimists like Hardy and Dreiser implies a belief in the possibility of a better society such as Sophocles apparently never dreamed of.

The movements in the symphony of modern literature are not, then, all *adagio lamentoso*. I say this, however, only to clear the way for a sober analysis; for there is no denying the pessimism of the modern temper. These very qualifications must in turn be qualified. The hope of a better society, for example, springs less often from a robust optimism than from a confusion and discontent at times almost hysterical; much of the enthusiasm that supports it is simply neurotic. The idea of Progress was at first a pure, shining revelation, either a new demonstration of the glorious powers of the human mind or a new manifestation of the glorious ways of God that brought the heavenly city within nearer view. But even the eighteenth-century philosophers insisted too much; and the Victorians, who insisted still more, were plainly trying to drown out their secret misgivings about what God and England had wrought. Today men often embrace the future chiefly to escape the horrors of the present. Like the persecuted Hebrews in the time of Daniel, they seek refuge in apocalyptic visions. Many cling to the idea of Progress as a hope; fewer build on it as a vital faith. And others contemplate chiefly its logical complement: decadence.

Underlying all such anxiety, however, lies the chaos of unbelief, from which the immediate practical problems are almost a blessed distraction. The pessimism of the past was largely an unreasoned pessimism. It was an emotional recognition of the mortality of man and the suffering that is his portion, and it appears as plainly in folk-music as in tragic poetry. But pessimism today has a more solid philosophical basis and emanates from a more compact body of uncongenial knowledge. As it diffuses, it becomes emotional and unphilosophical, but at its source it is more rational and systematic. Above all, it is more devastating. It plumbs still darker depths and raises still more awful phantoms than man had dreamed of.

The most obvious source of this pessimism is man's new notions about the universe and his position in it. The story of what has happened to his world is an all too familiar one. Briefly, he is no longer the very important fellow that once he was. He still feels himself a part of an immense order, which he may still capitalize and refer to as God, but he is no longer sure that he knows its purposes, and still less sure that those purposes are his purposes. He is no longer the special concern, "the pet and privy councillor," of deity. Life itself, once the unquestioned glorious end-product of creation, he now thinks may be, in the striking words of Sir James Jeans, no more than "a mere accidental and possibly unimportant by-product of natural processes which have some other and more stupendous end in view"—or even "a disease which affects matter in its old age."

Such notions man's common sense—or his egoism—is likely to dismiss as fantastic. It is again an old story, however, that from these remote and rarefied regions science has moved steadily toward the more intimate realms of human experience. From astronomy to biology to psychology its progress has been inexorable. If we can believe I. A. Richards, man's egoism will presently have to withstand still more terrific onslaughts, digest still more lumpish masses of uncongenial truth:

> The most dangerous of the sciences is only now beginning to come into action. I am thinking less of Psychoanalysis or of Behaviorism than of the whole subject which includes them. It is very probable that the Hindenburg Line to which the defense of our traditions retired as a result of the onslaughts of the last century will be blown up in the near future. If this should happen a mental chaos such as man has never experienced may be expected.

Still more corrosive than its specific discoveries, however, is the rationale of science, the modes of experience it has imposed. It has not only broken up many of the oldest emotional associations of the race but made difficult their necessary replacement. Few men can actually live in the world it continues to create with no day of rest—the world of electric charges whirling in a field of force, in which time and space are relative, and cause and effect perhaps an illusion.

> Nature, and Nature's laws, lay hid in night:
> God said, *Let Newton be!* and all was light

—so ran Pope's hymn in a happier day. Many would now answer with J. C. Squire:

> It did not last: the Devil, howling Ho!
> *Let Einstein be!* restored the status quo.

Yet men have at least caught the general idea. They live in a world that is no longer explained in terms of human hopes and desires; the essence of the scientific attitude is that such considerations are rigorously excluded. Of no type of thought, indeed, are contemporaries more conscious and more distrustful than of rationalization. At the outset of his *Quest for Certainty* John Dewey accordingly finds it necessary to discard all the philosophical systems of the past.

The difficulty, however, is that if men now think differently from their ancestors, they still feel very much the same. Intellectually they may grow rapidly more subtle and sophisticated; emotionally they do not. Like their primitive ancestors, for example, they are instinctively ritualists. Ritual regulates behavior and is the source of faith—as Sumner noted in *Folkways,* it *makes* religion, it is not made by it. Even the emancipated today unconsciously follow it and are steadied by its influence. Yet the whole way of life of modern men, their habits of thought and conduct, are hostile to it. They perceive chiefly flux and change, they feel chiefly the need of individual adjustment. They brush their teeth regularly, they go through the prescribed paces in office or factory, they make habits of their thousand mechanical gadgets—in their surface lives they are creatures of fashion and routine; but in their more deeply human relations there is no ordained ritual, no spirit of reverent conformity. Although the faith in science has itself become a religion, with high priests to conduct it, its abstract forms and symbols do not satisfy the deepest needs of the being, and are often, indeed, incompatible with the reverent emotions they are supposed to excite. Men still feel the basic need of building their lives on some system of natural pieties; it is difficult for any such system to take root in the habit of suspended judgment and "organized doubt," the insistence on taking life straight, that is considered the first duty of the intelligent modern.

Hence when Eddington, Jeans, and other leaders of science began to toy with metaphysics and find room for God, they found few grateful readers. They were greeted instead with derision, scorn, even indignation. They were suspected of softening of the brain, they were charged with apostasy. The layman has been by now only too well trained, and demands that all attitudes be supported by *fact.* Yet this makes for an impossible strain on man in his present state of knowledge, when there are insufficient objective references for all his emotions and instinctive responses. "The justification of any attitude *per se,"* writes Richards as a practical psychologist, "is its success for the needs of the being." These needs vary with the individual and his situation; and to attempt to base all our attitudes on matters of fact is to "run extreme risks of later disorganization elsewhere."

One need not look far in modern literature to discover evidences of such disorganization. Writers have been forced to examine their premises anxiously, and this necessity is sobering even when their conclusions are not bleakly pessimistic. "In periods of firmly established meanings," Kenneth Burke observes, "one does not *study* them, one *uses* them: one frames his acts in accordance with them." Almost as sustaining as this unconscious acceptance of a set of meanings, it might be added, is a vigorous attack upon them in the cause of another positive set. But even such crusading has become difficult for the self-conscious modern. In the early 'twenties skepticism was fashionable and exciting. It was a kind of luxury that a society complacent in its seeming prosperity could afford to indulge. Now it is a drug on the market. "Organized bad taste" is no longer good taste; puncturing faiths is no longer good clean fun. Even intelligent men are now responding with pathetic eagerness to promises of security and light—to dictators in the world of affairs, to soul-healers in the world of literature.

2

The essential difference between pessimism today and the pessimism of the past appears most plainly in the modern conception of tragedy. Greek tragedy is at bottom an act of piety. Not merely is it permeated with a sense of the divine government of the world, but the adequacy of this government is not seriously questioned; the poets do not put embarrassing questions to the gods. Their characters are the hapless victims of monstrous fatalities ordained by the "dark, unfathomable mind of Zeus," and to a modern reader often appear innocent. One can justify even so horrible an act as Jocasta's exposure of her infant son, for it was committed to avert the still more horrible intention of the gods as expressed by the oracle. Yet the grief aroused by these spectacles was in the Greeks not a rebellious grief; with their fatalism they managed to reconcile a conviction of human responsibility for human suffering. There are grounds here for indignant protest, but the poets acquiesce. There are grounds for despair, but they somehow retain a faith in the fitness of things.

The world of Shakespeare, more "cheerless, dark, and deadly" than that of any other great poet before recent times, is indeed less orderly, less susceptible of comforting interpretation. As on the religious and ethical problems implicit in his tragedies he preserved a strange silence—possibly because his audience did not encourage him to speak out, possibly because he had no pat answers to offer—the reader is left to form his own impressions; and about impressions there can be no conclusive argument. Yet most readers have felt that Shakespeare does in the end reconcile himself to the controlling order. Its workings are manifestly complicated and often painfully incomprehensible. They involve an appalling waste of good; noble figures like Hamlet and Brutus and Othello are wantonly thrown away. Still, Shakespeare never definitely rejects the idea of a Providence, never definitely represents the ruling powers as merely blind or indifferent. His order is in its largest aspect a moral order, and its compulsion a moral compulsion. *Human evil* is always the chief disturbing element and the primary source of Shakespeare's tragedy. "We remain confronted," writes A. C. Bradley, "with the inexplicable fact . . . of a world travailing for perfection, but bringing to birth, together with glorious good, an evil which it is able to overcome only by self-torture and self-waste." But eventually this evil is eliminated, if at terrible cost, and a balance is struck, an equilibrium restored, with "all passions spent."

In a word, such pessimism as colors the tragedy of the past was qualified by some notion of a divine plan in the working out of which man was the chief actor, and to which his sufferings were referred and thus given dignity and meaning. This was a vital intuitive faith that preceded reasoning and went deeper than religious belief. Some were less conversant than others with the intentions of deity, but the humblest agreed with the glibbest prophets about the importance of man in the scheme of things. Behind all puzzled speculation and recurrent misgiving was a clear certainty by the light of which man could follow the paths to glory in this world if not the next. And this fundamental certainty of the greatness of man and the divinity that shapes his ends is what makes ancient tragedy never a confession of despair but an assertion of faith. As has often been remarked, the world's greatest tragedies were the products of two of the most confident ages man has known—the Periclean and the Elizabethan.

Here, then, is the peculiar characteristic of much tragedy that men now write: it no longer resolves its dissonances into a triumphant major chord. It insists not merely that great suffering is and under the unalterable conditions of human life always must be, but that it is compensated for by no ultimate good. It denies that behind this suffering is any exalted or intelligible purpose to which man can submit with pride. Submit he must, but to a blank necessity.

The essence of tragedy, Schlegel declared, is a conflict between necessity without and freedom within; the terms of this conflict are today radically altered. Men have had, in the first place, to temper their notions of the freedom within. They perceive how largely they are products of their environment, and they have learned how subterranean and amazingly tortuous are the workings of their minds. To be captain of one's soul, writes Irwin Edman, "has become impossible now that personality itself seems to be more like a river than a ship." But more troublesome is the form now assumed by the external necessity. Men can no longer respect the forces that crush them. An awful Fate has given way to the unsanctified compulsions of the social and natural environment; the decrees of the gods have dwindled into the commands of their neighbors and bosses, and the blind necessity of natural and economic laws. Thus where there was one solemn mystery there are now a hundred vexing riddles. Where the older poets saw an order whose larger purposes were reasonable or even benevolent, the modern writer can see only a "meaningless welter," an "immense indifference." Where, accordingly, the spirit of ancient tragedy is ultimately that of reverent acceptance, the spirit of the moderns is like Conrad's of ironic aloofness, like Hardy's of vehement protest, like Hemingway's of alcoholic bravado, like Dreiser's of complete confusion and dismay. There are few to justify the ways of God to man.

The dangers of such a pessimism are obvious enough. It may simply depress human vitality, dry up the springs of energy at their source. It may shrivel into sere and barren despair. And this is actually what one finds in much modern fiction: an insistence upon the merely painful, an utter joylessness, devoid of passion even in its negations. Some writers come to no sort of decent terms with life, make no sort of peace. They neither chant a solemn litany nor voice an indignant protest. The burden of such brilliant studies as Ernest Hemingway's *The Sun Also Rises* and Aldous Huxley's *Point Counterpoint* is chiefly world-weariness, disenchantment, futility. Still emptier of values or meanings is William Faulkner's *Sanctuary,* a riot of violence and horror for their own sake. A more remarkable work, Celine's *Journey to the End of Night,* is remarkable for a superior savagery; it is the apotheosis of downright disgust with life. And perhaps most dismal, if less striking, of this melancholy kind is Julian Green's *The Dark Journey,* a relentlessly objective, brilliantly "scientific" study of the mean struggles of mean souls, born seemingly of an entire lack of emotion. Here is tragedy at the last remove from a *Hamlet* or an *Antigone,* never warmed by compassion, never lighted by poetry, never lifted by a sense of greatness in pain or solemnity in mystery.

These novels are not, to be sure, fairly representative; one may reasonably doubt that the future is theirs. Yet throughout its range modern fiction has not the glamor, the sweep and pomp, the grand and compelling figures of ancient tragedy. As a more realistic and a prose performance, it could indeed scarcely be expected to deal in such heroics. More significant, however, than that the modern hero no longer sweeps the boards in purple robes or makes significant gestures, no longer sways the destiny of nations, is that he is often a base, miserable fellow. The mantle of Hamlet is now worn by a Clyde Griffiths, the splendor of Antigone has shriveled into the meanness of an Emma Bovary; and the comment of stately choruses has dwindled into the gossip of the neighbors. Modern novelists are less confident of the glorious possibilities of man and feel more at home when making absorbed studies of the ordinary, the weak, the morbid, or even the ignoble.

To this generalization there are notable exceptions—the men of Conrad's best work, for example, have much of the stature, force, and glamor of the Shakespearian heroes. But, on the whole, writers appear to be more often impressed by the pettiness than by the magnificence of man, by the futility of his efforts than by the splendor of his aspirations. They distrust the grand passions, and like the hero of *A Farewell to Arms,* who "was always embarrassed by the words sacred, glorious, and sacrifice, and the expression in vain," they are prone to feel a little uneasy and ridiculous when writing largely about life. "Rhetoric" has become a term of disparagement. The mere mention of the word "spiritual" makes men uncomfortable, and "soul" has become the property of ministers, as "heart" of the writers for the pulps. They shrink from passionate utterance as something adolescent; they live in fear of being somehow taken in. Chiefly they appear to be interested in the maladjustments of what we have recently discovered to be our highly complicated minds. They prefer subtlety to vehemence, the nuance to the flaming line, the minor to the major key.

This is another of the mixed blessings of that extraordinary "improvement in natural knowledge" in which Thomas Huxley had so fervid, joyous a confidence. It has made many distrustful of the inherited idealisms that could otherwise sustain them in the bleak immensities they have discovered. When the biologists and psychoanalysts have done with love, for example, they are less ready than their ancestors to think the world well lost for it. The terrible plight of Edipus, which the Greeks invested with all the majesty of tragedy, is now a symbol of one of the many ugly complexes from which they suffer. The behaviorists have turned their deepest emotions into conditioned reflexes, comparable to the salivations of a laboratory dog. No conclusion about behavior has more weight, William James once lamented, than one derived from the twitchings of a frog's leg—especially if the frog was decapitated. In general, the tendency of science has been to substitute physical and psychical compulsions for freedom of choice, to explain personality in terms of glands, hormones, and complexes, and to enforce an unpleasant awareness of the unlovely origins of human impulses. In *Point Counterpoint,* for instance, Aldous Huxley, a great lover of music, describes the rendition of a masterpiece. "The fiddlers drew their rosined horse-hair across the stretched intestines of lambs"—and what happened? "The hairy endings of the auditory nerve shuddered like weeds in a rough sea . . . and Lord Edward ecstatically whispered 'Bach!' " This is a professional irony and in itself of slight significance; yet it is this kind of thought that curdles the idealisms of many artists—and in some measure explains the torment in Huxley himself.

3

In the presence of these melancholy exhibits, one can more easily understand Krutch's famous pronouncement that it is impossible for the moderns to write Tragedy. Not only have they lost the vital faith that inspired the old masterpieces, but, he declared, they cannot recapture it by a mere intellectual conviction that it would be desirable to do so. And although *Mourning Becomes Electra* convinced him that he had been wrong, this clinical interpretation of an ancient legend only strengthened the fears of others that a glory has permanently departed this earth. Modern pessimism, we often hear, makes impossible a great literature. The conception of a universe purposeless or indifferent to human values cuts the ground from under these values, without which a great literature cannot exist. It makes of all idealism at best a gloomy consolation, a mere whistling in the dark.

This is clearly a serious issue, and the property not merely of clergymen or professional viewers-with-alarm. I shall return to it at the end. Yet I should meanwhile remark, again simply for the purposes of preliminary survey, that the growth of pessimism has not been uniformly cankerous, and that only the tender-minded should find modern tragedy an altogether sordid, ineffectual, and merely distressing performance. Man has had to surrender his flattering hopes of a magnificent destiny and accommodate himself to a lower range of dream and desire. In the immense drama of the spheres his own drama has come to seem an inconsequential and possibly alien interlude. But in being thus driven back upon himself he has sought new sources of inspiration and support, and often made virtues of his necessities. If only because of the predicament in which he finds himself, he has cultivated such values as tolerance, compassion, and charity.

One reason why modern literature rises less often to the level of the heroic and sublime is simply that it is so deeply rooted in our common humanity. The last hundred years have been marked by a growth in understanding and therefore in sympathy. In the everyday world this appears in the more humane treatment of paupers, delinquents, mental defectives, and the wayward and unfortunate generally; in the intellectual world in the rise of the social sciences; and in imaginative literature in a lively, sympathetic interest in all classes and types of men. This interest may be chiefly scientific, but more typically it is humanitarian. Despite their objective manner, many modern novels are saturated with pity—a pity that embraces the humblest creature in them.

Many contemporaries no doubt enjoy their glow of pity because, as William James said, it enables them to feel virtuous at the expense of very little effort. At its worst, this spirit of compassion melts into a facile, mawkish self-pity—a dispirited resignation, or a sniffling over a cold, cruel world. At times it attaches itself to paltry objects or softens into the sentimentalism that has provided us with so many pure-hearted prostitutes. It raises the difficult issue of "selective sympathy"; though one may distrust the specific criteria of the cloistered Paul Elmer More, or suspect any man who sets up as a stern judge of his fellows, there is a plain objection to an undiscriminating humanitarianism. At its best, however—as in the works of Dostoyevsky, Hardy, and

Hauptmann—this compassion is a healthful, cleansing, and sustaining feeling. It has at least lightened the burden of the new knowledge, taken some of the curse off the depressing notions men have got.

This attitude has at any rate considerably altered the ethical content of modern literature. As Jehovah goes the way of Zeus, His commands naturally cease to command obedience or even respect. At the same time there is none (except perhaps the psychiatrist) to inherit the mantle of His authority. In an age that no longer pretends to know ultimate meanings, the moralist can no longer assume the comfortable posture of the oracle, no longer carry his case to a heavenly Court of Appeals. Such wisdom as he may express does not flow from a holy fount but must justify itself on empirical grounds. If he is realistic, he must accordingly recognize that his judgments can be only provisional and relative. In the absence either of complete knowledge (even the psychiatrist suffers from this) or of supernatural authority, moral laws are no longer immutable and no longer have absolute validity. For better or worse, the categorical imperative is no more.

A natural result of this confusion of the preachers' tongues has been much babble and angry polemics. We have again in our laps the whole immensely difficult problem brought by our emancipation from Prejudice and Superstition, the tyranny of priests and kings. The impulse of much modern fiction is accordingly an impersonal, undogmatic effort to understand life for what it inexorably is. Writers have cultivated the ideal, derived from the practice of science, of suspended judgment. They seldom write the tragedy merely of sin and retribution, seldom make out plain blacks and whites. In so far as they preach, they preach the doctrine of every man his own moralist.

Now, the moral world of ancient literature is indeed not so simple and tidy as it is often made out to be. Pedagogues seize too eagerly upon Aristotle's comfortable notion of the "tragic flaw." Aristotle was too little a poet, too much an orderly philosopher and logician, thoroughly to understand tragedy; he could find no place in his precise system for the grossly fortuitous and unreasonable elements in the fates of Edipus, Antigone, and Orestes. Imperfect though these characters are, their crimes followed almost inevitably the curse laid upon their families by the gods, a curse of which they were themselves guiltless; only by being less sensitive, less noble, could they have averted their tragedy. Similarly the destructive forces in Shakespeare are far too ruthless to be considered mere avenging deities, and they exact a penalty out of all proportion to the offense; if it is justice that an old king and all whom he loves should be brutally destroyed because of the mistakes of his dotage, it is justice by no civilized human standards. The chief fault is not in these great figures but in the world about them. In short, in the poetic as in the actual world, the little measuring rule of the tragic flaw is hopelessly inadequate.

Yet the old masterpieces at least lend themselves to a conventional moralistic interpretation. They are founded on relatively simple, fixed notions of right and wrong; the forces of good and the forces of evil are sharply opposed; and there is little serious disposition to question the essential rightness of the laws of man or of God by which their heroes live and die. The issues in modern fiction, however, are far more complicated. Most writers now regard volition and conscience as largely the product of external forces beyond the individual's control, derivatives of the social context, and his actions as therefore not susceptible of a downright judgment. They attempt to penetrate to underlying causes, distinguishing between the evil of a deed and the criminality of its perpetrator, and they question the theory of punishment—as even so humane a man as Henry Fielding did not. With him as with the Elizabethans a scoundrel existed only to be hanged, and his hanging was an edifying spectacle; now writers try to understand the scoundrel in terms of his environment, and to correct that environment. Hence society itself is often the evil force in their fictions. Such unfortunates as Tess Durbeyfield and Jennie Gerhardt suffer primarily because of the rigorous moral law imposed by the community; their authors question the law itself, the standard of judgment. And this is another reason why good, placid people are pained and bewildered by much modern fiction: it is forever asking questions that they prefer to think closed, disturbing the ordered serenity—or violence—of their moral judgments.

This wider humanity, if not greater veracity, of modern fiction is reflected as well in the banishment of the villain to melodrama. Shakespeare introduced these implausible figures less as a concession to a primitive moral sense than as the stock instrument for effecting the necessary complication and conflict; from either point of view, however, this conflict falls short of inevitability and universal truth. Modern realists have accordingly discarded this easy device. They feel that man's sufferings seldom result from a great sin or the machinations of a villain or any head-on collision of virtue and vice, but that they arise rather from a maladjustment with the social environment, or from the inevitable conflict of interests and desires in a group of characters upon no one of whom is especial guilt to be fastened. The reader of Shakespeare ordinarily identifies himself with the hero, as does the simple spectator of melodrama. But in modern tragedy he is asked to identify himself with all the characters at once—with Sue Bridehead as with Jude Fawley, with Soames and Irene as with young Jon and Fleur Forsyte, with Hurstwood as with Sister Carrie. Where he is urged to become partizan, it is on behalf rather of a principle than of an individual.

The pleasant way of describing this whole change is to say that modern novelists have subdued the violence of the primitive urge to damn heretics and deliver transgressors to an angry tribal god, and that out of a profound sense of the community of human frailty and suffering they have cultivated the ideal of tolerance. A rude critic, however, might call it but another symptom of the sickness of the age. He might point out that the growth of tolerance is usually the sign of the decay of faith, and that those today who do have a strong faith—the Communists, for instance, or the New Humanists—are much less charitable in their judgments. And he might also point out that others revel too luxuriously in their freedom from categorical imperatives. They junk too wantonly the accumulated wisdom of the past simply because it comes to them with the stamp of a discredited theological authority. They are too ready to suspend judgment, too eager to disclaim all personal responsibility. One yearns at times for the refreshing common sense or even the dogmatism of a Sam Johnson, and would like to say as plainly, "The woman's a whore, and there's an end on it." For despite their emancipation men have still to face the inexorable logic of facts. They may shift the responsibility for their deeds, but they cannot escape the consequences. The problem of evil in one form or another is still a fundamental concern of literature; and today as in the past we are finally called upon to make some sort of judgment.

Whether fortunate or unfortunate, this emphasis upon the values of catholicity, forbearance, and compassion is plainly a result of the skepticism and pessimism of the modern temper. If it is regarded as an essentially Christian spirit, it marks most conspicuously the work of novelists like Hardy and Dreiser who have utterly rejected the Christian faith. The pessimist often becomes a misanthrope; but he is also notoriously apt to be a more charitable fellow than the optimist who is in touch with the Absolute, and who has therefore a laudable eagerness to share the truth, a reasonable impatience with those who fail to see it.

III

REALISM

I

I HAVE already indicated the obvious connection between the pessimism and the realism of the modern spirit. Both have been stimulated by the tremendous growth of scientific investigation, pessimism more particularly by its findings, realism as well by its methods—its habit of patient scrutiny and analysis. As men became more isolated on their whirling speck in the infinite, and more uncertain of the final meaning of their lives, they naturally tended at once to take a gloomier view of their lot and to become more absorbed in the immediate realities that alone they could get a firm hold on. The decay of faith intensified the claims of the actual.

As it is rooted in the elemental impulse to imitate or reproduce, observable in the art of the prehistoric cave-dwellers, realism too is familiar in world literature. It marks plainly the Old Testament, and obtrudes even in medieval religious drama, designed for an audience supposedly convinced that this life was but a trial heat run off in preparation for the final race of glory in heaven. With the development of prose fiction, the literary form best adapted to its uses, it was given a new impetus, and in turn quickened this development. Yet realism as we know it today is something new. Historically it has been a source of comedy or an occasional method, a device used to make convincing the fantastic and unreal; now it is an end in itself. As the banner of a self-conscious and militant school, as an instrument of wholly serious purposes, as in some form the approach to art of the great majority of important writers, it is a relatively recent development and a peculiar expression of the modern era.

This generalization is simple and obvious enough. But when one attempts to describe more exactly the change that has occurred, all simplicity ends. So luxuriant has been the growth of the realistic spirit, so diverse and often conflicting are its manifestations, that it is extremely difficult to keep a firm grasp on the immense literature it has inspired. When novels with seemingly as little in common as *An American Tragedy* and *Remembrance of Things Past, My Antonia* and *Ulysses,* are all described as realistic, one obviously cannot set fixed boundaries to this literature. The meaning of "realism" has in fact never been very precise or generally agreed upon; as one looks at the word hard, one grows a little dizzy. All artists have at bottom the same subject matter, all deal somehow with life; and so far as they give the impression of actuality they are in a sense realistic. Who is to say that a "realist" like Dreiser gives a truer impression of life than a "romanticist" like Shakespeare?

Yet if all great artists arrive finally at the same goal, and the distinctions among them resolve largely into differences of approach, these differences nevertheless lead to important consequences. The realist begins with the concrete and familiar in experience; his inspiration is less a cloudy imagining than observed fact. Although he does not and cannot exactly reproduce actual experience, although as an artist he inevitably recasts and imaginatively shapes, his primary effort is to represent without markedly idealizing, to remain close to actuality and impart its savor. Essentially, realism implies only so general a tendency or purpose—the purpose, as Professor W. L. Myers expresses it in *The Later Realism,* "of conveying to the reader, whatever else may be accomplished, a strong sense of things actual in experience and within the range of the average life." Its record may be drab or exciting, ugly or beautiful—"so long as it give the essential impression of actuality."

This is admittedly a broad definition that does not permit exact application or tidy category. Because of the very nature of modern literature, however, the traditional labels do not fit its innumerable forms. As reality has come to seem increasingly complex, the representation of it has naturally embraced new materials and demanded new modes. Yet "realism" even in this general sense helps to define and distinguish modern fiction; and to give it a more precise meaning, to apply it only to a particular specialized technique, only obscures the basic issues, and necessitates the addition of still more isms to the flock that already confuse and bewilder us.

It is at least clear that the modern writer, by whatever devious route, approaches actuality in a distinctly new spirit. One can readily isolate the realistic impulse behind the work of most earlier novelists, from Fielding through Jane Austen to Trollope. They reproduced, with more or less verisimilitude, familiar experience; all had a strong sense of fact. Yet despite the shrewdness of their observation, all were likely at any moment to subordinate fidelity of representation to humor, to sentiment, to melodrama, or, generally, to mere diversion. All tacitly accepted their position as public entertainers, hired to put on a good show. Tom Jones is a natural young scamp, but he is led through an elaborate series of artificial adventures and finally handed over to his angelic Sophia; David Copperfield travels a familiar road into maturity and marriage, but many of his fellow-travelers are clowns and freaks. Their creators had a sentimental or satirical ax to grind; realism was not yet its own sufficient justification. Toward the end of the nineteenth century, however, there grew up, under the wing of Zola, a new school of novelists who militantly insisted upon absolute fidelity to fact for its own sake and above all other considerations. They looked at life more closely and recorded their findings more minutely. They studied large segments of experience that had hitherto been ignored or at most viewed with distant politeness. They scorned their readers' desire for edification and entertainment, and outraged their fine feelings. In general they worked in the spirit of science, with its ideal of thorough, dispassionate inquiry. And that here was a new kind of realism was heralded by the invention of a new label: naturalism.

Although "naturalism" is even today a term of opprobrium, its apostles at least succeeded in establishing the artist's right to an uncompromising treatment of reality in all its forms. The movement still survives, is still a significant expression of the scientific spirit. But the naturalists are important chiefly because they hacked a path through the jungles of artifice and convention, enabling later writers to make more balanced, penetrating, and inclusive studies of life. Thus we have the solid and faithful, if still conventional realism of *The Old Wives' Tale, Of Human Bondage, The Forsyte Saga.* And thus we have also innumerable divergent developments which, realistic at their source, lead into fields so strange and remote that it becomes difficult to encompass them in a single classification. For at the same time that the modern novelist has come to regard the writing of novels as an exacting fine art, he has also been made acutely aware of the elusiveness of human personality, the complexity of human behavior. Accordingly he often feels that a catalogue of externals will not render the essential, inner truth that he perceives, and he finds it necessary to supplement when not actually to discard traditional methods, and to voyage into uncharted seas.

"Life is not a series of gig lamps symmetrically arranged," declares Virginia Woolf; "life is a luminous halo." Her whole effort is accordingly to render the "myriad impressions" that we daily receive, the "semi-transparent envelope" veiling all our activities. She is, in short, an impressionist; and as such she joins the large company, including Conrad, Proust, and Lawrence, who have extended into literature the method of the French painters: a projection of the artist's immediate sense impression as opposed to a literal reproduction of surfaces or an intellectual analysis of what underlies them. The impressionists substitute the subtle evocation of atmosphere for inventory, the direct rendering of sensation for analysis; they strive to achieve a greater intimacy with the experiencing self rather than with objective reality, to impart a full *realization* instead of a mere comprehension of experience. All greatly extend the limits of realistic investigation—Lawrence so far that he approaches the mystical. Yet even when they deliberately distort appearances for the sake of essences, the aim of these writers remains fundamentally realistic. They have simply developed finer instruments than the earlier realists and penetrated farther below the surface of the familiar. They are simply striving to convey in purer form the impression life makes upon us.

More difficult of classification, however, are other more extreme developments in recent fiction. Kaleidoscopic pictures like Evelyn Scott's *The Wave* and all the later novels of John Dos Passos give only momentary trouble; these novelists are merely assembling their bits of reality in unusual combinations. Similarly when Aldous Huxley in *Point Counterpoint* and André Gide in *The Counterfeiters* toy with the principles of musical composition, and when Proust actually writes a Time Symphony, they are nevertheless presenting a realistic picture of a cross-section of their society. But beyond these experimenters is a more advanced group whom in *The Twentieth Century Novel* Professor Beach aptly describes as "expressionists." In certain chapters of *Ulysses* James Joyce definitely departs from the world of appearances and employs the principles of abstract composition illustrated in the paintings of Picasso: the creation of a "generalized atmosphere," the presentation in some abstract form of the underlying meaning of a scene. And Joyce is but one of a number who, eager to distil the very quintessence of actuality, are led to the use of extra-realistic devices and enter the realm of the, strictly speaking, unreal.

In this misty mid-region one can hardly continue to talk easily of realism. Obviously a line must somewhere be drawn; no less obviously its location will be arbitrary. More important than such geographical distinctions, however, is the recognition that even these extreme developments are outgrowths of the realistic spirit and not romantic revulsions against it. They introduce not a violent reaction in mood but a refinement in technique. Despite its thick overlay of amazing artifice, *Ulysses* is at its core a realistic work, and as clearly as *An American Tragedy* a product of the realistic spirit; Joyce's point of departure is essentially different from that of Shakespeare or Racine, Dumas or Scott. Most of the so-called impressionists and expressionists keep their feet pretty solidly on the earth. They are not fleeing the familiar or commonplace but striving to render it more adequately and immediately. The gist of their dissatisfaction with conventional realism is simply that it is not *real* enough.

2

The following of the labyrinthine ramifications of modern realism is a fascinating, if bewildering business. It should not, however, make one contemptuous of the large body of more conventional work animated by the realistic spirit, or forgetful of the significant innovations even in this work. These may be summed up as a greater exactitude and inclusiveness, a sharper and more thorough specification of the whole experience of man. And perhaps most obvious is the democratization of literature that I have already mentioned: the honest, serious treatment of all classes and types of men.

The hero of classical and medieval drama was of course a person of high rank; the plain assumption was that only "the harm of hem that stoode in heighe degree" was worthy of being dignified as Tragedy. Bourgeois or domestic tragedy had its beginnings, indeed, as early as the Elizabethan period, in such plays as Heywood's *A Woman Killed with Kindness;* by the eighteenth century it had become definitely self-conscious.

> We ne'er can pity what we ne'er can share. . . .
> Therefore an humble Theme our Author chose,
> A melancholy Tale of Private Woes

—so runs the prologue of Rowe's *The Fair Penitent;* and Lillo and Moore in the drama, Richardson in the novel, all worked in this lachrymose kind and had a wide influence on the Continent. But their works are preposterously moral, sentimental, and high-flown. What, asks the wicked temptress of the hero of *The London Merchant,* are his thoughts of love?

> If you mean the love of women [replies the unforgettable George Barnwell], I have not thought of it at all. My youth and circumstances make such thoughts improper in me yet. But if you mean the general love we owe to mankind, I think no one has more of it in his temper than myself. . . . In an especial manner I love my Uncle. . . .

Such stuff is veracious only as a reflection of bourgeois mentality on its lower levels.

With the rapid growth of a large middle-class reading public, however, and the accompanying rise of prose fiction, literature came to dwell more and more comfortably on the plains of every-day life. After making the necessary concessions to prevailing notions of the edifying and genteel, Victorian novelists treated more or less realistically the lives of average middle-class folk. Yet the range of their realism was still limited. They seldom followed their hero into his work-a-day life, and the lower classes they introduced only incidentally, as comic figures or occasionally as objects for the exercise of fine sentiments. Not until the dawning of the modern era does the hero of austere fiction become commonly a proletarian who is treated honestly, sympathetically, and without obvious condescension, in the conviction that the ruin of the ordinary man is as poignant and noble a theme as the spectacular downfall of the great. "Before art as before the law all men are equal," declares Hauptmann in *The Rats;* like Hardy and others at the time, he was self-conscious and felt obliged to defend the status of his heroes. Today his gospel is taken for granted. For perhaps the first time in literary history, a real meaning has been given to the sonorous commonplace: *Humani nihil a me alienum puto.*

In the past, moreover, the whole social organism received scant consideration; except for incidental details of costume and manner, drama was enacted virtually in a vacuum. Only in recent times have writers properly recognized the incalculable influence of heredity and environment. They can no longer accept the simple idea of Nemesis, but look everywhere for cause and effect. Hence the stream of sociological fiction that has broadened steadily since the time of Balzac and borne an increasing volume of criticism and protest. Zola and Howells, Gissing and Galsworthy, Dreiser and Wells—strange bedfellows these are, yet all are offspring of the teeming family of social historians and critics. While belligerently asserting the rights of the individual, they have treated him more and more as a social fraction, with increasing stress on the social implications of his struggles. Tom Jones can no longer wander blithely and haphazardly through his society and finally settle his simple destiny by winning a fair Sophia; he must follow a logical course, wrestle with the monsters of political economy as well as with the hobgoblins of his own conscience, keep a wife after he wins her, and like as not carry a pack of pamphlets on his back.

As they sought causes modern realists of course found everything immensely complicated. This is why the drama has surrendered its traditional supremacy to the novel; it is too simple a form to mirror the whole truth, in all its intricacy, that they have a passion for telling. They have commonly discarded even the dramatic structure of the novel, so magnificently illustrated by Hardy's *The Return of the Native,* in which the action rises steadily to a definite climax and culminates in a definite catastrophe. Although so neat a disposition of material is obviously effective, many consider it too arbitrary, too unlike the impact of actual experience. And so their conflicts are likely to be less sharply defined, less firmly conducted, less surely resolved. At times, indeed, the element of conflict almost dissolves in a sea of uncertainties and complexities; the characters are blown hither and yon, and become so uncertain of their destination that they go nowhere at all. Many readers are left wondering what has actually happened to Clarissa Dalloway or Stephen Dedalus, and why. This indecisiveness results partly from the absence of clear-cut moral standards—the freedom or laxity that makes the conflict of Emma Bovary seem to many sophisticated readers unreal

—but more often it results from the novelist's deliberate intention to give the impression of average experience. Even when he is treating of tragic experience he often blurs or tangles the issues. For he is treating, typically, of ordinary men, and ordinary men are less often destroyed in one dramatic, decisive struggle than they are worn down by attrition. They are seldom the victims of swift and spectacular misfortune; they are usually denied the luxury of swift and glamorous death.

This same distrust of simple, trim, and too symmetrical patterns has led novelists to break down the sharp distinction between comedy and tragedy, and to avoid definite endings involving either the marriage or the death of the hero. They perceive that human happiness like human failure is never absolute, and they have done with all pretense of finality as untrue to our deeper experience. Just as many painters have given up representation and many composers melody, so have many novelists given up finished actions or even plot; all are suspicious of the simplicities of the past. But the novelists more specifically are seeking to mirror life in its endless flux and infinite variety, and life denies them any sort of conclusiveness. They have erected the mere trickery of *The Lady or the Tiger?* into an artistic principle. Rarely, to be sure, do they leave so bold a question mark —they blur even their interrogations; but they leave a cloud of little marks. For every lady there are now a dozen tigers.

3

Many of the tendencies in modern realistic fiction are obviously contradictory. If the study of the average man is a distinguishing characteristic, the study of abnormal types is no less so. If there has been a marked trend toward the socialization of fiction, there is also a strong inclination to explore the crannies of individual consciousness. If many writers are carrying on exhaustive and exhausting researches into subtle states of mind, a whole school of primitives deliberately eschew intellect and write baldly of primal emotions and violent conflicts. These innumerable pulls in opposite directions are precisely what make so difficult a survey and estimate of modern literature, so hazardous a prediction of its drift or direction. Yet the matrix of the great bulk of this literature—of the work of Bennett as of Faulkner, of Wells as of Virginia Woolf, of Proust as of Hemingway—is a realistic spirit; and it is chiefly because reality presents today so many facets and reveals so many mysterious depths that the representation of it has assumed so many forms.

In celebrating the obvious rewards of the realistic method, however, many readers overlook its relation to the modern dilemma. Realism appears to have a solid foundation in fact, it gives naturally a strong illusion of Truth; here, it would seem, is a rock for the artist to stand on while others flounder in a sea of uncertainties. Actually, the realist is peculiarly liable to be a victim of the confusion, instability, and heterogeneity of his age. A great work of art is a formal creation, not a parcel of information; and what many of our realists are recording so conscientiously is simply the forms of our confusion, the evidences of our instability, the scattered particulars of our heterogeneity. Although some of them seem innocently content with this occupation, blissfully unaware of its deeper implications, their work is nevertheless testimony for the prosecution of their society. They are immortalizing its chaos.

Writers in every age are liable to the error of supposing final and immutable the manners and morals they depict, of failing to keep clearly in sight the unchanging elements of human desire and emotion that underlie the forms of a particular society. The intricacies and uncertainties of modern society enormously complicate their problem. They tend, in the first place, to lose that sense of the deep permanence of the order about them, that settled habit of piety, out of which great literature most easily grows. Yet their consciousness of rapid and incessant change seldom rescues them from the illusions of the present. They are themselves caught up in the swirl. They are bombarded by such a hail of scattered impressions, their attention is distracted and enfeebled by such a multiplicity of concerns, that detachment and command become extremely difficult. Amid the relative simplicities of the nineteenth century Thoreau was already vehemently protesting that our lives are frittered away by detail; it is precisely this detail that engrosses a whole school of industrious reporters.

The lesser realists are accordingly interesting chiefly as they indicate, by their bobbings, the innumerable swirls and eddies in the confused current of modern thought. They have usually a fine scorn of the academic; their very up-to-date work is nevertheless destined to provide footnotes for the scholars of the future. But even the more authoritative realists, who appear to cut through the snarls and tangles of our daily existence, seldom get far enough below the surface to escape the temporal and parochial. Not merely the costumes of their characters but the terms of their conflicts soon fit their work for the old family album. They describe painstakingly what presently seems just quaint; they announce sonorously what presently becomes obvious or irrelevant; they hurl themselves headlong against a wall of prejudice that is presently torn down—leaving them, like Nora in *A Doll's House,* charging into thin air. Rapidly their once pertinent and even revolutionary novels gather dust and assume more historical than literary interest. This is already the fate of Gissing and Howells; already it is overtaking Sinclair Lewis.

Reflections like these help to explain the growing dissatisfaction with the methods and ends of ordinary realism. I have shown how some more recent novelists have rid themselves of the usual paraphernalia of realistic investigation and employed extra-realistic devices. Still others, however, have not merely extended realism but more plainly transcended it. Seeming to feel that no literal representation can give a clear, rounded, luminous expression to the essential truths of human experience, they have attempted to get at these truths more directly, and to present them in not merely an abstract but a more specifically ideal form—a form in which the mind can contemplate them undistracted by illusory appearances. They have concerned themselves more immediately with purely spiritual concepts. In short they have observed, though from different motives, the precept of Browning's Renaissance prior:

> Paint the soul. Never mind the arms and legs.

Thus Ibsen, who established his reputation in a solid realism, ended his career in a world of cloudy symbols. Hauptmann supplemented the rigorous naturalism of *The Weavers* with the shimmering poetry of *The Sunken Bell.* Hardy gave the final statement of the philosophy of life expressed in *Jude the Obscure* in the immense if uncouth poetry of *The Dynasts.* All the diverse experiments of Eugene O'Neill have been efforts to escape what he has called the "banality of surfaces." And in *Masses and Man* Ernst Toller presents even the passionate revolutionary propaganda of the proletariat in a number of "visionary abstracts of reality."

This tendency is indeed most apparent in the drama (one thinks immediately of Kaiser, Pirandello, the late work of O'Casey), and it is here no doubt chiefly a recognition of the inability of the drama to compete with the novel in the field of realism, and hence an effort to reestablish it on something like its old basis. But it appears in various forms in the novel too: in the protests of Lawrence, Proust, Gide, Virginia Woolf, and others against the assumptions of a literal realism; in the prose-poem supplements of Dos Passos and Wolfe; in the development of Thomas Mann from the conventional sociological chronicle of *Buddenbrooks* to the immense allegory of *The Magic Mountain.* In any event it is to be distinguished from the various retreats into shallow romanticism as from the stunts of the frowsy-minded cults. The writers in question are not turning their backs on their society or seeking surcease from its ills in a dream world. They are not destroying the realistic spirit or even aiming to destroy it. They are simply supplementing it.

They are by no means, of course, uniformly successful. They suffer from the same strain and confusion reflected in the unimaginative, earthbound realism the insufficiency of which they help to make clear. All are characteristic expressions of the modern era in its groping search for meanings and purposes; and the job is too big, they have to work too hard. Many of the expressionists in the drama simply lose themselves in the blue and confuse spirituality with mere balminess. They present only shadows of the ideal—pale and cloudy abstractions, like Pélléas and Mélisande, too insubstantial to be live symbols—and their ideal is itself misty. Others can neither subdue nor harmonize their realistic impulse, and give us an indigestible scramble of real and ideal. O'Neill's young Margaret in *The Great God Brown* rhapsodizes as the spirit of eternal youth—and as a silly adolescent will chirp in the same breath, "Dion is my Daddy-O!"; Nina in *Strange Interlude* is at one moment maundering about God the Mother, at the next worrying about contraceptives and complexes. And if the novelists generally keep their feet more firmly on the ground, this ground is itself, once more, none too firm.

IV

PSYCHOLOGY

I

ALTHOUGH the vogue of the "psychological study," the whole fascinated interest in the intricate, mysterious workings of the human mind, is another manifestation of the realistic, scientific spirit, psychology deserves a separate chapter. In its origins an adjunct of philosophy, it became in the nineteenth century the child of physiology; toward the end of the century it cut loose even from this indulgent parent and began a lusty independent existence. Today it is a word to conjure with, and the spirits it conjures are legion. Despite all the hocus-pocus about the "psychological moment" and the formulas for a fearless personality, the chatter of fancy illiterates about reflexes and complexes, the new science embraces some of the most significant developments in modern literature. Novelists of all stripes draw heavily upon it; critics are head-over-heels in debt to it.

An interest in the springs of behavior is of course no new thing under the sun. These springs were once limpid, however; one could see to the bottom of them with the naked eye. Motives in classical narrative and drama, for example, were thoroughly socialized, and even when character began to be individualized—notably by the genius of Shakespeare—they were still generally taken for granted: critics were almost two hundred years in discovering the problem in *Hamlet*. French fiction has indeed been given to analysis since *La Princesse de Clèves*. But it was not until the last century that novelists became more interested in exploring man's consciousness than in narrating his deeds, that personality and emotion became really complex, and that analysis became patient, minute, and unsentimental. The appearance of Stendhal in France, George Eliot in England, was a portent; the number of their progeny today is truly portentous.

The change that has accordingly come over character in modern fiction is plain enough. In Fielding and Thackeray, the patterns of characterization are relatively simple and trim; emotions are readily recognized and defined, motives readily explained, personalities readily tagged. Becky Sharp may be a woman of infinite variety and resource, but there are no shadows in her soul; if she fools most of her companions, the reader always sees through her. The neat, rounded, transparent types still persist in conventional realism, still make pleasant companions. But many novelists now consider them too artificial, and the traditional explanations of behavior inadequate. They have in the first place become interested in abnormal psychology, with its important implications for theoretically normal men. They have learned, moreover, that the dividing line between normality and abnormality is far from clear or fixed, and that much seemingly irregular behavior is lawful and natural. They are therefore apt, like Proust or Gide, to throw into sharp relief the irrational, incongruous elements of personality; they give us jagged characters impossible to fit into snug categories—characters not consistently and comfortably eccentric, like Mr. Micawber, because they are not exhibited as freaks and placed in side shows. Above all, novelists have discovered the immense well of the unconscious. Into this they may, like Lawrence, plunge directly and almost disappear from sight; or they may, like Sherwood Anderson, remain on the surface only to watch what comes up out of the depths and to picture the havoc wrought upon conventional designs for living. And the culmination of such interests has been an effort to expose the whole of human consciousness—the popular stream-of-consciousness is only the most literal of the several methods employed. The final effect of all these innovations is at any rate the same: a breaking up of the familiar, more or less symmetrical patterns of personality, and an emphasis upon obscure, inconsistent, unpredictable, often inexplicable impulses and emotions. Character becomes wavering and shadowy in its outlines, fluid even at its core. Thus we have Stephen Dedalus and Paul Morel, Ivan Karamazov and Lafcadio Wluki, Nina Leeds and Albertine Simonet—creatures whom the reader brought up with Tom Jones, David Copperfield, and the various Amelias often finds baffling, fantastic, or positively unreal.

These notions of personality and consciousness artists have not necessarily got direct from the psychologists. Many novelists—notably Dostoyevsky—anticipated the experts, and a host of critical middlemen have since translated the new concepts into a gentleman's English, made them fit for human nature's daily food. The influence of official psychology, moreover, is often diffuse, difficult to isolate. Pavlov's work on conditioned reflexes, for instance, or the more militant behaviorism of John B. Watson, has inspired no specific school of writers. As a new version of the materialistic, mechanistic thought of the nineteenth century, from which the early naturalists drew so heavily, it has perhaps helped to keep alive and vigorous the naturalistic impulse. It has in any event thrown light on the processes of adaptation, it has emphasized the environmental influences upon consciousness and personality. Hence it has no doubt left some mark on realistic fiction; that Watson's popular crusade to enthrone Environment as the sole arbiter of destiny had a contemporaneous literary parallel in *An American Tragedy* would seem not accidental.

More specific and demonstrable, however, is the influence of the thought usually associated with William James, though not entirely original with him. From his concept of consciousness as a continuous flow stem the streams of consciousness that flood the novels of James Joyce, Dorothy Richardson, Virginia Woolf, and Conrad Aiken, and trickle through the novels of innumerable others. No less familiar in modern literary experience is the concept of the subconscious that he did much to systematize and popularize; though conservative psychologists still protest against such notions, or at least hold that they are perforce outside the realm of any self-respecting science, writers have enthusiastically appropriated them. And perhaps most pervasive and profound is the influence of his doctrine that experience is always a vital unit, whose essential quality is falsified by analysis, and that the immediate perception gives a truer impression of reality than do its intellectualized derivatives. If James was not directly responsible, he at least prepared the way for impressionism, and the widespread reaction against a literal, bureaucratic realism.

But far more conspicuous is the mark of a school of whom the conservatives are even more suspicious: the psychoanalysts. A great deal of modern literature would be almost unintelligible to one unfamiliar simply with their vocabulary. Rationalization, libido, complex, inhibition, sublimation, projection, defense-mechanism, maladjustment, repression, compensation, intravert and extravert—to mention but a few of the terms they have introduced, or to which they have given a new meaning, will indicate the twist they have given to modern thought. They have not only provided the specific themes and symbols of innumerable fictions, from May Sinclair's *The Three Sisters* to Eugene O'Neill's *Mourning Becomes Electra,* but opened up the whole dark world of the unconscious, of which almost every living writer has made his Cook's tour. It is a question whether they have more distressed or delighted the contemporary by their revelations of the strange workings of his mind; it is beyond question that they have profoundly impressed him.

Psychoanalysis has gone the way of all schools in a restless age and is already split up into groups that attack one another more fiercely than they do their common enemies. Most influential is still that headed by the founder, Freud. The emphasis upon sex in modern fiction is not merely a reaction against Victorian prudishness; it is also an outgrowth of Freud's doctrine that sex is the mainspring of our unconscious life, the primary source of our hidden conflicts. Also influential, however, has been the theory of Adler, who locates this source in the "inferiority complex," with unconscious efforts at "compensation" and a tendency to "overcompensate." And though it is more difficult to trace his influence, especially fruitful for the artist would seem the psychology of Jung, who emphasizes normal rather than abnormal experience, who makes the animating principle of our unconscious lives not sexuality or any other specific instinct but an "undifferentiated life-energy" that may assume countless forms, and who considers the unconscious a reservoir of collective memories —symbolical material drawn from mythology, folk-lore, history, the arts, and the whole experience of the race. But all these schools have united in emphasizing the concept of a divided or "split" personality struggling with itself, often unconscious of its own purposes, often seeking to fulfil these purposes by means that it refuses or is unable clearly to define.

Such notions may appear to be merely sophisticated versions of old truths, and their fancy trappings merely elaborate ways of saying the obvious. Often they are. The split personality is no recent discovery; many heroes of the past struggle with themselves—and some suffer from what we now call complexes. Similarly Freud's therapeutic technique is an embellishment of the very old idea that it is helpful to get something off one's chest; and from another point of view his doctrine of sublimation, with the triumph of the conscious over the unconscious, is a kind of restatement of the old religious view of the struggle between the powers of light and darkness, good and evil. But that Freud's thought leads back to old and common experience certainly does not lessen its value, or even its originality. These derive less from his specific dogmas than from his whole, consistent way of looking at things. Artists have at any rate found his system stimulating, if only because it is more dynamic than the behavioristic psychology it in some ways resembles, and constantly stresses wilful action, purposeful striving—the element of conflict by which drama lives.

Of as exciting speculative interest, however, is the still more recent *Gestalt* psychology. I can think of no novel or novelist that it has as yet inspired. Its professional standing is still uncertain, its theory still in need of much experimental confirmation. Yet it draws from some of the strongest intellectual currents of the time—the anti-mechanistic trend in biology and physics as in philosophy and literature—and it is rich in implication and suggestion for the literary critic. It would seem to offer, for example, an excellent basis for a theory of esthetics: its insistence upon discrete *wholes* as the essence of experience—wholes not only differing from the sum of their parts but determining these parts—obviously corresponds with our immediate esthetic experience. The "meanings" critics assign to a poem or novel are seldom the actual meanings it has for us—or for them. More specifically, the extension of *Gestalt* theory into the field of personality also has literary analogies (as well as a close correspondence, incidentally, with the thought of James and the theory and practice of Adler); the stress upon dynamic patterns of behavior that must be studied as totalities and not broken up into little chains of causes and effects, the view of personality as an integrated whole to be distinguished utterly from the aggregate of characteristics into which it may be analyzed, confirms the reaction against purely intellectual analysis and all mechanical or abstract presentation of character. And still more specifically, it buttresses the work of the impressionists. When Ramon Fernandez, the most acute student of impressionism, declares that it forms in us *"psychic equivalents* of things containing within themselves the principle of their elucidation," he is pointing to a cardinal doctrine of the *Gestaltists;* they regard immediate, naïve impressions as the primary means of apprehending reality, and introspection as artificial and secondary. Hence they confirm the value of the sensory impressions to which the artist of every age is especially sensitive, restore to primacy the old ways of viewing life that are naturally congenial to him. They can help to rescue him from mechanical or merely fashionable responses, especially from the excesses of intellectualism that today often obscure his peculiar function.

We are here, of course, in the realm more specifically of criticism than of creative literature; it is chiefly upon and through the critics that the new science has exerted its influence. Most marked, again, is that of psychoanalysis. In its light biographers and critics are busily analyzing artists past and present: turning them inside out, dredging their unconscious selves, ferreting out their secret frustrations, demonstrating that nothing is as it seems.

As so many artists, especially in more recent times, are obviously neurotic, these studies are often suggestive—and should distress none but those acolytes who fear that explanation somehow degrades art, destroys its unique and ineffable value. Although the Freudians have not really uttered the secret of the motives, processes, and values of art, they have at least thrown some shafts of light through the cloudy talk that has for centuries shrouded this secret.

All this fashionable activity should not distract one, however, from the less spectacular reinforcements along the whole front of literary criticism. The psychologists themselves have made studies of genius and the artist type, and produced many treatises on esthetics—treatises that often make pretty hard going for the layman, but at worst no harder than those written by the philosophers. I. A. Richards for one has become an outright literary critic, creating a considerable stir by his blunt, if not always plain, talk about poetry. In general, the psychologists have furnished critics with sharper tools, contributing to the equipment notably of Kenneth Burke, perhaps the most acute critic in America today—the most penetrating in his analyses and precise in his definitions.

It is indeed difficult for the uninitiated to find their way around in this field, with so many conflicting and overlapping perspectives, so many schools vociferating that their half-truth is the whole truth. Although, to the non-partizan, few of the opposing doctrines seem utterly irreconcilable after their metaphysical sprouts have been lopped off, they still do not fit cozily into a composite picture; and although the eclectic has the comfortable feeling that he is displaying obvious good sense, he also feels the embarrassment of all middle-of-the-roaders and has to sacrifice the value of a consistent point of view. At present theory is rampant; what with the youth of the science and the nature of its subject matter, all is tentative, fragmentary, highly questionable. But the chief contribution of psychology is not the specific knowledge that critics have picked up. It is rather the new way of looking at things that has enabled them to see around the corner of habitual beliefs, helped them to escape the tyranny of habitual verbalizations. Psychologists have unveiled holy mysteries, stimulated direct thinking. And so, though they have given some critics merely a new and particularly unlovely jargon, they have led others to attempt to give something like specific gravity to the counters that for centuries have been flung about in fine careless raptures.

2

At first glance, all this energetic psychological investigation may appear to be simply another advance in the march toward Truth, another exciting promise of the brave new world that science is to fashion for us. As one begins to study its fruits, however, he is likely to have occasional misgivings, and in the end certain to be facing again the modern dilemma. In the scientific laboratory, psychology is indeed only another department of knowledge, another technique of control; in the novel, despite all the new insights, the preoccupation with the whys and hows of behavior is another symptom of the disintegration of modern society.

As Burke points out in *Permanence and Change,* our especial interest in *why* people do things clearly indicates our uncertainty about the whole problem of motivation and right conduct: "In great eras of drama, the audience *know* why characters act as they do." Stable cultures bring stable and standard patterns of behavior; motives are as socialized as manners. Although characters may be momentarily confused and bewildered, or rebellious, they finally perceive their motives as clearly as the audience always do. Yet modern readers make puzzles even of the old plays. They make of Shakespeare an earnest psychologist, and unearth intricate problems—about Hamlet, about Iago, about Shylock—that never occurred to his audience, and that often make nonsense of his plays. As Shakespeare had a profound intuitive understanding of the human mind, the implications of these problems are no doubt there—Hamlet is *not* so simple as his contemporaries thought him; just as plainly they were not Shakespeare's primary intention or interest.

In the modern novel, however, there is plenty of room for such speculation, and plenty of warrant for debate. There are no longer standard patterns of stimulus and response. With the extraordinary diversity of interest and occupation, the constantly shifting surface and periodic upheavals, the uncertainty about the future, the death of old gods and multiplicity of new ones, the whole painfully confused and confusing process of revaluation, conduct has naturally become more and more individualized. The question of motives has accordingly been thrown wide open. Each man must work out his own salvation, each becomes fair game for all specialists or partizans. One probable reason for the popularity of behaviorism was that it in a sense shelved the whole problem of motives, or at least delegated this problem to the expert; it at once relieved the individual of responsibility and encouraged the hope that in time behavior might be perfectly regulated. One probable explanation of the rise of both Fascism and Communism is that they arbitrarily impose "right" motives, manufacture the ideal personality; the totalitarian state demands a total response and gives at least the illusion of the simplicity and stability of the past. At any rate the novelist treating seriously the behavior of the modern man naturally must explain it. Hence he is likely to regard his materials as an opportunity for analysis as much as for drama, and his demonstration is likely to be viewed less as a formal work of art than as psychological or sociological data. In any event his explanations of the behavior that he has himself invented and motivated will not be accepted by many of his readers. They will be juggled among the various competing schemes of interpretation—Marxist, Freudian, behaviorist, or what you will.

If this preoccupation with diagnosis points to the presence of fever symptoms, the diagnoses themselves are in view of the sharp disagreement among the doctors seldom satisfying—or reassuring even when they are intended to be. The new knowledge of the springs of behavior has so far proved a very mixed blessing in literature. In an earlier chapter I remarked that some writers have been distressed by it. No less unfortunate, however, is that others have been simply bewitched by it. Their enthrallment would be dangerous if only because the findings of psychologists are so fragmentary and hedged by controversy; it is the more dangerous because they seldom drink deep even from this muddy Pierian spring. They reduce the human soul whose complexity they admire to a new set of simplicities, differing from the old chiefly in being more grotesque and in having fancier names. *Mourning Becomes Electra,* for example, is a crudely oversimplified reinterpretation of the classical legend, and would perhaps embarrass Freud as much as it would bewilder Sophocles. Similarly Ludwig Lewisohn, in his *Expression in America,* talks bumptiously of fixations and complexes, fastens a suspicious eye on all bachelor artists, and explains away everything he dislikes in American literature by referring it to either a Puritan heritage or a sexual maladjustment.

Critics generally are far too free and easy with the vocabulary of psychoanalysis—especially the many terms with which one may disparage the motives and activities of those whose interests differ from one's own. The psychoanalysts themselves are arbitrary when they select some one principle, whether sex or the drive for power, as the center of the web of impulses, and then assume that seemingly different activities are forms of sublimation, self-deception, or dishonesty. They slight the whole social context that frames and verbalizes our motives, one age disapproving what another had applauded; they forget that the selection of a different point of reference turns their explanations upside down —the Freudian who psychoanalyzes the Marxist is himself likely to be displayed as an evader of still grimmer realities, playing a bourgeois make-believe. And the bedazzled amateurs make still balder this error of mistaking relatives for absolutes. All one's opponents are simply "rationalizing"; a shy fellow is obviously suffering from an inferiority complex, but so too is a blustering fellow; a writer of tragedy is sublimating, a writer of comedy is compensating for, some secret frustration; radical reformer and romantic "escapist" alike are indulging in wish fulfilment. With this vocabulary it is easy to describe whatever one wants and however one wants it. It is less easy to say how much these paraphrases really explain—or above all what they have to do with the all-important matter of value.

Perhaps the plainest symptom of fever, however, is the specialization, not merely in irrational and incongruous, but in neurotic, definitely abnormal behavior. The modern hero is likely to be less an agent or spokesman than a patient, his story less a drama than a case history, his whole world a kind of psychopathic ward. Thus *Mourning Becomes Electra,* again, is a Freudian extravaganza, a riot of complexes culminating in the gratuitous horror of the suggestion of incest; by translating the classical legend into these terms O'Neill lends it timeliness—and effectually empties it of universal significance. Robinson Jeffers uses his splendid gifts of expression to produce a series of nightmares, distinguished among other things by his nice sense of the more horrible forms of perversion. The often-praised "strange and rich psychology" of William Faulkner is rich especially in abnormalities, and it comes presently to seem strange only when he approaches normal experience. The ancients themselves are viewed from this angle—and even by academic critics. Professor J. Q. Adams interprets *Hamlet* as a study in melancholia, buttressing his case by constant quotation from Krafft-Ebing, and taking a manifest pride in the myriad-minded Shakespeare's anticipation even of modern psychiatry.

Even when they stay closer to normal experience, the advanced novelists are likely to make so esoteric a study of its obscure regions, or reproduce so literally its kaleidoscopic elements, that they fail to give it a solid, substantial significance. Like Lawrence they may set out into the Unconscious—the "unanalyzable, indefinable, inconceivable" that now supplies the need of mystery once served by exploded superstitions; but this is often the bourne from which no traveler returns—and it is not our natural home. Like Dorothy Richardson they may generate streams of consciousness that flow nowhere in particular but simply and endlessly flow. There is in general a tendency, in poetry as in fiction, to mistake seeing life minutely for seeing it whole, to blur the main outlines of experience while exploring its shadows or exhibiting its many bright or curious bits, to make these subtle studies an end in themselves and not bring them to bear on the major choices, actions, and conflicts that organize human lives. Lawrence does indeed relate his discoveries to a passionate and provocative, if lopsided, view of life, and Proust, despite his obsession with all but the normal forms of love, does create a whole world. But Dorothy Richardson, and even Virginia Woolf, become themselves victims of the fragmentary, disconnected mental experience they recreate, and leave at the end an impression of tenuousness when not of downright inconsequence. And Joyce definitely takes the last step backward and presents a stream of sensations for its own sake. In *Ulysses* he still made some effort to integrate and point his miscellaneous material by superimposing the *Odyssey* motif; in his latest project he effectually divorces his reproduction of sensation from any problem of motive or any account of significant conduct.

The very subtlety of which contemporaries are so fond raises questions. The modern investigations of the soul of man make the old masters seem blunt or obvious, and no doubt are a sign of the growing intellectual maturity of the race. But what price subtlety? One thinks of the ultra-refined and distilled novels of Henry James. Although his eviscerated characters reflect his own temperamental limitations, one wonders whether any web so finely woven as his could hold a great passion—whether any such refinement of point of view and delicacy of analysis could encompass the fulness and tempestuousness of major experience. One thinks of the innumerable women novelists who with exquisite sensitiveness render fluttering sensations, who dip and dart into the crannies of fine consciences, who cultivate the nuance and the half-tone. One thinks of all the intimate plays performed in all the little theaters—and one recalls the immense edifices of the Greeks, or even the popular playhouses of the Elizabethans.

The drama of the past is in its great moments marked by the simplicity of all passionate utterance. The crisis is naked; the characters stand out in bold relief and squarely face the final issues of life and death; the emotion is primal and whole. To these simplicities the poet gave flaming expression. He was unafraid to make large and loose statements about life. It is a tale told by an idiot, a song dancing down the wind, a fevered dream.

> Nothingness, nothingness
> Ye children of man, and less
>   I count you, waking or dreaming!
> And none among mortals, none
> Seeking to live, hath won
> More than to seem, and to cease
>   Again from his seeming.

And the end to all pain, the answer to all doubt, is Death. It might seem, then, that great drama is a little primitive and naïve—and certainly it is. But so still are men; and so is all intense emotion, all their deepest experience. All the myriad impressions of sensitive minds, the intricacies of consciousness, the fascinating shades of character and emotion, pale before the immense and inexorable fact of man's common destiny.

The novel, to be sure, does not lend itself so readily to these compressed simplicities—its latitude is its chief advantage. At any rate one can, and today one must, admit more complexity, more subtlety. Yet something of the old simplicity and directness would still seem desirable, in fiction as in drama. Despite his new intellectual raiment, man is still a poor, naked, forked animal, and the final issues of his life the same. Intellect alone does not sustain him; he needs catharsis as well as understanding. And here again the preoccupation with the windings of consciousness and the hidden sources of behavior, the preponderance of intellectual interest in so many subtle studies, the emphasis upon what comes to seem information or argument more than art, the popularity of "authentic" as the badge of approval—all this is symptomatic of a confused, unquiet age that is profoundly uncertain when it seems most sure of itself. Those modern novelists, like Thomas Hardy, who continued to deal simply and powerfully with the basic tragic facts of human life—with the "pathos of mortality"—already seem to many a little old-fashioned and naïve. Contemporaries appear less interested in the great emotion itself than in an analysis of its genesis and intricate ramifications. If despite the reigning incertitude—and the reigning sophistication—they feel moved to large and passionate statement, they are likely to be restrained by the fear that such statements are too blunt and will not nick the precise center of their wavering target. And so they scrupulously analyze, explore, and explain; or they carefully modulate their tone and write what Elizabeth Drew has aptly labeled the "Novel of the Three Dots."

The characteristic expression of the realistic spirit in general is the habit of acute analysis (I use *analysis* loosely for the moment to include impressionistic rendering of complex or obscure sensation); the many forms of modern realism are differentiated chiefly by the objects and methods of this analysis. Zola, Dreiser, and today the proletarian writers are occupied especially with external forces. In them exhaustive documentation and the scientific pursuit of a chain of causes often clog the imagination; the individual may almost disappear from sight in the minute study of the squalid circumstances that shape his destiny. And when he comes into his own and is granted inwardness, it is only to face new hazards. He may be subjected to the remorseless analysis of the psychoanalyst—an analysis that makes the forces within him seem almost as impersonal. He may be studied primarily for his subconscious self, and be broken down into a misty bundle of disconnected impulses. And if he is endowed with a distinct, coherent personality, he may still not be represented in a significant action or allowed to make a significant decision.

Hence modern realists as a whole do not merely stain the white radiance of eternity; they tend to refract it, break it into particles that in sum may equal the whole but seldom resemble it. The special gloominess of much modern literature owes partly to the disproportionate emphasis given the innumerable unpleasant components into which experience has been split up—warts that not merely disfigure but conceal the complexion of reality. But this is in turn only one aspect of a more serious fault: the failure of many writers to supplement their penetrating analysis with a balanced, harmonious synthesis. Their sociological studies may treat of purely local infections; their streams of consciousness may trickle into inconsequence; their kaleidoscopic impressions may never be shaken together; their luminous halo may fade into thin air. They have all the glory of the specialist in their private domains, but their triumphs only emphasize the main problem of an age infested with specialists. And this problem, again, is to link all these domains within a broad view, to organize all that is valuable in this wealth of knowledge and experience into some satisfying scheme, to deepen and widen the channels of communication and cooperation.

Part Two

THE BASIS OF EVALUATION

V

PLATITUDES AND FIRST PRINCIPLES; A NOTE ON LAWS AND FORMULAS

I

I HAVE so far attempted to describe in general terms what modern fiction is like and how it got that way. In subsequent chapters I shall illustrate and amplify these general statements in studies of representative novelists. But, as these introductory chapters have no doubt made apparent enough, notions of value inevitably color even simple exposition; in the mere act of stating fundamental problems one has in mind some notion of "what this country needs"—even if no very specific notion of what the country is likely to get. My main purpose is at any rate appraisal, and so it is now necessary to drop the melancholy pretense of wholly impersonal survey, and attempt to establish criteria.

Henry Hazlitt once discoursed wittily on the prevalence of "Standards (Loud Cheers)"; the cheers emphasize again the profound uncertainty of the age and the profound disagreement upon all standards whatsoever. One is accordingly obliged to begin with a number of elementary observations. The history of criticism is among other things the history of the many disguises assumed by a few hoary fallacies; and like deathless dowagers, these fallacies are still with us, grimmer and lustier than ever. The identification of technique with value or means with ends, the insistence that art must be immediately useful in the service of some specific cause, the assumption that truth is absolute and has finally been cornered—these are only the more conspicuous forms of critical confusion. Literature is indeed going to survive the most fantastic of current operations on it, as it has survived centuries of misapprehension and abuse; but if the critic with an eye to the obvious is meanwhile not reduced to helpless exasperation, he is at least embarrassed by the necessity of pronouncing platitudes.

One should in the first place be able to look at the word *modern* without getting red in the face. Just as to some men on the street it means only progressive and up-to-date, to others only newfangled and cock-eyed, so do many critics respond to it as to a push-button. Some are dazzled by all innovation, and applaud the splendid spirit of William Saroyan when he announces from his flying trapeze that he has cut loose from all tradition, and that his is to be an altogether new stunt; they talk as if new methods automatically invalidated the old, and the history of literature were a sweeping advance, with the bones of outmoded genius moldering in its wake. Others as arrogantly condemn all departure from tradition, and like the New Humanists talk as if this history were a steady decline from some state of glory (upon whose geographical and temporal location they incidentally disagree); in demanding a return to the old "truths," they forget that the stress today is inevitably different, simply because of the different groupings and particularities of the constants of experience, and that original genius is always likely to make unusual demands of its audience.

But the problem of appraising modern literature is far more difficult than avoiding these grotesque extremes, or even than getting a bird's-eye view of a scene in the midst of which one lives. There arises the troublesome question of permanence and its relation to value. As I. A. Richards argues, there is no exact ratio between them. Because of its pertinence, a contemporary work may have more real value than much intrinsically superior work from the past; an artist is likely to profit by the pass-words and ready-made attitudes of a given audience, and hence to become obsolescent with the inevitable alteration of this context. By the same token, even the great art of the past is often obsolescent; only he can really appreciate Dante who has built up a very special equipment and steeped himself in the archaic attitudes out of which the *Divine Comedy* grew. And there is surely something ridiculous about the many scholars who look down their noses at modern literature while they carry on exhaustive researches in Medieval Drama or Sentimental Comedy or the Gothic Romance.

Yet just as surely there is a close connection between value and likelihood of endurance. Even one who has all of Richards' scorn for notions of immortal essences and eternal truths, and explains permanence instead by the "uniformity of the impulses from which the work of art starts," may still believe that the most valuable experiences are usually those least dependent upon specialized interests. The "impulses" most uniform are the oldest and deepest; a work of art that draws deeply from the well of racial experience is likely, not only to transcend its immediate purposes and outlive its particular symbols, but even in its own day to provide a richer, more deeply satisfying experience than will a work that exploits merely fashionable attitudes. Richards himself warns against the common tendency to judge art by its immediate signs and effects: the momentary consciousness it occasions, the thrill it provides. Intensity, power, poignance, ecstasy—these and other qualities by which critics approve usually accompany value, but they do not guarantee it, they are not its trademark. A football victory may produce "ecstasy," a toothache or a thriller may be "intense," an account of a murder or a rape "powerful," a piece of Hollywood sentiment "poignant"—and the quality of the experience is *at the moment* much like that in great art. Value lies rather in the residue or after-effects of an esthetic experience: the reflective emotions it evokes, the attitudes it induces, the possibilities it opens up. Hence the novel that is too closely identified with the peculiar interests and attitudes of its time and is not deeply rooted in the constants of experience will be less spacious, suggestive, or resonant. Its impact will be solid but not lasting, its reference pertinent but not extensive, its value real but not rich.

This observation is especially pertinent to the social studies so characteristic of modern fiction. Even when it becomes evangelical, this sociological interest is certainly not deplorable. Novelists are living in the twentieth century, and it has undeniable claims upon them. They cannot always be "citizens of eternity," they should not be saddled with solemn obligations to posterity—they can trust posterity to write for itself. At the present crisis of civilization it is simply precious to warn the artist off immediate issues. Yet the highest privileges of art are not immediate, deliberate, or specific, and the limitation of these sociological studies is that they commonly have little reference beyond the thesis they work out. Often they are too diagrammatic, too syllogistic; characters are impaled on the "spire of meaning" that rigidly shapes rather than merely crowns the entire work. And those that are less synthetic are still likely to have relatively narrow implications and to slight the age-old patterns of experience. With Hardy as with Shakespeare we look down the whole stupendous vista of life; they leave us brooding over the eternal questions of life and death. Ibsen, Gissing, Wells, Shaw, Galsworthy, Lewis, and innumerable contemporaries often leave us chiefly with some notions about the imperfections of our social order—notions that not only soon lose their point in a changing though still imperfect society, but cramp the imagination even while they are still pertinent. These writers sharpen our perceptions, quicken our conscience as citizens; they do not intensify and order our whole experience.

An H. G. Wells may indeed fulfil himself more completely as a social philosopher than as a creative artist. Other novelists, however, have a different if not a more exalted calling. Hence it is unfortunate that they are today so often impelled to adopt purposes likely to result in the presentation of information and argument rather than the creation of a work of art.

2

Ever since the first critic began to systematize his prejudices, the most despotic of critical fallacies has been the confusion of means with ends, the erection into universal law of the practice of a particular age. Although most forms and methods are in their origin unconscious or accidental, once they have been stamped by genius and become firmly established they appear to be the inevitable, the only "right" mode, and hence the necessary sign of value. Critics merely rationalize and codify what the creative artist usually takes for granted. And this pious process ends in pure fetishism. The history of art, with its endless diversity from country to country and its endless change from century to century, makes nonsense of it; yet this multifarious experience has served less to discourage the habit of false worship than to provide alternative idols. The proprieties and the unities that French drama carried over from the Greeks—the whole practice that was imposed upon the Greek dramatists themselves chiefly by the presence of the chorus and the physical properties of their theater—are only a more obvious example of the tyranny of a convention, the mistaking of technique for value, that has warped the judgment of every art form in every age. And the moderns, despite their radical break with tradition and their bold experimentation, make the same elementary error. The advanced critics, the very apostles of freedom, make a gospel of modernism and so simply substitute new fetishes for the old. What chiefly unites the various partizans is a vigilant suspicion of certain conventions of the past—a fear of rhetoric, for example, or of formal contrivance.

Perhaps the most serious delusion of this kind today is the common attitude toward realism. Realism is only a useful method, a technique; but heavily loaded as the name itself is with the assumption of "truth," many regard it as the necessary approach to art, the necessary badge of seriousness and maturity. The realistic spirit has become a kind of holy ghost in the new trinity fathered by science. In its crudest form, this new fetishism has inspired all the fact-mongering in modern fiction, the substitution of laborious documentation for imaginative creation. It then appears in the confusion of material with meaning, of verisimilitude with value—the confusion generally of literature with life. In one form or another it enters almost all the critical disputes over what is or is not "authentic," and obscures in a denser fog the functions and values of art.

However irritating the pontifical manner and occasionally unfortunate the vocabulary of Matthew Arnold, one must begin with his dictum: It is the business of art in some manner to offer a criticism of life. It must integrate, consolidate, interpret, and hence illumine our experience, give form and significance to facts that in their mere contiguity are meaningless. It is properly not an imitation of nature; in the words of Nietzsche, it is "a metaphysical supplement to the reality of nature." It has its own laws, its own logic, its own "truth." Its function is always in some measure to idealize—to select and filter, to exclude or minimize the trivial, irrelevant or grossly fortuitous, and in this way to detach meanings and values. This is not, of course, to demand of the novelist explicit instruction. He is not to be a Polonius, peddling precepts; his business is to state problems, not to solve them. But simply to make a vital statement, his work must have an intellectual or spiritual center, must provide a point of view, must organize and not merely duplicate experience.

Now, one need not worry about the novelist's refusal to shoulder this responsibility. He cannot help himself. As has often been observed, there is no such thing as plain, unvarnished fact; one cannot present life "from nobody's point of view." However squeamish his fears of being didactic or ardent his aspirations to complete objectivity, the novelist inevitably makes a comment simply by the kind of story he chooses to tell, and inevitably imposes some pattern that is in itself an interpretation. Even *Ulysses,* Edwin Muir has remarked, is less confusing than Dublin. Like all novelists, Joyce has made a statement—as life does not.

The quality of this statement, however, is another matter; and here the realistic method has misled many of its practitioners. With a fine zest they join the parade of the real, but they simply get lost in the crowd. They offer us the spectacle from but a slight remove. They fail to draw out its deeper implications, to give it a large symbolical significance, even to reveal the wonderful strangeness of the familiar and commonplace. One has only to recall the flood of transcripts of Mid-Western farm life that followed in the wake of *Main Street:* transcripts faithful, painstaking, honest—and ineffably dreary. Although the moderns have developed an excellent habit of impersonal curiosity and patient observation, and produced a whole school of shrewd, adroit reporters, the fruit of all this industry and skill is often but a "meaningless pageant of the real" and a slavery to its illusion. However large or dense, a slice of life is only a slice, and its size is no more index to its value than the length of a bus ride is to quality of observation.

The pedestrian realists, to be sure, are straw men for any kind of critical game. Yet there is a general disposition even among more important novelists to select material for its intrinsic interest rather than for its relation to an esthetic purpose, and among critics to applaud any work simply because of its verisimilitude or its scientific validity. The stream of consciousness, the minimal plot, the habit of analysis, the application of Marxist philosophy—all are justified less on esthetic than on scientific grounds, less because they heighten artistic effectiveness than because they correspond more closely to our notions of actuality. Realism has led, once more, to a confusion of the experience of art with the experience of life; and although this confusion may be flattering to the artist, it obscures his true function. It gives rise to bastard forms that bear only a superficial resemblance to either parent. "A mere headache is more 'authentic' than a great tragedy," writes Kenneth Burke; it is also a very different kind of experience and by no means a fit subject for tragedy. The novelist orders experience in accordance with formal principles that correspond to complex processes of the human mind but do not necessarily have a counterpart in the everyday business of living. He *creates* a world with laws of its own. The reader demands of a novel a design, a unity and completeness, a logic, that he does not look for in the lives of his neighbors.

Realism is accordingly only an approach to this different world—an approach at that of but a recent few in the long line of great artists. It is a fruitful method, especially adapted to the novel form and to the peculiar interests of the modern world, and certainly not to be disparaged *per se*. But it is no guaranty of value or of truth.

3

The popularity of all that passes for "psychology" in fiction is a striking example of the fetish of the "real." The psychologists themselves are likely to keep clearly in mind the nature of esthetic experience, the norms by which one can more clearly perceive the many vagaries in modern literature. But literary men have frequently lost perspective and exploited for their own sake the new methods and materials that should properly be but a means to an end. Thus they become absorbed in analyses or demonstrations that too often provide a predominantly intellectual interest. Thus they penetrate ever farther into the subterranean world and explore most avidly the murky recesses of the neurotic and pathological, the perverted and abnormal.

"Morbid" is the popular word for these artists, and indeed they often display an unhealthy fondness for pricking the mental pimples and scratching the mental sores of this age; but to identify them with their material, as if they had neither imagination nor impersonal curiosity, only obscures the important issue. The response to such work is not necessarily disagreeable, nor the attitudes it fixes necessarily unhealthy. But it is a limited experience. Clinical fiction lacks the element of deep constancy necessary to great drama, it leads away from "the main march of human affections" and touches our own experience at too few points, it brings into play and harmonizes too restricted emotions, it obtrudes the restricted values of hygiene. Although we may pity its unhappy creatures, we cannot thoroughly identify ourselves with them or regard them as universal symbols. Thus Hamlet not merely looks uncomfortable in the ultra-modern dress in which Professor Adams has draped him; he shrinks and dwindles. As an idealist planted in a corrupt, materialistic society, as a man of thought suddenly called upon for resolute and violent action—as almost any of the hundred other persons that scholars in their ingenuity have made of him, Hamlet can be a great tragic hero and voice the tortured doubts of all ages; as a psychopathic case he must lose his compelling attraction, for he ceases to represent suffering and aspiring humanity.

But *Mourning Becomes Electra* once more offers the most striking demonstration. O'Neill has a passion to transcend temporal interests, to treat "big subjects," to study "the relation between man and God," to recapture for his fellows the heroic and sublime. Yet even had his manipulation of the Freudian symbols been less heavy-handed, he could not have realized his lofty purposes; his whole conception stands in his way. His play has a lurid, sinister beauty and power, but it is impossible to endow with profound spiritual significance a case history, impossible to make compelling symbols of diseased characters who die like poisoned rats in a hole. The fact remains, of course, that so generally sensitive a critic as Joseph Wood Krutch apparently got from the play the lift and glow of high tragedy; and mere argument is unlikely to destroy his impression. But what explains O'Neill's practice also explains Krutch's criticism. He is not only likely to be taken in by all solemn discussion of the modern dilemma and to enjoy all tinkering with his forlorn soul (he was about the only reputable critic to be impressed by *Dynamo*); he is also saturated with the new psychology and accepts its partial explanations as the whole testament of behavior. If because of these special interests *Mourning Becomes Electra* was for him an experience of unusual value, it for the same reason disappointed more normal expectations—and at that one may question the richness and permanence of its value for Krutch himself.

Perhaps the most common way, however, in which the new psychology has led critics astray is the habit first of substituting, then mistaking explanation of *why* a work was written (which on the lower levels becomes a matter of discovering the mistress who "inspired" it, or in scholarly circles the official literary "sources") for appraisal of its meanings and values, and their relation to our whole culture. In the first place, the explanations are inadequate as such. The Freudians, for example, reveal much about the artist's personality as a private *citizen* but much less about his work as an *artist.* In their contentment with mere paraphrases, they fail to show how or why the undifferentiated sex impulse becomes the individual impulse to form. They do not explain the immense diversity, in both kind and quality, of work rooted in presumably the same type of complex—the mystery of the creative impulse or inner will as opposed to the external frustration. But beginnings must in any event always be distinguished from final references. That a work of art grows out of a certain context does not mean that it ends there, any more than all behavior is equally selfish because it can all be traced to selfish impulses. Milton, Blake, Shelley, Flaubert, Melville, Rimbaud, Proust, Lawrence—all suffered from some form of maladjustment (most of them, too, were bourgeois); but however amplified, this statement is still only a footnote to a proper criticism of their work. Millions of maladjusted bourgeois have written trash or written nothing at all.

Unfortunately, moreover, this whole approach has led to some aspersion as well as to neglect of the final references of art. Having discovered that artists suffer from "maladjustment," the critic —or even the artist himself—becomes suspicious of their "compensation," with its implication of evasion of reality. But all activity can be interpreted in these terms. "Every notary bears within him the débris of a poet," wrote Flaubert; if one likes, the notary's scribbling industry is a compensation for the frustration of the poet—and what of it? The artist is indeed likely to be more obviously maladjusted simply because he is more finely attuned, more keenly aware of the disharmonies in his own soul and in his age. But if such stresses condition his work and need to be understood, they do not explain its value or necessarily set a limit to this value.

4

Partly as a reaction against the excesses of bourgeois morality, partly too as a refuge from the oppressive authority of science, there was cultivated toward the end of the nineteenth century the doctrine of the unmorality of art. Flaubert's ideal of a pure or absolute beauty apart from matter, the virtuoso performances of the Symbolists, and the posturings of Wilde and the art-for-art's-sakers were all forms of this new religion of art. It is an elegant religion and provides an apparently impregnable fastness; the artist becomes his own priest, and in an age of experts his own expert. It is also a very futile religion, and finally more unflattering to the artist than the vulgar assumption that his activities are *im*moral. This assumption at least implies that he is a positive influence upon conduct, a force to be reckoned with; to cut him off from moral ideas is to put him in a vacuum, to make his work at best merely decorative. Yet the sanctuary is still tenanted. Croce has served as its high priest, the Dadaists for a time made it noisy with their pranks, and sophisticates and esthetes always keep it semi-fashionable.

Now, one need not worry about the threat of so rarefied a faith. It is opposed by the immense weight of common experience: the instinctive feeling of the artist that what he is doing is vitally important, the instinctive response of the great majority of readers, plain or cultivated, to whom intense esthetic experience is not merely a diversion. One has but to consider the ubiquitous evidence of bad art: the vulgarization of taste, the diffusion of shoddy ideals, and the fixation of crude and unrealistic attitudes that the movie, the radio, and the printing press have made into one of the mightiest of modern industries—one has but to contemplate this appalling spectacle (or indeed attempt to escape it) to realize that the arts are vitally tied up with the practical business of living. Hence far more prevalent today is the opposing fallacy, to which the esthetes have perhaps contributed by exciting a backfire: the fallacy that art should enlist in the service of some immediate, specific cause. And here one runs head-on into the angriest critics of the moment—the extreme Marxists.

Their challenge cannot be declined simply because their eyes are often bloodshot and their voices hoarse. In the present crisis, as Waldo Frank has soberly pointed out, there is a need of direct action, "transcending the solid, quiet, slow certainty of art." It is not enough in any event to invoke the old bogey of "propaganda," for all art is in a real sense propaganda. The writer is always trying to influence his readers, make them see and feel as he does; and Milton, Pope, Balzac, Dickens, Tolstoy, and indeed most great writers have preached directly. Even Shelley, the romantic model of the poet, was as evangelical as Shaw.

Yet the artist's communication is generally most effective when it is tacit, indirect, undeliberate, even unconscious. Thus *Paradise Lost* remains a great poem not because but in spite of Milton's arguments—its grandeur is today almost measured by the magnificence of Satan that makes nonsense of his intentions. Explicit and insistent propaganda is likely, moreover, to weaken the artist's peculiar force. When he does not simply substitute canned dogma for his own perceptions, he often simplifies them and forces them into too rigid a mold. Conceivably, indeed, he may be less "useful" for the purposes of reform than writers indifferent or actually hostile to these purposes, for such writers may incidentally arouse a dissatisfaction with the *status quo,* as for example T. S. Eliot does, and thus open the door for all salesmen of nostrums. But the essential point is that all great art prepares the mind in a general fashion by intensifying consciousness, promoting finer adjustments and raising standards of response, inculcating values and ideals. As Kenneth Burke reminds his fellow Leftists, "There must be a literature which upholds such an equipment in the abstract, if the social reformer is to find something in us to which he can appeal when advocating reforms in the particular."

The basic fallacy of the zealots, however, is again one that in all ages and under innumerable flags has obstructed an elementary understanding and appreciation of literature. It is the fallacy of appraising a literary work on the basis of its *specific* meaning, as explicit in argument or implicit in the author's conscious intention, and then arbitrarily condemning it in so far as it is found to contain "error" or "evil"—in other words, in so far as it is at variance with the critic's own guaranteed brand of "truth." It is the fallacy of assuming that the rich, subtle harmonies of esthetic experience can be resolved into such crude valuation as may be measured by a particular dogma. The Marxist doctrinaires are choosing for themselves such cozy bedfellows as Irving Babbitt, Joseph Goebbels, Will Hays, and countless preachers and old-fashioned moralists. All sniff under the bed for a naturalist, a Red, an atheist, or a bourgeois; all have essentially the attitude of the simple reader who judges a work of art by the plainness and soundness of its moral.

Great literature is never wholly expressive of any one philosophy. Its value clearly does not lie in the information it conveys or the dogma it demonstrates—else one should go direct to scientists and philosophers, and the masterpieces of the benighted past would be as dead as conscientious scholars strive to make them. Although ideas, especially moral ideas, are implicit in all literature as in any significant account of human life, they are by-products rather than end-products; and they are not necessarily the ideas consciously planted by the author. One need not accept the specific conclusions that a Tolstoy or a Hardy appends to his imaginative creations in order to appreciate these creations and respond to his poetry and passion. The "synthetic and magical power" of imagination reveals itself, Coleridge said, in "a more than usual state of emotion, with more than usual order; judgment ever awake and steady self-possession with enthusiasm and feeling profound or vehement." This elevated state often associates itself with a particular doctrine, but it is not actually occasioned by this doctrine. It is a good in itself and only secondarily reinforces particular concepts of good.

The only valid objection to any philosophy in art accordingly arises in so far as it fetters the artist's imagination, insulates his understanding, blunts his perception, curdles his emotion. What threatens a writer is finally not the "wrongness" but the narrowness or exclusiveness of an attitude—not the erroneous conclusions it leads him to but the experience it shuts him off from. He deals preeminently with the immediate, the personal, the concrete; the final test of his work is not the soundness of his arguments but the vitality of his concrete representations of experience. All one can safely say is that certain attitudes threaten this vitality more than others, and that the ideal philosophy for the artist would appear to be that which allows him to deal freely and unaffectedly with the entire range of experience. Hence the Marxists may fairly point out that the contemporary writer whose vision does not embrace the economic warfare is to that extent limited in his understanding of the realities among which he lives and from which he draws sustenance, and that the attitude of fastidious distaste or timid evasion is plainly a dangerous one. In the same spirit, however, one may point out that also dangerous is the passionate partizanship that warps the vision of many of the comrades; the red blood even of proletarian fiction is often sucked out by despotic arguments, its vigorous representation cramped and distorted by being forced into the frame of a syllogism.

The critic will naturally view the attitudes or philosophies of modern writers first of all in relation to the special interests, problems, and needs of the time. But it is his job finally to view their work in relation to the larger purposes of art and to detach the values that are often obscured by immediate issues. That the interests and prejudices of Hardy and Dostoyevsky, Lawrence and Proust, do not correspond with his own is no warrant for the critic *ipso facto* to suspect their work. He must often discount the avowed intentions of the writer, who himself as often transcends as he falls short of them. It is of course easy in this way to dismiss too airily all the eccentric attitudes of a writer to whom one is temperamentally attracted, and to prove whatever one wants —the Unconscious is in the present state of knowledge a vast storehouse of arguments for any cause. Yet the whole history of literature makes it plain that one must accept precisely this hazard.

5

Literary historians have always been prone to talk as if literature were the product of a few gifted men, ordinarily banded in "schools" taught by the critics. They stress the "influence" of selected individuals, they point to sacred authorities, and they assign to large movements generic motives that would certainly have seemed strange to most of the participants in them. Today, however, most critics realize that such explanations are merely convenient abstractions, and that we only begin to perceive the real causes of literary movements after these movements have sunk into the trough of the next groundswell—just as historians discover the causes of wars long after the statesmen that declared them and the soldiers that fought them have moldered in their graves. With the rise of evolutionary theory, the tendency in all fields of thought has been to think in organic terms, to seek large patterns, and to emphasize the deep, unconscious processes that govern both society and the individual. Cultures somehow just grow; and even in a self-conscious, critical, and scientific age they continue to be shaped less by reasoned, weighted choices than by obscure, affective, non-rational motives—the "residues" that are the subject of Pareto's prodigious study. In his *Anthropology,* Professor Kroeber notes that in proportion as "the alleged products of their intellects are involved, when one might most expect foresight and reason and cool calculation to be influential, societies seem swayed by a conservatism and stubbornness the strength of which looms greater as we examine history more deeply."

In such a view, the critics and even the great creative artists play a much less decisive part in shaping the course of literature than their prominence would suggest. They are largely the symbols or agents of the forces they appear to create. The critic helps to interpret and stabilize the practice of others, to crystallize and canalize the creative energy, and so to a certain extent he molds the literature he judges; but, like the sheep dog, he has only the illusion of control and is subject to the same power that governs his flock. He no more makes literature than the grammarian makes language; both rationalize what somehow makes itself. Even the great pivotal figures in modern thought, like Rousseau or Marx, do not so much create universal sentiment as they are created by it, recognizing what has already come to be, making their fellows aware of the direction in which they are already facing. Similarly—and still more obviously—creative artists are spokesmen of the time spirit, fuglemen rather than commanders-in-chief. The very great geniuses, like Shakespeare and Michelangelo, indeed break out of these bounds, but for the same reason that they defy category they defy imitation; they affect the course of artistic development little more, and often less, than do less awe-inspiring figures. One doubts that English literature of the last two centuries would have been significantly different had Chaucer, Shakespeare, and Milton not written. When a genius appears greatly to influence a later age it is because the age is ripe for him, peculiarly ready for his influence, and uses him as an authority to go where it was already going. This is not to belittle the achievements of the great or to deny the force of individual personality. It is simply to say that the effectiveness of genius derives chiefly from its splendid service as the instrument of still greater forces—forces once called God and now more commonly by less intelligible names. What ultimately shapes literature is these blind, deep-seated, complex forces that shape our whole civilization.

Hence we have the spectacle today of critics everywhere burrowing underground in an effort to discover the hidden laws governing the movements in literature and life. Taine was one of the first to attempt to skirt the blind alleys of purely subjective interpretation and work out a scientific system of criticism; today his children are legion, and they have much sharper and shinier tools. Most fashionable at the moment is the method of "dialectical materialism" practiced by John Strachey, Granville Hicks, and the Marxists generally. No less systematic is the Freudian approach, which has fixed a thousand eyes on the artist's love-life. Pareto now bids fair to inspire a new school. Sociology, biology, psychology, anthropology—all have started up still other hares, all give us prophets voluble and brash.

It is an exhilarating and up to a point an illuminating spectacle —much light has been thrown upon the springs and texture of imaginative creation, the conditions out of which literature grows. It is also embarrassing to the critic who has himself no law, no specific formula of criticism. From this profusion of perspectives and programs it is difficult to form a composite picture, for if at times they overlap, more often they cross tangentially or remain on different planes. Furthermore, the prophets are constantly swallowing one another. The Freudian psychoanalyzes the Marxist; the Marxist dishes up the Freudian as a bourgeois; and as one rubs his eyes, he hears from the New Humanists that it makes no difference—they are both "naturalists" and hence of the devil. "Disputes are multiplied," in the words of Hume, "as if everything was uncertain, and these disputes are managed with the greatest warmth, as if everything was certain." The mere civilian of letters has accordingly a pardonable impulse to cry plague upon all these houses.

The pall of nineteenth-century materialism is indeed upon most of this ambitious effort. The system-builders tend to reduce all phenomena to a few mechanical elements as the handiest blocks to build with, and then to translate intricate interdependencies into simple relations of cause and effect. They mistake relatives for absolutes, names for things, and presently they ignore their own ignorance. At most, moreover, they explain the artist's origin but not his effectiveness, the nature but not the quality of his work. In short, in their excitement over the discovery of some superior salt to sprinkle, critics forget the elementary matter of getting close to the creature's tail. And the serious harm is that their formulas contract not only their judgment but their actual esthetic experience. Their conditioned reflexes become too firmly fixed; like Pavlov's dogs, they salivate upon a stimulus only within a narrow range.

Yet criticism must somehow embrace and reconcile all these doctrines, for all have some element of truth. Even the plain fallacies of which they are also compounded are significant, as they point to the kind of meaning that literature actually has for many contemporaries. The effort at synthesis is in fact under way. Stephen Spender (of the holy trinity worshiped by the younger writers: Spender-Auden-Lewis) is one of a number calling for a combination of Marx and Freud. Yet the simple processes of addition will not do. The difficulty with any formula, any specific principle or law designed to make criticism objective and absolute, is that if it is genuinely inclusive it will perforce be so broad, intricate, and many-sided, have so many corollaries and qualifications, that its application will permit neither neatness nor certainty. We have no common denominator for all the heterogeneous factors, no means of isolating any one of them. In short, it is impossible, at least in the present state of knowledge, to apply any rule-of-thumb. One can make out forces and conditions, tendencies and probabilities; one cannot absolutely measure, explain, predict, or prescribe.

As a concrete illustration of the difficulties besetting the formulist, and of how the very brilliance of the light he often throws deepens the shadows in all the experience outside the illuminated area, Marxist criticism will again do best. During its early stages, in the first flush of revolutionary ardor, this criticism was naturally crude: a simple matter of separating artists into proletarian sheep and bourgeois goats, complicated by some haggling over doctrinal orthodoxy, but constantly enlivened by whoops from the bandwagon. Michael Gold's savage attack upon Thornton Wilder some years back was the signal for the slaughter of all the "bourgeois" artists still unaware that their society was hell-bent for destruction. Some of the foremost Marxist critics, notably Strachey and Hicks, have not yet really outgrown these grotesque simplicities. But even the more temperate disciples continue to make the elementary error of attempting to explain everything from *one* point of reference. In making the quest of food and its derivative institutions the key to all human behavior—just as the extreme Freudians open all doors with the no less primary but unrelated principle of the sexual impulse—they establish a hierarchy of causes that is arbitrary even from a deterministic point of view. They ignore the multiple and intricate interdependencies so brilliantly analyzed by Pareto, failing to see that if the thought and feeling, the materials and methods, the whole equipment and response of the artist are *conditioned* by his social context, they are not, strictly speaking, *caused* by it—any more than economic or sexual manifestations are caused by esthetic ones. Hence they not only still denature the workers whose vigor and virtue they hymn, but fail of the genuinely organic view on which they pride themselves. It is as if the physiologist made the stomach the central organ of the human body and explained the structure and functions of all other organs by their relation to it.

It is possible, indeed, to interpret Marx's philosophy more liberally, for his was not the rigid, mechanical materialism of other nineteenth-century thinkers. He did not regard psychical phenomena as identical with physiological processes, and he dreamed of supplementing his analysis of the economic structure of society. But if in a broader view dialectical materialism loses its distortions, it also loses its wonder-working power. The harder one looks at it, the mistier and more metaphysical it gets. *Dialectics* is only a way of thinking, not an instrument of incontrovertible proof; *materialism* is only a convenient assumption—a scientific figure of speech, not a scientific fact. The whole concept may too easily dissolve into another of the many verbalizations that confuse thought—already many Marxists substitute the manipulation of elaborate linguistic machinery for direct thinking. As employed by Marx himself, his method brought brilliant results; when set up as an absolute principle, an open-sesame, it becomes dangerous. At best it is chiefly another way of saying that the critic ought to be as thorough, systematic, and comprehensive as possible (which few will deny), and use all the findings and resources of modern investigation in an effort to correlate all causes and effects. In short, it finally lands the critic in the hole of subjective interpretation he has tried to crawl out of, with nothing but a shelter somewhat more shell-proof.

However exasperating their dogmatism, the exponents of the economic interpretation of literature have indeed done a valuable service. They have added a fresh perspective, pointed to important relationships hitherto largely ignored, discredited a number of "eternal verities," supplied a needed antidote for the excesses of both esthetes and pedestrian scholars. But they cannot be regarded as exciting pioneers clearing the path that is finally to lead to truth. They are instead specialists, whose diagnoses must be correlated with those of specialists in other domains, and even with the opinion of the old family doctor familiar with the whole personality and life history of the patient. They have provided only another slant, another bias, that must be included in a much larger view.

VI

A THEORY OF VALUE; HUMANISM

I

IN pointing out the limitations of the scientific systems of criticism currently popular, I have so far only touched upon their most serious insufficiency. The formulists often explain more or less satisfactorily why men write as they *do*. They explain much less satisfactorily why men *write* at all—the nature of the creative impulse itself. Above all, they prove little about how men *ought* to write, or how we are to weigh the products of different writers in different cultures. They may retain their scientific air but they lose their scientific authority when they approach the all-important problem of determination of value.

Values and sanctions are indeed implicit in all the systems, and usually they are insisted upon. Most of the analysts have got tied up with a cause. Freud's program is frankly therapeutic, but even the objective analysis of Marx periodically shades into evangelism; one cannot at every moment be sure that he writes of what is and is going to be or of what ought to be—and in his disciples today this confusion is much more pronounced. Inevitably men have preferences and must make choices. But evaluation ultimately rests on concepts of the good life, and though these may have some scientific basis, they cannot be tested in a laboratory or conclusively verified by any empirical method. In short, the thoroughgoing critic finally lands in the realm of exalted guesswork.

Yet the critic must obviously have some theory of value—especially today when the arts have been put on the defensive in a science-dominated world at the same time, curiously enough, that they are clamorously called upon to serve various causes. No less obviously, I should say, this theory ought to be empirical. In the face of the whole history of thought, or of even a superficial survey of the attitudes and behavior of one's neighbors, it is difficult to postulate an absolute Beauty or Good, a universal Idea independent of human experience; about the dictates of Pure Reason there has been even more dispute than about the commands of Jehovah. With this in mind, one can at least profit by the mistakes of a long line of distinguished theorists. For the philosophical critics of the past have usually located value in some specific manner or dogma: in an ideological content derived from a particular culture and almost certain to evoke a different response in a different context. In effect, they have by an all too familiar process erected into metaphysical entities, and thence into categorical imperatives, their temperamental preferences or the preferences of some age, shutting out experiences that whole ages plainly found valuable. Hence the first requisite of any adequate hypothesis is that it be broad enough to embrace all the multifarious products of creative imagination throughout human history, modest enough to premise that in this disorderly, imperfect world we have no real knowledge of absolutes but only an incorrigible tendency to identify them with our favorite sentiments.

Toward such an hypothesis I. A. Richards has at least made a brave start in his *Principles of Literary Criticism*. He begins with "appetencies": wants conscious or unconscious. Their only psychological restraints are other and conflicting appetencies. "Anything is value," accordingly, "which will satisfy an appetency without involving the frustration of some equal or *more important* appetency." Importance is determined, after allowing for certain obviously prior physiological needs, by "the extent of the disturbance of other impulses in the individual's activities which the thwarting of the impulse involves." That organization will then be best which thwarts or starves fewer important impulses, is least wasteful of human possibilities. "The most valuable states of mind . . . are those which involve the widest and most comprehensive coordination of activities and the least curtailment, conflict, starvation, and restriction."

Herein lies the vital importance of the arts. They are "our storehouse of recorded values," and if rightly approached, "supply the best data available for deciding what experiences are more valuable than others." For they are the records of the most sensitive and discriminating men, exercises of the spirit impossible to, or at least incommunicable by, the ordinary man. "They spring from and perpetuate hours in the lives of exceptional people, when their control and command of experience is at its highest, hours when the varying possibilities of existence are most clearly seen and the different activities which may arise are most exquisitely reconciled, hours when habitual narrowness of interests or confused bewilderment is replaced by an intricately wrought composure." And as fine conduct springs only from fine ordering of impulses, not from such crude organizations as can be summarized by ethical maxims or as commonly pass for "instruction," the poets, as Shelley said, lay the basis of morality. Through such intricate processes, imagination is indeed the chief instrument of moral good.

Now, in view of the fanfare with which Richards announced this approach, the results are somewhat meager and disappointing—not to mention a little stupefying when he draws a diagram of what goes on in the mind when one reads a poem. If he keeps clear of the metaphysical wastes in which other seekers of the True, the Beautiful, and the Good get lost, he does not himself come very close to his quarry. As a general statement his theory is neat, plausible, comprehensive; the trouble is that all his key words need more precise definition. While apologizing for the present ignorance of the processes of organization, Richards still insists that his system of measurement enables one to compare not only different experiences belonging to the same personality but different personalities: that is the better experience which engages more of our possible personality, that is the better personality in which more can be engaged without confusion. This yardstick indicates clearly enough the stature of the greatest geniuses; in Homer, Dante, Michelangelo, Shakespeare, and Goethe are both abundance and order. When one applies it to more controversial figures, however, one immediately runs up against incommensurables and is presented with the eternal arbitrary choice: wide and varied possibilities at the price of disorder, or well-ordered impulses at the price of narrowness. Is Pope's a better personality than Shelley's? Mozart's than Wagner's? Is the experience provided by *Phèdre* more valuable than that provided by *The Brothers Karamazov?* By a Greek temple than by a Gothic cathedral? The problem is further complicated, in social behavior as in art, by the inevitable presence of the element of sacrifice; as Richards recognizes, this automatically lends an added value to the activity for which one has sacrificed other impulses. But how does one determine what impulses to sacrifice, and to what extent? In short, the whole problem resolves itself into the question of what are the most "important" impulses. Nobody knows. Nobody could in any event give a categorical answer, for it will vary with the possibilities of the individual, his immediate situation, and his whole cultural context. The critic has to deal with all the idiosyncratic, temporal, variable factors that make judgments of value relative and provisional.

Yet Richards' theory is still less vague than some, less arbitrary than others, less merely emotive than most. It not only lays a broad foundation upon which future investigation may erect a more solid, imposing structure but more clearly isolates the basic, universal, timeless elements of esthetic experience and permits a freer understanding of new combinations and new particulars. It seals the necessary divorce of value and specific meaning or moral or any one view of life. It sets up a general scheme into which one can fit the more specialized doctrines of Marx, Freud, and other prophets—the "economic man" and the "libido" in this view furnish highly important impulses for organization and composure. If even in its premises it has no absolute authority, neither does any other theory; and it at least avoids pretensions to the absolute and everlasting that in the light of human history are as dangerous as they are arrogant and grotesque.

The common objection to Richards' theory is of course that it is "naturalistic." So must be any theory that does not introduce supernatural sanctions. But it is naturalistic in no narrow mechanistic sense. What it means, when translated into less technical terms, is simply this: that that way of life is most valuable which permits the freest, fullest, most harmonious development of the possibilities of the human spirit. It is therefore a scientific—or pseudo-scientific—restatement of one of the noblest traditions: humanism. And in this tradition, as it is being adapted to new conditions by such writers as Thomas Mann, lies, I believe, the soundest approach to the fundamental problems of modern literature.

As an ancient and honorable term, "humanism" has been appropriated for strategic purposes by thinkers of many complexions; it is one of the many words in common critical discourse that have so many undifferentiated meanings as to be almost meaningless. In these days every man appears to be his own humanist—and is ready with genealogical credentials. Yet the term is worth preserving, and not merely for its emotive usefulness, for it has symbolized a recognizable attitude—the attitude of Chaucer, Erasmus, Rabelais, Montaigne. This, broadly, is an emphasis upon distinctively human interests and ideals, as opposed to either the purely mechanistic or the purely supernatural. The humanist is interested in all philosophies as in all religions, not as final answers but as servants of human needs, not for their absolute truth but for their possibilities of adaptation to a rich, harmonious way of life. His dispensation is catholic, tolerant, urbane, flexible. Hence he will commit himself to no exclusive dogma, no one scheme of conception, but will adapt his values to changing conditions of life, recognizing that any live tradition must be rooted in the present as well as the past.

This fine talk is admittedly vague—and will still be vague at the end. Humanism as I conceive it is a state of mind, not a dogma, and by its nature incapable of exact or full definition. As a general attitude making for wholeness, harmony, and equilibrium, its stress shifts as it combats the particular forms of bigotry, oppression, and excess of its age. Even its vocabulary is perforce blurred by controversy. One man's tolerance is another's timid evasion of responsibility; one cannot fix the point where catholicity becomes mere lack of discrimination, or insistence upon values downright dogmatism. Yet humanism states positive preferences, asserts positive values, and need not land one in the *impasse* of solipsism. It is a recognizable attitude, once more, exemplified by great thinkers and writers of the past, persisting even in this age of embattled experts. It can be related concretely to current problems.

2

The twentieth century is unquestionably one of the most vigorous in human history. Unquestionably, too, much of its energy is scattered, centrifugal, explosive, self-destructive. It is inspired by no common ideal, rooted in no common faith, focused on no common purpose. Individual effort is more than ever competitive and invidious, unsocial when not anti-social. Men tend to strike highly individualized rather than socialized attitudes; many virtually ignore the group, others strive to be different from it. Collective effort is confined to shifting groups and conflicting programs—a welter of competing loyalties. Although previous societies were never so compact as they seem now, when we can clearly make out their central pattern and conveniently ignore the tangled fringes, they nevertheless had a much more solid and extensive common ground—a broad communal green. This green is today a highway for hurrying transients, lined with jerry-built camps.

This is not even to mention the immediate problems we have on our hands—the problems, generally, of running an immensely complicated industrial society that has been set up without forethought or design. These are not the province of the literary artist. Yet though their more "practical" members are usually unconscious of it, societies are founded on some philosophy; and imperfect philosophies result in such concrete realities as wars and depressions—even, if indirectly, in such physiological disturbances as epidemics, such physical disturbances as floods and dust storms. A patented philosophy cannot, of course, be slapped on like a celestial mustard plaster; it must work its way into the *mores,* establish itself by ritual, and this slow process would try the patience even of T. S. Eliot.

Meanwhile, if at a given crisis the artist's activity is likely to seem irrelevant or even distracting, in a long view it is nevertheless more practical than the bustle of many who are impatient with him. Occasionally he deals directly and vigorously with immediate issues; more generally his effectiveness comes by indirection, through the creation of predispositions to behavior, the establishment of a background of values and ideals. His work is at any rate no mere exhibition or side-show but an integral part of the whole art of living. And it must accordingly be judged on the basis of a philosophy comprehensive enough to embrace the extraordinary profusion of attitudes expressed in the literature of the present as of the past, yet positive enough to provide a coherent scheme—an amalgam of values and not merely a medley of preferences.

The multiplicity of half-truths in contemporary criticism would in any event be difficult enough of synthesis, but this difficulty is heightened by the exclusiveness of the various partizans. Each group asserts that its slice is the whole loaf. Each shouts for a particular mode of communication, a particular scale of meanings, and denies the validity of other modes and scales. All are persuasive, often irrefutable once granted their premises; none is really comprehensive. All seize upon some one element in a complex of manifestations, some one point on a sliding scale, and arbitrarily make it primary. Choices are necessary, of course, and simplification inevitable, but the basis of simplification must be broader than most of the partizans prescribe. Above all, the critic must always be aware that he *is* simplifying, and guard against mistaking his verbalizations for entities, his metaphors for fact.

In the absence of complete knowledge, above all of any knowledge of the ultimate principle of life, one chooses a point of departure to suit one's purposes; and almost any approach will be fruitful. The argument for humanism, then, is that it is the most inclusive, the least biased, and therefore especially desirable in an age of experts. It can embrace the findings of science, encompass at once all that is valuable in more specialized attitudes and all that is still pertinent in the rich heritage of the past. For this reason it cannot have an utterly precise, constant meaning or lend itself to pat, downright generalization. It will be blurred at the edges simply because it must embrace so many perspectives and deal with so many immeasurables. It cannot offer the whole explanation of its values, for science has not provided such explanations. But if it can work no wonders, it is nevertheless richer in values, more responsive to the deepest needs of the human spirit, than specialized schemes that promise such wonders. It permits the creative artist the freest development of his possibilities; it helps the critic to return to the essentials so often clouded by controversy. If in the end one is oppressed by the uncertainties of guesswork, the hobgoblins of temperamental preference, so must he feel in all discussions of final meanings and purposes.

The ideal humanistic critic has been admirably described by Santayana in *The Genteel Tradition at Bay:*

> A legislating naturalist would be like a physician or horticulturist or breeder of animals: he would remove obstructions and cut out barren deformities; he would have a keen eye for those variations which are spontaneous and fertile, gladly giving them free play; and he would know by experience those other variations into which nature may be coaxed by grafting and watering. In all his measures he would be guided by the avowed needs and budding potentialities of his client.

But this language—and especially "naturalist"—will fall harshly on the ears of the assorted company known as New Humanists; and here is the best means of defining this approach more precisely. Although the New Humanists have a sincere desire to cherish spiritual values and rescue the world from spiritual anarchy, what chiefly distinguishes them is the inadequacy and frequent irrelevance of the standards they attempt to impose, the futility of their endeavors to block off large areas of experience, defy the new knowledge, and deny the inescapable conditions of modern life. While taking the name, they reject the essence of the old tradition.

They not only have, in the first place, a habit of talking vaguely and abstractedly about the exigencies of an age of hard, bitter fact; they seem far more concerned with preserving their brand of culture intact than with adapting it to a living, changing society. They appear to regard culture as a fancy growth that does not have its roots in the vulgar realities of biology, economics, psychology. They nurture their spiritual values as if they were tender flowers that must wither under the foul breath of democracy, industrialism, or scientific investigation. They talk in genteel accents of the Great Tradition, as it has come down from Greece, as if it were a hothouse plant and not an organic social growth, and as if it could be kept alive in a vacuum. If they are right, if modern society is necessarily and irreconcilably hostile to the humanistic tradition, then indeed there is nothing to do for those who cherish it but to fold their tents and silently steal away to monasteries until the tide of barbarism has receded.

Meanwhile, however, one can raise more specific objections to the New Humanists' creed. Especially questionable—and mystifying—is their ethical absolutism, the haughtiness of their dispensation. They "might pass," Santayana remarks mildly, "for rather censorious minds, designed by nature to be the pillars of some priestly orthodoxy"; they even seem to feel "called upon to correct nature by the authority of a private oracle." And what do the oracles command? Babbitt talked constantly of the "inner check." Paul Elmer More recommended the "inalienable authority" of "a law within nature but not of nature in the naturalistic sense of the word." Others dress up in even fancier words what appears to be at bottom simply the old notion of conscience. But aside from their failure to prove the authority of this moral law and their apparent assumption that it is independent of environment, they never clearly define it, they never tell how to recognize its dictates. Resolutely they turn their backs upon any inquiry, like that of the anthropologists and sociologists, into the origin and development of moral ideas, or upon any practical effort, like that of the psychoanalysts, to inform the inner Censor; instead they indulge in sheer logomachy. Their descriptions of the "inner check" recall the purely verbal attributes of Divinity assembled by rapt scholastics: absolute, indivisible, immutable, infinite, omnipresent, and all the other counters in the metaphysical game that William James described as a "shuffling and matching of pedantic dictionary adjectives." They become hypnotized by their own magic; they mistake their symbolic accessories for eternal entities; they substitute verbalization for vision. Like the king in the fable, they sincerely believe that they are wearing fine raiment; they need some outspoken child to tell them that they have nothing on.

The most nearly specific principle of the New Humanists, on the basis of which they condemn almost all the important writers of this century, is their horror of "naturalism"; and it incorporates their central inconsistency. Most of them either reject religion or extend it a lukewarm welcome as a helpful but unnecessary ally; officially they do not acknowledge its sanctions. But if they refuse to admit the authority either of divine revelation or of "naturalistic" science, where does this holy "ethical will" come from? "I cannot understand," T. S. Eliot once wrote of them, "a system of morals which seems to be founded on nothing but itself"; and he went on to grease the horns of the inescapable dilemma: "Either everything in man can be traced as a development from below, or something must come from above. There is no avoiding that dilemma: you must be either a naturalist or a supernaturalist."

This is an exact statement of the case. Eliot, moreover, is entitled to his own choice. He has plumped for the supernatural. But when he insists that all avowed humanists must vote this same ticket, he raises another issue. It is true that most humanists of the past have paid at least lip service to the church. Yet a really passionate faith, really intense religious conviction, is hostile to the humanistic spirit. One who has got hold of absolute truth is unlikely to be amiable, urbane, tolerant of the guesses and experiments in living of others—as Eliot's own Puritan ancestors make sufficiently clear. Theological history is in this view chiefly a record of suppression, bigotry, even fanaticism; the excesses of the pious have until recently been the chief object of humanistic attack. Even the very cool, synthetic religion of Eliot himself has fortified in him the positiveness and exclusiveness that he rightly objects to in the New Humanists. In "Thoughts After Lambeth," for example, he comments on the doings of a conference of Anglican bishops as if he were their uncle. "We" are plainly the chosen; the sarcasm and wit practised on the lost sheep of modernism have a typical theological heaviness. More than one reader must have been surprised when he heard Eliot, in another essay, accuse Arnold of priggishness.

In the end, however, this discussion becomes largely academic. What Eliot ignores is the *impossibility* for many men today of the religion he recommends. In "Second Thoughts About Humanism" he indeed mentions the objections of some friends: if humanism alone is insufficient, what of those who with the best will cannot make themselves believe? But he never takes care of these poor devils. He merely reiterates that belief in the supernatural is desirable, and takes its validity for granted. He even waves aside the whole question of what faith to hold. "For us, religion is Christianity," he says simply; so apparently one grabs the faith of one's ancestors, whatever it be. But no faith adopted merely for purposes of convenience can inspire a great art.

It is accordingly more profitable to waive the ultimate and transcendental and accept a frankly naturalistic basis for humanism, justifying its values on empirical grounds precisely as men do in their everyday lives in the only world that they know or are fitted to know. I see no reason why men cannot leave in abeyance the question of what and why things are, and substitute for their service of the gods (upon the proper nature of which the faithful have seldom agreed) the notion simply of the dignity of human potentialities. The religion of classical Greece was one of the forms rather than the source of its ideals, the flower rather than the root of its culture; many humanists of the Renaissance introduced God into the scheme of things more or less perfunctorily and had no real need of divine sanctions for their way of life. By disregarding the religious accessories of this tradition, moreover, one will be freer to adapt it to present conditions; and to adapt it to the modern world, whose terms of existence are strange and often seemingly incompatible with the modes and symbols of man's oldest experience, is the first duty of one who cherishes it.

To illustrate: one of the forces to be reckoned with in any broad view of modern life and literature, and any effort at revaluation, is, once more, the Communistic movement. Although Marxism appears in public chiefly as a heated state of mind, behind all the trumpets and eagles lies a specific, comprehensive program. It is in fact the most systematic effort today to provide an institutional framework for a scheme of reorientation. At the same time the Marxists are often harsh, bigoted, narrow; in actual practice they appear to find no room for humanistic values. In the way of so many reformers presumably fired by humanitarian zeal, they repel humane men by their very inhumanity.

Now, like it or not, fanaticism is as necessary to the world as tolerance. The revolutionary may be like the many doctors who love to operate, but operations are often unavoidable; in periods of crisis the good humanist is seldom qualified for active leadership. His rôle is a different and less heroic one: that of following in the wake of the zealots, like Lincoln after Garrison, cushioning their inspired excesses and translating their inspired lunacies, repairing what they have wantonly destroyed and consolidating what they have gloriously won. And so with Communism. It may or may not be a workable scheme of cooperation, or in an industrial society the soundest basis for the good life; in either event it does not *by itself* constitute the good life. Although it may guarantee economic security, it does not automatically provide a rich culture. Although its collectivistic philosophy lends itself to poetic-religious metaphor and may lead to a more idealistic management of our vast technological resources, it needs to be both qualified and supplemented before it can become the instrument of a satisfactory art of living. The citizens of the perfectly regulated classless society cannot lead a full life simply by an ecstatic contemplation of all the wheels going around.

This adjustment of Marxism to the deeper needs of the age is indeed already in process. Its early champions had a naïve reverence for orthodoxy, a naïve confidence in formulas and open-sesames. Like Marx himself, they overemphasized the "economic man." Pamphleteers wrote almost exclusively of the material needs of this nameless creature, making the Cause a kind of glorified S.P.C.A.; even novelists and poets reduced the individual, as Waldo Frank recently protested, "from an organic integer of cosmos to a mere quantitative factor of the collective mass." They made Communism chiefly a matter of technology, they neglected the *whole man*. In short, they gave the extreme statement to the very elements in the scientific scheme of conception that needed correction or supplement. But more recent converts, like Frank, Kenneth Burke, and Edmund Wilson, have begun to discredit these bizarre simplicities. They are fitting Marx's thought into a larger frame, making it more genuinely organic, adapting it to spiritual needs. In effect they are striving to integrate it with the humanistic tradition.

A comprehensive criticism of Marxism accordingly leads to the still larger issue of the whole scientific rationalization. Science is by no means necessarily hostile to humanism—else this would become mere quackery. It is idle to talk of ignoring or repudiating its findings—of repudiating *fact*. It is as yet even dangerous to combat the inculcation of the purely scientific attitude. A vast deal of ignorance, superstition, and prejudice remains to be overcome; millions have yet to acquire the habit of dispassionate inquiry, the ideal of intellectual integrity, the discipline of verified knowledge and reverence for truth. Yet once one has completely accepted the point of view of science, admitted its value and its necessity in the modern scheme of life, he has then to take a further step into a realm more distinctively human than the realm of knowledge: the realm, broadly speaking, of sentiment and natural piety.

The common complaints about science spring from certain disagreeable truths it has thrust before us, certain cherished illusions it has destroyed, certain venerable authorities it has discredited—in general from all the aristocratic toes it has stepped on. These often jealous or tender complaints nevertheless reflect a fundamental objection that even the tough-minded can raise to the present scientific rationale. This is to its dehumanization of experience, its neglect of or actual hostility to the oldest needs of the race. Science satisfies man's intellectual needs; his emotional needs it often ignores, or even condemns as primitive, naïve, humiliating, beneath the dignity of intelligence. It has gone so far in its exciting pursuit of truth that it has lost sight of its humble origins. It is so preoccupied with understanding and controlling nature that it has forgotten the nature of the creature it is supposed to serve. It is absorbed in such rare visions and has raised men's heads so high that it overlooks the elemental and obvious. It has replaced ancient superstitions by another even more oppressive: the superstition that man is a perfectly rational creature who can live on knowledge alone.

Such criticism, once more, implies no *denial* of science. It simply calls for a supplement to science—or, as in the work of psychologists, a broadening of its base. Hence the significance of men like Richards and Burke, who are striving to work out a corrective philosophy; they bare their heads before science, but they also recognize that its truths are ultimately arbitrary and limited, and must be subordinated to the needs of a naturally ethical animal to whom purpose and piety are more important than fact. Hence too the significance of the mystical tendencies in modern literature—for example the intuitionism in the thought of Bergson and in the poetry and fiction of Lawrence—that the scientific rationalist is apt to consider merely atavistic. Despite its absolute validity for the individual, mystical experience has indeed a limited social value, simply because of its ineffability; it does not give knowledge, strictly speaking—in arguing the superiority of states of mind in which they are interested, the intuitionists too often refuse to call things by their right names. These tendencies are nevertheless supported by the latest developments in science itself: the positivist can no longer feel altogether at home in the world now being fashioned by physicists and astronomers. They have at any rate a real value, especially today, when customary ways of seeing and doing are being called into question. As Burke points out, mysticism enables one to see around the corner of accepted verbalizations, it is "the farthest reach of the search for new perspectives"; and so if it can bring no solutions, it can at least exhibit modern experience in a new light, open up new possibilities, and weaken the tyranny of current attitudes that seem natural, necessary, inevitable, while they have no less obviously got us into grave difficulties.

3

To argue for the humanistic approach to modern fiction is not, of course, to demand that all novelists be catholic, urbane, disinterested. The ardor of the humanist is likely to be chiefly negative. "Their sympathy with mankind," writes Santayana of the Renaissance fathers, "was not really universal, since it stopped short at enthusiasm, at sacrifice, at all high passion or belief." But the artist is apt to have precisely such a passion and belief, and like as not these will be invested in some creed that is transitory, lopsided, or even harsh. Milton devoted his splendid gifts to the vindication of a theology soon to become antiquated; Dostoyevsky preached passionately a spirituality that found little room for either flesh or mind and that would certainly embarrass the good humanist who was measured by it. Both pay the penalty of narrowness and distortion. Yet both provide experiences of unmistakable worth. The critic must again often discount conscious intention and explicit meaning for the sake of the concrete representations, the insights and the emotional evocations within a given range, the formal harmonies and the verbal eloquence, the imaginative sweep and glow—in general for the valuable attitudes that may be induced by a work of art whose specific import one does not accept. Definite spiritual values—fortitude, magnanimity, gallantry, and the many forms of altruism and idealism—may still find a lofty place in an angular or too rigid philosophy. The official philosophy of Thomas Hardy, for example, is in its extreme statement grotesque, and the spirit in which he preached it at times crabbed; his fictions nevertheless represent eloquently a number of humanistic ideals.

If one demands of the artist strict conformity to the norms of poise, decorum, serenity, and restraint, humanism will manifestly be only another name for the classical tradition. Yet the very essence of this approach is its refusal to make invidious comparisons of classic and romantic art. Although these classifications are useful and important, they are not self-contained principles, they do not correspond to eternal archetypes, they are not to be ranged at opposite poles like Good and Evil, Light and Darkness. They can be understood only as the natural products of different cultures, one of a strong collective, the other of an individualistic ideology. No one way of life or art can be laid down as necessarily and under all conditions superior. Neither the classicist nor the romantic, accordingly, has a corner on wisdom and dignity. Although at their best these are both admirable attitudes, both have limitations that the opposing school harps on, both can be and usually are abused. Critic and creative artist prefer according to their temperament and especially to the conditions of their time. In the sound and fury of these times, one can make a good argument for the classical discipline as a needed corrective. One can also argue that the romantic temper responds more satisfactorily to the immediate needs of the present, and is indeed its inevitable expression: a profoundly unsettled age provides no solid assumptions for serenity, poise, and order. One must in either event recognize that both attitudes spring from fundamental impulses, both can provide excellent experiences, and both must be included in a larger perspective.

Whether classicist or romantic, the artist is always related to a group, always striving to communicate with his fellows, and always judged ultimately by the range and effectiveness of his communication. He may talk fondly of pure "self-expression," but the very self he is expressing has been molded by his society. His experiences are modified from their inception by the racial habit, reinforced by his own probable need, of communicating them, and in the process of communication are further modified by the particular concepts and symbols provided by his society. He works within a given framework; his attitudes are shaped by it as plainly when he rebels against as when he accepts the reigning *mores*. And when he is most hostile to or contemptuous of the ways of his fellows, he nevertheless seeks to justify himself by convincing others and obtaining their endorsement. If many modern writers appear to be highly specialized performers, this exclusiveness is the very measure of their limitation and of the disorganization of their society.

As the modern writer is therefore inevitably judged first of all by his relation to the interests and needs of the age, it is the more important to have a comprehensive view of these interests and needs, a long view in which peculiar forms and immediate pressures are clearly recognized but are also seen in perspective. The present scheme of life is obviously neither perfect nor valueless, and above all not permanent. Modern technology is potentially a splendid tool and not necessarily an incubus, a monstrous vampire sucking our blood; at the same time it is properly only a tool, not an end in itself, and to make the improvements still necessary to its efficiency will not mean an automatic paradise. The brave new world satirized by Aldous Huxley is scarcely more depressing than the Utopias of Wells and Shaw. Hence the critic concerned with the rich development of human possibilities will be sympathetic not only to attitudes that exploit the valuable elements in the present scheme, or that seek to effect reforms within its frame; he will be sympathetic as well to attitudes that would wrench this frame where it is cramping, or restore valuable elements from former schemes. He will perceive the worth and the need, for instance, of both Lawrence and Dreiser, Tolstoy and Shaw, Mann and Dos Passos. He will measure not only the artist's immediate values but his ultimate contribution to a satisfactory way of life or art of living.

"Universality" is a large and loose word. It does not lend itself to definite measurement or incontrovertible demonstration. Yet it plainly corresponds to a positive fact of human experience: the fact of fundamental unity behind the most bewildering and complicated diversity. The strangest differences among men only emphasize their basic similarity. Although they take new shapes and involve new intricacies, the essentials of purpose and pleasure have not changed since prehistoric times. In another million years, indeed, a new species of man may evolve. This creature can then be trusted to shift for himself. Meanwhile the writer has to deal with a creature whose neurological processes are essentially what they were before he became self-conscious about them and gave them fancy names. The great writers will accordingly be those who despite the new appearances of things penetrate to the permanencies of interest and emotion. Necessarily their stress will shift with changing particularities, and they will employ different symbols, seek different routes of communication; they will nevertheless address the same abiding needs. A view of life that refuses to insist upon the pattern of any one dogma or upon any arbitrary fixation of attitude will therefore best enable the critic to recognize and appreciate such deeply valuable experience in whatever guise. For a rigid, narrow creed does not merely warp judgment—the judgments of extreme Marxists or New Humanists are upon the basis of their experience sound enough. It raises barriers to participation, it governs the initial response, it alters the esthetic experience itself.

VII

CATHARSIS: THE PLEASURE OF TRAGEDY

I

AS a final preparation for the analysis and appraisal of the text of modern fiction, it will be helpful to crystallize the general principles of humanism into more specific values, handier touchstones; and for this purpose the most serviceable reagent, I believe, is one of the basic but most baffling of literary forms: Tragedy. Traditionally accounted among the noblest of the arts, tragedy has through the ages inspired in critics an eloquence that would be a still more handsome tribute to its value if it did not so often obscure the source of this value. Today men are less likely to mention it in hushed tones, or even to mention it at all; yet it still deals with a fundamental problem of human experience: the problem of evil and justification, of suffering and reconciliation, that confronts the enlightened modern as stubbornly as it confronted his benighted ancestors, and that has indeed been greatly complicated by his enlightenment. Still more specifically, tragedy deals with the problem of death; it faces squarely the fact that all art, and all religion, strive to conquer or evade. It is the last stand of the will to immortality at the root of the creative impulse.

Now, "the pleasure of tragedy" is a phrase that seldom emerges from the classroom, and must ease its way apologetically into a society feverishly concerned with the various new deals in life and letters. But the questions it raises are not the exclusive property of professors. It is easy, of course, to be too pontifical when talking of the exalted function of the artist; to the Elizabethans poetry was the "quintessence of knowledge"—and perhaps their most characteristic poetic utterance was "Hey nonny nonny!" Great tragedy, however, has always grappled with the final issues of human destiny. It has given passionate utterance to the most cherished faiths, the noblest aspirations, and the darkest misgivings of the human spirit. And if men are today suspicious of the heroic attitudes it has assumed, they are for that reason more at the mercy of the fears that have inspired it. No age has had a more imperious need of catharsis.

In approaching this subject, however, one has immediately to hurdle the barrier erected by C. K. Ogden and I. A. Richards, with the heads of most great critics of the past stuck on the paling as a grim warning. Poetry, they insist, cannot give us knowledge or truth; it "tells us, or should tell us, nothing"; and that modern poetry which to many old-fashioned readers seems pointless and profitless they hail as a return to the conditions of greatness, because it is "abandoning the obsession of knowledge and symbolic truth." The beliefs stated in art must be recognized as "pseudo-statements," "provisional acceptances." As for tragedy, our notion that we are seeing into the heart of things is merely an indication of a satisfying adjustment in the nervous system.

At first glance, this attitude would appear withering, a blight upon all esthetic experience. It seems to make literature merely a kind of game played by overgrown children, a running away from the stern visage of reality, at best a useful drug or an incidental pastime. Deeply to enjoy art or respect their experience, most men must believe that it is somehow "real" or "true." Yet if one chews the plain talk of Ogden and Richards it should prove less indigestible. Our experience with Greek and Shakespearian drama, with the "Intimations of Immortality" and "To a Skylark," with *Tristram Shandy* and *The House of the Seven Gables,* with indeed the great bulk of literature, makes clear that we do not demand or expect of it strict truth. None but the literal-minded are greatly bothered by the obvious untruth of many of its assumptions; most readers take for granted the necessity of "provisional acceptances" or "objectless beliefs." Hence what distresses the pious is chiefly the bald way in which Ogden and Richards say these things, their refusal to take off their hats and hush their voices when they enter the temple of art; and the dispute between them is largely verbal.

Actually, Richards (whose *Principles of Literary Criticism* is simply an expanded study of the emotive function of language distinguished in *The Meaning of Meaning*) by no means denies the importance or value of art. He attributes to it, in fact, a function "far more vital" than that of science. He is merely trying to distinguish these functions, and insisting that if they are not confused, one need in no way interfere with the exercise of the other. Poetry, he declares, suggests to us valuable ways of dealing with things. It induces fitting attitudes, and for this purpose it is not necessary to know precisely what things are; the continued pertinence of great poets who made very unscientific statements about life is sufficient proof that these attitudes need not be based on fact.

Yet Richards' distinction is misleading, and as arbitrary as the exactly opposite but equally plausible distinction of Max Eastman, who argues that only science can induce really fitting attitudes and tell us how to deal with things. Although it is unfortunate that words like *knowledge, truth,* and *reality* serve as symbols for both logical and emotive purposes, hence giving rise to wranglings over Intellect and Emotion, Logic and Intuition, and other antitheses as artificial as an invidious comparison of Belly and Lungs, his restriction of them to science alone is too despotic. As he himself repeatedly declares, we never know *what* things are; we know only *how* they behave. It follows that even the statements of science are in the last analysis "pseudo-statements." If the relations it investigates in the material world are measurable and constant, the relations between human beings with which literature deals are still not based on pure guesswork. Some element of exact knowledge and logical thought enters into them, and is incorporated in the artist's representations; more important, the mere recognition that some attitudes are more "fitting," that art increases our capacity for dealing with things and so for controlling our experience, implies a kind of knowingness that cannot be distinguished too absolutely from verifiable knowledge or measurable truth. A great deal of modern psychology (including Richards' own theory of value) consists of stating, in more precise terms, what poets have stated indirectly, figuratively, loosely; and that the scientific restatement is more demonstrable and trustworthy does not warrant so flat an assertion as that poetry "tells us nothing." This assertion not only encourages a merely decorative art but slights the perceptions and insights that are not always less valid because they are intuitive rather than reasoned.

What leads Richards into overstatement is his especial concern with the more purely formal arts, like music, painting, and poetry. The novel too is a more formal art than the ordinary reader appreciates. It not only takes incidental advantage of the mesmeric effect of rhythm, harmony, and word-color in style; as an esthetic whole it has (or should have) an internal harmony, and satisfies the complicated formal expectations it raises. Yet fiction is also a specific representation of experience and makes a specific comment upon it. Although its validity and worth do not depend upon this representation and comment in their *most* specific form —upon the author's ideas about God, capitalism, marriage, or birth control—they have a close connection with the clarity of his perceptions, the penetration of his insights, the firmness of his grasp upon the major elements of emotion and desire. The control and command of experience for which Richards so greatly values the artist implies some approximation to the facts of experience, even if these facts have as yet not been explained, verified, or measured. An obvious inconsistency in characterization, an inadequate motivation, a crude representation or shallow interpretation diminish the value of a novel simply because they are *untrue*. The action of Meredith's Diana at the crossways makes for a pleasing formal pattern; that the novel goes to pieces at this moment is sufficient indication that the laws of fiction are not purely formal. And the values of great fiction involve the representation of the more specific values of conduct, such as generosity, fortitude, loyalty, and love, that are again inconsistent with the statement that poetry "tells us nothing."

Hence there arises the difficult issue of subject matter, the importance of the "great subject." In painting, as Richards says, there is no absolute need of representation. Even here, however, his own theory of value would seem to imply that, all other elements being equal, a "great subject" will afford greater value: the total response to such a painting should be fuller and deeper, embracing formal beauty in the narrow sense *plus* emotional and intellectual significance, and thus opening up wider possibilities, engaging more of our personalities. But there can be no doubt of the importance of subject matter in fiction, where form is less prominent and some kind of representation inevitable. All experience is not equally deserving of treatment. One can no more make great tragedy out of the struggles of paltry souls than one can produce great sculpture on cherry stones. Hence the complexity of the problem facing the critic of modern fiction. He must be aware in the first place that representation is still only a means to an end, and that when he praises certain novels for having a profounder "truth" he is not dealing with absolute or precise concepts, but simply making general distinctions that are obvious only when one compares Thomas Mann with Harold Bell Wright. He must consider the kind of experience represented in relation to current interests and needs. And he must consider this experience finally for its intrinsic possibilities—the width and depth of the potential response to it.

In this spirit, at any rate, I approach the problem of tragedy. As Richards points out, the value of tragedy is still clearly a *general* character of response. It brings no specific message to all readers alike; although critics find a hundred different "meanings" in *Hamlet,* they nevertheless agree upon its value. At the same time tragedy offers more than an ineffable beauty. It is a representation of painful experience, and it tells us something definite about this experience even if what it tells is not scientific fact. The attitudes it induces are vitally related to the practical problems of living.

2

It is a familiar complaint that in modern literature one no longer finds "authentic tragedy." If authenticity is measured exclusively by the precepts of Aristotle, or by the practice of Shakespeare, there is good reason for the complaint. Yet writers are still treating, with high seriousness, the sufferings of man in a world that is at many points in painful disharmony with his hopes and desires. Hence I use *tragedy* in this admittedly loose sense: a narrative or drama treating seriously events terrible and piteous. If this definition robs the term of something of its academic dignity and denies it its time-honored right to a capital letter, the important issue concerns substance, not form. Granted that modern tragedy differs, in many striking respects, from the tragedy of the past, can it nevertheless arouse emotions comparable in intensity and in kind to those aroused by *Antigone* and *Hamlet?* Does it offer equivalent values? Does it, in other words, satisfy the same needs of the human spirit?

To answer these questions, however, one must first determine what are these emotions, values, needs; and here one runs into the paradox of tragedy: that it gives a pleasure to which its representation of misery would seem fatal. Plainly it does not aim merely to distress. It offers some kind of compensatory good, satisfies some need, fulfils some desire—otherwise men would neither create nor attend it. Moreover, the common experience is that the pleasure great tragedy affords is not meager but intense, not a morbid satisfaction but a noble exaltation. Deliberately the tragic poet calls up the worst, only to exhilarate us. Eloquently he sums up the case for the opposition, only to dismiss it. Somehow he justifies suffering and death.

Hume, Burke, Schlegel, Hegel, Nietzsche, Schopenhauer—these and many other illustrious thinkers have explained this paradox. But to philosophize, Leslie Stephen once remarked, is to declare half the assumptions and conclusions of the wise men of the world to be transparent fallacies; and so it has been with these particular wise men. Their theories are so different that one doubts that they are talking about the same experience. If in the face of such distinguished contradiction and confusion it seems impertinent to add still another opinion, one may at least, however, point out the obvious sources of confusion. The philosophers have generally consulted the exigencies of their systems of thought more closely than they have the tragic poets themselves, been too eager to make tragedy the handmaid of a particular ethical or metaphysical view. The authority of Aristotle himself is qualified by his natural acceptance of Greek modes of thought and expression as immutable and right. It is a withering thought. But it is also a helpful and challenging one. It should guard one against the supposition, in the face of all the diversity of vision among the tragic poets and the still greater diversity of critical interpretation, that tragedy must embody any one ethic or support any one view of life. And so it forces one to go deeper to find the common ground on which the universal, enduring significance of great tragedy rests.

In general, the pleasure in all creative literature, aside from the purely formal satisfactions, lies in richness and fulness of experience, a new insight and a new wonder, a sense of "heightened powers in heart and mind." As Matthew Arnold said, poetry so deals with things "as to awaken in us a wonderfully full, new, and intimate sense of them and of our relations with them." And tragedy, in the more technical language of Richards, is the most splendid because the most complete and stable organization of experience that art can afford: it is "perhaps the most general, all-accepting, all-ordering experience known," the most exquisite reconciliation of seemingly irreconcilable impulses, supremely poised because it involves more of our personality and is least exposed to destruction by impulses excluded. Thus we feel godlike as the imagination soars into the immensities and embraces the whole stupendous mystery, terrible as it is. Our mood is at once somber and exultant. It is

> that blessed mood
> In which the burthen of the mystery,
> In which the heavy and the weary weight

Of all this unintelligible world
Is lightened . . .

Naturally, then, different men will find different sources for the pleasure of tragedy. In this intensification and amplification of experience all can find what they want, the confirmation of their deepest convictions. Hegel is given a vision of eternal justice and steps over the corpses into a world of perfect harmony and rationality, where the philosopher can live in entire comfort. Schopenhauer is fortified in the surrender of the will to live in a hostile universe unworthy of our attachment. Nietzsche finds the highest happiness that comes to him with the annihilation of the real, of the most beautiful phenomena in the world of appearance. Each stains the white light of poetry with the color of his own temperament; and the humble reader does likewise.

All this, however, is still largely paraphrase. The most difficult question remains: *how* does tragedy, the one art form that treats exclusively of harrowing experience, effect this wonderful reconciliation and composure? By what specific means does it induce us to accept the seemingly intolerable? These means are obviously complex. There is no doubt a kind of self-congratulation in the exercise of sympathy, an exalted feeling that we are very fine fellows. There is the simple satisfaction in mere finality—an account squared and written off the books. There is again the whole intricate adjustment to purely formal content: the satisfaction in subtle harmony and appropriateness, in a chord resolved, in a circle completed; the tragic hero *must* die to satisfy desires initially created. But the more specific source of the peculiar tragic value, the touchstone for the terms into which we inevitably translate what begins as an adjustment in the nervous system, the explanation of the all-important after-effects of the experience of tragedy, is its display of the dignity, the potential greatness and glory of the human spirit. Great tragedy gives an exalted meaning to suffering and death, perhaps by discounting them on a heavenly check or by referring them to some transcendental scheme whose final purposes are reasonable and just, but most universally, most significantly, and most surely by exhibiting them in the light of spiritual values that are their own justification. It throws into relief the mysterious element in man that leads him to do the heroic and unpredictable, to embark gallantly upon impossible enterprises, to suffer martrydom for impossible causes. It transports us into an ideal world, a heaven within man, where apparent defeat is resolved into triumph—the triumph of the human spirit over material circumstance. Hamlet dies; but more important than his torment and death, more inspiring than the angels who may or may not sing him to his rest, is the mere fact of his magnificent existence.

"I accept the universe!" Margaret Fuller flamboyantly exclaimed. "By gad, she'd better," commented Carlyle; and so she had. Yet she had a real choice. Many men do *not* accept the universe, many more resign themselves to it grudgingly. A voluntary acceptance of the obligatory is an act of self-assertion, a vindication of self-respect, a declaration of independence. And this is the declaration of tragedy. It affirms that man is equal to a destiny cruelly hard, at once subservient and superior to a perhaps soulless universe.

> The mind is its own place, and in itself
> Can make a Heaven of Hell, a Hell of Heaven

—this is its faith; and it is what makes tragedy more than a painful tale and gives it ultimately a kind of happy ending.

This consolation has nothing to do with moral uplift in the depressing sense. It has nothing to do, once more, with the vindication of any particular set of ethical values. Tragedy always deals, to be sure, with the problem of evil, and the author's concept of evil is ordinarily plain enough. It is likely, moreover, to be a noble concept. But it is also likely to be limited, to a later age extraneous or unacceptable. If the good that tragedy insists upon is the good only of a certain age, obviously it would have little meaning in a later age. Hence the enduring import of ancient tragedy derives less from the arguments than from the great personalities it presents. What matters is not the particular ideals of the tragic hero or his creator but the unquenchable idealism of the human spirit. The hero's splendid force may be consumed in evil or in good causes—in the selfish ambition of Macbeth or in the noble devotion of Antigone; in either event it is frustrated and illustrates no tidy moral precept. What matters is the mere existence of this force. Whether effectual or ineffectual, heroic life is beautiful.

Indeed, heroic life *must* be ineffectual in order to appear in all its beauty. "The great failure," declares the painter Lachman in Hauptmann's *Michael Kramer,* "can be more meaningful—we see it in the noblest works—can move us more deeply, can lead us to loftier heights—deeper into immensity—than the clearest success." Or, as Schlegel said, spiritual elevation can be determined only by the opposition it meets and is therefore seen most clearly in defeat, where it reaches its greatest height. In the glories of material triumph it is much less conspicuous. Hence Othello captures the imagination more than Henry V, the Napoleon of Waterloo and St. Helena more than the Napoleon of Austerlitz. Only when the giant has fallen can we measure his stature.

Now, this celebration of Spirit may seem to lead one far from the neurological origins of esthetic experience and the realities of everyday living, and to land one in the realm of cloudy symbols where language ceases to convey ideas but merely touches off emotional reflexes—the realm where for centuries critics have practised lyrical exercises under the delusion that they were dealing with absolute truth. Actually, however, this is only a translation of a psychological theory of value into the terms of common experience. It is a more specific description of the form and texture of the attitudes evoked by tragedy, a more complete description of the total experience and its after-effects; and it still does not imply a literal identification of poetry with absolute truth, or of value with any patented brand of truth. To say that great tragedy demands a great personality, with a capacity for feeling greatly, is another way of saying that the most valuable experiences are the richest and fullest, those that order the most varied and conflicting impulses and engage the most of our personality. The defeat of a little man with limited possibilities, the frustration of simpler or meaner aspirations, naturally provides a more restricted experience—just as, still lower on the scale, the death of a lap dog can induce only simple, sentimental attitudes. And a cynical view of life that denies the splendid possibilities of the human spirit, reduces magnificent passion to a few mean or mechanical impulses, and substitutes for pity and awe the wry laugh and the bitter pleasure of disillusionment—such a view automatically makes great tragedy impossible.

This concept, moreover, is not remote from ordinary experience, in life or in literature, or a sentimental glorification of it. The revolutionaries, for example, who are likely to distrust all talk of "spiritual values" as an evasion of "reality," are themselves striking examples of the power of idealism: sacrifice is the most convincing proof of any value, and by actual living they prove the reality and strength of what tragedy represents. The daily papers are filled with examples of preposterous gallantry in all walks of life. Similarly the common man, to whom this talk may seem high-falutin, shares in the fundamental immortality-urge that is at the root of tragedy as of all forms of creation. The simple citizen plants a tree, erects a stone, builds a monument, preserves his name in a son; the scientist and the scholar strive to attach their names to a bit of undying truth; the artist more directly immortalizes both the race and himself. All, however obscurely, seek to escape the inexorable and intolerable fact of death. And tragedy, which at first seems a paralyzing admission of this fact—which, in fact, repels immature minds who see in it only this admission—most defiantly celebrates the spiritual element in man that alone can give the illusion of escaping mortality. It proclaims the triumph over death itself.

The pleasure of tragedy indeed finds constant expression in the language of common men. "It doesn't matter whether you win or lose, it's how you play the game"—something like this goes the depressing refrain. Expressed in such terms, this pleasure is likely to seem hollow, insubstantial, adolescent: the approach to life of the boy scout. Rationally considered, it is at any rate illogical. It may be a mere whistling in the dark. But this proves only that men are not rational beings—proves the presence in all men of the incalculable spiritual element that especially distinguishes the great tragic heroes. However inexplicable its origin and irrational its expression, the idealism of the human spirit is not fiction but fact.

3

Such language will embarrass many contemporaries. Although appropriate to the ancient masterpieces, it would hang limply enough on the frames of some recent performances. Plainly, much of what passes for tragedy today does not affirm the values I set up as criteria. Yet I believe that in so far as it does not, it falls short of greatness and but proves this test. A decadent art, an art rooted in preciosity or cynicism or despair, may conceivably satisfy purely formal demands, rounding out the circles and fulfilling the expectations it has raised; a vital art must be rooted in a reverence for the human spirit, some faith in life beyond its possibilities of arrangement in pleasing formal patterns. Here, then, is the issue: Is it still possible for the modern writer, despite what we like to think of as his corrosive clear-sightedness, to offer something comparable to this ideal pleasure? Can he, in the terms imposed by the new knowledge and the new conditions of life, still assert equivalent values?

This is not, I repeat, a merely genteel issue to be debated by cloistered critics. It embraces all that is vital in more specialized approaches—Marxist, Freudian, Neo-Humanist—and goes behind them all. If it cannot be the whole concern of any responsible critic among the imperious issues of the moment, or if it is at times approached in a spirit of fastidious aloofness from these issues as something vulgar and unbecoming the attention of a philosopher-gentleman, it must still be the background of the thought of all who would be more than quarter backs calling the next play before shouting stands—of all whose social consciousness or scientific interests are rooted in natural piety and broadened by a conviction that culture is more than an elegant accessory. Meanwhile it helps the student of modern fiction to avoid being merely deafened by the hullabaloo about him, and more clearly to distinguish the deepest from the loudest or shrillest notes.

At any rate, this is the question I have put to the representative writers who have shaped the modern novel: what positive meanings they have found and what positive values asserted, what harmonies they have resolved from the discords and what syntheses effected from the chaos of modern experience, what they have won from the fear of death and contributed to the triumph of spirit—in sum how far they have conduced to catharsis as well as to understanding. The answers are of course multifarious, impossible of tidy classification or categorical judgment; and this is as it should be. Literature must be free to mirror the incessant flux and conflict of human thought and emotion, and neither its affirmation nor its negation of any formal creed determines *per se* its value. Yet some attitudes are more fruitful than others. Some strengthen, others weaken vitality. Some make for a freer and fuller response to the possibilities of experience, others lead to narrowness, frustration, and waste. Some contribute to a satisfactory art of living in its widest aspect, others produce a performer's or specialist's art to be savored by an elect few. On the basis of the broad principles I have outlined one can, I believe, make these necessary distinctions and still avoid a dogmatic exclusiveness.

Part Three

THE TEXT

VIII

GUSTAVE FLAUBERT

I

THERE are almost as many "fathers of the modern novel" as there are historians of it. As each genealogist has his own blood test, and as the proud parent will in any event bear little resemblance to most of his immense progeny, it would seem profitless to swell the argument. If necessary, however, one could make out a good case for Gustave Flaubert. No other single novel did more than *Madame Bovary* to determine the course of modern realism. On the Continent it had a direct and great influence, especially on Zola and his followers; indirectly through them it helped to shape the novel in England and America. It provides, if not an inevitable, at least a highly convenient point of departure for a study of modern fiction.

Flaubert's contribution stands out most sharply when he is set beside another of the "fathers," Balzac. The originality and historical importance of Balzac are undeniable. In his self-appointed rôle of secretary to his society, he was conscious not only of the "great and terrible labor" he was undertaking but of its novelty. The *Comédie Humaine* is documented with a thoroughness the novel had not yet known; he was the pioneer who taught novelists the habit of close observation and faithful recording. Yet if his great work is simply saturated with realistic detail, it is in its ruling ideas and its main outlines an old-fashioned philosophic, even a romantic work. When he was attacked for portraying so much evil, Balzac protested, quite truly, that he was actually presenting a world better than it is. He was always more careful than life to deplore sin and finally to punish wrongdoers; he was always holding up religion and monarchy as the eternal, necessary principles of the perfect society. He was not, in short, making the objective historical study of his society that sometimes he liked to think he was.

It was thus left to Flaubert to introduce, for better or worse, what might be called pure realism; and this he did in the first place by insisting on an absolute objectivity: a complete separation of the artist from his work, a complete suppression of his personality and private convictions. Although this doctrine of impersonality appears to have been chiefly the rationalization of a sentiment—the pride and distrust of a timid, sensitive spirit—it was the one great consistent doctrine of Flaubert's artistic career. Even his excruciating concern with style did not stand in its way; style as he conceived it was an absolute and unique, not a personal expression: an endless pursuit of the one right word, the one and only "manner of expressing a thing in all its color and intensity." If he lapsed into an occasional generalization or implied comment, for the most part he remained aloof, rendering with remarkable precision and concreteness the experience of his characters, and allowing this experience to make its own point.

Now, impersonality is of course a relative matter; as an absolute it is unthinkable this side of divinity. Every artistic creation is in a sense a chapter of an autobiography, for it inevitably shadows the personality and philosophy of its creator. Thus there is no mistaking Flaubert's judgment of the miserable life of Emma Bovary: irony, pervasive and occasionally explicit, is his constant attitude. Yet this revelation is almost always indirect—and this has been the way of realists since his time. Most have agreed, in theory if not in consistent practice, with his repeated assertion that comment should be implicit in the materials, the deeper meaning of the novel made clear by selection and composition. Impersonality is in fact logically necessary to a consistent realism. The editorial footnotes of Balzac as of the Victorians are not merely an unnecessary buttonholing; they finally come to seem a kind of tampering with the facts. The pure realist should at least give the impression of a wholly objective, disinterested, and faithful recording of what *is,* a selfless devotion to actuality. He must, in other words, have something of the appearance of the scientist—as Flaubert himself said. Art, he declared, should be given the "methodical relentlessness, the *precision* of the physical sciences."

Precision is indeed the right word for Flaubert. He perfected the new creed as well by the thoroughness of his realism, his refusal to compromise in any way with the plain, homely truth as he saw it. Although he did not, like Balzac, habitually count buttons, nor break up his narrative with such thick slabs of description, he was as methodical in his observation and as scrupulous in his reporting; both were far more painstaking than the relatively carefree Victorians. But the materials of Balzac are as romantic or even sensational as those of Dickens. However drab his incidental detail, his main actions are highly dramatic and his crowded canvases splashed with vivid color. If this *mélange* is the very essence of his art, it also considerably lightened his task as a realist; and Flaubert refused the aid of such gaudy trappings. He did not depend for interest upon intrigue or artifice; he made little or no concession to plot; he introduced little satire or humor, puppetry or caricature, to provide the easy diversion of Fielding or Le Sage. With a relentless, unswerving persistence he followed his stern ideal of fidelity to the sober truth of ordinary life.

Similarly Flaubert's characters are more definitely individualized than Balzac's, and exhibit a more faithful realism. Balzac's main characters are ordinarily types, at times conventional ones; as he himself was careful to point out, they include, for example, a number of paragons—to balance the sinners and keep the lesson plain. Although he costumed them with elaborate care and photographed every pimple, he was far less painstaking in particularizing their minds and souls. The affection of Père Goriot for his daughters is as extravagant as their hypocrisy and ingratitude; thoroughly convincing on the plane of his daily activities, he becomes in the big scenes a mere caricature of the Outraged Parent. But Emma Bovary is more than a type of general significance. She is also an individual with an existence entirely and minutely her own. We know her inside out as we know perhaps no character in the novel before her. Although, as Henry James pointed out regretfully, Flaubert never attempted a really complex character (Emma is by James's standards indeed a most uncomplicated person), his characterization is subtler than the average even today, and certainly much less broad and obvious than Balzac's. The whole study of the romantic temperament in Emma: her sentimental religiosity; her dramatization of her illness after the failure of Rodolphe, and her attempt to find solace in a romantic piety; the gradual shrinking of her dreams, and the degradation from romanticist to sensualist and almost to courtesan—this is one of the early triumphs of analysis in fiction. With Stendhal, Flaubert stands among the first great psychological realists.

It is especially by his impartiality toward his characters, however, that Flaubert helped to shape the ideal of modern realism. If he was impartial simply because at heart he despised all his creatures, at least he seldom indulged in special pleading. He simply presented his people for what they were and allowed them to speak for themselves. This explains the famous trial for indecency and all the furor that for a while obscured the originality and significance of *Madame Bovary:* Flaubert had failed specifically to condemn the immoral conduct of his heroine and to point the lesson in her career. In his view true realism could not teach edifying precepts. Neither could it corrupt. It was precisely as moral or immoral as experience—which is neither. To most contemporary novelists this is self-evident truth, even though they have still to defend it from periodic attacks by an incurably moralistic citizenry; but Flaubert helped to establish this principle, and it is another measure of the distance that separates him from Balzac. Although the breadth of his interests and sympathies made Balzac fair-minded in his practice, he was still an avowed and sincere moralist, preaching especially the need of Christian faith. The writer, he declared in the Preface to his *Comédie Humaine,* "should regard himself as an instructor: and mankind does not need to be instructed how to doubt"; these "noble words" form the rule of his art. But however noble, they are not the gospel of most modern realism.

Even in the brilliant technical achievements and the highly self-conscious artistry of *Madame Bovary* Flaubert left his mark on subsequent realism. Few, indeed, have attempted to rival this marvel of composition. In nineteenth-century England its example was practically ignored; and the later naturalists emphasized observation almost to the exclusion of composition and style, reverting to Balzac's practice of hewing roughly to an emotional center and letting the chips fall where they would. Many today are as suspicious of the well-made novel as of the well-made play, feeling that even so beautifully concealed an artistry is still too artificial, even so cunning a design still too simple, to represent the essential truth of human experience or reproduce its deepest impressions. Yet Flaubert taught realists something by his avoidance of intrigue and his perfect balance of character and plot. He impressed them with the value of compactness and the uncompromising pursuit of a single theme. He has at least shown them that a rigorous realism is not incompatible with great art.

Finally, *Madame Bovary* is an impressive novel in its own right —not only one of the first expressions of a new spirit, but one of the most enduring. Flaubert's achievement appears most plainly by contrast with a more recent sensation: *Main Street.* Sinclair Lewis's theme is quite similar—the conflict of a second-rate woman with a third-rate environment—and he gave it a shrewd, effective treatment. As one of the pioneering works of American realism, *Main Street* is historically important; it let in light and air where they were sadly needed, it led the way to more honest, robust studies of American life. Yet now that it has won its victory it has lost most of its point. American readers go to Flaubert, not for an account of French provincial life in the nineteenth century, but for an insight into universal experience. Foreigners come to Lewis (and still, one gathers, in droves) more in the spirit of tourists, eager for a picturesque view of the curious American animal in his rural haunts—and the view they get is almost as distorted as the set pictures of homespun heroes that were the fashion before him. Lewis's satirical purposes make this familiar comparison somewhat unfair, but it is nevertheless significant. It illustrates the difference between a topical and a timeless realism, between brilliant journalism and art.

In short, Flaubert clearly saw and carefully avoided the bogs that beset the realist, and did not get mired in mere compilation or transcript. Fact, he observed, is nothing in itself; only its relations are important—its position in an esthetic whole. Although his method was the method of patient and precise notation, and although at times he carried it to an uninspired excess out of pure pedantry (in the over-long speeches of the apothecary Homais, for example, he appears to delight in parading his technical knowledge), most of his documentation was taken in a steady stride and subordinated to a steadily conceived artistic and philosophic end. Charles Bovary's hat is the famous example of detail skilfully selected to render character, but throughout the novel Flaubert manages an admirable balance between character and background, persons and things. Unlike Balzac, who mechanically separated these elements in his narratives, he gives at almost every point the impression of an organic view: life represented at once in its particularity and its intricate wholeness. One accordingly remembers *Madame Bovary,* not as a merely accurate, but as a wonderfully vivid, complete, and just study of what life in a provincial town meant to a flabbily imaginative, sentimental woman, married to a clod who by the very act of marrying her lost the one element of mystery and romance that had attracted her to him. One may indeed question how far such a subject is worth doing; one cannot deny that by Flaubert it was almost ideally done.

2

The sources of Flaubert's realism are both historical and idiosyncratic. He had obvious literary antecedents in Stendhal and especially in Balzac. He shared consciously in the reaction against the romantic movement—the miserable Emma Bovary was a product of the romantic literature that by the middle of the century was giving its last gasp. Yet if like most French writers he fits snugly into a neat literary pattern, coming midway in the transition from romanticism to naturalism, his position there is also due to accidents of temperament. As a stern discipline, realism would naturally appeal to so severely conscientious an artist; pure romance might seem relatively too free, too easy. More particularly, however, Flaubert's realism appears to have been the thwart, unnatural child of his almost pathological hatred of its bourgeois subjects. He had a horror of the vulgar and mediocre, but he was also fascinated by them. He actually suffered from this painful sore, but he was forever scratching it. Fools exist for the pleasure of our contemplation and scorn, he declared; and so he got his chief joy out of tirelessly unearthing, analyzing, and exhibiting choice specimens. The final monument to this diseased passion is the amazing and appalling *Bouvard and Pécuchet,* the famous epic and encyclopedia of human stupidity. He drove himself through enormous researches, reading 1500 books simply to unearth every sample of absurdity in the intellectual history of mankind. "One must be mad to undertake a work like that," de Maupassant quotes him as saying; and he spent the last six years of his life on it.

Yet the paradox of Flaubert goes deeper than this. If there was a remorseless realist in him, there was also an incorrigible romanticist who could never reconcile himself to realism; accordingly his work falls into more or less repellent halves. To follow Émile Faguet's beautifully neat, if oversimplified and too symmetrical, analysis of this cleavage, the romantic in Flaubert appears plainly in his strong imagination, his love of the mysterious and macabre, his pleasure in melancholy, his passionate fondness for the East and the exotic generally. It appears as well in his concern for style, the almost mystical significance he attached to the Word. Yet his realistic conscience would never permit him to indulge freely or for long these fancies so wildly dear. He made some effort indeed to harmonize the conflicting elements in him —his realistic novels are typically studies of romantic temperaments, his romantic novels are documented with endless detail; for the most part he canalized them, serving first the realistic, then the romantic Muse, but both unwaveringly, austerely—and always unhappily. The regular alternation of his novels is thus not fortuitous. While he was engaged on a realistic work he expressed constant distaste for his task and looked forward eagerly to writing a romance; when he had got under way on this romance he spoke of it as bitterly, and again pined for a different project; and his exasperation was always intensified by his anguish over the problems of style that attended romance and realism alike.

Hence the curious inconsistencies in Flaubert's career. His principle of impersonality he observed faithfully from beginning to end: both a perfect realism and an untrammeled romance demand it. For the rest his practice was as contradictory as his criticism confused; he could be content with neither way. This realist did his best to shut out the world about which he wrote. This romantic was also a furious enemy of that personal expression which is most characteristic of romanticism. This hater of the bourgeoisie had nevertheless their attitude toward romantic behavior, and in his persecution of Emma Bovary epitomizes their conventional morality. As Faguet summarizes it, the romanticist in him found reality flat and the realist found romanticism shallow; the artist in him found the bourgeois grotesque and the bourgeois found artists pretentious; and all united in a misanthropy that found the whole world ridiculous.

More specifically and more profoundly, however, Flaubert suffered from an esthetic ideal that always haunted him. He yearned for an absolute beauty, a beauty of diction and form apart from substance; in his letters he expressed a desire to write a book about Nothing, or almost nothing. "The most beautiful works are those with the least matter. . . . I believe that the future of art is in these channels." This was at least a prophetic remark. It anticipates Symbolism and the whole reaction against naturalism and science. Probably all artists have had some such desire, secret or unconscious, as they struggled with stubborn materials or chafed at the claims and the fetters of their age. But in Flaubert it was a deep desire; and it made his frustration inevitable. It was incompatible, not only with the immense documentary labors he was driven to by other impulses, but with the very medium he had chosen to work in. The novel is the literary form in which matter, concrete representation of experience, is unavoidably most conspicuous; in which diction and lovely proportions can never be ends in themselves; in which perhaps no other writer has even dreamed of achieving such an absolute beauty. Hence his revulsion against each completed work. It was not a simple opposition of realistic and romantic impulses; it was the impossibility of achieving his ideal through either. The novel has not been written that could really satisfy Gustave Flaubert.

Despite his terrifyingly arduous labors, Flaubert accordingly failed ever to make full use of his great gifts, or to match his initial triumph in *Madame Bovary*. His devotion to the task in hand was intense but never wholehearted; at least one part of him was always outside his work, viewing it with a yellow and a jaundiced eye and making destructive comment. And *Madame Bovary* is his best novel chiefly because it was his first. Its theme incidentally provided opportunities for the exercise of most of his conflicting impulses: the realist could dissect the follies of the romanticist, the misanthrope could stick pins in the bourgeois, the esthete could give the whole a perfect shape. But all these operations were carried on with more freshness and enthusiasm than Flaubert ever managed again simply because he had *not* yet quite found himself—found, that is, the self whose painful disharmonies were to become more acute. The novels that follow are more definitely cankered and frustrate; all are as disappointing as they are imposing.

Flaubert's romances, *Salammbô* and *The Temptation of Saint Anthony,* accordingly suffer from a kind of monotony of execution especially noticeable because of their flamboyant or grandiose materials. *Salammbô* was the realization of his dream of the Orient and was written, he declared, for his *own* pleasure; it was also the product of his usual prodigious research—and this has kept the pleasure indeed exclusive. Despite the gorgeousness of its style and imagery, this story of old Carthage is a fatiguing work. It is documented as minutely as any catalogue of Balzac's, and Flaubert defended the accuracy of his details far more jealously than he did the power of his imaginings. The main characters are either wooden or shadowy, and get lost on this huge, elaborately set stage (he himself admitted of Salammbô that "the pedestal is too great for the statue"); even the many glamorous or ghastly details miss the effect they ought to have, for they are clammy with the sweat of his labors. Although he no doubt wrote more accurate history than Scott, Flaubert failed in the primary duty of the historical romancer: he did not achieve a live, imaginative re-creation of the past.

The Temptation of Saint Anthony is no less fatiguing, only in a different way. A philosophical poem, a vast reservoir of abstract rather than concrete material, it is another sacrifice to Flaubert's demon of thoroughness, and also comes out lumpish and leaden. But it suffers too from the feebleness and eccentricity of his thought. In reworking the ancient legend, Flaubert attempted to replace the visions of nude women that disturbed the old saint with all the false, superstitious doctrines that trouble the mind of man; the result, one suspects, is even more chaotic and nightmarish than he intended. He who yearned to write about nothing has again given us a surfeit of matter. And this helps to explain the lack of real zest or verve even in this work, whose theme had haunted him for many years, and which with *Salammbô* was apparently closest to his heart.

Although *The Sentimental Education,* the realistic novel sandwiched in between these two, is a more successful achievement, if only because its less grand design was easier to execute and less menaced by cross-purposes, it is marred by the same fatal monotony and mania. It is a journal of everyday life worthy of the author of *Madame Bovary,* and it is distinguished by a surprisingly effective creation of a good woman. Yet most readers cannot help feeling that the education they are asked to observe is in a way as tedious and even as profitless for the observer as it was for the hero. By Flaubert's central design Frederic Moreau is a nonentity; and this sorry fellow is our constant companion throughout this long journey. From by his side we must look out on this vast panorama of human feebleness, folly, and futility.

If this is an uninspiring experience, it is exciting, however, in comparison with that we are subjected to in *Bouvard and Pécuchet,* the last and by his immediate disciples apparently the most admired of Flaubert's works. Here we follow the intellectual adventures of two morons, almost indistinguishable in personality as in mentality. Flaubert endows them with a fortune so as to enable them to gratify a rather strange thirst for knowledge; as they embark on their systematic researches, he is able to have pass in review all the sciences—and to seize unerringly upon every absurdity and contradiction, every error of fact or fault of logic, every foolish or unguarded statement that has come down from the past. It is an ingenious if fiendish display, and one must no doubt regard with awe so colossal an enterprise and so heroic a devotion to it. But after a few chapters one gets the idea, and after a few more one is weary of its endless illustration. In this illustration, moreover, Flaubert loses all perspective; delightedly he takes a snapshot of Homer nodding, and magnifies every slip of even the wisest and greatest of men. What begins as a devastating satire on human stupidity becomes a pointless mockery of all human thought. What remains at the end is simply the monument of Flaubert's misanthropy.

Extreme as it is, *Bouvard and Pécuchet* only emphasizes the chief limitation of all Flaubert's work, and even of *Madame Bovary.* His only passion was for pure art; for the human experience whose representation was inescapable in the art form he had chosen, he had only a scorn and hate amounting to mania. This mania, moreover, led him to multiply the representation of the objects it fed on, cram his books with matter absurd and grotesque, ugly and mean, thus intensifying the dissatisfaction of the artist while affording only a morbid gratification to the man. And to complete this melancholy picture of frustration, one can scarcely even respect the man. Flaubert's misanthropy was not wrung from bitter experience or fired by a dark passion. It was simply an extension of youthful cynicism, a prolonged adolescent hangover. Most men outgrow their early disillusionment, or at least sober and deepen it by mature thought; Flaubert did not. As a youngster shocked by the Facts of Life he wrote of the pleasure of dissecting and exposing "the gangrene of lovely places"; as an aging man he had the same adolescent obsessions, the same adolescent desire to shock. His misanthropy was ingrowing, self-nourished, and strengthened chiefly by habit.

Whatever his subject, Flaubert accordingly never wrote with the gusto or exuberance of the greatest creative artists. It is idle, of course, to lament his meager output or distrust his agonies over style. He could write only as he did; if he had written differently he would not have been Flaubert. Yet his infinitely polished art was an outgrowth of the same temperamental deficiencies that led him to cut himself off from the world and for most of the year live as a hermit. If it justified his precious aloofness, it was not the real reason for this aloofness. It was a kind of compensation for his fear of experience and inability to cope with its responsibilities.

In his Journal, Arnold Bennett quoted from Flaubert's letters a comment on the single, very perfunctory sentimental episode in his life: "Un amour normal, régulier, nourri et solide, me sortirait trop hors de moi, me troublerait, je rentrerais dans la vie active, dans la vérité physique, dans le sens commun enfin, et c'est ce que m'a été nuisible toutes les fois que j'ai voulu le tenter." This remark (addressed to a woman) Bennett cites as a fine example of Flaubert's *maladif* quality, and the reason why he is not of the first rank. It is at any rate this attitude, more than his limited range or his relative simplicity, that distinguishes him from many of the later realists, or among his contemporaries from the great Russians. Howells, Dreiser, Galsworthy, and Bennett, like Tolstoy and Dostoyevsky, have a broad humanity, an eager curiosity and sympathetic interest, a perpetual wonder and awe, that illumine their darkest pages. Their impersonality does not resolve itself into a chilly remoteness; they can be impartial and yet have a warm love for their characters, arouse an interest in them as persons such as one seldom feels for Flaubert's most life-like creations. They display, in short, a kind of love of reality, or at least a courageous willingness to accept it on its own terms, that makes their realism invigorating and gives it a foundation in humanistic values. For such values Flaubert substituted the Word and the Fact; and in the novel these are by themselves not enough.

3

The misanthropy that with each novel further distorted Flaubert's mask of impersonality, twisting his expression into a fixed grimace, is apparent even in *Madame Bovary*. Through most of the novel, to be sure, he remains the impassive observer. Although he introduces a pretty sorry cast of characters, they are recognizable if not fairly representative, and they are not wholly ignoble; he has by no means libeled human nature. Similarly his veiled irony is a familiar and for such a story even an appropriate attitude; it would not necessarily indicate bitterness or scorn. Toward the end of the novel, however, Flaubert drops the veil, and his irony runs wild. Inflexibly he refuses to grant Emma Bovary the least shred of consolation or beauty, to soften in any way the misery and horror of her last moments. What had been an inexorable realism takes on the appearance of perverted invention. He introduces the gratuitous horror of the blind man; he follows the dead Emma to the grave with a series of mean mockeries; he ends on a note of pure cynicism by bestowing on the contemptible Homais the cross of the Legion of Honor. By this time it is plain that here is no scientific analyst, nor even a stern moralist paying to the last penny the wages of sin, but a creator who despises his creatures.

Despite such unpleasantness, however, Flaubert is not strictly to be associated with the pessimism of the modern spirit, or studied as an early symptom of its sickness. Such pessimism as colors his work is purely temperamental, not philosophical, and has no clear connection with the new knowledge or scheme of life. His attitude was not the product of the disagreeable notions about man's position in the universe that science was introducing; it was simply the natural reaction of a timid introvert who one imagines would in any age have despised his fellows—and found a small company to share his views. Flaubert was not a philosopher. His concern was not the cosmos or the gods but art and style, the lovely form and the right word, and these in turn were to him not symbols or means but separate entities and ends in themselves. Thus there are no cosmic implications in the fate of Emma Bovary. It is pitiable but not surprising or even, strictly speaking, unjust; it is rather the logical, almost inevitable consequence of her own flabby folly. Her tragedy is not the tragedy of all mankind. It does not involve the final issues of human life, nor imply a larger cruelty or injustice. It leaves no residue of the mysterious and inexplicable.

Yet to the gentle reader it is as distressing as works that do insist upon these more awful implications, and even for the tough-minded reader it does not have the dark splendor of many actually pessimistic performances. To none can it give the lift and glow of high tragedy. It arouses pity, but no awe; it illumines, but it stirs no great imaginings. And the reason is simply the littleness of the souls, the smallness of the affair, Flaubert has chosen to deal with. It is not the obscurity of its actors or the remoteness of their habitat, but the meagerness of their emotional, imaginative, spiritual capacity. The defeat of ignoble aims, the frustration of mean souls, cannot grandly move and inspire. Emma Bovary is indeed not simply contemptible: she has some dignity and force and is at least superior to her environment. Similarly the shabby specimens with which Flaubert surrounds her are at worst imbeciles, and are occasionally likable: the gross stupidity of her husband Charles is shaded by a simple decency, and her father has actually a kind of nobility. Yet one can say as much of many animals; and even had he told his story with more compassion Flaubert could not have made it a deep or rich experience. He has given his subject an unsurpassable form and got out of it almost all there is in it, but there is relatively little in it. Inevitably the story of Emma and her tawdry lovers is of no great consequence.

This limitation is still more obvious in Flaubert's later realistic novels, in which he employed still paltrier materials. The abject hero of *The Sentimental Education* is simply a more ignoble and ineffectual edition of Emma Bovary. Flaubert achieved in him another triumph of perfect rendering; he even managed to give the impression of size to his story; but the size only makes more resounding its hollowness. Why, wondered a sincere admirer, Henry James, should Flaubert choose to register so much experience through not merely so unsubtle but so mean a consciousness? There remains, of course, the fairly impressive figure of Madame Arnoux; but her presence is finally only another expression of Flaubert's misanthropic bias. Because he had permitted himself the novel experiment of introducing a really good woman, he thought, with some misgiving, that he had written a "semi-idealistic" novel. By now he had clearly fallen into the common error of identifying the real with the sordid.

The point, then, is that more depressing and more paralyzing than the pessimism that takes a gloomy view of human destiny is the cynicism that has no respect for human nature. Flaubert has little helpful to say, either directly or indirectly, to those wrestling with the fundamental problems of our civilization. His way cannot be the way of most, for it is no way; it is a denial of almost everything except a brilliant art that will become meaningless unless provided with a background of human values. He has illuminated with a beautifully clear and steady light some of the byways of human experience. He has led the way to modern realistic investigation. He has taught novelists much about method and composition, providing them with superb models that can be employed for more fruitful subjects. But he does not answer the questions that are today so urgent, nor even point a way by which men may profitably approach them. He cannot satisfy the deepest needs of the human spirit in this or any age.

IX

THOMAS HARDY

I

WHEN Thomas Hardy began to write, many of his older contemporaries were sounding modern notes—the note of social reform, for example, in the novels of Dickens, Reade, and Mrs. Gaskell. He did not make a dramatic entrance, or abruptly announce a new creed. His *Far From the Madding Crowd,* published anonymously, was by astute critics attributed to George Eliot; and from this first major novel he worked his way slowly, to discover not long before his readers that he was living in a different world. Yet it is not arbitrary to study him as the first modern novelist in England. The plain reader instantly recognizes that if Hardy's novels are not what he would call up-to-date, they are far removed from *David Copperfield* and *Vanity Fair.* His break with Victorianism was more radical than that of two contemporaries, George Eliot and George Meredith, who were also in important ways pointing to a new era.

Meredith was indeed far enough in advance of his time to have to wait almost until the twentieth century for an audience. *The Ordeal of Richard Feverel* was published in 1859, the same year as *A Tale of Two Cities;* not until nineteen years later did it go into a second edition. Meredith did not indulge in the rambling, sprawling chronicles so comfortable to the Victorians, but strained their attention by his habit of distilling and refining a single issue under the guidance of the Comic Spirit. He disturbed and bewildered them even more by his scorn of mere narrative, his emphasis upon psychology. His goal was the quintessence of reality (he talked of the futility of "a conscientious transcription of all the visible, and a repetition of all the audible"), but he did not arrive at this goal by the straight path of patient, orderly analysis. His method was instead intuitive, a seemingly haphazard succession of leaping, flashing motions difficult to follow; and in this sharper, intenser, subtler notation he anticipated not only Henry James but Conrad, Lawrence, and the impressionists. Finally, he felt the impact of the new ideas that were reshaping civilization, and he honestly faced their consequences. Many of his attitudes were what we like to think of as modern—he fought, for example, for the emancipation of women. And in two lines of *Modern Love* he wrote a kind of preface to the whole modern era:

> Ah what a dusty answer gets the soul
> When hot for certainties in this our life!

Yet Meredith was rich in genial certainties, remorselessly eager to share them; and here he parts company with the harassed moderns, fading back into another and more comfortable world. He incidentally had the Victorian habit of constantly interfering with his story, pawing over his materials, turning his characters around, telling the reader at every point what to think: he was incessantly didactic if only because he was so sure of himself. More important, his message, robust though its optimism is, has been pretty thoroughly corroded by "the acids of modernity." His proclamation of the divine harmony between man and nature, his confidence in the splendid promise of evolution, his rapt display of the glory of love—these faiths come to us in accents that sound almost foreign.

A further reason for passing thus lightly over Meredith's work is that it is a kind of isolated and unique achievement, less significant in the history of the novel than its virtues might suggest. Meredith is never mediocre; he is a great personality and a rich source of wit and wisdom, fancy and sentiment; but he is not a great novelist. His many excellent qualities do not fuse; his novels are glittering collections of incidental beauties whose sum is greater than the whole. What splits them, even more than the essayist who forever obtruded comment and the stylist who grew to have a horror of simple statement, is a divided personality, a fundamental disharmony between the impassioned poet and the comic philosopher. Passion and intellect did not unite in him as they did in Dante, but pulled in opposite directions. Thus *The Ordeal of Richard Feverel,* the richest in poetry and passion of all his novels, breaks up into mutually repellent halves; Meredith could not make up his mind whether he was writing comedy or tragedy, and ended by writing both—and neither. Even *The Egoist,* generally admired as his most consistent and characteristic work, falls apart in its big scenes. Sir Willoughby Patterne is a wholly comic creation, but Laetitia and Clara, the objects of his exalted conceit, are conceived and analyzed in an altogether different spirit, realistic or even sentimental; the reader is insistently asked to take their sufferings seriously. Once he is emotionally involved he cannot retain the Puck-like detachment of the Comic Spirit; and he then realizes of what flimsy and artificial stuff the story is made. In short, Virginia Woolf is right in placing the "brilliant and uneasy" figure of Meredith among the great eccentrics rather than among the great masters.

Less brilliant, but also less uneasy a novelist was George Eliot. She too was one of the "advanced thinkers" of her day, and in her honest wrestling with doubt and her revolt against convention foreshadowed the coming unrest. She was also perhaps the first important writer in England to take the novel with entire seriousness—Fielding and Thackeray, for instance, were often all too earnest but as often willing merely to entertain. She consciously introduced a new order of realism, insisting upon a more logical relation between character and plot, and pointing out how in their fondness for the dramatic and the picturesque her contemporaries shied away from the subdued tones of ordinary experience; hence she set for herself the ideal of the early Dutch painters: a faithful, loving representation of humble, commonplace lives. How nearly she approached this ideal is indicated by the very annoyance we feel at her occasional lapses into melodrama; we are acutely distressed by an incident like the galloping, last-minute rescue of Hetty Sorrel that in Dickens we should scarcely notice.

Perhaps the chief contribution of George Eliot, however, lay in her preoccupation with the obscure workings of the mind, her patient analysis of motive and impulse, her intense interest in the profounder problems of man's mental and spiritual life, by which she expanded the substance of fiction and deepened the truth of character as had no English novelist before her. Where Dickens and Thackeray introduce us to jolly or surly companions, she gives us sober, responsible citizens of the spiritual and intellectual world. Where they brightly depict appearances or merely describe states of mind, she plunges below the surface to seek out hidden causes. As early as *Adam Bede* she was concerned with the complexity of mental processes, with their tangle of obscure, wayward, and contradictory impulses, and in her analysis of Arthur Donnithorne even anticipated the modern concept of the unconscious. Nor was this a fortuitous concern. As a highly intellectual novelist, she was in close touch with the scientific movement of her day.

This is an impressive pioneering accomplishment. Yet despite her forays into strange territory George Eliot always returned to ground solid and familiar enough for all but the most timorous of her readers; they soon found that they could dwell quite comfortably in her spiritual home. To link her with Hardy, on the strength of incidental similarities of interest, is to miss the very heart of their work. George Eliot not only clung to the Victorian manner—the constant habit of comment, the constant disposition to be edifying; she retained the essential quality of Victorian thought. The mild heresies that at first shocked her contemporaries can today scarcely be detected by the naked eye. She had doubts, but she fought her way through scientific rationalism to an essentially Christian faith; she lived very conscientiously in a state of sin, but her "emancipation" was skin deep and ultimately only another proof of her piety. One need not contemplate the rabid, pathetic conventionality of her last days to discover that she was at heart always a conventional and a deeply religious woman.

All George Eliot's novels make clear that she was a relentless moralist, and that her ethical teaching was of a quite orthodox kind. From beginning to end she preached the power of Conscience, the sacredness of Duty, the sublimity of Self-Sacrifice; and she never questioned the authority nor examined the origins of this trinity. Although her moral earnestness is by no means to be laughed away (it might well be injected into the hardened arteries of some enlightened contemporaries), she missed the whole issue of morality as it appears today. She had a vision of the complexity of the human mind, but she had an even brighter vision of a few clear certainties, and could march unerringly to the holy cabbage at the center of the maze. Her ethical system is simple and rigid. She assumed without question its absolute and universal validity; she placed volition and conscience entirely within the control of the individual; she almost disregarded the immense influence of environment and the whole significance of *mores*. The gulf that separates her from Hardy is measured by the creation of Sue Bridehead in *Jude the Obscure*. Sue's final surrender of Jude and happiness in the interest of what she conceives to be duty is an act of renunciation that to George Eliot was the highest test of character. To Hardy it was the last step in the degradation of Sue and the misery of Jude, and but another testimony to the appalling cruelty of the scheme of things.

2

Thomas Hardy himself was by no means, of course, a full-fledged modern. Apart from the occasional quaintness of his vocabulary and stiffness of his manner, he is in important respects an old-fashioned writer. The first great tragic novelist in England had strong ties with the tragic poets of the past.

In an age that was beginning to busy itself on smaller scales and within narrower scopes, Hardy is distinguished by the largeness with which he treated elemental and eternal forces, the boldness with which he presented the extremes of human passion. He considered his characters primarily in their relations to Time and Destiny; even his feeblest dramas are enacted in the presence of the gods. More than any other modern, indeed, he resembles Sophocles and Shakespeare: in the sweep of his imagination, the magnitude of his designs, the universality of his themes. Although his heroes are obscure, simple folk, inhabiting a small rural area insulated from the fields of spectacular activity in the modern world, he endowed them with an intensity of passion and a greatness of soul that make them heroic; and he gave a spaciousness to his restricted scene by concentrating his attention upon the timeless problems of life and death, the play of elemental passions before the majestic background of nature.

Hardy is thus only incidentally a realist. He employed some of the methods and subscribed to some of the main tenets of the new creed, notably its catholicity; but the abundant realistic detail with which he re-created his Wessex was to him only a "shadowy accessory." "My art," he wrote in his Journal, "is to intensify the expression of things . . . so that the heart and inner meaning is made vividly clear." To reveal the essential features the novelist must deliberately alter and distort; an inventory of the "simply natural" is no longer interesting and cannot even be exact, since art is at best an approximate copy. "Hence 'realism' is not Art."

In his *Thomas Hardy: Penseur et Artiste,* F. A. Hedgcock suggests an illuminating contrast of *The Return of the Native* with *Madame Bovary*. Both novels relate the story of a woman who tries vainly to escape from an uncongenial environment into a freer, fuller life; both give a detailed account of this environment. But Flaubert's is a thoroughly realistic and typically modern study. Tragedy results solely from the play of character and the pressure of social forces; one situation grows out of another with all the inevitability of cause and effect. In *The Return of the Native,* however, the master of the show is an incalculable supernatural force, whose interferences are as capricious as they are irresistible. The dice are loaded against Eustacia Vye; and she plays her futile game, not against society, but against the gods. Similarly, external nature, which in *Madame Bovary* serves occasionally as a striking backdrop, is in *The Return of the Native* a constant presence, one of the main actors and the most impressive. The magnificent description of Egdon Heath in the opening chapter—"A Face on Which Time Makes But Little Impression"—announces a central theme; the dark, austere spirit of the heath broods over the story until its tragic close. Hardy thus gives his drama a sublime simplicity, a solemn and majestic beauty, that Flaubert could never get into his more subtle and painstaking record. Here, roughly, is the difference between poetry and science.

Here is also what makes Hardy's greatness difficult to define. Flaubert's virtues are precise and measurable; with Hardy one perforce falls back on swelling adjectives, as in all efforts to communicate the glow of poetry. Yet I make these distinctions only to emphasize, finally, the qualities that stamp Hardy too as a modern. He had much in common, once more, with earlier tragic poets, and especially with the Greeks. Like Sophocles, he had a profound sense of Fate. Both perceived a force that opposed human will, that in often fantastic ways frustrated human designs. Both recognized the futility of attempting to combat its incomprehensible decrees. But to Sophocles the gods were intelligent, if not merciful, and he retained an unwavering faith in the essential rightness of their government. Of such faith Thomas Hardy had not a jot. Where, accordingly, the spirit of Sophocles was ultimately a reverent submission, the spirit of Hardy was a passionate, at times almost a shrill protest. "'Justice' was done, and the President of the Immortals (in Æschylean phrase) had ended his sport with Tess"—this is Hardy's final comment upon the terrible fate of his heroine; and these bitter words state an irreconcilable difference that in its largest aspect is the difference between modernity and antiquity.

To Hardy, then, men are not the instrument of divine purposes; they are merely the hapless victims of blind forces. They cannot shape their conduct with reference to just and immutable laws; they can only prepare themselves against "stupid contingencies." Although they are of course partially responsible for their fates, an implacable deity forges both character and circumstance, destroying as unreasonably as it creates. Eustacia Vye was imperiously selfish; Tess Durbeyfield had but a "slight incautiousness of character" that only the sternest moralist would call a tragic flaw. Where Aristotle declared that misfortune overtaking the innocent and virtuous can only shock and outrage us, Hardy insisted that life *is* shocking and outrageous, that the innocent *do* suffer and the noble go crashing to their ruin simply because they are noble and therefore less capable of paltry compromise. He specifically forbade man to assume the final responsibility for his destiny.

> It is usually so [he comments when Clym Yeobright ceases to complain of his fate and gives way to self-reproach], except with the sternest of men. Human beings, in their generous endeavor to construct a hypothesis that shall not degrade a First Cause, have always hesitated to conceive a dominant power of lower moral quality than their own; and even while they sit down and weep by the waters of Babylon, invent excuses for the oppression which prompts their tears.

What makes this view of life significant is that one cannot romanticize Hardy as a sensitive spirit bruised by unfortunate experience, nor isolate a tragic period in his life and make conjectures about some Dark Lady. Neither can one dismiss his pessimism as a mere accident of temperament. He was definitely influenced by the advanced thought of his age, directly through his reading in science (he was one of the first to acclaim *The Origin of Species*), indirectly through contact with men like Leslie Stephen who were playing the prelude to the symphony of Doubt and Despair. Thus his ideas became more precise, coherent, and positive. What was in his early poems a youthful feeling of the unfitness of things crystallized into a formal philosophy. What had been an assortment of vague generalizations, connected only by their uniform gloominess, became a coordinated metaphysic.

The complete statement of this philosophy is to be found in *The Dynasts*. In the stature of its actors, the magnitude of its issues, the vastness and magnificence of its whole conception, *The Dynasts* is comparable to the great epics of the past. It is also an epic unlike all others, that only the modern spirit could have produced. Hardy dramatized so immense a conflict as the Napoleonic Wars simply to show how purposeless and insignificant it was. He chose as protagonists the great of the earth simply to emphasize their littleness. Napoleon, like his commonest soldier, is but a puppet of the "great Foresightless," a minutest fiber of the anatomy of the Absolute; his colossal designs affect the course of destiny not a whit. Hardy's final conclusion is that the Immanent Will is not malicious but simply indifferent, not omniscient but blind and unwitting.

> It works unconsciously, as heretofore,
> Eternal artistries in Circumstance;
> . . . like a knitter drowsed,
> Whose fingers play in skilled unmindfulness,
> The Will has woven with an absent heed
> Since life first was; and ever will so weave.

And the tragedy of man is that during the unconscious weaving he somehow developed consciousness. This gratuitous cruelty was indeed mere accident, a Tragic Chance of which the Will is ignorant; but the accident happened.

The Dynasts ends, to be sure, on a note of hope: perhaps the Will may become conscious too, and thus sympathetic with its creatures. But after the World War, which extinguished the feeble rays of optimism that had occasionally filtered through his gloom, Hardy declared that he would have omitted this cheerful thought; and he had never really built on it anyway. The interludes of gaiety he permitted his rustics were "no part of the actual drama." These simple folk might for some time be expected to live in contentment, but only because among them "a perfect insight into the conditions of existence will be longest postponed."

3

Now, there is inevitably something a little ridiculous in the postulation of so utter a pessimism. In his curious anxiety to convince us how miserable we are or ought to be, Hardy at times recalls, despite his dignity, a character in P. G. Wodehouse who was forever "going around searching for the leak in life's gas pipe with a lighted candle." A mere ride in a cab would induce this sort of cosmic observation in his Journal:

> Drove home . . . behind a horse who had no interest in me, was going a way he had no interest in going, and was whipped by a man who had no interest in me, or the horse, or the way. Amid this string of compulsions reached home.

And at that, such resolute determinism is preferable to the crude fatalism that governs much of his work. Hardy had the sophomore's love for irony—irony of the most obvious sort—and this was constantly the inspiration even of his mature poetry. "Ah, Are You Digging on My Grave?" is a sample of the grotesquerie that with the disillusioned adolescent passes for the essence of Life; many scenes even in the great novels are conceived in as ludicrously grim a spirit. Hence one often feels that it is not Fate but Thomas Hardy who is persecuting his characters with so almost fanatical a zeal. Although there is warrant in actual life for his most sinister scenes, there is no warrant for the dismal generalizations that he deduces from these exceptional instances.

Hardy indeed objected heatedly to treating his works as if they were a "scientific system of philosophy." "Art is concerned with seemings only," he tells us in his Journal; he had simply used the theories of his age for artistic purposes. Plainly, however, his views were not so provisional, else he would not so repeatedly have gone out of his way to state them. What is important, at any rate, is less that they narrow the truth of Hardy's tragedy than that they tend to weaken its vitality. Some of his scenes approach the pure horror of a nightmare—a horror that simply numbs the tragic emotions. As early as *Far From the Madding Crowd,* in the episode in which the dying Fanny Robin drags herself along

Casterbridge Highway, he was testing the reader's powers of endurance in the harrowing; by the time of *Jude the Obscure* he was scouring every resource of a perverted imagination to intensify and prolong the life agony of his hero. And in the midst of such extraordinary incidents his characters are likely to appear theatrical, puppet-like. They are the agents of a rigidly preconceived and ordinarily bizarre scheme; Hardy works them so hard in the execution of this scheme that they lose flesh. As he was less interested in studying the human soul than in narrating its awful destiny, he too rarely achieved that nice balance between character and plot that gives drama the appearance of inevitability. The fault lies partly, indeed, in a still somewhat old-fashioned technique. Almost to the last he was hag-ridden by plot, and his notion of a good plot was one crowded with unusual and exciting incident; he had a natural fondness for miscarried letters, mistaken identities, overheard conversations, and amazing contretemps generally, and did not scorn the most shopworn devices. Yet his extravagant pessimism, his arbitrary irony, is always the chief threat to his art.

Hardy was clearly unfortunate in the age in which he lived, and suffered from its opposition. He had constantly to satisfy the irritating objections of hyper-delicate magazine editors—for example the one who, fearful that the scene in which Angel Clare carries Tess and some milkmaids across a flooded lane would put lurid ideas in the heads of his readers, suggested for decorum's sake the use of a wheelbarrow. He had then to contend with the unforeseen furor created by his later novels. More and more indignant voices shouted that he was an agent of the Devil; *Jude the Obscure* evoked a storm of abuse unequaled for violence and savagery since the publication of Swinburne's *Poems and Ballads* thirty years before. It is difficult for us today even to understand the state of mind of the lady who reviewed the novel for the New York *World:*

> What has happened to Thomas Hardy? . . . I am shocked, appalled by this story! . . . It is almost the worst book I ever read. . . . I thought that *Tess of the D'Urbervilles* was bad

> enough, but that is milk for babes compared to this. . . . It is the handling of it that is the horror of it. . . . Aside from its immorality there is coarseness which is beyond belief. . . . When I finished the story I opened the windows and let in the fresh air, and I turned to my bookshelves and I said: "Thank God for Kipling and Stevenson, Barrie and Mrs. Humphry Ward. Here are four great writers who have never trailed their talents in the dirt."

Although Hardy perceived the ludicrous aspect of this hysteria, he could hardly be expected to get a wholehearted amusement out of it. "A man must be a fool to deliberately stand up to be shot at," he noted in his Journal; and in mid career he gave up the novel in bitterness and disgust.

Long before this, however, the harm had been done: the more insidious harm of the want of a riper culture. Among the first to feel the full impact of the new forces at work, he was constantly on the defensive; in his consciousness of the smug disapproval of his audience, his views naturally tended to harden in an exaggerated form, and in this form to persist even when in time they met more general acceptance. It is this violence of reaction that gives him at times the appearance of the village atheist, as Chesterton called him. Proudly he calls attention to his innovation in *The Dynasts* of referring to his blind deity as It; very self-consciously he takes his periodic flings at Christianity. One can agree with many of his comments and yet deplore their militance and harshness. One can wish, in general, not only that he had held a more balanced view, but that he had held it more urbanely.

Yet it is easy to make too much of Hardy's extremes. Although they mar his work, they do not destroy its greatness. Logically, his beliefs should paralyze all effort; actually, Hardy was as illogical in their application as most similar thinkers are. His very contentiousness would seem to be a flamboyance unbecoming a mere fiber of the Immanent Will. Similarly his characters, who should logically be mere automatons, still manage on the whole to give a lively illusion of being free, responsible, and spontaneous spirits. In general, the consequences of his pessimism are not what some critics assume, or what he himself assumed. Many mature readers are indeed depressed by his novels; but what explains their distress is either that they take him too literally at his own word (as they do not take Sophocles), or that they have been too thoroughly conditioned to the more obvious consolations of ancient tragedy. For in the end his grim narratives do affirm the ideal values of tragedy. Despite their drastic terms, they have uniformly the "certain, cathartic, Aristotelian qualities" that Hardy strove for even in *Jude the Obscure,* the most gruesome of his novels.

In the first place, his terrible pictures are veiled by compassion: a deep, sober feeling, unlike the simple pathos of Dickens. It appears in his sympathetic treatment of the meanest peasant in his novels. It is projected philosophically in the Spirit of the Pities, who plays so prominent a rôle in *The Dynasts.* It inspires such poignant words as those spoken in *The Mayor of Casterbridge* by Mother Cuxsom, at the death of Susan Henchard:

> Well, poor soul; she's helpless to hinder that or anything now. And all her shining keys will be took from her, and her cupboards opened; and little things a' didn't wish seen, anybody will see; and her wishes and ways will all be as nothing!

It has its sublime monument in *Tess of the D'Urbervilles.* If the immense sadness of this story is touched with bitterness, it is also softened by tenderness, lifted finally into a realm of beauty.

This flood of compassion, in which all of Hardy's thought and emotion unite, stems from his deep reverence for human life, his conviction of its dignity on its lowliest planes. The story of man is to him infinitely sad, but it is never commonplace, never mean, never a matter for mockery or scorn. He insists (again perhaps illogically) that man is nobler than the Will that creates and controls him. His novels are filled with records of generosity and unselfish devotion among all classes, and most strikingly among the humblest, from the half-witted peasant in *The Mayor of Casterbridge* who cares for the dying Henchard, by whom he had been treated harshly, simply because he remembered a kindness Henchard had once done his mother, to the unobtrusive, uncomplaining Marty South, who showed all the marks of poverty and toil, yet "touched sublimity at points" as she spoke the beautiful words that close *The Woodlanders*. By such examples of unwavering loyalty, of patient endurance, of selflessness, of pure beauty of soul, Hardy elevates and ennobles our common humanity. He demonstrates what he explicitly asserted: that the tragedy of obscure, unpretentious men can be endowed with a majesty and grandeur "truly Sophoclean."

Hardy's pessimism thus has little flavor of cynicism. "No man can be a cynic and live," he once remarked; and it is doubtful, surely, whether a man of his own dismal convictions about man's fate could carry the burden of cynicism as well. Instead Hardy inclines to sentimentalize his Wessex folk. He idealizes not only their quaint, rich humor but the purity of their feelings. He is prone to magnify their simple virtues to the point where they recall that depressing romantic creation: nature's nobleman. At times he even grows tiresome in his reiteration of "how little acquirements and culture weigh beside sterling personal character."

The chief limit to Hardy's understanding of men, indeed, was a kind of provincialism. He knew and loved best his simple rustics simply because he was so much like them; and he had something of their distrust of the city dweller. Although from time to time he conscientiously made excursions to London in search of material, apparently he observed with a fishy eye; most of the weak, shoddy, or vicious characters in his novels are intruders in Wessex, who feel as little at home there as does Hardy himself when he enters the sophisticated society from which they have come or to which they aspire. They are alike in their incapacity for the more solid virtues and in their lesser vitality. Troy, Wildeve, Fitzpiers—all are cut from the same cloth, and cut to measure. They are a little stagey and synthetic, at best lifelike rather than alive.

Yet of the primary elements of human character Hardy always had a firm grasp, and his respect for these elements is what affords the chief consolation in his tragedy. His pessimism only strengthened his trust in the simple, because the oldest, values. The patience, the kindliness, the loyalty, the unpretentious heroism of people of unheroic stature, dull the edge of the misery of his darkest dramas and give them the glow of tragic beauty—give them, in short, those "certain, cathartic, Aristotelian qualities" he hoped to give them. His novels generate a universalized feeling in which pity and fear and admiration merge into awe; they transport the reader into an ideal world above the painful particulars, and beyond the reach of death. If life is a "thing to be put up with," as he constantly insisted, it can be put up with with more fortitude and better grace for the existence of such compassion and such faith as his.

4

If I have labored both the pessimism and the idealism of Thomas Hardy, my excuse is that they are at the core of his art. He presents the critic with little opportunity for subtle or fancy analysis in the latest modes; neither Freudian nor Marxist can do much with him. His importance lies in his very simplicity, that takes one directly to the final issues of modern life and literature. Yet Hardy's work has other facets of special interest to the historian of modern fiction. I have so far treated his art and philosophy as if they were static—and up to a point one may fairly treat them so. His great novels are of a piece; all are the product of essentially the same view of life, all are dedicated "To sorrow." Nevertheless there were several developments in his career as novelist that are significant because their general tendency was to remove him still further from the past, stamp him more plainly as the spokesman of a new era.

In the first place, his novels grew steadily more somber in tone. In the final chapters of his earlier works he brought in fiddlers and measured out grudgingly a certain portion of happiness to the surviving characters. Gabriel Oak wins Bathsheba Everdene (and welcome he is to her); Diggory Venn is rewarded with Thomasin Yeobright. This happiness is indeed of a sober kind not designed to gladden the hearts of the sentimental; and however grateful one may be for the dim sunshine that is finally let into these novels, it is still incidental or even incongruous—the result, Hardy explained, of "certain circumstances of serial publication." In time, however, he refused to make even this slight concession to the tastes of his Victorian audience. The tragic chords that were once resolved in a quiet octave now swell and crash into dissonance. The bright lyrical note grows fainter, the pessimistic undertones grow deeper, and the delightful interludes of rustic humors that regularly relieve the tragic action of his earlier novels become more and more infrequent, until in *Jude the Obscure* they disappear entirely. In this work, the culmination of his career as a novelist, he for the first time made no use even of the poetic beauty of the Wessex background, but with a remorseless single-mindedness and intensity concentrated on his one grim theme. The uncompromising realism of *Jude the Obscure* is a distinctly more characteristic expression of the modern age than either the elemental drama of *The Return of the Native* or the luminous poetry of *Tess of the D'Urbervilles.*

By now, indeed, Hardy may be linked with the naturalistic movement, even though he was not clearly inspired by it. He still did not conceive realism as an end in itself or introduce the sordid for its own sake; the "grimy features" of *Jude the Obscure,* he asserted, were intended to stress the contrast between the ideal life to which Jude aspired and the squalid life to which he was fated—hence the "characteristic part of a barrow pig" that Arabella throws Jude as her first love token. Yet no contemporary English realist bared uglier realities, and none spared his readers less. And in this novel too Hardy for the first time follows the modern tendency to subordinate incident to psychology, and to rely for interest, not upon superficially exciting action, but upon an unwavering and passionate pursuit of the truth as he saw it.

One important reflection of this more realistic spirit is Hardy's gradual disuse of fantastic tricks of fate in favor of a more logical chain of events. His early conception of capricious external forces was not only naïve but at odds with the positive, scientific spirit of the day. Fate had appeared as an almost personal power, a wanton and sardonic Jehovah, and in this shape could be apostrophized, if not propitiated, by an unhappy young poet; this supernatural scheme was a kind of hangover from Hardy's early religious training—an exchange of one superstition for its opposite. But as he matured, he became more and more aware of natural law and its relentless logic. In his later novels tragedy grows more directly out of character and environment, and the issue is less often obscured by the merely fortuitous. In other words, Hardy's extravagant fatalism gave way to a kind of scientific determinism. The Immanent Will became less an arbitrary force than the sum of all natural forces.

This distinction in Hardy is not to be pushed too far. As a realist he occasionally used the language of determinism in his first novels, and as a poet he continued to use the language of fatalism in his last ones. Thus in *Tess of the D'Urbervilles,* where tragedy is the direct result of natural forces, Hardy still speaks of the President of the Immortals; and in *Jude the Obscure,* which is seemingly governed by an inflexible determinism, one still feels the ominous presence of a supernatural power. Something like the Greek Fate remains in the background: it still commands the show, it still assigns the parts, and in its designs there is always an inexplicable irony. Although the philosopher in Hardy came to conceive of an Immanent Will that worked by natural law, the poet continued to brood over the mysterious and unknowable, and in his impassioned moments gave this insensate power a personality in which a massive indifference gathers into a direct antagonism.

Yet his more scientific attitude altered the content and scheme of Hardy's novels. As he began to govern his tragedy by the play of natural forces, he naturally took note of the social environment; and as he focused his attention upon the individual in society, he was naturally impressed by social injustice. Tess and Jude are in the last analysis still the victims of cosmic forces, but they are immediately the victims of social laws. They are sacrificed to the blind purposes of the Immanent Will, but the agent of these purposes is human stupidity embalmed in tradition and convention. Hence Hardy developed a polemical interest in contemporary social problems that brought him into another of the main currents of modern literature. His early dramas are timeless and universal; except for their vivid local color, they might be enacted on almost any stage in any period. In his last novels, however, Hardy concerned himself seriously with matters of peculiar significance to his own age. And on these matters he expressed a characteristically emphatic opinion.

Although there are hints in Hardy's earlier novels, especially in *Two on a Tower,* that Victorian conventions did not seem to him the crowning glory of civilization, this new note is not struck clearly until *Tess of the D'Urbervilles.* Here it appears as early as the title page, with its defiant subtitle: A Pure Woman. This is the burden of the whole story, that Tess is a pure woman; and Hardy caustically arraigns society for its cruel treatment of her. He is indignant that men should by arbitrary conventions, pitilessly enforced, make still more difficult a life already intolerable enough. He deplores the phantoms of an acquired conscience, mere "moral hobgoblins," that torture Tess. At every opportunity he enforces his main lesson: that the first principle of wisdom is to discard all terrifying religious dogmas and to distinguish between natural laws and artificial conventions. It becomes faintly amusing, indeed, when he employs even the contemptible Alec D'Urberville as a spokesman, having him point out to Tess the need of teaching children more of the "facts of life."

Jude the Obscure is still more specifically a social tragedy. It is, in fact, the first important realistic treatment in English fiction of the problem of marriage—marriage had hitherto been introduced merely as an incidental complication or as the sign of a happy ending, on the assumption that the winning of the right girl was the end rather than the beginning of serious problems. Hardy's main thesis here is essentially the same as in *Tess,* but he worries it even more furiously and appends even more copious footnotes. Society shackles the individual with unnatural laws, "rusty and irksome molds" against which all his instincts revolt. In attempting to force their own feelings into these molds, Jude Fawley and Sue Bridehead succeed only in shattering their lives.

Similarly Hardy's characters become more distinctively citizens of the modern world. Although in Clym Yeobright he faintly reproduced the first throbs of "the ache of modernism," he devoted little attention to its peculiar spiritual attitudes. With Jude and Sue, however, he takes the pulse of characters who could have lived only in this age. Both suffer from the feverish restlessness and uncertainty of goal typical of it. Sue is the "intellectualized, emancipated bundle of nerves that modern conditions were producing, mainly in cities as yet." She cannot, like Hardy's other women, simply follow her instincts and take love and marriage as a matter of course; her enlightened intelligence plays restlessly and raises conflicts that never troubled the equally unhappy Eustacia Vye. She is in general a more complex and elusive personality than English readers were yet accustomed to; in his analysis of her apparently incongruous elements, Hardy anticipates the concept of character later to be stressed by Lawrence, Virginia Woolf, and other psychological explorers. And when, under the stress of too great suffering, Sue finally lapses into a maudlin religiosity and flutters back to the paths of formal righteousness, it is only to exchange positions with Jude, who has by this time given up entirely the principles by which he once unquestioningly governed his life.

> I am in a chaos of principles [he tells Sue]—groping in the dark—acting by instinct and not after example. Eight or nine years ago when I came here first, I had a neat stock of fixed opinions, but they dropped away one by one; and the further I get the less sure I am.

He speaks here for the heroes of scores of contemporary novels.

Hardy's attitude toward these offenders against the prevailing moral law is of the kind that is today only too familiar: his bitterness is all for society, his sympathy all for the honest transgressor. Yet, though he brought to the consideration of social problems his invariable compassion, his excursion into this field was in many ways unfortunate. With this added grievance against life, he was too often mastered by the strength of his feelings.

Hitherto he had ordinarily remained aloof, except for an occasional gloomy generalization allowing his stories to tell themselves—as they most excellently did; his modest, self-effacing attitude threw into relief the limitations of the brilliant but erratic Meredith. Now he can no longer contain his indignation at the ways of both gods and men, and it explodes in a shower of complaints and polemics. He fumes and frets over the demons, and hence is less able to exorcise them. He becomes often didactic; he repeats his charges against society and fate with a monotonous insistence; he flings ill-natured sarcasms at more optimistic prophets, particularly Wordsworth and the romantic poets; he quarrels with his public and stoops to querulous explanation and protest; and in general he lays about him bullishly at every opportunity. However generous and laudable his indignation, it clouds the austere, passionless calm that had been his habitual manner, and that is the manner most becoming to tragedy. Ultimately it tends to defeat its own purpose.

"The purpose of a chronicler of moods and deeds," Hardy declares in *Jude the Obscure,* "does not require him to express his personal views upon the grave controversy above given." It is an excellent doctrine. But having stated it, he proceeds to ignore it. He expresses his personal views so freely and fully that the philosopher and moralist threaten to submerge the artist. Action is sacrificed to discourse that often resembles formal disputation; character loses vitality in the service of abstract ideas; and all elements unite to point the moral too neatly. From time to time Jude and Sue cease to be individuals and become mere spokesmen in a knockdown debate, Hardy against all comers. Hence the reader is dropped from his grandly imposing imaginative world into the relatively narrow and ordinary world of his ideas; and once there he is at the mercy of everyday logic, beyond the spell of Hardy's magic. Even when Hardy's arguments are cogent, as for the most part they are, they are stated so explicitly that they appeal primarily to the intellect, thus impeding the direct emotional impact that would provide an intuitive conviction—something far more convincing in fiction than a reasoned conclusion. Cold reason goes on, moreover, to detect the basic fallacy in this kind of argument. As artist, Hardy has skilfully arranged the characters and set the scene; but with this stacked evidence the philosopher cannot logically impose all the conclusions he wishes to. One cannot attach a general moral application to a special case presented from a single point of view. It is the author, not Nature, that has brought about the terrible dénouement. In short, Hardy has proved nothing. And though ordinarily this is a meaningless comment, it is pertinent when the novelist has so obviously set out to prove something.

At times, moreover, Hardy becomes incoherent, and is betrayed into serious inconsistencies and contradictions. He is whacking so many heads that it is not always clear exactly who is the real villain. He asserts that Society caused the misery of Tess, and of Jude and Sue: were it not for its unnatural laws, their unhappy experiences would have been simply a liberal education. But how can mankind be at fault if it is controlled by compulsions it cannot master? And why, if the Immanent Will who imposes all instincts is blind and merciless, is it the truest wisdom to act upon natural impulses? Briefly, Hardy involves himself in the inevitable difficulties of one who represents man as a pawn and at the same time condemns him for not moving as a knight.

These are serious flaws. Again, however, I should insist that like his other flaws they do not reach to the base of Hardy's art, and that only a myopic critic will fail to see beyond them. In disputing their preferences for his early or his later manner, critics forget that his essential attitudes remained the same, and that his values survive the drastic realism of *Jude the Obscure* as they survive the extravagant fatalism of *The Return of the Native*. After his rages Hardy returns to the grave impassivity of high tragedy. The bitter complaints die away, a majestic and monumental calm remains. If in the heat of his indignation he is carried away into incoherence and exaggeration, his basic views are at the end clear enough. Ultimately, Society is but one of the actors in a larger drama, an agent of the blind purposes of the somnambulistic Will. There is always this greater malignancy than the malignancy of men's judgments. For "these harshnesses of mankind are tenderness itself when compared with the universal harshness out of which they grow; the harshness of the position toward the temperament, of the means toward the end, of today toward yesterday, of hereafter toward today." In short, the President of the Immortals is unmistakably the real villain, and man his tragic victim.

Most important, however, is that in narrowing his immediate interests Hardy did not narrow his final aims. His later novels go much deeper than the particular problem that inspired them; their reference is larger than that of the social tragedies of Ibsen and Galsworthy, or the treatises of Wells and Shaw. The poet in Hardy takes one to the heart of the mysterious, unalterable tragedy of all human life; and at the end here one remains. Even the fierce intensity of *Jude the Obscure* fires much more than its immediate subject. The reader must indeed follow an argument whose logic is dubious—the chief cause of the unhappiness of Jude and Sue is after all not the marriage law but their own peculiar temperaments. The plot scheme, with its perfect symmetry in the relations of the four main characters, is also too neat and obviously fabricated, and strains credulity. But as Hardy once remarked, "It is not improbabilities of incident but improbabilities of character that matter"; and his hold on the primary passions is here as firm as it was among the melodramatic incidents of his earlier work. His novel succeeds in rising through all this murkiness and artifice to a universal plane, where it treats austerely the struggles that eternally sear the human soul. In his preface to the original edition Hardy declared that his main purpose was "to deal unaffectedly with the fret and fever, derision and disaster, that may press in the wake of the strongest passion known to humanity; to tell, without a mincing of words, of a deadly war waged between flesh and spirit; and to point the tragedy of unfulfilled aims." It is a just summary of the final impression that actually the novel leaves. If he has expressed the thought of his own age, Hardy has also expressed powerfully the emotions of all ages. One forgets the discussions of marriage to which he returns with a wearisome persistence. One remembers the story of two strange, twisted, tortured, baffled lives that is simply a modern version of the age-old story of man's seeking and not finding.

In short, Hardy was through all his limitations a great artist, and as an unconscious artist he constantly transcended these limitations. The poet and philosopher in him were never in complete accord, and it was the poet who finally triumphed—flooding his novels with a light, now crepuscular, now luminous, that blurs the edges of his rigid theories and gives a haunting depth to his circumscribed scenes. If his thinking was at times confused and his arguments weak, he nevertheless richly fulfilled the primary duty of a novelist and presented remarkably vivid, compelling impressions of life. If the framework of his novels is generally angular, he softened it with warm feeling and clothed it with majestic poetry. The drama of *The Return of the Native,* set against the somber grandeur of Egdon Heath, belongs among the sublime conceptions of tragic poetry. In short, there is no escaping the largeness of Hardy. He dwarfs innumerable contemporaries who have special gifts manifestly denied to him, and who perhaps make him seem antiquated. Aldous Huxley has a more brilliant, incisive intellect, Virginia Woolf more subtlety of perception, John Galsworthy more urbanity and poise, Arnold Bennett a better rounded vision of life, even Theodore Dreiser a keener awareness of the drift of our society—and countless others have more grace of style, and more technical adroitness and ingenuity. But by virtue of his elemental creative gift, his imaginative power and emotional force, Hardy towers above all these. In an age of brilliant experiment he still stands out as the greatest tragic novelist in English.

X

NATURALISM: ÉMILE ZOLA

I

WITH the dawning of the Victorian era and the solid intrenchment of the middle class as literary arbiter, the English novel became wedded to the democratic ideal and chose realism as its natural home. The furnishings of this home, however, were definitely in the style of the period; as I have already pointed out, realism had fixed and narrow limits. The middle class was incurably materialistic and had a strong sense of fact; it enjoyed having its picture taken and exhibited in the great galleries of literature. But it was also incurably sentimental and romantic. It wanted to be dressed in its very best clothes for this picture, and all the members of its virtuous, prosperous, and happy family posed in an "artistic" group, their faces shining and well scrubbed. In short, it enjoyed the recognition of familiar fact, but it wished this fact to be exhibited in some comforting or flattering light, and such fact as was not susceptible of this elegant treatment it wished to be ignored. Poverty must be ludicrous or picturesque, and when virtuous must finally be rewarded; sentiment or morality must never bow to disagreeable truth.

Although the greater writers were superior to their public, they generally submitted to its tastes. "We must pass over a part of Mrs. Rebecca Crawley's biography with that lightness and delicacy which the world demands," Thackeray confides; and though he ridicules a society "that has, perhaps, no particular objection to vice, but an insuperable repugnance to hearing vice called by its proper name," he nevertheless makes it a point "only to hint at the existence of wickedness in a light, easy, and agreeable manner, so that nobody's fine feelings may be offended." The realism of the Victorian novel is therefore not only diluted by the incidental reticences that almost embarrass this generation; it is vitiated at its source by being forced to subserve an essentially unrealistic attitude toward life.

In the early 1880's, however, there was added to the growing spiritual distresses of the Victorians the appearance of a distinctly new realism: a realism uncompromising and remorseless, whose object was not entertainment or edification but truth, and truth of the most unpleasant sort. These new writers insisted upon taking life raw and straight, without a chaser of sentiment or humor. Because their predecessors had disregarded the uglier realities, they plunged into them wholeheartedly and brought to light the most sordid, brutish experience. They found their subjects ordinarily among the lowest classes. These classes had entered fiction before, to be sure, and occasionally in an important rôle; but Dickens sacrificed fidelity of representation to melodrama, humor, or sentiment, and even George Eliot subordinated it to ethical preachment. The later realists accordingly attempted a rigorously objective study of the poor, and had a passion, as some critic has remarked, "to mention the unmentionable with as much detail as possible."

What was happening in England was happening all over the Continent, and with an even greater fanfare of trumpets. This is what we know as the naturalistic movement. Although *naturalism* is today often used as a synonym for *realism,* thus adding to the confusion of an already cluttered critical vocabulary, it may still be given a more precise meaning: the meaning it had for the very self-conscious writers who themselves appropriated this symbol, and who provide a remarkable instance of a group planning and executing their work in accordance with a more or less definite program. The emergence of this school was indeed a natural culmination of the growth of the realistic spirit; once stimulated, the taste for reality comes to demand stronger food and to reject a polite or superficial literature. It was a natural reaction against the fantastic excesses of a febrile romanticism. But it was also the natural expression in literature of the materialistic, positivistic thought that ruled the intellectual world of the last half of the century—the thought of Comte and Taine, for example, that influenced George Eliot and Thomas Hardy without inducing them to accept all its logical consequences. This thought was in turn the product of the advance of science. The exciting theories of Darwin and Laplace had thrilled the mind of Europe and raised wild hopes of the power of reason, guided by the methods of experimental science, to penetrate all mysteries and solve all problems—hopes summed up in the extraordinary statement of Renan: "The world today has no more mysteries!" And herein lies the chief significance of the naturalistic movement. It marks the definite entrance into literature of the chief force of the modern age, the scientific spirit, which by virtue of its astounding achievements in the material world was beginning to dominate almost every field of human thought. The naturalists not only made use of the findings of science and thus recognized the immense influence of heredity and environment; they also adopted its method: the method of patient observation and analysis—"the modern method," as Zola proudly declared, "the instruments of universal inquiry of which the century makes such feverish use to penetrate the future."

The most conspicuous name in this movement was of course that of Zola. He did not pretend to have an exclusive copyright of the new technique. With a glad piety he acknowledged his masters, Balzac and Flaubert, and by his own admission was more immediately anticipated by the Goncourt brothers. Yet he was the recognized leader. He became the symbol of all that was horrendous in the whole creed and deliberately stretched out his neck for the ax of the conservatives. He was not only the most conscientious, consistent, and extreme practitioner of naturalism but its most tireless and outspoken apologist. In *The Experimental Novel* he wrote its official handbook.

Zola here makes clear and explicit the scientific impulse that governs naturalistic art. His gospel is Claude Bernard's *Introduction to the Study of Experimental Medicine*. Bernard had insisted upon what now seems obvious, that medicine was not an art but a science, and that the experimental method must be applied to animate as well as inanimate objects. Zola carries the argument a step farther and sets up in the laboratory the literary man as well: the novelist's primary aim must be to experiment scientifically on human beings in given circumstances. "In one word, we should operate on the characters, the passions, on the human and social data, in the same way that the chemist and the physicist operate on inanimate beings, and that the physiologist operates on animate beings." Zola is done with ideal hypotheses and philosophical speculations and all such prejudices and delusions of the imagination. One can easily see, he boasts, "how little part imagination has" in his novels. He has made it his business simply to collect the most complete and exact data obtainable, arrange these data logically, and thus present not guesswork but verifiable fact, not fiction but truth. The writing of novels is properly not an art but a science.

This process obviously demands of the novelist a complete objectivity—and here Zola seized gladly upon the example of Flaubert, and acclaimed him master. With Flaubert, however, impersonality had been a purely esthetic concern (at first pleased, he became more and more uneasy at the thought of having fathered so wild a brood as the young followers of Zola, once exclaiming, "Cursed be the day that I had the fatal idea of writing *Madame Bovary!*"); to Zola, impersonality was simply the necessary attitude of the scientist. "The passionate or tender intervention of the writer weakens a novel," he writes, not because it is unartistic, but because it "introduces a strange element into the facts which destroys their scientific value." The novelist is only a recorder who is forbidden to judge and to conclude. His work "becomes a report, nothing more; it has but the merit of exact observation, of more or less profound penetration and analysis, of the logical connection of facts." Everywhere Zola insists on analysis alone. "In the actual condition of the science of man the obscurity and confusion are still too great to risk the slightest synthesis. . . . To give your reader a scrap of human life, that is the whole purpose of the naturalistic novel."

At the same time Zola insisted that this scrap will not be a mere photograph. The naturalist first observes but he then experiments, and experiment implies some selection and disposition of material. Temperament and genius will find their rôle, partly in eloquent expression, but especially in the choice of the subject for demonstration, the management of the experiment, and the deduction of consequences. Experiment is only the method, the tool. Yet it is always the necessary tool. It alone can give real validity to a novel, it alone can prove genius. The poets and philosophers did not verify; and although the naturalist can add but a scrap of new knowledge, penetrate but a short distance into the unknown, this slow conquest of truth is infinitely preferable to high-flown guesswork.

Most important theoretically, however, is the determinism implicit in the naturalistic creed; but this too Zola took easily in his stride. A mechanistic materialism was the prevailing thought of his age, and especially of Taine, the critic who most impressed him. "Vice and virtue are products like sugar and vitriol," Taine declared in the famous preface to *A History of English Literature;* Zola stated no less roundly that an absolute determinism governs the brain of man as surely as the stone in the roadway. At the same time he was not blind to the devastating implications of this doctrine. If men are made out to be mere mechanisms and their actions mere reflexes, they must ultimately be relieved of any real responsibility for their behavior, denied any real possibility of control. Their destiny becomes a formula, their story a parade of empty symbols. The very conquest of truth to which the naturalist is to contribute his glorious bit would seem pointless, for it can result only in a more precise definition of the terms of their bondage, a more elaborate demonstration of their helplessness. And whence, in the amoral world of determinism, comes the incentive or obligation to submit to the discipline of truth, when illusion may provide an anesthetic against its rigors? To evade this futility, Zola attempted a hairline distinction between determinism and fatalism. Fatalism indeed means the absolute impotence of man, but determinism he defined after his master, Claude Bernard, as simply the necessary condition or cause of the appearance of a phenomenon. Once man has discovered this cause, he can act upon it, and thus modify his surroundings and control his fate. Hence complete knowledge will make him monarch of all he surveys.

This is a comforting escape from the materialism of late nineteenth-century science. It is also a little confusing. Apparently there are two realms of behavior: one unintelligent and determined by physical or physiological causes, the other free and conscious and acting upon these causes. Of these the second would seem far more significant, far worthier of artistic treatment. But how can such voluntary, and therefore unpredictable, conduct be made the subject of scientific experiment? Logically, Zola can safely apply his method only to such instinctive, unreasoned conduct as is governed by determinism—and this is actually what for the most part he does, and after him his followers. Here, then, is another explanation of the preoccupation of the early naturalists with the more primitive forms of life, the more animal kinds of behavior. Not only had such materials been denied a just, adequate treatment by the serious artists of the past, but they were the most readily adaptable to scientific treatment, the most obviously illustrative of the workings of hereditary and environmental forces.

2

Now, we no longer condemn Zola as an immoral fellow whose large nostrils quivered ecstatically at the least whiff of filth; the hysterical abuse of his contemporaries and their fears for the tender purity of their society seem today as quaint as the horror and anxiety aroused by *Jude the Obscure*. Nor do we dismiss him as a mere sensation-monger. Although as an ambitious young writer he deliberately sought publicity by shocking the pious, and throughout his career got a kind of melancholy pleasure (and incidentally a handsome fortune) from his rôle of pariah, his purposes were at bottom unquestionably sincere. Indeed they were noble, not to say optimistic. Naturalism was not merely going to give an honest report and add its bit of truth; ultimately it was going to guide all human activity and master good and evil, "to regulate life, to regulate society, to solve in time all the problems of socialism"—and so on through as long a list of ambitious and laudable ends as can be found in eighteenth-century prefaces.

Yet the limitations of his creed are all too obvious and irritating. Zola's ideal is in the first place impossible of realization. "We do not make a choice" about what we shall tell, he boasts of the naturalists; but they could not help making choices. Judgment and synthesis are as yet too dangerous to be attempted, he warns; but they are as necessary as they are inevitable. Although only literal factual truth was to him worth attention, even in this narrow realm it is clearly impossible to give any fiction an indisputable scientific validity. One can never logically attribute an unalterable, objective truth to any demonstration worked out from an imagined set of circumstances. Even the science in Zola is already obsolete. Heredity is the dominating force in the great *Rougon-Macquart* cycle, and of a number of scientific theories he apparently leaned most heavily on the *Treatise on Natural Heredity,* by Dr. Prosper Lucas. Much of the theory of Dr. Lucas has been discarded, however; and the whole problem of heredity has yet to be solved by science—if indeed it ever will be solved. But had he chosen more wisely Zola would still have been unable to verify his experimental results, as he insisted was the chief duty of the novelist. How is the novelist to check up on these results? Why, indeed, should he even attempt this experiment and compete with the scientists in their own field, when his only conceivable advantage over them lies in his imagination—which Zola distrusts as the author of delusion?

Moreover, Zola's method is hopelessly inadequate, and will remain so as long as so much experience remains immeasurable. Science has not explained everything, and even its explanations have to be supplemented. A personality psychoanalyzed and ticketed is still not a living, integrated personality; a table resolved into an aggregation of electrons still remains a table, which is something quite different. And in his worship of fact, and his shallow conception of imagination as a mere departure from it, Zola misses the whole function of creative literature. He is blind to the essential processes and values of esthetic experience. In the light of modern psychology, indeed, his conception of the human mind is highly unscientific.

The naturalistic creed has accordingly failed to satisfy man's needs; it is not the answer to the modern prayer for certainty. The mechanistic, positivistic thought upon which it is based is contrary not only to prevailing intellectual tendencies but to the latest findings of science. Although like many of his contemporaries Zola lost his religion, it was only to substitute a faith even more extravagant. In a period of despondency caused by personal misfortune he wrote his one actually pessimistic novel, *La Joie de Vivre;* but presently he returned to this faith. Truth was just around the corner, and Science would in time catch up with it; the pursuit was slow and painful, but one could always march to the stirring strains of the hymn to Progress. Today all this sounds a little grotesque. To most even of those who have visions of a Utopian state the premises and the specific terms of Zola's faith appear as naïve as the eighteenth-century worship of pure Reason.

The entire naturalistic movement is by no means, of course, to be judged by the extreme statement of Zola's views. Few of his followers went so far in theory, nor in practice did he himself. *The Experimental Novel* was one of a number of polemical treatises designed to present a striking exposition of his creed, and by their very violence to attract customers and trumpet his novels. In later life he privately mocked them, and his last work completely disavows them. Even in his earlier novels, as Matthew Josephson has pointed out in his excellent biography, Zola swallowed his scientists whole in the full flush of his creative activity, and often appeared unaffected by so unwholesome a diet. His creed was largely an afterthought, a rationalization of his instinctive practice; Claude Bernard, for example, he discovered after he had worked out the conception of the *Rougon-Macquart* history and was well along with its execution. Yet his instinctive practice was at least pseudo-scientific; science permeated the atmosphere in which he lived and was inhaled with every breath. Even in their exaggerated form, his doctrines are a significant expression of his age, and they had a wide influence. Many novelists were infected by both his precept and his example and bogged down in one or another of the morasses in the path of the literal realist.

In deploring the excesses of the naturalistic movement, however, one should not forget the importance and value of its contributions; and to these might well be given the last word. If the early naturalists did not themselves present a whole, harmonious, well-proportioned account of human life, they at least cleared the air of a deal of rank mist and made it easier for later and greater writers to present such accounts. They helped to emancipate the novel from cramping taboos, and to establish the novelist's right to treat unaffectedly of all forms of experience. By their insistence on a strictly impartial, objective study they led a healthy revolt against the more conventional patterns of characterization and the more conventional modes of moralistic interpretation. By the abundance and precision of their documentation they brought about what Henry James called a "sharper specification of the signs of life," teaching writers to look longer and harder at a scene and making them less likely to confuse what was there with what they wanted to see there. The ultimate effect of their work was both to amplify and to intensify the art of fiction: to bring the novel more in line not only with modern thought but with actual experience, to broaden and deepen its humanity and truth.

3

In examining more closely the career of Émile Zola, one should be only momentarily surprised to discover that the early ideals and efforts of the father of naturalism, the "Slimy Giant," were feebly and fantastically romantic. Hugo, de Musset, Lamartine, George Sand—these were still the magical names for the spirited young men of his time. In his lengthy, polished letters to Cézanne, the closest friend of his youth, he constantly remarked upon the hideousness of reality and the evil of the art that would represent it literally. "When one stirs up the scum some of it always remains and soils the hands"; as for him, he was going to turn his glance "away from the manure pile, to cast it upon the roses." In short, he reveled in the vocabulary of the outraged critics of his later work. But this rapt aloofness was short-lived. What destroyed it was partly the brutal poverty that for many years gave him few roses to cast his glance upon. Partly too it was the desire of an ambitious youngster to push himself into the spotlight by striking a sensational attitude, to achieve one of those spectacular "effects" upon his public in which Zola always delighted. But above all it was the influence of the scientific thought of his time, the growing fondness for fact and the Real Thing; and in literature the exciting revelation of *Madame Bovary.*

Zola's first conception of the realism he would pursue was eminently reasonable. "All art is one," he had exclaimed earlier; "spiritualist, realist are only words!" He was aware that it was impossible to attain exact truth in a work of art. One simply saw life "through a given glass or screen," he wrote. "And the screen of realism is most sympathetic to me." Presently, however, what had been merely a technique became a passion, an end in itself, the whole duty of the novelist. In *Thérèse Raquin* and *Madeleine Férat,* his first novels of importance, he was already well along the road to naturalism. *Thérèse Raquin* is a bourgeois nightmare, impeccably respectable in its morality, ludicrous in its insistence on gruesome details (to wit, the chapter on the morgue, and the constant reference to the "green, putrid flesh" of the omnipresent ghost); at the same time it is a kind of operation or experiment on conscience, performed with more or less logic and certainly with thoroughness, and decked out with pseudo-scientific trimmings. And the horrors of *Madeleine Férat* are even more clearly "scientific." Here Zola is playing excitedly with the "physiological laws" that govern character, and making conscious use of the vocabulary of determinism. From here it was but a short step to the twenty volumes and twelve hundred guinea pigs of *Les Rougon-Macquart.*

Although Balzac undoubtedly suggested the idea of this cycle, Zola had from his early youth, when he was projecting epic poems, dreamed of doing some work on a grand scale. Much as he admired the polished perfection of the work of Flaubert and the Goncourt brothers, he felt the need of much more scope. His genius was not for exquisite artistry but for large effects, sweeping movements, teeming masses. He was not one to carve heads on cherry stones—he was one to hew figures from a mountain side. And so he conceived *Les Rougon-Macquart,* "The Natural and Social History of a Family Under the Second Empire," an account of the careers of the legitimate and illegitimate branches of two families, and their evolution into various forms of disease, filth, vice, crime—and occasionally ideal success.

> Ah, it is a world [he wrote of it when it neared completion], a whole society, a civilization, and all life is there with its good and evil manifestations, in the fire and forge that molds everything. . . . Yes, our family may now suffice as an example for science whose hope it is to fix mathematically the laws of nervous and blood variations in a race, as a result of an original organic lesion, thus determining according to the social environment the sentiments, desires, passions of its members, all the natural and instinctive manifestations whose products are called virtues and vices. . . . It is also a historical document, covering the Second Empire from the coup d'état to Sédan; for our tribe, originating among the common people, invaded every station of contemporary society. . . .

Nor do these ecstatic words exaggerate the scope of Zola's work. It gives a closely documented account of all the important trades and professions, and the manners and customs of every stratum of his society, both urban and rural. As we know from Zola's elaborate notes, moreover, this whole vast effort was carefully planned beforehand. He enlarged his original intention and wrote twenty instead of ten or twelve volumes, but at the outset he knew precisely what he was going to do and how he was going to do it. Henry James himself was not a more deliberate, self-conscious artist. And James, curiously enough, paid almost extravagant tribute to this work so utterly different from his own. "No finer act of courage and confidence," he wrote of Zola's high project, "is recorded in the history of letters."

Zola was of course from the beginning aware of how his work was to differ from that of Balzac, the historian of morals and "registrar of good and evil." His was to be "less social than scientific"; he would not come to decisions and conclusions, but would content himself with "a simple exposé of the facts," a scientific demonstration of what *is*. Yet he realized the need of a "philosophical tendency" to give direction to his books; and so he deliberately worked out the naturalistic creed, completely rationalizing, as he went along, the scientific approach congenial to his temperament and his time, and constructing a theory of fiction in which at bottom he did not entirely believe. Everything had to be sacrificed to the consistency of his great epic; he would leave no loopholes, permit himself no second thoughts. And for the unifying principle of his countless episodes he settled, more specifically, on the great force of Heredity. This, a "modern" and "scientific" doctrine, was to dominate his drama as the "absurd" notion of Fate had dominated Greek drama.

This highly self-conscious formulation of doctrine would seem a strange procedure for the supposedly objective naturalist, who is "forbidden to judge and to conclude." It is in itself a refutation of the inspired nonsense of *The Experimental Novel*. Zola was on firmer ground, however, in his plans for the construction of his epic. Here his originality was to lie in his large chapters, his carving out of huge, solid, meaty chunks of life.

> Instead of the flowing analysis of Balzac, establish twelve or fifteen powerful masses; therein the analysis may be made step by step, but always from above. Everybody in the world analyzes in detail nowadays; I must react against this through the solid construction of masses, of chapters; through the *logic*, the thrust of the chapters, succeeding each other like superimposed blocks; by the *breath of passion* animating all, flowing from one end to another of the work.

Here Zola departs from his master, Flaubert, and with Dostoyevsky and Tolstoy leads the way for the later realists. Reality was more truly his muse; he would not sacrifice it to neatness of pattern, nor for any consideration of Art lose a drop of the precious blood of life. Unity and clarity he achieved instead by a ruling idea—a passionate purpose large enough to include all of life that mattered to him. And this, with reservations, has been the way of novelists otherwise as diverse as Bennett and Proust, Dreiser and Mann, Galsworthy and Joyce.

The quality of the twenty volumes of the *Rougon-Macquart* is of course uneven. Some, like *L'Assommoir* and *La Débâcle,* were written with verve and gusto; others, like *L'Argent,* were turned out wearily and mechanically, simply to complete his unwavering design. Similarly they differ in mood, according to the kind of flower or weed in the garden of the two families that he happened to be cultivating; he ranges from the drabness of *Pot-Bouille* and the violence and brutality of *La Terre* to the sheer fantasy of *La Rêve.* Yet all fit into the same plan and all are unmistakably by the same pen. They may fairly be discussed as a unit.

Their faults are plain enough. Zola has of course not "experimented" on his characters; he has simply observed and imagined. As Brunetière pointed out, in order to experiment on a character like Coupeau, the drunkard in *L'Assommoir,* "you would have to keep him locked up in your cellar, send him out for a walk with a nurse, and feed him stated doses of alcohol at stated intervals." Hence the objection is to the fruits and the manner of Zola's observation. A fat, near-sighted, and naturally sedentary man, he had had little first-hand experience of life. He had therefore deliberately to go out in search of the immense material necessary for his *magnum opus*—with his purposes he could not, like Flaubert, pursue his researches in the library. This job he did with a dogged conscientiousness. Notebook in hand, he prowled and peered indefatigably, exploring the scene of each new novel. He consulted every conceivable source of information; he took prodigious notes; and he had, indeed, remarkable powers of assimilation. Yet his information was often either deficient or inaccurate. As he grew famous, he was harassed on his expeditions by flocks of reporters, curious onlookers, and zealous busybodies generally, all eager to see the great man at work and to help or mislead him; even at the outset of his career he was at the mercy of informants who had none of his passion for scientific exactness—*Nana,* for example, reveals clearly the lurid imaginations and too fond memories of those who led the bourgeois novelist into the glamorous world of sin. The more serious objection, however, is that this is a very mechanical way of writing a novel: at its most laborious, the business of documentation is less exacting than the responsibilities of imaginative creation. After a short correspondence course, one can easily master the naturalistic technique and turn out a decent specimen of the documented novel, a profitable parcel of information. Hence scores of facile contemporaries quickly vulgarized it; and, as Matthew Josephson remarks, many of Zola's own novels virtually wrote themselves.

Yet when most accurate, Zola's records are still not truly representative, for they are invariably striking and highly colored. His materials are even more melodramatic than those of Dickens and Balzac; he never rivaled the achievement of Flaubert in *Madame Bovary* or of George Eliot in *Adam Bede*. When his story is drab it is sensationally drab; when his people are lowly, they stop short only at growing horns and tails. As Sainte-Beuve pointed out to him, he had not rendered faithfully the setting of *Thérèse Raquin:* he had taken a narrow, commonplace street and plunged it into a dense and fantastic blackness. Nor can one agree with Zola that he always exaggerated "in the direction of truth," for the aspects of experience he chose to emphasize are ordinarily not only the vilest but the least significant. Partly this was the fault of his creed—the animal passions, to repeat, lend themselves most readily to naturalistic treatment. Partly too it was the violent opposition of his public, which stirred his native belligerence and drove him to underscore all that it disapproved of. But Zola plainly had as well a romantic fondness for ugliness and evil, and a driving instinct to exploit them. His best pages are typically his blackest.

Hence his novels teem with misery, violence, brutality, idiocy, and ineffable squalor. Although he himself often sickened of this bloody carnival, conscientiously following a particularly gross with a more or less idealistic novel, these works of penitence were almost without exception his feeblest dramas, with little of the vividness or vigor of *La Ventre de Paris, L'Assommoir, Nana, Germinal, La Terre, La Débâcle.*

Its critics accordingly have reason for describing *Les Rougon-Macquart* as an epic of animality. Although Zola was by no means blind to the loftier aspirations, he in effect minimized the very important differences between men that are the source of our values and ideals. And in so far as he immersed himself in essentially paltry materials, his work is wanting in spiritual significance, especially for the contemporary reader who takes for granted the privileges for which he so bravely fought.

Under no circumstances, however, could Zola have taken a place among the greatest novelists. Henry James once said that "the deepest quality of a work of art will always be the quality of the mind of the producer"; if "quality of mind" is broadened to include more than a fine intelligence, this is an obvious truth. It also makes for an imponderable standard, which begins to dissolve when one looks at it hard. Yet by it we perforce measure the masters, and by it we recognize that Zola has not their stature. His responses to life were neither fine in themselves nor finely ordered. He was powerful and intense, but seldom profound. His imagination was fertile and strong, but it was still earthbound. His visions were immense, but they still did not melt into eternity. He did not strike into the very deepest layers of experience from which, paradoxically, men emerge on the loftiest heights.

Despite his zest of creation, Zola lacked, more specifically, the warm feeling of most great novelists and dramatists for their characters as *persons,* symbols of mixed humanity who are also suffering and aspiring individuals. He regarded the innumerable offspring of the Rougon-Macquart families more as pawns in a vast game; his attitude was much like that of the mathematician toward his x and y. His fire was chiefly for the demonstration of his theories, the completion of his immense design (not to mention the next shock he was preparing for his audience). I say this with all respect for the heroic rôle he played in the Dreyfus case, when he became, in the words of Anatole France, a "moment of the conscience of mankind." Even here his splendid emotion was aroused again by an abstract ideal; Alfred Dreyfus was to him less a suffering human being than a symbol of the cause of Justice, Liberty, France. For the representatives of humanity that he himself created Zola at any rate seldom manifested a comparable passion. Hence we are intensely interested in his best passages, but we are seldom deeply moved.

When one leaves the rarefied realms, however, and returns nearer the ordinary level of our experience in literature and life, it should be to recognize that if Zola is not one of the Titans, he was still one of the giants of his century, and remains an imposing figure in this one. *Les Rougon-Macquart* has not been laid away in the museum of literary history. It still stands on its own feet, and stands firmly despite its dubious scientific program. This was for one thing a vast program, and more flexible than is commonly realized; Zola conceived it as "the huge hold of a ship" in which he could manage to cram almost everything. Although much of the cargo was dumped in according to a formula, he often forgot or scrapped this formula. Like so many artists, he rose by intuition as far above his impossible intentions as he fell short of them. He invented a technique as artificial as the heroic couplets of Pope, a manner that imitators were able to reproduce almost exactly; like Pope, he continues to live when most of these imitators are hopelessly forgotten. In short, the father of naturalism was more than a naturalist, and did more than beget sterile offspring.

The detail of Zola's work is indeed seldom impressive. He displayed little subtlety or brilliance; he seldom forged fiery and imperishable words, and his style made less and less claim to distinction. He is like Balzac, and today Theodore Dreiser; any given page of his work is likely to be ordinary, and whole passages may be dull or irritating. Yet the total effect, the complete inventory of all these often dreary minutiæ, is undeniably imposing. One cannot escape the cumulative power and the bigness of his finished work, and this memorable impression derives from large effects to which the pedestrian passages contribute almost as much as the many powerful scenes and terrific climaxes. As Zola himself realized, his originality lay in his ferocious passion for "enormity and totality," his flair for great masses, his ability to project these masses in bold relief and in steady, sweeping movement. He could take a deep breath and plunge to the bottom of a whole society; he could afford to be careless of the value of all he held in his huge fists when he came heaving to the surface. He peopled an immense world, teeming, throbbing, groaning with life, and to all that he assimilated or even imperfectly understood he gave a wonderful sense of reality. It is a gross, sinister world, more gloomy and terrible still than Dostoyevsky's; but it is fiercely alive. Its inhabitants are often grotesque, bestial, revolting; but they have an unquenchable vitality. Zola's creation has at the end a kind of dark sublimity, a monstrous and appalling grandeur.

For the impulse behind this creation was essentially lyrical. Behind the scientist who conceived a rigid theory and a sterile formula, behind the clerk who with laborious conscientiousness collected volumes of notes, stood a poet who had dreamed an intoxicating dream and who by intuition constantly supplemented the theory, the formula, and the notes. Zola's public appearances were indeed almost invariably in the rôle of the ruthless scientific naturalist; and this was the rôle he most fancied himself in. But secretly he cherished more exalted hopes. The young man who had projected epics continued to write to his friends of "the starry leap from the springboard of exact observation," continued to dream of "reconciling poetry and science," and was obviously delighted when sympathetic critics began to point out that beneath this so thick and hairy hide there dwelt a poet. His whole achievement is in fact more romantic than scientific. He invented more than he observed, he transformed more than he reproduced, he made over a world in his own image.

Many readers and critics still see only the man of pseudo-science, the man with the notebook, the man who delighted in forcing raw, bleeding chunks of animal life down the public throat. They take Zola at his own vociferous word. Yet those who can digest the chunks and stop their ears to the voice should find that *Les Rougon-Macquart* is conceived and executed in the grand style, and is genuinely epical in more than size. The coldly objective manner finally gives somehow the impression of towering passion; the undistinguished style culminates in an effect of "headlong eloquence"; and in his best work all the manifold crudities are drowned in a resistless flood that sweeps us into a vividly imagined world—a world that is definitely idealized if it is not strictly ideal.

The least that can be said of Zola was spoken at his funeral: "Everything of him was disputed, save that he was excessive and colossal."

4

The last phase of Zola's career, in which the scientific naturalist blossomed out as a Utopian crusader and prophet, and the "experimental novel" culminated in apocalyptic visions of the future, is extraordinary in itself, not to say of an amusing irony. But it is especially important because it coincides with the general decline of naturalism and the rise of tendencies still more significantly "modern." For many years Zola had dominated the literary world of France. The adventures of the spawn of the Rougon-Macquart still outraged the pious and evoked screams of abuse, but the two families had become an accepted institution; readers who had lived with them over a couple of decades felt that, like the poor, they must always be with us. The publication of *La Débâcle* (1892), the next to the last of the long series, was the apex of Zola's triumph; the most eagerly awaited and widely translated of his novels, it placed him, in the eyes of many contemporaries, in a class alone with Tolstoy, the other giant of the age. Yet the applause was almost absent-minded. The cheerers were already marching in a different direction, leaving Zola on a lonely eminence, like a classic waiting to be embalmed, and with but a handful of faithful attendants to perform the tardy last rites. For some time the younger writers had ceased to call him master and follow his bold lead. At first merely restive, they had at length become openly hostile; and this hostility had come to a head a few years before in the famous, fatuous, and terrible "Manifesto of the Five," a brutal assault on his powers both as novelist and as husband.

Naturalism had played itself out. Zola could continue to fill immense canvases, but his followers were endlessly treading the same mill, either documenting subjects thoroughly explored, or in their search for new grist falling into such vulgar excesses as Paul Bonnetain's *Charlot s'Amuse,* a naturalistic study of onanism. (Bonnetain, ironically, was one of the five bright young men who signed the "Manifesto.") Yet the reaction against Zola had a far more significant source than mere restlessness or boredom. It grew out of a profound disillusionment in Science as a messiah; and it resolved itself into a protest against materialism in every field of thought, and in literature into an attack on the fundamental premises of naturalism. It became the second romantic movement of the century. Hence exotic novelists like Pierre Loti became popular. Esthetes in England as in France began to burn with a hard gemlike flame and to babble of art for art's sake. Bergson appeared with his doctrine of the fluidity of reality and the superiority of intuition over reason as a means of apprehending it. Brunetière led a crusade for the claims of mysticism against science, and many of the mystics fell into the arms of the church—Huysmans, Zola's close friend, created a sensation by announcing his conversion to Catholicism. And perhaps most important in subsequent literary history were the Symbolists, led by Mallarmé. But, silly or serious, all these were manifestations of a revolt against all that Zola conspicuously stood for.

Now, Zola always had too keen a desire to lead the vanguard for him to remain comfortable for long in his deserted camp in the rear. Yet his abandonment of this camp was by no means an act of apostasy, nor did it demand a violent wrench. Almost in spite of himself he was impelled in a new direction—a direction, at that, which to one who really knew him should not have seemed strange. Though in public he had steadily thumped on the same big drum, he had long been aware of the limitations of the naturalistic creed. He had also wearied of its practice: when with *Docteur Pascal* he wrote Finis to the history of the Rougon-Macquart, he felt enormously and justifiably proud—but he also felt relieved. In mid-career he reveals in the notes for his novels that he was himself oppressed by the dismal materials demanded by his design, and he voiced the intention "to tell the truth and still to hope." For Zola was at bottom never a pessimist or a misanthrope. He always had a robust, optimistic faith, a lusty feeling for "the joy of action and the pleasure of existence." It was only natural, then, that he should attempt to supplement the systematic negations that are the inescapable burden of the major novels of *Les Rougon-Macquart*.

Matthew Josephson argues plausibly that the change that took place in Zola was due at least in part to a physical change and an adjustment in his private life. He had been fat, he had been childless; and the impertinent authors of the "Manifesto" had touched a highly sensitive sore spot. Perhaps, they had suggested, his animality and filth, his "violent preference for obscenity," were but a compensation for his unfortunate virginal youth and "a malady of the lower organs"; in his "anxiety over certain functions" he had been driven to "magnify their importance." The effect on Zola was unmistakable. He began to diet and grow thin, he took himself a mistress, he even dropped the Rougon-Macquart to act for a time the whole-hearted lover. When shortly his mistress presented him with the child his wife could not, his joy was pathetically immoderate. It is thus no mere accident that the "collapse of Zola's famous stomach" coincided with the decline of naturalism. The new, thin Zola, the father of a child, overflowed with energy, optimism, joy. This hearty, radiant, public-spirited citizen could no longer content himself with gloomy anatomical operations. He had always celebrated fertility; now he sends up a passionate hymn to the bull breeding, to "love, which is stronger than death," the "eternal life-force"—and on this note, surely not the result of scientific investigation, *Les Rougon-Macquart* ecstatically ends. "Henceforth," Josephson concludes, "it was foregone that Zola should be the poet of human 'fecundity' and of Utopianism."

Yet even the career of "Zola fat" led quite logically to its seemingly illogical conclusion. The impersonal manner, the refusal to judge and conclude, had never been really natural to him. He had always been filled with passionate certitudes, and eager to share them. "My husband loved to sermonize all his friends," Mme. Zola remarked; throughout his "experimental novels" he had in effect been sermonizing his public as a crusading scientist. The didactic implications of his work became steadily plainer and sharper. *Germinal,* with its magnificent picture of a strike, made him willy-nilly the champion and prophet of the downtrodden throughout Europe. Thus his new faith in humanity and himself only strengthened his evangelical tendency. As a naturalist he had ruthlessly laid open all the "social sores"; now he would thrust the remedies down the gullets of his public. As a scientific novelist he had ostentatiously refrained from explicit moralizing; as a crusader he would now bend all his energies to pointing the moral, baldly, emphatically, relentlessly.

The faith that Zola began to preach was a humanitarian faith, and the specific solution he offered was Socialism. He thus entered another of the main currents of modern thought and literature. His prolonged researches into the conditions of his society had brought him into close and constant contact with its appalling miseries and injustices. Although his early novels aroused resentment among humanitarian reformers by their unrelieved picture of the grossness and bestiality of the poor, his sympathies soon became apparent; and the publication of *Germinal* confirmed the widespread suspicion that the terrible Zola was now also a Socialist. With the growing unrest, the labor movement had become a political reality, and the doctrines of Socialism were daily winning converts; into a study of these doctrines Zola now threw himself in a spirit that he again believed scientific but that at bottom was again romantic. Through the concluding volumes of *Les Rougon-Macquart* he retained, at least nominally, the attitude of impartiality, but his new program made inevitable the final abandonment of naturalism. If only to correct the false impression made by *L'Assommoir,* Zola felt that he must definitely surrender the luxury of detachment and become an avowed partizan.

In turning his back upon naturalism, Zola thus did not join hands with its enemies. He kept in the vanguard, still the leader of a small band of adventurous spirits, but he was far afield from most of the other pioneers and occupied a position almost as lonely as that in which he had planted the standard of the Experimental Novel. In 1891 a journalist conducted an inquest on Naturalism: Was it sick? was it dead? could it be saved? The replies of most of the famous writers were derisive; some pretended ignorance of the existence of the animal. Zola's was admirably restrained—and significant. "Naturalism finished? . . . Possibly." Prophetically, he foresaw a possible reaction against science, an impatience with its slow progress, and himself stated the soundest criticism of naturalism: its abuse of positive fact, its negation of idealism. Yet he reaffirmed his faith in the toilsome conquest of truth, whose banner naturalism had for a time carried, and he scorned the alternatives proposed by his contemporaries.

> As a foil to the immense positivist labors of fifty years they display the vague label of "Symbolism" and some nondescript verse. They bring to a close this enormous century, formulate this universal anguish of doubt, this shaking of minds passionate for certainties, with the obscure babbling, the four sous' worth of verses of some café habitués!
>
> The future is to those who seize the soul of modern society, and, detaching themselves from too rigid theories, consent to a more logical, more sympathetic acceptance of life. I believe in a picturing of truth, broader, more complex, a greater overture to humanity, a sort of *classicism of naturalism.*

Meanwhile, what was he himself going to do? "Well, if I had the time, I would do the *other thing,* what they want, what they need."

Zola found the time. When he had done with the Rougon-Macquart history he embarked on "The Three Cities": *Lourdes, Rome, Paris*. There is some question whether they offer what the world wants and needs; but they present, unmistakably and in immense detail, the preface to Zola's program. His basic methods were still the same. He made field expeditions to each of the cities; he held innumerable audiences and took elaborate notes; he swamped his novels with the resulting documents. He retained, too, his naïve faith in science: it was during this period that he submitted himself as a guinea pig for a naturalistic experiment by fifteen medical and psychiatric experts, the results of which were published in the curious treatise of Dr. Toulouse: "Psycho-Physiological Study of Émile Zola, with Reference to the Relationship between Abnormality and Genius." But the scientific, naturalistic method is now subordinated to the quest of faith, of certainty, and it is supplemented by interminable discussions. The main characters debate incessantly; when they are alone, it is only to hold earnest self-communion. Zola misses no opportunity to spell out his meaning in capital letters and then to underscore it. Specifically, the conclusion he arrives at in his trilogy is the scarcely surprising one that orthodox religion cannot provide salvation for the modern world. In *Paris,* symbol of enlightenment, he points out the true path to the future: "The Old Testament dream of the Evangel is to be swept away by clear Latin rationalism, aided by modern science."

This is of course pretty vague, and only a prelude to the Utopian symphony. Pierre Froment, the hero of the work, does finally reach, however, some specific certainties; and these form the basis of an extended and, as ever, carefully planned study in Zola's last cycle, "The Four Evangels." This work was begun after the miserable and glorious Dreyfus affair ("Shakespearian tragedy orchestrated by Offenbach"), which left Zola a battered but a better man; and it is the final statement of his sublime optimism. Each of the four sons of Pierre Froment writes one of the new gospels for the glorious City of the Future. *Fécondité* is an endless hymn to its title; when we finally take leave of the aged hero, he is beaming at the company of his descendants, numbered in the hundreds. *Travail* is an idyllic picture of the Communistic state. *Vérité* is a dramatization of the Dreyfus affair, and represents another triumph over the forces of ignorance and oppression. The fourth Evangel, which was to complete the picture of the heavenly city under the title of *Justice,* was cut short by Zola's death.

Both these cycles are insufferably tedious, and to me unreadable—I confess to having been unable to do more than skim any one of the novels that compose them. W. B. Yeats once observed of John Donne that he could be as metaphysical as he pleased because he could also be as physical as he pleased; had he but kept one foot on the ground Zola could have claimed a similar privilege. But where Donne was physical and metaphysical at once, in Zola the tendencies were separated by an abyss bridged only by an almost absent-minded habit of observation that presently became a mere pretense. He took off into the airy blue never to return to this earth; his pilgrimage to Utopia was a final farewell to actuality. In short, the messiah swallowed the novelist whole as the novelist had once swallowed the scientist. In his apocalyptic novels there remains scarcely a trace of the amazing sense of reality Zola had once given to almost everything he touched. All is shrouded in a warm, blessed, but dense fog.

Even as prophecy and propaganda these novels are arid; Zola lost both his talent and his grip on reality. The faith of his last years is as extravagant as his youthful faith in the scientific method. If he occasionally anticipated an actual event, like the establishment of Communism, his dream picture bears little resemblance to its realization. For he had no real grasp of the larger movements of modern civilization, and in his transports he gave scarcely a glance to the conditions under which an Evangelist will actually have to work. Hence he offers only the cloudiest blueprints for the society of the future. His faith is touching as an example, but it provides no solid foundation for a faith for modern men; where his premises have not been rejected, his terms remain shadowy or grotesque. His heavenly plumbing is almost as antiquated as that of Shelley, who was going to install paradise simply by abolishing priests and kings. It is difficult, indeed, even to pay him the pious tribute of calling his tragic death "untimely." Literature almost certainly lost little or nothing by it; he himself was spared the bitter necessity of putting away his grandiose dreams and again facing reality, a reality more terrible than any he had pictured in his most brutal passages: the World War.

Yet it is difficult, too, to wish that Zola's career had ended otherwise. Surely he had earned the right to feed on ambrosia; his arduous and prolonged service to Reality entitled him to a metaphysical spree. And surely the Evangels do him credit as a man. They lend dignity to the naturalistic movement he fathered. If they provide an ironical ending for the Experimental Novel and emphasize its insufficiency, they also make clear that the naturalist is not necessarily the monster that even in this sophisticated age he is often considered. They encircle with a faint halo, however unwanted or undeserved, the brows of Erskine Caldwell and William Faulkner.

XI

NATURALISM IN ENGLAND: GISSING, MOORE

I

IT is difficult to overestimate the extent of Zola's influence in his day. It is even more difficult to explore it. Naturalism was translated into a dozen languages and made hundreds of converts, as diverse as Blasco Ibañez, George Moore, and Maxim Gorky; only a Saintsbury could read the countless novels it inspired. And this is not to mention its influence upon the drama. Like so many novelists, Zola himself attempted to write plays, with intense concern and indifferent success; far more important is that indirectly he sponsored the début of a number of the greater modern dramatists, notably Gerhardt Hauptmann.

In France itself, the movement left few monuments of any importance besides Zola's own work. Alphonse Daudet for a time harshened his pathos and humor with diluted doses of naturalism, but he remains a minor figure; the storm raised by *Sapho* whistles hollowly on the modern ear. The Goncourt brothers, who self-consciously laid the basis for the new creed, were concerned chiefly with their "personal" style, and were at any rate not great enough artists to transcend so deliberate a program; soon thrust into the background, style and all, by the incomparably more vital Zola, they are read today chiefly for the gossip and criticism in their Journals. On the other hand the many young men who enthusiastically adopted this program—Céard, Hennique, Bonnetain, Huysmans—succeeded chiefly in performing an innocent burlesque of it. They caught only the externals of Zola's manner; they prided themselves chiefly upon outdoing him in ferocity, unearthing still uglier samples of depravity; and before the master, they tired of this dismal practice and were off to worship new gods. Huysmans, the most important of them, announced his revulsion as early as 1884, with his strange and mystical *À Rebours* ("Against the Grain"). And Maupassant, the most gifted of Zola's youthful disciples, left only a handful of brilliant pieces among all the shoddy journalistic merchandise that still attracts the drug-store trade. One of these pieces is the famous preface to *Pierre et Jean:* perhaps the most measured, penetrating criticism of the naturalistic credo in its own day.

In England, however, Zola's influence was more clearly salutary—if only because it was diluted. Novelists borrowed his method and subject matter without clearly subscribing to his mechanistic philosophy or his devotion to science; naturalism in England was only an extreme form of realism, not a definite, self-contained program. Yet Zola was the first foreign novelist to make a really notable impression on the self-sufficient Victorians. Balzac, Stendhal, and Flaubert might have sharpened and deepened their realism (and given them some notion of form as well), but these masters they blandly ignored. Although the novelists poked their fingers through some of the thin walls in Victoria's fairyland of piety and prosperity, and cast occasional uneasy glances at the ominous clouds behind which the sun was beginning to set, on the whole they lived comfortably enough among their complacent neighbors. When at length these walls began really to crumble, and the clouds to darken the whole sky, they naturally hearkened to the loudest voice from across the channel; and this was of course Zola's. Upon the translation of his novels in the 'eighties was accordingly focused the exasperated controversy that ushered in the modern era in fiction.

One of the first to feel Zola's influence was also perhaps the most important: George Gissing. To the casual reader his work may seem distinctly Victorian, but what it owes to the earlier writers is chiefly its form. This was not a fortunate inheritance; the unwieldy furnishings of the Victorian three-decker were quite unsuited to Gissing's meager frame, and as Thomas Seccombe remarked, he "nearly collapsed in wind and limb in the heart-breaking attempt" to adjust himself to them. Yet his materials were essentially modern. Aware that he was witnessing "the dawn of a new phase of our civilization," he constantly and explicitly dealt with the forces reshaping it. Although in his particular contribution, the sociological novel, he was anticipated by Mrs. Gaskell, Kingsley, Reade, and other respectable Victorians, he dealt more broadly and consistently with large social units, he had a clearer view of the social implications of his conflicts, he documented his studies with far greater thoroughness, he made fewer concessions to prevailing tastes and was himself less infected by these tastes—in general he left a more nearly adequate record of actual conditions. Always primarily an intellectual novelist, he clearly stated and extensively argued ideas that were to make their mark in the twentieth century. He anticipated H. G. Wells, for example, by some twenty years in his views on marriage, and as many years before Shaw he was treating poverty as a social crime.

Hence Gissing's characters and themes often afford a melancholy pleasure to the spiritual invalids of today who are interested in the genesis of their symptoms. His heroes were among the pugnacious "advanced thinkers" of the time who were in the name of science beginning to attack the premises of religion—and were gloriously sustained by the heat of battle, happily exempt from the bitter spoils of victory. But more particularly Gissing concerned himself with temporal and mundane matters: the immediate problems of a social system that was out of joint, and of which he was himself a bitterly complaining victim. Here he entered and gave an impetus to one of the main movements in modern literature. His tragedy is social tragedy; and like so many subsequent writers, from the later Hardy to Galsworthy, Dreiser, Shaw, and Wells, he preached the gospel of social reform.

Chief among his themes is the curse of poverty, and the "myriad miseries" that result from it. This is the motif of his first novel, *Workers of the Dawn* (1880), and is insisted upon to the end of his career. Much of his work might serve as an introduction to a Communist manual. Although he offered no definite program of amelioration and apparently had none, he recorded, with voluminous ugly detail, the degrading, brutalizing effects of poverty. His most terrible picture is *The Nether World;* a succession of scenes strung like beads on the thread of unutterable squalor, it was the most powerful social document yet to appear in English fiction. More than any English novelist to this day, indeed, Gissing stresses downright physical suffering, privation, and disease. Particularly in his early books, written when he could himself rarely count on three meals a day, his heroes are seldom free from acute want. Only Gissing, Seccombe observed, could have described a heroine as having a face that gave signs of "habitual nourishment on good and plenteous food."

In his later novels, written when he had finally escaped his garret, Gissing enlarged the scope of his social criticism. He turned his attention particularly to the problems of marriage and the relations of the sexes generally. These novels, the best of which are perhaps *The Odd Women* and *The Whirlpool,* contain subtle studies of jealousy—again derived from his own unfortunate marital experience—but they are primarily novels of ideas. They suffer, indeed, from an excess of argument that has now become commonplace; they are too much like tracts, and have too little life apart from the thesis they support. Like so many subsequent writers, Gissing forgot that his primary duty *as a novelist* is to study human nature in the concrete and only secondarily to convey abstract ideas. Yet that he succumbed to the dangers implicit in the sociological novel does not destroy Gissing's historical importance as a pioneer. He is a lineal ancestor of the clamorous brood of proletarian writers who are helping to shape the novel of the present, if not of the future.

2

Gissing still has an unsavory reputation as a follower of Zola in his most lamentable tendencies; he is still commonly regarded as a specialist in low life. Unquestionably he did go to the school of naturalism, and he got some of his lessons by heart. Most of his novels are indeed bleak, oppressive with their burden of squalor and misery. As some critic has noted, he uses no color in his pictures; he paints them all in black and gray and white—with just enough white to set off and intensify the black. Yet he was by no means a thoroughgoing naturalist. He neither swallowed Zola's dogma nor aped his example. Only in the loose popular sense of the word, and then with reservations, can he be called the father of English naturalism.

Zola's ideal of a completely objective, scientific recording of fact is as impossible as it is artistically undesirable; Gissing shot still wider of the mark than the master or his early disciples. Although he managed to keep himself out of his story more than most of the Victorians, his personality unmistakably intrudes, and his voice is often raised in anguished protest. Unmistakably he judges and concludes. His later novels in particular are heavily freighted with sociological discussion, with the characters serving as mere mouthpieces, and their drama as a sounding board. For Gissing was at heart an earnest moralist. Even after carefully selecting and marshaling his facts to point to the right conclusion he was not content to let them speak for themselves. He not only stacked the cards; he refused to play the game at all.

Most curious, however, is the notion that Gissing's chief stock in trade consists of the vile, brutish elements of experience and supports a materialistic philosophy. However sordid their circumstances, his main characters are not themselves ignoble, or even merely commonplace, and they are not puppets. Passionately and often loftily they aspire; in suffering and defeat they still have dignity and force. And Gissing's women are often ideal or actually sentimental creations—Thyrza, for example, might have stepped out of Dickens.

In *New Grub Street,* Harold Biffen announces the naturalistic ideal: "absolute realism in the sphere of the ignobly decent." He complains that Zola himself had not treated ordinary life with fidelity and seriousness: "his vilest figures become heroic from the place they fill in a strongly imagined drama." So Biffen set about to record honestly "the day-to-day life of that vast majority of people who are at the mercy of paltry circumstance"—without idealizing it or without making it ludicrous. This is a mild version of naturalism, but at that it is not a statement of Gissing's accomplishment. "The absolute realism" of his record is marred, for example, by his persistent use of conventional melodramatic devices to motivate or wind up his plots—such as the lost will, at a critical moment suddenly recovered, in *Demos*. But Biffen does not state even Gissing's aim. Reardon is plainly Gissing's spokesman, and Reardon admits that he could not realize this ideal. "Certainly you couldn't," agrees Biffen. "You—well you are a psychological realist in the sphere of culture. You are impatient of vulgar circumstances."

These words give the obvious clue to Gissing's art. As he had spent many years among the poor, he naturally wrote of the life he knew only too well; and he never tampered with the facts as he saw them. One must admire his integrity and fortitude as a pioneer in an unpopular field—the more because he was dependent for his livelihood on the sale of his novels, and was expected by his publishers to please the easily distressed subscribers to Mr. Mudie's library. Yet the proletariat was in itself never his chief interest. Only in one novel, *The Nether World,* does he devote most of his attention to it. In all the others the hero is not a typical but an exceptional figure; the lower classes appear chiefly as the background against which he is unhappily framed, and provide the terms of his conflict. Gissing's tragedy is less of the downtrodden poor than of this superior, sensitive spirit who is born among them and struggles to escape them. As Frank Swinnerton points out, his best works are studies of abnormal temperament—characteristically a modern nervous temperament. He is most at home with his Edwin Reardons and Godfrey Peaks, lonely outcasts like himself, enmeshed in an uncongenial environment.

Gissing was, in fact, temperamentally incapable of a genuinely sympathetic or even a veracious treatment of the poor. He could never imaginatively identify himself with them. Although he was among the first to recognize the proletariat as helpless victims of industrial civilization and to set his dramas against this background, he could never have fought in their ranks. Few things, indeed, would have distressed him more than the Communistic doctrines that have gained force from just such protests as his; it is ironical that he should be, as in a sense he is, one of the fathers of proletarian art. For as he himself freely confesses in *The Private Papers of Henry Ryecroft,* he had no real love for the people or deep interest in them. "Every instinct of my being is anti-democratic," he declares. He revolts against social injustice, but he adds, "I am no friend of the people. As a force . . . they inspire me with distrust, with fear; as a visible multitude, they make me shrink aloof." Thus the whole heavily loaded argument of *Demos* concerns the waywardness and bestial stupidity of the mob.

This fastidious aloofness, this acute distaste for his material, is everywhere apparent in Gissing's novels, and goes far to explain the deadening misery of some of his scenes. These scenes are neither warmed by a sympathetic understanding nor illumined by a vivid imagination, and so they often come out clammy, lumpish, simply painful. Gissing had for facts almost as great reverence as for ideas, but he lacked the tenderness or the gusto to make his facts live and moving. He was almost feminine in his constant distressed emphasis upon filth and sweat and bad smells. One pictures him tramping the squalid alleys, observing with a painful conscientiousness, but always holding his fingers to his nose. The reason for his aversion to the poor, he explained, was that he "came to know them too well." A truer reason is that he never came really to know them at all. He made them, not viler than they are, but duller, drearier, unhappier. Humorless himself, he could never understand their humors. Always intensely subjective, he could never adopt their point of view. He never saw them as they seemed to themselves. The superficiality of his observation, the meagerness of his sensibility, is particularly apparent in the famous description of the Bank Holiday in

The Nether World. It is a striking picture of the banality and vulgarity of the pleasures of the poor; but it is only a partial picture. The simple humanity of the scene quite eludes the squeamish Gissing. And this unconscious distortion is the limitation of the entire novel as a record of proletarian life.

To appreciate this inadequacy, one has only to read Frank Swinnerton's *Nocturne*. Swinnerton's material is intrinsically as drab as Gissing's, and his treatment of it as unsentimental and unsparing. Although he has a humanitarian interest in humble people, he does not, like some humanitarians, exaggerate their humble virtues and romanticize their humble lives. He exhibits them in all their stupidity and coarseness, omitting or extenuating no qualities that offend the delicate susceptibilities of polite society. Thus his account of vulgar lovemaking in the chapter called "After the Theater" is entirely veracious. But it is also very touching. The simple humanity glows through the shabby dress. For while Swinnerton was completely detached he was also able completely to enter the minds of his characters, and he felt at home there. Slight as it is, *Nocturne* has accordingly a beauty and truth that the no less honest Gissing was never able to achieve.

3

The subjective approach, I have already remarked, is one of the distinguishing signs of modern fiction. Although Fielding and Thackeray constantly embroidered their narratives with personal comment, their work is in a deeper sense highly impersonal. They preserved a philosophical if not an artistic detachment, and could enter their stories so freely if only because they so definitely stood outside them and commanded the show. They had a far firmer grasp of their material than most contemporaries who on esthetic grounds fastidiously eschew their intimacy with the reader. For in the complexity and confusion of the modern world, such detachment and such a tight hold of objective reality become increasingly difficult. The artist is driven back upon individual consciousness as, with all its intricacy and mysteriousness, the most solid reality he can be sure of; and finally he is often driven back upon himself. Even the common man today has an itch to write autobiography.

With this tendency, however, Gissing clearly is not to be associated. His subjectivity has no necessary connection with his concept of reality or the concepts of his age. Actually, he strove to present an objective study of the society in which he lived; his failure to achieve this aim resulted from temperamental deficiencies that were in turn the product of accidental circumstances. His novels grew out of his poverty, and poverty is scarcely peculiar to modern society. Similarly his desperate seriousness, in which Gissing also anticipates many later novelists, was primarily accidental. Given the unfortunate circumstances of his early life, he would in any age have lacked the geniality of the greater Victorians.

Here at any rate we approach the reason why Gissing has little to say to those concerned with the deepest issues of modern life, and more specifically the reason why his tragic novels lack the universal, transcendental quality that gives great tragedy its undying glow—and its undying meaning. He was not, in the first place, fascinated by the whole spectacle of life, nor did he brood over it largely. His concern was not with the eternal problems of mankind, stranded in bleak immensities, but with the particular woes of a particular class in a particular society. He presented a special case with special pleading; and if the case has not yet lost its point, at least its terms are now different. Yet what finally limits Gissing's significance is not the narrowness of the field of his observation or the sordidness of many of its objects. It is the deficient vitality of his concrete representations. It is the restriction less of his philosophical than of his imaginative reach, and his want of poetical power. Although modern novelists often confine their attention to small segments of unheroic life, at their best they still manage to make the segment suggest the whole. This Gissing was seldom able to do. His conceptions do not expand or mirror larger conceptions.

It is of course easy to say simply that Gissing was not a genius.

What he lacked more particularly, however, was the impersonality, the self-forgetful detachment, that can make potential the most restricted or even the most private experience—the detachment, for example, with which Proust viewed his highly subjective materials. Gissing's criticism of life was blurred and narrowed by an intensely personal point of view. His very realism was the direct result, not of an artistic impulse, but of his unfortunate experience in the garrets of Grub Street. All art is indeed in one sense subjective, inasmuch as it inevitably originates in self, expresses self, and is conditioned by personal experience. Great art, however, does not end in self; its ultimate reference is larger and outward, it mirrors the consciousness of the race. John Milton was a colossal egoist, but in *Samson Agonistes* he expressed much more than his own sufferings after the collapse of the Commonwealth; in his "Ode to the West Wind" Shelley voiced not only his own yearning but the yearning of all tortured, frustrate humanity. Gissing failed to rise above and master his experience, failed sufficiently to merge it with that of the race. He was not an impersonal philosopher soberly recording the eternal story of the defeat of human endeavor in a world indifferent to human aspiration. He was not an impassioned poet sublimating the eternal woes of man—there is neither great passion nor serenity in his novels. He was simply an egoist who had suffered misfortune, and his tragedies were a gloomy projection of this misfortune: of the prolonged suffering of a proud, fastidious, supersensitive spirit who had to struggle with the most vulgar and brutal realities.

This morbid absorption in his own experience, this incomplete catharsis in his own soul, is what makes Gissing's work so forlorn, to many readers so depressing. There is pity in it, indeed, but too often it resembles self-pity; and too often it is flavored with bitterness. There is "terror" as well, but it is chiefly scare of a world that had used him harshly. He is seldom austere; he is more often resentful and afraid. "The world frightens me," confesses Henry Ryecroft, and in many of Gissing's pages one feels a kind of shrinking from life. To achieve greatness, the tragic novelist must in a deep sense love life, must at least embrace it in all its awful beauty. But Gissing, in the words of his sympathetic biographer, Frank Swinnerton, always "saw life *through* his own poverty and sufferings"; and in this view he was unable to come to terms with it.

Gissing's whole career as a novelist was in fact an accident. He did not have the instinct of the novelist; he turned to fiction simply as the most marketable commodity. Heroically he persisted in his thankless task, but he never really subdued his material, never managed to give even the impression of ease. His novels are built up awkwardly about some preconceived plot, and are filled with hackneyed devices; they creak under the weight of tedious exposition and a superabundance of dialogue, both rendered with an uninspired conscientiousness; and the characters ordinarily enter the scene as if by appointment with the perspiring author. Had fortune been kinder to him he would almost certainly not have produced his cheerless fiction. He would probably have become instead the retiring classical scholar he always longed to be, and indulged in the mildly pleasant speculations of a still kindlier and mellower Henry Ryecroft.

Clearly, then, Gissing does not belong in the company of the great. Neither is he a significant representative of the modern spirit in its profoundest concerns. Although he occasionally indicates a pessimistic view comparable to Hardy's, his fiction has little philosophical implication; it is significant that his later novels, written after a pension had made him secure, are at once more cheerful in tone and inferior in quality—his best novels were written by 1893, when he was only thirty-six years old.

Yet within his limited range Gissing has solid virtues. His chief gift is a keen intelligence, coupled with an absolute integrity, but he has also considerable emotional force. The same intense absorption in his own suffering that warps his vision and embitters his tone gives his best pages an undeniable power. One can deny his tragedies universal significance; one cannot easily dismiss or forget them. At his best, moreover, Gissing succeeds in rising far enough above personal grievance and morbid self-pity to make a surprisingly subtle, restrained, and dignified study of the world in which he lived and suffered. *New Grub Street,* for example, is not only a moving but an admirably just record. Although the novel is in a sense Gissing's *apologia pro vita sua,* he is unsparing of both the weaknesses as man and the limitations as artist of his spokesman, Edwin Reardon; at the same time he does complete justice to his foil, Jasper Milvain, and even makes likable this thoroughly practical, worldly literary merchant to whom artistic ideals are as much a luxury as are moral scruples.

Less well known but still more impressive is *Born in Exile.* Its hero, Godwin Peak, is of commanding stature, and its drama has a sweep and stir uncommon in Gissing. Peak is a gloomy, vehement fellow of exceptional ability who struggles desperately but futilely to raise himself above the squalor in which he was born. His story is thus another projection of Gissing's own experience as an involuntary exile among the alien and despised poor; and like the other novels it suffers somewhat because Gissing stood too close to this experience. He does not appear fully to have realized that Peak's hungry ambition to lead a life of ultra-refinement and ease is at bottom vulgar and ignoble—one suspects because he himself had dreamed this pitiful dream. Yet on the whole he succeeds in lifting his drama into the greater world of the timeless aspirations of the human spirit. He has a firm imaginative grasp of Peak's character and makes one feel deeply the force and fire of the man. The tragedy of the frustration of so much force approaches grandeur.

Despite such considerable successes, Gissing's importance remains, indeed, primarily historical. A few of his novels may survive on their own merits, and *The Private Papers of Henry Ryecroft,* with its mild if mellow flavor, will probably long be read, especially in academic circles; on the whole he will live chiefly as a landmark. Yet he is a notable landmark. He mapped a new province and pointed in the direction in which many later writers were to travel. If his work belongs with neither the deepest nor the loftiest expressions of the modern spirit, he nevertheless anticipated and helped to define this spirit. He was carried along in the middle of one of the main currents of the modern world, and he had a clearer idea than most of his contemporaries of where this current was flowing. He was still immersed in it, unable to rise far enough above it to make an impersonal survey, but as a sensitive observer he left an intelligent record of the conditions of which others may take a larger view. Like so many forgotten pioneers, he helped to do the dirty but necessary spade work.

4

Most of the individual performances of Gissing's contemporaries are, of course, hopelessly forgotten or at best embalmed in textbooks. A few can still be read with interest—notably the short stories of Arthur Morrison and George Douglas Brown's *The House with the Green Shutters,* a powerful study of Scottish rural life and a healthy antidote to the unfailing sweetness and whimsicality of Barrie. But there remains one novel that seems to me the finest product of the early naturalistic movement in England. This is George Moore's *Esther Waters.*

Curiously enough in view of his reputation as an esthete—a reputation clearly, if laboriously, earned—Moore was for a time strongly influenced by Zola. As a young man he met him, corresponded with him, and almost worshiped him; Boswell himself did not approach Samuel Johnson in a holier spirit, nor more humbly seek advice (later to be ignored). "Why," Zola once wrote him, "don't you set to work at once upon a novel about Ireland; a social novel, truthful, audacious, revolutionary? . . . England would be shocked by it; never did such an occasion offer itself to move a whole people." The less audacious Moore waited for more auspicious times to write *Hail and Farewell,* but meanwhile he was writing in the naturalistic manner; and although one is scarcely surprised to find him at the very outset of his career scandalizing his generation by his frank treatment of delicate moral issues, one does blink to discover in him so eager a student of vulgar life. *A Mummer's Wife* is, in fact, a vivid and vigorous presentation of such life worthy of Zola. *Esther Waters,* however, remains Moore's masterpiece in this kind. A product of youthful exuberance, *A Mummer's Wife* is fresher and more spontaneous, more picturesque in its material and more brightly imagined. But *Esther Waters* is more deeply felt. It has the soberness and fulness of maturity, and reflects a more profound, compassionate understanding.

It is the life story of an illiterate servant, Esther Waters—the first of her class to be seriously studied in English fiction. A single pardonable misstep in Esther's youth results in the birth of an illegitimate son; her remaining years are a desperate, heroic struggle to care for him. Finally, through shame and sorrow and terrible hardship, she fights her way to a subdued happiness. The story fades out in a kind of silvery gray twilight haze, at once melancholy and serene. The peace Esther has found is the peace of resignation born of prolonged suffering, but she is at least free from pressing care, and content in the knowledge that the son to whom she has devoted her life has grown to promising manhood. Unlike Kate Ede, the heroine of *A Mummer's Wife,* she has not weakly succumbed to her environment. By the strength of her patient endurance, her selfless devotion, her stubborn gallantry, she has triumphed.

This element of greatness in the humble Esther is precisely what makes her story memorable. The characters of *A Mummer's Wife* are on the whole decent and good-natured enough, never merely swinish, but they are all little and commonplace souls who cannot greatly stir our imagination and arouse "thoughts that wander through eternity." With Esther Waters we enter a range of feeling at once deeper and loftier. She is unlettered, inarticulate, often blunt in her perceptions, often stubborn out of pure ignorance; but she is never mean. Her capacity for noble emotion lifts her story above mere pathos, into the realm of tragedy.

In other words, the characters of *A Mummer's Wife* are guinea pigs in an orthodox naturalistic experiment; Esther Waters has an incalculable force that cannot be measured and determined by any instruments science has yet provided. She is beyond the reach of logic and law. Yet Moore did not sacrifice the absolute realism and impartiality demanded by the high priests of naturalism. He made no concessions to popular sentiment, no attempts to spare the reader the grosser realities of the life he was describing. He remained as objective as Zola himself, and even freer from suggestion of polemics. *Esther Waters* is not of the literature of protest or violent reaction. As Matthew Arnold once said of Tolstoy, the author seems to have written because the thing happened so and for no other reason.

Moore's novel is, in short, one of the most admirable manifestations of the modern realistic spirit in its concern with humble life. As a self-conscious esthete he often declared, with evident pride, that he did not care how the poor live. When he wrote this novel, however, he obviously did care. He stated as much in his preface to the 1899 edition:

> There can be no question that to refrain from judging others, from despising the poor in spirit and those who do not possess the wealth of the world, is certain virtue. That all things that live are to be pitied is the lesson that I learn from reading my book, and that others may learn as much is my hope.

Of the sincerity of this statement the tenderness of his treatment of Esther is sufficient proof. His novel is neither a passionless clinical study, nor a study of low life merely because it is low life and therefore likely to shock or startle. It was conceived in a humanistic spirit, it reflects a deep and rich conception of life, and it is lit with poetry. Hence it has a simple eloquence to be found in neither the embittered Gissing nor the more vigorous and imposing novels of Zola. It is the stuff of great fiction stamped by whatever school.

XII

NATURALISM IN AMERICA: THEODORE DREISER, AND PROLETARIAN FICTION

I

ACCORDING to the picture of American literature drawn by the militant young men of the 'twenties, fiction in the late nineteenth century was grown in a hothouse and nursed by pottering old gentlemen whose chief concern was to keep out sunlight and fresh air. Then with the dawn of this century honesty and truth came "flaming from the ethereal sky" and shriveled these elegant plants. A new and lusty species sprang up, with its roots sunk deep in the soil of American life; and it was the glorious destiny of this new generation to fertilize this soil.

This was a picture to intoxicate young men as only a crusade poster can. Unfortunately, however, the colors were laid on too thick and soon began to peel. A number of the nineteenth-century gardeners refuse to stay put in their hothouses. And their leader was the far from contemptible figure of William Dean Howells. Within the last few years the Marxist critics have dusted off this charming gentleman of the old school, to discover that he was a champion of the victims of the industrial order and among the first to become aware of the predestined class struggle. Both his dogma and his drawings were of course imperfect. He often lapsed into unorthodoxy; many of his lines are wrongly placed or too lightly sketched. But his soul was right. It appears that he was closer to the truth than the crusaders of the 'twenties who prided themselves upon its discovery. His voice was deeper, for example, than the very loud voice of H. L. Mencken.

Howells looks a little awkward, indeed, with this new halo.

Yet even before his realism was deepened by a growing social-consciousness, and above all by his discovery of the great Russians, it deserves respect. The charm that lingers in his earliest as well as his latest work is not merely the scent of old lavender. It remains even after one has penetrated a natural urbanity of manner and grace of style. Its essence diffuses from a genuinely civilized attitude toward life. His geniality was not a shallow complacence—he perceived and did not blink many of the glaring imperfections of his society. His tolerance was not a gentlemanly incapacity for conviction—he felt strongly about these imperfections. But though he saw it mixed, he still never lost his natural warm love for the "work-worn, care-worn, brave, kindly face" of the everyday world. Realism today is too seldom as mellow as the realism of Howells.

Yet the dust settles again and the halo fades. Even the enthusiasm of the Marxist cannot set pulsating vigorously blood that flows so thin. The novels of Howells remain pale and anemic. The reason is chiefly that his talents were not robust and could in no age have carried him beyond the ranks of the honorable second-rate, but partly too it is that he was in spite of himself taken in by the society in which he lived. He was always honest and sincere in his thinking, he did not shrink timidly from unpleasant reality; yet as a novelist he was himself infected by the tasteless tastes of this society and never quite escaped its unwholesomely wholesome influence. His urbanity was diluted by its notions of refinement; his realism was qualified by his acceptance as universal of many of its manners and morals. On his boldest excursions into the seething industrial world he carried with him the aroma of its drawing-room. Hence when naturalism reared its head at the end of the century it was at once recognized as a different species of writing, and frightened good people who had read Howells with but a polite distress.

Conspicuous in the first litter of naturalists was Stephen Crane. In *Maggie: A Girl of the Streets* he plunged into muddier waters than had yet been explored and rose from the bottom with uglier specimens than had yet been exhibited. It is indeed an amateurish performance that today seems ludicrous in its self-conscious and almost gloating display of brutal detail; but Crane also wrote a number of memorable short stories, and above all *The Red Badge of Courage*. A remarkable feat of imaginative re-creation, this account of a common soldier in the Civil War is no product of naturalism: Crane's method was scarcely the method of observation, and his aim was essentially impressionistic. Yet his novel was a realistic study of war at a time when war was still the subject primarily of romance.

More unmistakably the child of Zola, however, and still lustier, was Frank Norris; one of his first efforts, *McTeague*, bears prominently the livid birthmark of naturalism. *McTeague* is the story of a primitive creature—we know him simply as McTeague—who practises dentistry in a dingy byway of suburban San Francisco, and whose spiritual reach is measured by his one great ambition: to have an enormous gold tooth hanging outside his office. Marriage brings some approach toward a more civilized state, but under the pressure of a series of misfortunes he relapses into his animal-like habits, even acquires an animal-like viciousness, and like an animal kills his wife and is at length trapped. The final tableau of McTeague, locked to the body of a dead man on the burning sands of Death Valley, gazing stupidly at the limitless horizon, is unforgettable.

The entire demonstration is worked out with remorseless logic, yet with admirable restraint. When Norris underscores too heavily it is less, one feels, from a desire to shock than from a youthful distrust of the imaginative powers of his readers; his attitude toward his crude material remains rigorously objective. He has, moreover, the masculine vigor and gusto that Gissing lacked. He presents powerfully a segment of life necessary to a complete picture of America. And he does not fall into the too common error of implying that this ugly segment is representative of the whole. In short, *McTeague* is a triumph in the naturalistic manner.

Yet the very success of Norris in achieving his aim only makes plainer the limitations of this aim. His main characters are too gross and insensitive for their tragedy to evoke a deep response. Despite his primordial brutishness, McTeague is not indeed naturally vicious; he is simply stupid and inert. He even has glimmerings of gentler or nobler feelings—as in his love for his canary, which he carries with him to the end. Similarly Norris attempts to inject sweetness and light through the romance of old Grannis and Miss Baker, feeble and sentimental as this interlude is. But in effect he here treats the raw, bestial elements of human nature almost to the exclusion of the qualities that have produced its triumphs. *McTeague* never brings us into the sphere of lofty aspirations; and we are not struck with awe at the defeat of mean, ignoble aims.

Norris himself apparently soon felt this. Like so many who went to school under Zola, he wearied of his lessons even as he mastered them. His subsequent efforts were accordingly unscientific but far more ambitious. He gallantly projected a trilogy, an epic of Wheat, in which the tragedy of individual lives was to be subordinated to a larger purpose, a greater good. Thus, although most of the main characters of *The Octopus* (the introduction to the trilogy) come to a tragic end through their struggle with the monster of Big Business, the Wheat remains: "that mighty world force, that nourisher of nations, wrapped in Nirvana calm, indifferent to the human swarm, gigantic, resistless, moved onward in its appointed grooves." Despite its straining for sublimity—not to mention the difficulty at least one reader finds in prostrating himself before Wheat—*The Octopus* is fairly impressive; it has something of the sweep and stir of the epic. But *The Pit,* which follows the "mighty world force" into the Chicago market, falls off into mere sensationalism. It is more exciting than profound, and its excitement at times appears designed for popular appeal. Norris's premature death, which prevented the completion of his project, was thus perhaps a less serious loss to American literature than is commonly imagined.

In any event neither Crane nor Norris made a deep impression upon their audience. Both died young before the battle for naturalism was really fought out. The novelist who bore the brunt of this battle, which ultimately concerned the artist's right to make a thoroughly honest, unaffected study of American life, was Theodore Drieser.

2

Dreiser occupies today a melancholy position. He has been overtaken by the same ironic fate that has made somewhat pathetic figures of Bernard Shaw, H. L. Mencken, Sinclair Lewis, and other *enfants terribles* of only a decade or so back: advanced young men are now patronizing him and referring to him in the past tense. At the outset of his career he was at the center of a furious controversy. Because of their bluntness and directness, his early novels were virulently abused, when not officially suppressed. The professional reviewers were shocked by his realistic approach to sex and called it mere filthiness; they cried out against his "barbaric naturalism" and likened him to Zola at his most depraved; and in general they denounced him as a low fellow with a diseased passion to "paint only the backside of nature." At the same time the younger critics came whooping to his defense; he became the symbol of freedom, the hero of youth. As he persisted in his elephantine labors, readers gradually ceased to be distressed by his pictures of American life and began even to recognize a family likeness. Finally, with the publication of *An American Tragedy,* he was generally and almost reverently regarded as the foremost American novelist of his generation. And now, but a few years after his triumph, what reverence remains suggests the absent-minded tribute paid to senility. By a younger generation Dreiser is treated with condescension as a curious relic of a benighted age.

Shallow as this judgment may be, it is not surprising. While the vanguard has moved on, Dreiser as artist has stood still. He continues to do business with his original materials, continues to be convulsed over a number of ideas now generally taken for granted. Throughout his entire career he has written as if he could not help himself—written doggedly, perspiringly, ponderously, what is apparently the only kind of novel possible for him to write. This perseverance in his original purposes and refusal to make a single concession even to sympathetic critics gives his art, indeed, a kind of dignity; but it has also narrowed his art. Call it a colossal steadfastness, call it a mulish stubbornness; what ultimately it betrays is a sheer incapacity for development.

Yet Dreiser remains a significant figure in American letters. His historical importance is unquestionable. If he is no longer a revelation, his critics ought at least not forget that his achievements have made it easier for them to sneer at his obvious limitations. If we have advanced to a richer, deeper realism, he has done as much as any other writer to make this advance possible. He is of especial interest to the student of modern literature, moreover, because his novels so plainly give back the form and pressure of the forces that have shaped it. And these novels, finally, are apart from all historical considerations still worthy of serious study. Their merits are of an unspectacular kind likely to be overlooked in an age that relishes the subtle, the sophisticated, or the sensational, but they are nevertheless solid.

In appraising the intrinsic value of Dreiser's work, however, one stumbles at once over a number of irritations, and it is well to have done with these at the outset. Most obvious is his prose style. Although it is not so uniformly deplorable as in witty exercise critics have made it seem—*Twelve Men,* for example, contains much admirable writing—it is in general undistinguished, at worst positively bad; and with a discouraging insistence he is forever sounding his low notes. But scarcely less apparent are his utter want of taste and humor (Carl Van Doren has remarked the thousand times Dreiser describes something as "artistic") and his utter carelessness of form. His novels are shapeless, bloated with insignificant and dreary detail; the "Hindenburg of the novel" H. L. Mencken has aptly called him, blasting his way through his interminable stories by main strength. When Sister Carrie talks with a friend over a dumbwaiter, Dreiser must write a paragraph about dumbwaiters; when Jennie Gerhardt enters a hotel lobby, he must follow at her heels with a catalogue that stops only at the number of buttons on the bellboy's coat. It is difficult to imagine an inner vision bright enough to illumine such details. Although one can perhaps attribute this painful thoroughness to a revolt, in the interests of truth, against the too refined artistry and too unexceptionable "good taste" of such as Henry James, and although one may add that exquisite workmanship has generally been more characteristic of lesser than of greater artists, Dreiser remains a unique phenomenon. His sins in these respects are unparalleled in fiction with any claim to importance, and they stand out starkly in an almost complete absence of charm.

Equally annoying is the impenitent moralist that forever obtrudes unnecessary comment and allows only Clyde Griffiths of all his heroes to tell his own story. The notions that obsess Dreiser, moreover, are scarcely startling or novel. They are summed up in a passionate, almost blind distrust of what he calls "professional moralists and religionists." Brought up in a strict Catholic faith, Dreiser is still suffering from a hangover. His fierce joy in his onslaughts upon the delusions of the pious reveals plainly that he has but recently escaped these delusions—and by no means entirely escaped at that. Certainly he is much less Nietzschean than he likes to think. But it is today nevertheless embarrassing to watch him still pummeling antagonists long since dead. It is trying to listen to harangues about ideas that are now commonplaces but to him still a shocking novelty. "At this point," he exclaims, with obvious complacence, early in *Dawn,* "I am sure any self-respecting moralist will close this book once and for all!"—but the ordinary intelligent reader has been merely bored.

Still more distressing than Dreiser's habit, in Santayana's phrase, of letting off unnecessarily loud blasts of incidental steam is his inclination to destroy all ethical values. In the extravagance of his revolt he confuses religion with all morality. Everything goes overboard in a jolly, be-damned-to-you spirit. Although he obviously does have moral ideas, the view of life reflected in his novels is at times too purely negative, and it is arrived at, as the Folletts have remarked, "by too easy a series of negations"; he at times minimizes the ideal values that give significance to the passions he portrays. Thus in *The Financier* he presents us with the now famous image of the lobster leisurely devouring its predestined prey, the squid, as a symbol of the brutal predaciousness that most adequately characterizes the human animal.

Here one approaches the most troublesome problem of Dreiser's art: his materialistic, mechanistic philosophy. There can be no dispute about what are his conscious views; he is all too eager to make them explicit. In his autobiographical work as in his fiction he insists upon biochemistry as the whole explanation of human behavior. "Of one's ideals, struggles, deprivations, sorrows, and joys," he writes in *A Book About Myself,* "it could only be said that they were chemic compulsions, something which for some inexplicable but unimportant reason responded to and resulted from the hope of pleasure and fear of pain." To these "chemic compulsions" Dreiser constantly returns with the wearisome persistence of a schoolboy intoxicated with a new idea. The novelist's art would accordingly appear to be reduced to an experiment in a laboratory—an experiment, too, with no conceivable point unless it be the childish pleasure of looking at the new colors that result from mixing certain ingredients, and listening to the little explosions.

This concept Dreiser got from the official sources of Zola's naturalism; and though the trend of scientific thought today is clearly away from it, characteristically he continues to hold by it and even to flaunt it with the enthusiasm proper to mystical revelation. The depressing implications of this concept, once more, are plain enough. "Chemic compulsions" will explain man's triumphs as well as his failures—and rob both of any real significance. Even criticism of society ultimately must be touched with futility; indignation at social injustice would seem as pointless as a protest against the affinity of hydrogen and oxygen. Hence we should be able to get no inspiring or consoling meaning from the tragic spectacles that Dreiser habitually presents. His philosophy should squeeze his novels dry of splendor, if not of all ideal value, and make them at most merely pathetic. Yet it does not. His best novels make not only a deep but a different impression. They stir a keen pity and a troubled wonder, but also a feeling of awe that could never be aroused by the contemplation of the futile antics of mechanical puppets. They are never merely dismal. And the explanation of this paradox is simply that Dreiser does not consistently carry out his theories. His feelings as an artist do not coincide with his conclusions as a thinker—and his perception of his characters is primarily intuitive and emotional, not intellectual. In short, he builds better than he knows.

To put it baldly, Dreiser is a third-rate thinker. His reflections upon art and life, as dressed up for example in *Hey Rub-a-Dub-Dub,* are often shallow, muddled, sophomoric. For all his patience and honesty, he cannot really think through a problem, and he is too easily dazzled by novel ideas. Yet he is despite himself a great instinctive artist. Like Thomas Hardy, he has the birthright of a brooding imagination as the descendant of a family that for generations lived close to the soil in the grip of elemental forces; and although he shows a disconcerting readiness to sell this birthright for a mess of rather shoddy scientific ideas, he cannot deny his origins. If his theories about life cramp his art, the unconscious artist nevertheless breaks through these bounds. If he is at times swollen with a rank mist, he is also steadied by deep feeling. "The coachman is tipsy, the chariot drives home."

Dreiser is in this respect like his avowed master, Balzac: one may quarrel with their conscious intentions and conclusions, but one cannot deny the vitality of their fictions. Dreiser's early novels in particular were the product, not of a reasoned philosophy, but of an artistic passion; their soul is pure feeling. Although his ideas appear in embryonic form—he had already discovered biochemistry—they have yet to be rationalized. Constantly he calls Jennie Gerhardt a "big woman"—and convinces us that she is one. She is definitely a creature of circumstance, never mistress of her fate, but she is also superior to circumstance, greater than her fate. Despite the endless dreariness of the prospect she faces at the end, one accordingly feels a kind of exaltation in sadness, a response to the splendor of her sacrifice and devotion. Jennie has not been explained in purely mechanistic terms.

Precisely because they embody less of his conscious thought, these earlier novels are, to my mind, Dreiser's best work. *An American Tragedy* did most to extend and consolidate his reputation, and is indeed the most intense and overpowering of his works. Yet it inevitably suffers from his deterministic theories, which are here given their most rigorous, uncompromising application. Dreiser labors his thesis; elaborately he balances cause and effect to explain his characters; and the result is that these characters seem mere automatons. We pity Clyde Griffiths and Roberta Arnold, but we pity them much as we would helpless animals driven to the slaughter; we can scarcely love or even respect them. Their story has dignity only because of the deep sympathy with which it is told—because of the presence of a noble soul brooding over this ignoble affair. In *Jennie Gerhardt,* however, there is more than this somber and compassionate brooding. While *An American Tragedy* has the harrowing reality of an actual experience, the earlier novel excites the more valuable illusion of reality that results when experience is transmuted into the stuff of art. It contains more poetry, less mere documentation. Above all, it goes further beyond the harrowing, for it expresses an ideal faith as well as a sympathy.

3

Actually, the view of life that rules Dreiser's fiction is, despite his dabblings in biochemistry, fundamentally little different from that of many tragic realists of this age. At the heart of it is again an utter pessimism. All he can make out is a "vast compulsion which has nothing to do with the individual desires or tastes or impulses of individuals." He goes further than most, indeed, in his view that man is "a mechanism, undevised and uncreated, and a badly and carelessly driven one at that." The "mechanism" one can forget and still perceive this difference: that where others see an order, even if inexplicably cruel, Dreiser sees only an immense disorder, a meaningless welter. God is not only merciless but inept; man's struggles are not only vain but gratuitous. One might accordingly view him as the most thoroughgoing agnostic in modern fiction—were not agnosticism in a way too flattering a term for him. He gives the impression of being simply all at sea.

At times, it is true, Dreiser wavers and offers provisional answers, urging us to "have faith to believe that there is a larger intelligence at work" and assuring us that "there is something back of man." These wishful remarks, however, only lay bare the streak of peasant superstition that leads him to seek occasional refuge in a kind of feeble mysticism, as he did in his *Plays of the Natural and Supernatural*. He never dallies long with such, for him, flimsy speculations. One never perceives in his novels a "larger intelligence" controlling human destiny. In the end he simply records, powerfully, the chaos he sees, consciously extracting from it no other meaning than that there is no meaning. His whole credo, as in the *Bookman* some years ago he most aptly and concisely expressed it, is this:

> I can make no comment on my work or my life that holds either interest or import for me. Nor can I imagine any explanation or interpretation of any life, my own included, that would be either true—or important, if true. Life is to me too much a welter and play of inscrutable forces to permit, in my case at least, any significant comment. One may paint for one's own entertainment, and that of others—perhaps. As I see him the utterly infinitesimal individual weaves among the mysteries a floss-like and wholly meaningless course—if course it be. In short, I catch no meaning from all I have seen, and pass quite as I came, confused and dismayed.

This is a characteristic overstatement. Dreiser has been able after all to make some "significant comment"—it is embodied in his novels; and he himself has thought this comment important enough to spend most of his time writing—surely not for his own entertainment alone. Yet this is essentially the vision of life reflected in the novels. Its most striking expression is in *The Financier* and its sequel, *The Titan*. Frank Cowperwood, their hero, is the great business executive who most impresses the American imagination; he is the great man of his age. But like the heroes of *The Dynasts* he is made imposing only to emphasize his littleness. With all his tremendous force he cannot master life or even himself; he is as helpless a victim of inscrutable forces as the meanest wretch left in his blazing wake.

Hence Dreiser's work directly raises the final issues in modern literature. What can sustain him in this apparently intolerable world? What can rescue him from sheer despair, and therefore his art from futility? For he is clearly incapable even of the ironic detachment that enables many to view and up to a point enjoy life as a queer spectacle. He is not intellectual or aristocratic enough for this. His novels are almost untouched by irony; he is too simple a soul, and too intense, to make grim jokes about life.

The answer leads in the first place to Dreiser's compassion, which in itself goes far toward lightening the "burthen of the mystery . . . of all this unintelligible world." He does not substitute intellectual operations for living emotions and aspirations; his tenderness and his passion are especially conspicuous today, when one finds so much cold subtlety or cold violence. How some critics can call him unfeeling is to me incomprehensible. In *A Book About Myself* he writes (and his honesty at least is generally conceded), "I have cried so often that I have felt myself to be a weakling; at other times I have been proud of them [his tears] and of my great rages against fate and the blundering inept cruelty of life." Even behind the remorseless objectivity of *An American Tragedy* the sensitive reader should detect this mingled sorrow and rage; but his earlier novels are simply steeped in pity. Nor is Dreiser's feeling a facile, maudlin wretchedness, indulged for the sheer luxury of it. It grows out of an intense sympathy for the woes of mankind in all its unsatisfied aspiration and helpless degradation and downright physical misery.

More important than this compassion, however, is Dreiser's positive faith: a faith in life as a magnificent drama, and in man as an actor worthy of his rôle in it. Many critics have elected him to the dismal company of the apostles of despair—and he has taken a simple pride in this election and made appropriate speeches of acceptance. Yet he has not actually joined. Despite his vision of the terrible, meaningless cruelty of life and his insistence upon chemistry as the whole explanation of it, he hangs on to a confidence in its livableness, and even welcomes the challenge. Time and again he speaks his zest, for all his hurt. At the end of *The Genius* we leave Eugene Witla thinking to himself what a "sweet welter" life is—"how rich, how tender, how grim, how like a colorful symphony." Again in *A Hoosier Holiday* Dreiser tells us that "life at bottom, in spite of its seeming terrors, is beautiful." He even grows lyrical. "Give me . . . sound and fury, signifying nothing. Give me the song sung by an idiot, dancing down the wind. Give me this gay, sad, mad seeking and never finding about which we are so feverishly employed. It is so perfect, this inexplicable mystery." Admittedly these rhapsodies are a little boyish and windy. But this naïveté is the very essence of Dreiser. As Randolph Bourne early recognized, he is always a little youthful: in his fascination with sex, in his puzzling about the universe, in his thrilling to the crude and flamboyant. He has never lost his early lust for life. "Imagine incorrigible sensuous youth endowed with the brooding skepticism of the philosopher who feels the vanity of life," Bourne wrote, "and you have the paradox of Mr. Dreiser. For these two attitudes in him support rather than oppose each other."

The darkness at the end of his novels is thus not the darkness of despair. He is "confused and dismayed"; he is often stirred to "great rages against fate"; but he is never merely cynical or indifferent, and he does not throw up his hands. He has after all made his peace with life. He has even imposed his terms upon death. If he does not reach the level of the heroic and sublime, he at least maintains a simple dignity.

Despite his passion for photography, Dreiser is much more than a photographer. He too is at bottom a poet—an unlettered poet with an impediment in his speech, as anyone familiar with his official verse will shudderingly testify, but in his immediate response to life a genuine one. And this poet in him sees the dream behind things as they are and fills his books with a solemn sense of the eternal sadness and mystery arising from the eternal conflict between aspiration and experience. He gets into his often sordid stories a suggestion of brooding depths, a quality of spaciousness, that greatly enlarges their reference. Take even *An American Tragedy*. Its characters are base or vulgar, its incidents ugly, its argument perhaps dubious; yet with this dismal material Dreiser manages to stir a contemplation of the whole stupendous scheme of life. In short, Dreiser's drab stories are altogether worth telling and knowing. They may not impress us with the magnificence of man, but they do add a dignity and a deeper significance to the commonplace. Man is not godlike, but neither is he contemptible; and his story, if honestly and sympathetically told, is never mean.

4

As one of the few thoroughly indigenous writers at a time when much American literature was derivative, Dreiser raises another important issue: the need for a specifically American art. There is still considerable agitation about this (though more in music and the plastic arts than in literature); but as the many ringing declarations touch off more emotion than thought, it is seldom clear what a genuine American art is or should be. In the protest against imitativeness or shallow romanticism or any remoteness from the actual conditions of American life, the cheering is often too loud for work that is merely parochial. All one can safely say is that to be vital, any art must be deeply rooted, and that it is difficult for the writer to sink his roots deeply in any but native soil. If the art of the expatriate like Henry James is not inevitably touched with sterility, it at least suffers from the waste of frustration and the cost of transplanting; one cannot pack up his roots with his mental luggage and board ship intact. Yet this does not mean that the American novelist must paint a realistic picture of American manners or make a specialized study of American problems or speak only in an American dialect. He will do well to take off from native soil, profiting by the best elements in the native tradition; but if he is to become greatly significant, he must arrive at the end in a still larger and freer country that knows no nationality. Only so can he serve the deepest needs of his own people—as Cervantes, Goethe, and Tolstoy served theirs.

The necessity of repeating such platitudes is embarrassing. It is nevertheless a real necessity even in the highest critical circles —one of the penalties of brilliance or habitual astuteness is a likely blindness to the obvious. What is important, at any rate, is that Dreiser is thoroughly American without being merely provincial. He is in the line of Walt Whitman, hymning the lustiness and raw vigor of a young nation; he has left remarkably vivid accounts of such typically American growths as the young Chicago, with its ugliness and energy and crude but compelling glamor; but by the strength of his hold on the elemental emotions he has transcended national boundaries where more sophisticated writers have not. *Jennie Gerhardt* is memorable for its timeless comment upon all human life.

At the same time, Dreiser makes an emphatic comment upon American society that gives him special pertinence for his contemporaries. He is naturally quick-feeling, and his early experience of poverty at once sharpened his perceptions and deepened his sympathies. This experience of the terrors of the poor explains his rather naïve wonder and delight at material success. With obvious relish he follows Sister Carrie and Frank Cowperwood into high society; with loving care he describes the clothes they wear, the food they eat, the apartments they inhabit, and all the trappings of wealth—always with footnotes about the cost of things. But this experience also explains the power of his treatment of the downtrodden—his best single piece of work is his account in *Sister Carrie* of the gradual disintegration of Hurstwood. It explains the increasing weight of social criticism in his work. And it explains, finally, his active participation in the Left-wing movement.

Like most modern novelists, Dreiser refused from the outset to acquiesce in the orthodox judgment of his characters or to fit them into the orthodox scheme of rewards and punishments. But he went even further than most in his actual obsession with men and women who in earlier fiction would have existed only to be punished for the public edification. All his heroes and heroines are flagrant sinners. Sister Carrie and Jennie Gerhardt are kept women; Frank Cowperwood is a buccaneer of finance and a libertine to boot; Clyde Griffiths is actually a murderer. At the end of their stories all are unrepentant. All suffer, but not from consciousness of sin, and not as a necessary and proper consequence of their failure to conform. Sister Carrie and Frank Cowperwood are by all worldly standards indeed conspicuously successful; they reach the top in their professions, and are showered with all the material rewards that should insure their living happily ever after. That they are nevertheless unhappy is only because they have a greater capacity than a Hollywood hero for realizing the emptiness of their triumphs.

This almost ostentatious refusal to condemn unconventional conduct and append the comfortable moral is precisely what distressed Dreiser's early critics. Not only did he describe Vice with what then seemed frank detail; he appeared openly to countenance it. Few novelists, in fact, have presented people more simply and truly as they are. Yet he was by no means the unmoral fellow that his critics called him (and still call him), nor the iconoclast he liked to think himself. Although he talked loosely, he clearly did have moral ideas and pass moral judgments. Thus he constantly insisted that Jennie Gerhardt was a thoroughly good woman. And thus he affixed an external responsibility for her sufferings, blaming partly the incomprehensible powers that contrive the eternal dilemmas, but partly too the stupidity and inhumanity of a social structure that aggravates human woe in a universe already inhospitable enough.

In *An American Tragedy* this social criticism came to a head. Despite the enormity of his crime, Clyde Griffiths is not a monster, nor his guilt self-evident. Even when he himself yearns to apply to his tortured soul the Christian balm of repentance, he cannot say simply, "I have sinned." For his tragedy is not the just retribution that meets the sinner, but the profounder tragedy of the clumsy, inarticulate, always fevered and baffled struggles of the human spirit caught in an uncongenial environment. And Dreiser's whole point is that this environment was the real villain: the society that produced Clyde, molded him from the outset, and provided no natural outlet for his natural desires. His was an *American* tragedy. Although Dreiser does not, indeed, prove his case to our entire satisfaction, in his readiness to absolve the individual from all personal responsibility failing to explain why millions of other factory hands find it unnecessary to drown their girl friends, he was at least making an earnest effort to penetrate to underlying causes.

This effort finally landed Dreiser in the camp of the Communists, and so once more in the lap of controversy. But if it seems unkind to deny him the pleasure of again sharing in the advanced thought of his age, one still cannot regard this as a significant development. It has so far resulted only in some occasionally unfortunate publicity, and in a characteristic book on Russia that testifies more to the warmth and generosity of his feelings than to the incisiveness of his thinking; and he has already retired to the background. His brief appearance in the political arena did not at any rate mark a turning point in his career; it was simply a logical outcome of the attitude that has shaped both his novels and his interminable memoirs. All his work belongs, in a sense, to class literature. He has always shown a keen awareness of the inequalities and injustices in the economic structure of modern society, and a profound sympathy for the lower classes from which he came. At the same time he has never written as if human life were essentially a matter of economics, and a redistribution of wealth the cure for all human ills; he has seen around and through the working man, and never idealized him as the chosen to inherit the kingdom of this earth. "Proletarian art," Ernst Toller once wrote, "must ultimately rest on universal interests, must, at its deepest, like life or death, embrace all human themes. It can only exist where the creative artist reveals that which is eternally human in the spiritual characteristics of the working people." In this spirit Dreiser has written of workers and capitalists alike; and if or when his political views find expression in a novel, I doubt that they will make much difference in his art, for better or worse. They may alter his arguments, and possibly give them an unfortunate prominence; they are unlikely to cloud the vivid and powerful concrete representations of life that loom through his foggiest thinking.

It is always necessary, once more, to keep in mind the essential distinction between Dreiser the artist and Dreiser the thinker. As a philosopher he is often jaded and sophomoric, as a sociologist he may be unsound, but behind the muddled thinker one always perceives the simple, quick-feeling peasant; and this peasant-like quality, noted by critics both friendly and unfriendly, is the core of Dreiser's genius. It reveals itself in his simplicity of outlook, his frankness, his utter confusion in the face of complexity. It explains his blindness to the nuances of experience, and the bluntness of his sense of values; his understanding is broad and deep but rarely subtle. But it explains, too, much of his strength: his sympathy, his dogged honesty, his firm hold upon the primary emotions—his whole "thick, warm feeling for life." His response to life is always simple and impassioned. He is never sophisticated, but always fresh and ingenuous, boyishly enthralled by "the mystery of it all." He is hurt, but he is also endlessly charmed by the beauty of life. He is haunted, tortured by the cruelty of the cosmic scheme, but he is also intensely fascinated. And all this is in the novels: their essence is not thought but pure feeling.

No doubt Dreiser has suffered, even more than Hardy, from the lack of a ripe, humane culture. At the same time his emotional force, again like Hardy's, derives from his simple origins and his intimate acquaintance with life in the raw. One must obviously take him as he is, with all the limitations that appear to be an inseparable part of him. Despite these limitations, however, he is an important figure, still looming bulkily above more facile or gifted contemporaries whose way has been made easier by his pertinacious, uncompromising honesty at a time when American fiction was not conspicuous for this virtue. He has size if not shape, vitality if not art. In short, there are more brilliant and inspired students of human life, but few more patient and sympathetic. Although he writes as he thinks, clumsily, there is in him the passion of the great artist that gives his dark, jumbled, uncouth, springless narratives an enduring significance.

5

The most vigorous "school" of novelists in America today is undoubtedly the proletarian. John Dos Passos, Robert Cantwell, Grace Lumpkin, Susan Ertz, James Farrell, Albert Halper, Erskine Caldwell, Jack Conroy—these are but a few of the many writers who are drawing their inspiration from the cause of the workers. The school embraces various shades of enthusiasm, indignation, and doctrinal orthodoxy, and has a large and tangled fringe where liberal begins to merge with radical, humanitarian with revolutionary. Its members may portray the "class struggle" directly, dramatizing a strike as Cantwell does in *The Land of Plenty;* or they may represent the conditions out of which it has grown, drawing a picture of decadent capitalistic society, as in Briffault's *Europa,* or of life in the slums, as in Farrell's *Studs Lonigan* trilogy. They may in any event be certain of a fairly enthusiastic reception, in which the sharp criticism of the more doctrinaire comrades is balanced by the ostentatious leaning over backwards of the middle-of-the-road critics. They earn the currently popular badge of approval: "authentic."

Only the political implications of proletarian fiction are revolutionary, however; its form and even its content are familiar. Proletarian life has for many years been the subject of serious, sympathetic study, and even the gentle Galsworthy wrote of a strike. Hence, although the more fervent of these novelists might resent finding themselves in the same chapter with Dreiser, in a study of modern fiction this is where they belong. For they stem directly from the naturalistic movement—not indeed because of strict allegiance to Zola's creed, but simply because of the nature of their concerns. They have taken over the externals of this movement: naturally they deal primarily with the more brutal forms of reality, naturally they make a point of keeping their fact "unvarnished"; in a modified form, they exemplify as well the scientific inspiration and the deterministic philosophy. Often, it is true, they deck out their realism with new trimmings, borrowing technical devices from Joyce or stylistic devices from Hemingway. They adopt as well new attitudes—their novels occasionally have Freudian overtones. But they are seldom themselves important innovators, in the sense that Joyce, Proust, and Lawrence are innovators, for they have not made over the novel or notably extended its scope. The substitution of the concept of dialectical materialism for Zola's mechanistic materialism has not radically altered the texture of their fiction—most plain readers are unaware that they are observing a new kind of demonstration. Even when they perhaps anticipate a new age in literature by making their hero a whole class, subordinating the individual to the group, they are only following the example of Zola in *Germinal* or Hauptmann in *The Weavers*. In short, in politics the proletarian writers are definitely of the Left, but as artists they are as definitely to the Right of many of the bourgeois they despise.

This is by no means to disparage them. In literature especially, old forms are not necessarily dead crusts; the very radicalism of the arguments of proletarian fiction emphasizes the validity of traditional ways of telling a story. Yet a further reason for giving less space to these writers than the importance of Marxist thought by itself would call for is that they have not as yet produced really distinguished work. Their youth, the recalcitrance of their materials, the immediacy of their cause, the sound and fury of the conflict in the world both of action and of thought —all make for passion but not for command and control. At their worst they mistake profanity for vigor, plainness for integrity, literalness for truth—in general, journalism or pamphleteering for literature; the power of their narratives comes from the impact of their facts, less from their treatment, and hence is soon lost on one familiar with the facts. At their best they still belong with the honorable second-rate. Although *Europa,* for example, stirred most critics to call out their very best adjectives, it is far from a great novel; its interest, for the historian of the future as for the reader of today, lies chiefly in its materials, and Briffault's treatment of these materials is often crude and obvious.

Dos Passos, the most commanding figure in this group, has similarly been overrated. He can tell a story well, he is a first-rate reporter, and he has made a lusty, penetrating, vividly objectified comment upon American life; but he has neither the brooding imagination nor the elemental emotional force of Dreiser. Critics make too much of his experiments in technique—he is in this respect the most adventurous of the proletarian novelists. Professor Beach, for example, discusses portentously his "breadthwise cutting" of the slice of life, his deliberate discontinuity, his use of various devices: the Newsreel, a medley of journalistic items periodically accompanying the narrative; the interpolation of brief biographical sketches of prominent, representative men; and the Camera Eye, which registers impressionistically the underlying meaning or enveloping mood. By such means Dos Passos seeks to enlarge the reference of his major trilogy (*1919, The 42nd Parallel, The Big Money*), to include the whole sweep and render the essence of contemporary American civilization. But these means are neither original (they come chiefly out of Joyce) nor brilliantly effective. Although he conveys his idea clearly enough, one soon wearies of its illustration; and presently one is tempted to skip.

The chief limitation of Dos Passos, however, lies in his characterization. His many characters are with few exceptions shrewdly observed, carefully individualized, sharply projected—thoroughly life-like; but they are never compelling. One is not deeply interested in them as persons, and hence not particularly moved by their fate. For Dos Passos' own interest in them is primarily as types or symbols, little as individuals. Like Zola, he creates and manipulates them simply for the sake of the vast game he is playing. And although Society may be the hero of the fiction of the future, one may still doubt that in the best of this fiction the individual will be treated as a mere fraction, interesting only as a part of a whole. Art deals preeminently in the concrete and immediate. The great artists of the past who wrote in a strong collective spirit nevertheless created vital personalities, symbols compelling in themselves, like the Edipus of Sophocles or the Moses of the Old Testament. So can artists today—as Thomas Mann magnificently demonstrated with his Hans Castorp, and even Galsworthy with his two protagonists in *Strife*. But the characters of Dos Passos have little such vivid life of their own.

Quite different are the interests and aims of Erskine Caldwell, another of the proletarian novelists who clearly stands out from the mediocre. As artist he has been only incidentally concerned with the struggle of the workers. Yet this concern gives point and direction to his accounts of sub-human life in the South. The most moving passages in *God's Little Acre* are those centering about the strike of the textile workers. Caldwell also proves the truism that propaganda is most effective when implicit; no editorial in *The Daily Worker* has been more cogent than his bare narratives. Yet, like so many American writers, he has failed to develop: he promises to be perpetually promising. In *God's Little Acre* he made a confused effort at synthesis, but this only landed him in the arms—of all people—of D. H. Lawrence. His epilogue to a series of fornications and a heroic attempt to free the mill slaves is a dithyramb about the magic of breasts and the blood stream. Even such vagueness is preferable, however, to the monotony of his variations on the now famous Jeeter Lester. His latest work is almost a burlesque of his fondness for violence, grotesquerie, and horror. Its power is primarily the crude power of murder, of rape, of incest, of brutality and barbarism. Other writers could not realize so fully the potentialities of such material; but if it is a job worth doing, it is not worth the whole attention of a first-rate artist.

On the Continent, indeed, revolutionary fiction has been distinguished by a few deeply impressive performances, such as Malraux's *Man's Fate* and Sholokhov's *And Quiet Flows the Don;* and in Gorky it can boast a major writer. In America it is as yet interesting chiefly for its relation to the immediate issues of our society—and for the fundamental principles involved in its criticism. Yet already there is at least less occasion for repeating the obvious in protest against the doctrinaire. Proletarian artists and critics alike are becoming less narrow and inflexible, less crudely partizan in their judgment of the work both of comrades and of bourgeois. They are growing less fearful of style, and make fewer invidious distinctions between phrase-making and practical activity; they are realizing that poetry is an arduous discipline, not merely an outburst of rugged emotion or a spontaneous call to arms, and that only at the price of sterility can its inspiration be confined to a narrow range of experience; they are in general beginning to perceive that imaginative creation and political argument have a different logic, a different process, and a different value. In the novel more specifically they are outgrowing the cartoon stage, in which Capital and Labor were opposed as monstrous phantoms, and orthodoxy was demanded as naïvely as the Victorians demanded the edifying moral. The most earnest writers are developing a larger perspective, a sense of humor, a faith in the value of an unliteral or even an unorthodox art. Theater Union audiences still react like the simple spectators of the old melodramas, hissing the capitalist villain and wildly applauding the climactic revolt of the workers; novels as well as plays are still conceived in these simple editorial terms. But more and more writers are humanizing class conflicts, regarding them as tragic and not merely as evil, less often substituting canned dogma or official prophecy for their own immediate perceptions, and in this way getting a deeper, more universal and compelling truth into their fictions. *The Land of Plenty* is not a great novel; but in the spirit in which Cantwell treats a strike a great proletarian novel could be written—one that like all great novels transcends its specific theme and becomes something very different from history or argument, much more than Exhibit A.

Despite all its crudities and blatancies, and aside from its possible importance as a portent (a matter to which I shall return at the end), proletarian fiction has in many ways served as a healthy corrective. It has intensified the essential element of conflict that has been blurred and diffused in many modern novels. It has restored the primacy of conscious thought, will, and action at a time when novelists were prone simply to get lost in the jungle of the subconscious. Above all, it has provided a new generation of writers with a sustaining and integrating faith, and a vital subject matter. If they still flounder, it is no longer in the sophisticated futility of the post-war decade. If they still get maudlin, it is at least on red wine and not on cocktails and jazz.

XIII

REALISM OF THE CENTER: BENNETT, GALSWORTHY, MAUGHAM

I

POTENTIALLY of most importance in naturalism is the scientific determinism that provides its logical basis. This philosophy has plainly helped to shape the fictions of Zola, Dreiser, Julian Green, and others. In practice, however, most avowed naturalists do not consistently carry it out, and thus have not revolutionized the art of fiction; although the uninitiated reader should perceive that heredity and environment play a still more prominent part in their novels than in most modern fiction, he is unlikely to realize that the behavior of their characters is in theory absolutely determined. Even in most of Zola and Dreiser he will probably be unaware that a scientific experiment is being performed. And the concept of dialectical materialism now in favor is more dynamic and allows for some measure of human control; the characters in proletarian fiction often act as if they were free and responsible agents, who can make over their environment. Indeed, in *Out of the Night,* Professor H. J. Muller, a geneticist and Marxist, proposes ways and means of making over their heredity as well.

Hence there is some justification for the loose popular usage, in which the distinction between realism and naturalism is like that between firmness and obstinacy: if not a matter of sex, at least a distinction in degree rather than in kind. In the actual practice of contemporary fiction, there is no longer a clear division in philosophy and method. Those known as naturalists commonly use plainer language, give greater emphasis to ugly or scatological detail, and in general display a fondness for taking pictures of society with its pants down. Such distinctions, however, are governed by taste or temperament, and are not particularly useful. My honest realism is another's sordid naturalism —and argument is futile.

From any point of view, however, the conventional realist occupies today an unexciting middle ground. Although he can always be sure of a large following of plain readers, there is more buzz about either the more extreme naturalists or the adventurous experimenters. Often, indeed, he is regarded with a kind of good-natured tolerance that is but a polite form of contempt. He is, it would seem, an old dog who is for sentimental reasons allowed to stay in the house, and upon wagging his tail is absently patted on the head. For he is thought to have outlived his usefulness and is tolerated only because of affectionate memories of his frisky youth. As Herbert Gorman, for example, raptly contemplates James Joyce's *A Portrait of the Artist as a Young Man,* he recites this obituary: "It was necessary to comprehend [necessary for those who would appreciate Joyce] that the novel had (within the boundaries more or less arbitrarily set for it) fully flowered and blossomed, that in Gustave Flaubert, and, after him, Henry James, the ultimate possibilities of characterization and mental and spiritual exploration had been exhausted." In other words, the conventional realist today is worrying a dry bone.

Now this, once more, is precocious nonsense. If a survey of the last hundred years makes one hesitate to say with Ecclesiastes that there is no new thing under the sun, it is at least the same sun and it shines as brightly on the countless old things. For centuries genius has restated truisms—and it has not "exhausted" the simplest of them. Life is still an old wives' tale that can be endlessly retold. At the same time, however, it would be unprofitable in this study to discuss in detail the large body of work in the center of the realistic tradition. Its merits are solid and sufficient, but they are also obvious. Much of this work, moreover, contributes little to the quest of new values or to the revaluation of the old.

Dozens of honest, intelligent realistic novelists ply their ancient and honorable trade, with the incidental benefit, perhaps, of a few new tricks, and they are restful to the eye; but to the resolution of the underlying issues of modern life they bring little except their example of modest contentment. When they create something of a sensation, it is over some local, transient issues.

Thus the vigorous fictions of Sinclair Lewis, for instance, are of little importance for my purposes, and even that importance is largely symptomatic. Lewis has a splendid hatred of sham and a gift for vitriolic expression equal to his intensest hates; his satires have had a wide and generally salutary influence. This influence, however, has been like Mencken's largely negative. Once his point is granted and all the boobs and hypocrites are driven to cover —then what? What remains for the decent citizen who accepted his point at the outset and can no longer be sustained by the excitement of the chase? In *Arrowsmith* Lewis began to address the larger issues; but his later novels (*Dodsworth, Work of Art*) make plain what discerning readers of *Babbitt* suspected: that the positive values of Sinclair Lewis are at bottom those of Babbitt —a less blatant Babbitt, that is, shorn of his Elk and Booster buttons and sobered by the depression. This is a decent enough ideal and perhaps sufficient for an ordinary life. But thoughtful men can achieve it only after they have fought their way through problems that Lewis only skims. They accept in resignation what Babbitt aspires to.

There remain, however, a few names so prominent that it is impossible to ignore them in any study of modern fiction from whatever point of view. Arnold Bennett and John Galsworthy, for example, are still figures to be reckoned with. Old-fashioned as they may now appear, they nevertheless helped to crack the simple molds once made to contain life and shape its meaning. They raised, moreover, the larger questions that are my chief concern. "What Life Is" Bennett entitles the last section of *The Old Wives' Tale;* and this is finally the subject of all novelists. But some write in a more philosophical spirit than others, sound deeper undertones and overtones. The best novels of both Bennett and Galsworthy more clearly disengage the everlasting issues than do all but *Arrowsmith* of the novels of Sinclair Lewis.

2

Most of Bennett's work can be dismissed as lightly as he himself turned it out. Quite frankly he wrote to please the public, thereby to earn the means of living in the very best suites in the very best hotels. It is no doubt an ignoble aim; and one might distrust him entirely had he not, in his interest in material rewards, so illustrious a model as Shakespeare. Yet if he put together—and in his Journal carefully counted and complacently recorded—an immense number of words for purely popular consumption, he also took breath from time to time to write primarily for his own satisfaction. In this spirit he produced a few important novels and one great one: *The Old Wives' Tale.* It is one of the monumental novels of this age, remarkable for its firm, unhurried treatment of the whole range of ordinary human affairs.

Firm and unhurried too was Bennett's traffic with the modern world. As a private citizen he bustled, made eager use of the latest conveniences, kept abreast of the latest fashions; as a novelist he remained squarely in the main line of literary tradition and followed none of the fascinating offshoots. His youthful enthusiasm for the naturalists soon died; his desire, he noted in his Journal, was "to depict the deeper beauty while abiding by the envelope of facts." Neither did he attempt by novel or subtle means to pierce this envelope, which was to him always very tangible and solid. He did not explore the dark recesses of the soul nor exploit the intricacies of his private consciousness. The whole trend to subjectivism left him unmoved.

Bennett also failed to share in the downright pessimism of many of his contemporaries. As the life-story of two sisters, *The Old Wives' Tale* ends, appropriately enough, with their deaths; but death is only the inevitable last strand in a pattern in which pain and joy have been inextricably mingled. The sadness emerging from this story comes from the simple perception of what life always and irremediably is. Few writers, indeed, convey more poignantly than Bennett the "pathos of mortality" felt by Christian and agnostic alike. Bright, lovely young girls become old and worn and misshapen and all too often ridiculous. They have their fragrant memories, and they may feel that they have no right to complain; but what has been the end of all their fret and fever? *Vanitas vanitatum!* "Come, children, let us shut up the box and the puppets, for our play is played out."

The life of Sophia Baines is indeed more definitely a tragedy: the tragedy of frustration, of waste and sterility, in a woman of splendid promise. But the starved respectability in the last years of her sister Constance is scarcely even pathetic. Unlike Sophia, she aspired to nothing different; she would have been miserable without her daily round of worries about servants and lapdogs and tea things. And Constance, as Bennett states in his preface, was his chief interest, and her ordinariness the very reason for her position at the center of his bourgeois epic. Upon the journal of her commonplace activities he expended an even more indefatigable, exuberant industry than he did upon the occasional bravura passages punctuating the career of Sophia.

Here we confront the gigantic humdrum realism by which Bennett is known. His stories are saturated with detail, minutely observed and precisely recorded. We know the Five Towns as we know few other localities in fiction. We know the look of every person we meet, of every room we enter, of every street we walk. Bennett's inexhaustible documentation was not animated, moreover, by a scientific or sociological interest. He was not like Wells and Shaw a propagandist, nor like Galsworthy a social philosopher—his novels contain, in fact, few general ideas of any sort. He was excited simply by the perception of fact. I quote at random from the countless matter-of-fact notations in his Journal:

> Characteristic gesture of an old fisherman. He took off his cap, held it upside down under his mouth, dropped his plug (of

> tobacco) into it, and whipped it on his head again, all in the twinkling of an eye.

Or again:

> When a youngish horse is just starting out fresh from the stable in the morning, up a hill, with a light trap behind him, he brings his nose down under his neck, so that the line of the head is parallel with the fore-leg before it takes a step; his hind feet slip a little perhaps on the stones, and he pulls bravely. That is a beautiful sight. It was the first thing I saw, going out yesterday morning.

Hence some critics condemn Bennett as a mere statistician, commendable only for his mole-like industry—a "fact-ridden modernist," incapable of romance or even of reflection. Unquestionably his novels often sag with excess fat. The main characters of the *Clayhanger* trilogy, for example, are not interesting or significant enough to carry the weight of three lengthy volumes; Bennett here treats a very ordinary affair on a scale warranted only by the immense drama of *War and Peace*. Yet it is shallow criticism that makes of him only a grub. Despite his rapt interest in minutiæ he retains, at his best, a clear and broad perspective. He not only makes one see everything; he makes one see clearly what is significant. His details are not misshapen excrescences, as Dreiser's so often are, but live fibers of a rich and glowing whole; the solid masses of *The Old Wives' Tale* are rarely sodden or lumpish. For Bennett does not hack out thick slabs of local color for their own sake. With elaborate care he dresses his characters and sets his stage, but his characters do not then proceed to lose themselves in the scenery. He stands them on their own feet in the foreground, as individuals and not merely as provincial types, and he sacrifices as little of their substance to milieu as to plot or thesis. Few novelists, in fact, keep so firm a grip on the essential elements at once of character and of environment, so just a balance between the individual and the society that molds him.

Bennett's realism is accordingly justified by its deeper meanings. "The novelist," he remarked wisely in his Journal, "should cherish and burnish this faculty of seeing crudely, simply, artlessly, ignorantly; of seeing like a baby or a lunatic, who lives each moment by itself and tarnishes the present by no remembrance of the past." This baby Bennett was—and none has ever been happier with its toys. But he also had intimations of immortality. He was something of the "Mighty Prophet! Seer blest!" with the "Soul's immensity" of Wordsworth's exalted infant. Although he appeared to be wholly immersed in his little world, he still connected it with a larger view. Although with immense industry he recorded the temporal and particular, it was finally to leave a clear impression of the timeless and universal. He achieved at once a complete identification with his material and a high degree of ironic detachment.

Bennett's special gift, however, lay in his ability to make one see people as they see themselves. At bottom one always realizes how ludicrously trivial are the concerns of Constance Baines, how inconsequential her whole existence in any larger view; but one is almost as engrossed as she herself in her stuffy problems. Bennett brings vividly home the simple truth, as often forgotten as remarked, that human emotions are seldom commensurable with their occasion. The child breaks his heart over his toys, the adolescent over his failure to make the team or win the girl; the joys and sorrows of mature men often have causes that later seem as trivial. We should no doubt lament this folly and remember to make the proper discounts in our final judgments; we should also remember that this is the way people are. Similarly we should remember the fundamental identity of all human lives. Despite the significant differences in character and destiny, at the end all come to mean about the same thing. Bennett pictured the romance and the sorrow of life as simple people feel them —but the romance and sorrow felt by sophisticates are much the same. Thus he was able to make his ordinary, his apparently drab, dingy, and repellent material steadily interesting, and even glamorous and moving.

Bennett was by no means, then, the prosaic fellow of common report. For all his common sense and his fondness for fact, he was at heart a romantic. He not only revealed the wonderful strangeness of the familiar, the unsuspected depths of mystery and romance underlying the commonplace; he revealed it as if for the first time. He not only discovered, as Elizabeth Drew has remarked, "the living truth in platitude"; he found this truth exciting. Many moderns exhibit his interest in homely lives, but in few is this interest so eager and delighted. The mainspring of his art was accordingly no uninspired conscientiousness or unimaginative devotion to fact. It was an insatiable curiosity, an unquenchable wonder, an unflagging zest.

This romantic attitude toward ordinary existence helps to explain why Bennett, skeptical and ironic though he was, never approached the paralyzing extremes of pessimism. He was ignorant of the meaning of life, yet he makes it seem meaningful: "the creature hath a purpose, and its eyes are bright with it." He conveys a poignant impression of the sadness of human life, but a still stronger impression of its livableness. It would seem livable if only because his characters hang on to it so stubbornly in the face of the most discouraging circumstance. It seems livable above all, however, because of Bennett's respect for the human spirit in even its humblest shape. He found in lowly lives not only the strangeness and glamor but also the worth that ancient writers found only in the lives of the great. Thus Constance has a genuine dignity in her simple kindliness, devotion, and fortitude. Her mother is at times almost majestic in her forbidding respectability. And her often ludicrous husband is at his death actually heroic, in the same unpretentious, unspectacular way that she is. For Samuel Povey had "the vein of greatness which runs through every soul without exception. . . . He embraced a cause, lost it, and died of it."

All this is not to say, of course, that Bennett attained an Olympian wisdom or sublimity. His Journal alone makes plain why he does not belong with the Immortals. It is indeed a curiously fascinating personal document, despite its reticence, matter-of-factness, and lack of obvious charm. It reveals some excellent qualities: sound literary judgment, a humble admiration of the great Russians and of greatness wherever he recognized it, an unusual capacity for dispassionate, unillusioned estimate of his own work, and frequently a sensitiveness that belies his reputation as a smug, beef-eating Englishman. But it reveals even more clearly that he was a quite ordinary fellow, remarkable only for his prodigious sweating of modest talents that by no stretch of the imagination would have been death to hide.

The limitations of even Bennett's best novels are accordingly obvious. They are occasionally marred by shallow or insular comment, or by a flippancy of style revealing not so much a philosophical irony as the lifelong habit of professional journalism. More serious, they are infected by the gross materialism of most of their characters—a contagion from which Bennett himself was not free. He properly admired the tenacity and fortitude of his people, but despite his detachment he did not perceive steadily how paltry were many of the things they lived for. A full and satisfying life was to him too much a quantitative affair—a matter of living on twenty-four hours a day. At best he was never, like the Russians he admired, passionately concerned about ideals. While writing *The Old Wives' Tale,* he noted methodically that his novel must have an element of "lofty nobility"; and the sensitive reader is at times conscious of the deliberate injection of this necessary ingredient. Nor was Bennett's conception of nobility precisely lofty; the leap to the realms he appoints as the sublime is a short one, and Old Dobbin will do as Pegasus. He exclaims too much, and his ecstasies come too easily. Raptly he dwells on the "miracle" of Constance's last journey to the polls; the reader is touched by her feat, but finds it hard to pump up a grand emotion.

Bennett did not escape, moreover, the defects of his qualities. Simply because he remained so close to average experience and concerned himself primarily with establishing its atmosphere, he did not explore the deepest passional recesses nor soar into the loftier realms of aspiration. He was incapable, in fact, of rendering powerfully the great moments of human passion. Although it has breadth and abundance, his representation of life lacks the robustness and intensity of the masters. *The Old Wives' Tale* is in amplitude at least comparable to *War and Peace;* certainly it never approaches the heights of Tolstoy's masterpiece. Bennett was bright, shrewd, humane, engaging; but he had the reach neither of profound reflection nor of impassioned poetry.

Yet his range remains considerable. One is still impressed by the energy and variety, sensitiveness and gusto, sanity and health—in short by the richness and fulness of his account of human life. At the end one is especially impressed by his natural and sincere reverence for the human spirit; the "vein of greatness" that he sees in the humblest people gives his best work its elevation. He stoops to truth, but he finds it always fascinating and deserving of study. He exalts mankind, not by painting its most majestic representatives, but by ennobling its common humanity. He lends a grace and even a glory to the commonplace. Although he is not himself a great tragic poet, upon this humanistic base great tragedy can still be written.

3

Even the least successful of the efforts of John Galsworthy exhibit the qualities that won him his many admirers. He was always cool and quiet, always kindly and urbane; living amid an increasing din, he never shouted or lost his head. But on one work, *The Forsyte Saga,* rests his claim to fame. Although not until fourteen years after first discovering the Forsytes did he return to them, his other novels, if respectable enough performances, seem in view of this final achievement like so many five-finger exercises. His last novels are so feeble by contrast that it is a kindness to ignore them.

In its outward aspects *The Forsyte Saga* is a chronicle of the ripeness and gradual decay of the Victorian era, a study particularly of the possessive instincts—the sense of property—of the great middle class that was the backbone of this era. Galsworthy's saga is thus a modern species; the title, he is careful to explain in his preface, is used with suitable irony. Although the Forsytes are the main figures in a large scheme, they do not approach in grandeur the heroes of the old epics. They are admirable for their tenacity of purpose, the grim courage with which they face life, but their chief concerns and achievements are essentially paltry. Were they captains of industry who boldly formed and daringly executed large designs—like Cowperwood in Dreiser's *The Titan*—they still might be heroic figures; but they are merely shrewd and cautious. In their pinched, laborious accumulation of pence they cannot capture the imagination. And herein lies one of the obvious limitations of Galsworthy's saga. Great drama cannot be written of the possessive instincts thus manifested. What will cause the Forsytes most anguish is a fall in the price of consols; in this anguish the reader cannot participate deeply.

Yet though *The Forsyte Saga* suffers at times from slavery to period, it is more than the history of a family or even the criticism of an era. Galsworthy emphasizes the more universalized drama of certain individual lives—the lives, above all, of Soames and Irene, and of their children Fleur and Jon. In this view the main theme of the book is the impingement of Beauty and Passion on a possessive world; and on this theme Galsworthy builds a moving, genuinely tragic story.

Most poignant is the tragedy of Fleur and Jon in *To Let*. This is a modern version of *Romeo and Juliet*. Fleur is like Juliet the more direct and practical of the pair; Jon is like Romeo the poet and dreamer. Like Shakespeare's lovers they fall in love at first sight, before they learn of the insurmountable obstacle to their union, and this obstacle is again a family feud. But *To Let* is a realistic, not an idealized, portrait of young love—the sober substitute of the modern age for the glamorous romanticism of the Elizabethans. It raises more difficult problems and arouses more reflective emotions. For the love of Jon and Fleur is not the only issue; they cannot take it unquestioningly as its own complete justification and regard their parents merely as its traditional obstacle. Although directly responsible for the lovers' unhappiness, Soames and Irene call for as much pity as the lovers themselves; the tragedy of these tangled lives is thus amplified and intensified. In its sheer simplicity *Romeo and Juliet* is both more poetic and more dramatic; in conception at least, *To Let* has a deeper humanity.

Fleur and Jon continue to live at the center of *A Modern Comedy,* the sequel to *The Forsyte Saga,* which takes up the story of the modern generation of Forsytes. In the background stand a few survivors of the late Victorian age, some of them amused, some puzzled and irritated, some simply inert and hopelessly uncomprehending. But the main action centers about Fleur. Her one promise of real happiness lost to her with Jon, she finds in variety and novelty a round of insubstantial pleasures. About her is clustered a set as restive, frivolous, and miserably gay as herself. She is the symbol, accordingly, of the whole modern generation as Galsworthy sees it: a rootless generation that whirls and drifts and flounders, that "knows not what it wants, yet is intensely preoccupied with getting it," and that, in Santayana's phrase, redoubles its efforts as it becomes more uncertain of its aims. Such an age, declares Galsworthy in his preface, "must evoke a smile, if rather a sad one"; and so he calls his work *A Modern Comedy.*

A sad smile, and, one might add, at times a pretty wry one. It is often a dismal story, and a distinct falling off from *The Forsyte Saga.* One is uncomfortably aware of Galsworthy's conscientious effort to keep up with the times and maintain a gentlemanly attitude toward a generation that manifestly bewilders and distresses him. He seems old and tired and worn; his tolerance now costs him considerable effort; at times he gives way to something like petulance. No doubt the concerns of his characters are as trivial and absurd as he thinks them—but this is precisely the chief fault of his novel. A hundred pages or so, for example, are devoted to a slander trial in which Fleur is involved, and this incident is typical of her preoccupations. Of such slight and ephemeral stuff great fiction cannot be wrought.

Yet there remains the figure of Soames Forsyte. He has by now a kind of awkward grandeur as he retains his rock-like stability in a floating world, and his presence gives *A Modern Comedy* what impressiveness it has. The creation of Soames is the glory of the work as a whole, and Galsworthy's greatest triumph. For it is indeed a triumph to approach the heroic through so unpromising, ungrateful a subject. From beginning to end Soames is the man of property, measuring almost all things by material values. Although mellowed somewhat by the passing of years and above all by his whole-hearted devotion to his daughter, Fleur—the one feeling in him not tainted by notions of property—he remains essentially the same: stiff, mulish, crusty. At the outset he is a pitiable but always a chill, forbidding figure; in *The Man of Property* our sympathies are entirely with his wife Irene and her lover. But gradually, imperceptibly, we come to feel more tenderly toward him, without once an unpleasant awareness that our sentiments are being played upon. At the end he is an altogether sympathetic, even a heroic figure. He suffers much, in silence and with dignity and fortitude. He dies in the effort to save his daughter's life, which she has deliberately tried to lose after the frustration of her last desperate attempt to win Jon and happiness. During a fire in his art gallery, Fleur stands where the heavy frame of one of his treasured pictures is about to fall; Soames rushes forward to thrust her aside, and himself is crushed. Thus the man of property is killed by the thing he loves. And with his dramatic death the saga appropriately, and rather grandly, ends. It is the swan song of the old Forsyte traditions.

Now, though Galsworthy's saga is not downright tragedy, like most serious modern novels it leaves a somber impression of the ache and fever of life: of a cruel stress and strain, resulting occasionally in catastrophe and tragic death, but more commonly and even more intolerably in the weariness and fretfulness of thwarted effort. This spectacle Galsworthy views with a melancholy and ironic detachment. Hence the fatalism, though less formal and explicit than Hardy's, that pervades his stories: one feels the presence of supernatural forces whose designs are at times almost as freakish as those of Hardy's President of the Immortals. But hence too the infinite pity that distinguishes Galsworthy even in an age that has cultivated this sentiment. As some critic has said, "The very sight of a butterfly makes him think of wheels." At the thought he does not, however, fume and fulminate against society or the gods, as Hardy did. The indignation in his early plays was soon restrained by his native sobriety. In *The Inn of Tranquillity* (a fitting title for this collection of mellow commonplaces) he writes: "The true lover of the human race is surely he who can put up with it in all its forms, in vice as well as in virtue, in defeat no less than in victory."

Thus Galsworthy cultivated the scrupulous fairness for which he is also conspicuous. His fine, if limited, intelligence and his tender sympathy extended even to representatives of causes or ideals he deplored. He never fell into the common error of the zealous reformer, who conjures up inhuman abstractions, like Convention and Liberty, Capital and Labor, and separates his characters into sheep and goats according as they support or oppose his thesis. Galsworthy always felt chiefly the utter humanity of all the embattled and embittered, the mixture of idealism and grossness in the deluded and the inspired alike. A social philosopher, he was never like Shaw or Wells a pamphleteer; the only cause he pleaded was the cause of understanding and forbearance. In *The Pigeon,* a kind of modern morality play, he indicated his distrust of all simple guaranteed remedies, which "lose sight of the individual"; and in *The Foundations* he revealed the only solution he could see: simple kindliness, the foundation of society, is the chief corrective to the evils of the caste system. One may fairly point out the only objection to this beautiful solution: that, practically considered, it is no solution at all. One may add that at times Galsworthy is ponderously and almost excruciatingly fair in his exact balancing of sympathies. One may draw up the whole bill of charges pressed against the unhappy conscientious liberal today. Yet Galsworthy's impartiality is a valuable attitude for the artist, if not for the practical reformer. It enabled him to write tragedies where others wrote tracts.

This same breadth of understanding saved Galsworthy from the excesses of modern pessimism. His darkest visions are not cankered by cynicism or blank despair. His persuasion of the ultimate meaninglessness of human activities did not weaken his faith in the immediate validity of human ideals. "Life for those who still have vital instinct in them," he writes, "is good enough in itself even if it lead to nothing, and we humans have only ourselves to blame if we, alone among animals, so live that we lose the love of life for itself. As for the parts we play, courage and kindness seem to me the only virtues. . . ."

This is an admirably quiet and measured assertion of faith, and a testimony to the advantages of ripeness. It is refreshing, in so restless and strident an age, to encounter so cool, urbane, civilized a spirit as Galsworthy's. It seems almost ungracious, indeed, to point out its deficiencies. Yet deficiencies there are, and so serious that they vitiate his charming art and often make it merely charming. With the main articles of Galsworthy's creed, with his sincere conviction of the fraternity of man and his earnest recommendation of courage and kindness, there should be no quarrel; but in the living embodiment of his values there is often an almost sickly pallor, a tinge of sentimentality, that repels all but the gentlest seekers of salvation. The courage he presents for our edification is often merely schoolboy heroics, the kindness a wistful decency. And the compassionate and apparently austere creator of these spectacles dwindles into a kindly old gentleman who seems hopelessly to miss their real point.

Galsworthy once wrote a short story entitled "The Man Who Kept His Form." It is the story (as I recall) of the born Gentleman who falls far down the social scale but even in rags remains a Gentleman; who is at heart never so contaminated by vulgar circumstance that he loses his notions of what is not cricket. But I cannot be sure of the details, for on this theme Galsworthy played endless variations—in his later work with increasing persistence. Occasionally he embodied his faded ideal in so robust a figure as old Jolyon Forsyte, or so lusty a one as Sylvanus Heythorp. Occasionally he transcended it in a Soames Forsyte. But this constant, wistful concern for the genteel values reveals the softness at the core of Galsworthy's art. His protagonists are for the most part nice people, and they have nice sentiments, but their spiritual reach, their approach to life, is essentially that of the well-bred fox hunter. What accordingly stamps them with futility is the pettiness of their main concerns. They do not come really to grips with life, they never know it profoundly. Earnestly they wrestle with their private and genteel phantoms, which are to them of course very real, but to a hardy reader these encounters seem bloodless and remote—a kind of shadow-boxing in a hothouse. And perhaps most oppressive is the dreadful self-consciousness with which they keep their form. They recall Virginia Woolf's summary of the philosophy of life of her Mrs. Dalloway:

> As we are a doomed race, chained to a sinking ship (her favourite reading as a girl was Huxley and Tyndall, and they were fond of these nautical metaphors), as the whole thing is a bad joke, let us, at any rate, do our part; mitigate the sufferings of our fellow prisoners (Huxley again); decorate the dungeon with flowers and air-cushions; be as decent as we possibly can. Those ruffians, the Gods, shan't have it all their own way—her notion being that the Gods, who never lost a chance of hurting, thwarting, and spoiling human lives, were seriously put out if, all the same, you behaved like a lady.

Obviously it is difficult to give deep significance to the dramas of characters so inherently pallid and so insulated from the raw, brutal, terrifying facts of experience. Chekhov, indeed, wrote stirring and strangely haunting drama of a futile, decadent society. He had the gift of all the great Russians of penetrating directly to the hidden springs of emotion and illumining the deep undercurrents of thought and feeling. He was also able, however, to remain clear of the society he was describing. But Galsworthy was himself too infected with his particular brand of gentility to set it in proper perspective and make a really penetrating study of it. He had some notion of the futility of his society and the inadequacy of its ideals, but he did not entirely escape its limitations. His attitude toward it was, more than tender, nostalgic. And he himself appeared to take a gentle pride in always Keeping His Form.

In short, the gentlemanliness that is the source of Galsworthy's virtues is also, in its exaggerated and insular form, the source of his cardinal defect as a tragic writer. Although he clearly lacked the elemental creative gift that marks genius, his work is weakened more particularly by an excess of restraint, a deliberate shying away from violent emotion or tumultuous conflict. Like Conrad he was wary of extravagant emotional displays as of any form of self-indulgence, but his sobriety came less from a philosophical detachment or an austere artistic code than from the fastidious reserve of a too perfect gentleman. Although he is justly praised for his perfect self-mastery, one suspects that he did not have particularly unruly emotions to master. One does not even feel the effort of suppression, the presence of explosive forces under the impassive manner proper to tragedy. His melancholy is a gentle melancholy, quite lacking in wild, strange, rebellious moments. Even his fine impartiality comes to seem a mere fear of letting himself go—a more passionate writer would be less meticulously disinterested. Ultimately Galsworthy recalls Leslie Stephen's description of Sir Charles Grandison: a showman leading his perfectly tamed passions from scene to scene. This is no doubt unfair to the author of *The Forsyte Saga*—and this whole disparagement of his civilized art unnecessarily harsh. But one who recollects his reference to buttercups as "those little bright pieces of flower china out of the Great Pottery," his indulgence in the sentiment inspired by "Man playing his little, not unworthy, part in the great game of Perfection," will feel less compunction.

There is at any rate little grandeur in Galsworthy's tragedy, and however large its frame, no bigness. It is more often touching than moving; it is too seldom passionate and intense to arouse awe. In *The Forsyte Saga* he reached heights that justify his inclusion among the important writers of this age, but at the end his art seems slender, pallid, meager. This impression of deficient vitality no doubt owes partly to faults in technique. As Professor Beach points out, Galsworthy's constant shifting of scene and point of view before he has really sunk his teeth into his situations dilutes and diffuses their dramatic effect. But his failure solidly to develop his scenes is most conspicuous when he approaches what ought to be the great moments in his stories;

and here one feels that the explanation is again a too gentlemanly reserve, if not a simple inability to rise to the emotional heights demanded. His is an art primarily for drawing-room exercises. It is too refined to embrace the elemental conflicts and the terrible, turbulent emotions of great tragedy. It is unequal to the *Sturm und Drang* of the modern world.

4

Popular since the beginnings of English fiction, still popular in this sophisticated age, and because of its natural interest likely to be perpetually popular is the simple type of biographical novel (today characteristically often autobiographical) that leads the hero through childhood, adolescence, and young manhood, and leaves him, finally stripped of his swaddling cloths, facing in the direction in which presumably he is to fulfil his destiny. Samuel Butler's *The Way of All Flesh,* Somerset Maugham's *Of Human Bondage,* D. H. Lawrence's *Sons and Lovers,* and James Joyce's *A Portrait of the Artist as a Young Man* are among the conspicuous modern variations on this ancient theme. All, however, are conceived in a distinctly new spirit; the theme is at times unrecognizable for the variations. Tom Jones and David Copperfield travel a broad, well-beaten highway that has many windings but finally straightens out and leads direct to the rainbow; each fulfils his simple destiny by winning the right girl. The modern hero, however, often turns off on strange byways where he has more fearful adventures. If in the end he arrives at the same destination, it is in a very different mood; and he is lucky to arrive anywhere at all. What Lawrence and Joyce did to this simple form I shall discuss later, but the less exotic performance of Maugham may appropriately be considered at this point.

Although *The Moon and Sixpence* and *Cakes and Ale* are excellent novels, most of Maugham's work is in a relatively light vein, and is addressed to a fashionably smart audience. Its virtues are less brittle than many suppose; at the same time they are scarcely solid or deeply significant. *Of Human Bondage,* however, is a wholly earnest and an important novel. It is in some ways superior to *The Way of All Flesh,* which is more highly regarded in aristocratic critical circles. Despite some memorable characters and scenes, Butler's novel is a novel of ideas with most of the defects of that genus. Although his ideas were in advance of his time and are still stimulating, they are too often presented in essay form, too seldom dramatized. Moreover, they no longer bear directly on the deepest issues of modern life: Ernest Pontifex, Butler's hero, finally achieves integrity and happiness by the relatively simple expedient of throwing off the shackles of conventions that unhappy contemporaries have begun by discarding. *Of Human Bondage,* however, is much more than a forum or a slaughter-house of decrepit conventions. Although it contains abundant discussion of ideas, Maugham vitalizes the intellectual content of his story by embodying it in vivid personalities and suffusing it with emotion. This emotion, furthermore, has its roots in something more fundamental than a maladjustment with the forms of a particular society. As the biography of a typically nervous modern, *Of Human Bondage* naturally deals with the peculiar difficulties of the contemporary world; but at bottom it deals with the problems that eternally torture sensitive and thoughtful men. It considers the terms of life in this or any age.

Yet in one significant aspect Butler and Maugham are alike—and join Lawrence and Joyce. In effect if not in theory, all reject determinism. Where the naturalists emphasized primarily the compulsions of heredity and environment, they emphasize finally the will of the individual who rebels and struggles to achieve his own peculiar destiny. Their heroes are conditioned by their society, but they are never simply its pawns. They may insist upon a higher responsibility from their society, but they also maintain their responsibility to themselves. Even when they choose to conform, their choice is a free choice. Whether they win or lose in their struggles, they have asserted an independent will.

Philip Carey, the hero of *Of Human Bondage,* is like Ernest Pontifex one who wins. After a stormy youth he finally looks into a future that promises as much serenity and happiness as man has a right to expect. Maugham's premises are nevertheless thoroughly pessimistic, as Butler's are not—and here again he speaks more pertinently, if not more wisely, to this generation. Philip finds peace only after he has stamped out his bright illusions, swallowed his splendid hopes, and soberly accepted life for the harsh, pointless business that Maugham thinks it is. Human life is in any larger view utterly meaningless: this is the central idea of his novel. Man has no special destiny, and by living serves no glorious end. He cannot direct his life with reference to a transcendental order. He lives, for all practical purposes, at the heart of a vast nothingness; and only when Philip Carey has "wrenched from chaos the secret of its nothingness" does he find peace.

It is important, however, that he does find it. Despite his bleak pessimism, Maugham does not resign himself to mere futility. In the cosmic scheme man is impotent; he can nevertheless work his life into a beautiful pattern, even though it die with him and be known only to himself. A Persian rug, Maugham points out, has no meaning in itself, but it affords the weaver esthetic pleasure; in the same spirit man can order his life. Philip Carey dreams of different patterns, rich and varied, and begins consciously to weave the more fascinating of them. But one by one he rejects them, and ultimately finds happiness, as do the more fortunate of Hardy's heroes, in the simplest of all: man was born, he toiled for his bread, he married and reared children, and he died. We leave Philip about to marry a simple, wholesome, good-natured girl and live the life of a country doctor.

This doctrine of life for art's sake may be insubstantial and unsatisfying to mankind at large. It is certainly a highly self-conscious way of carrying on the search for happiness, and demands a considerable talent for mental legerdemain. Maugham's own subsequent career might indicate that it does not provide the firmest of foundations for absolute integrity and complete self-fulfilment. Yet it is significant as an honest, thoughtful answer to the dilemma of the modern man: Maugham managed to find a way out of a seemingly impossible situation. Others will work out different and perhaps more universally acceptable solutions; he has at least supplied another argument that the thoroughgoing pessimism of the moderns does not, at its soberest, necessarily poison the springs of vitality.

XIV

JOSEPH CONRAD

I

A DECADE after his death Joseph Conrad already fulfils the conditions necessary to becoming a classic: he is more admired than read, and read chiefly in the classroom. Few openly disparage him; as few make any reference to him at all. Yet he has substantial claims to greatness. Of his contemporaries none saw life more steadily or recorded his vision with a sincerity more passionate and austere; and none preserved a more complete detachment from the tangled ephemera of the modern world. From first to last he adhered rigorously to the purpose stated in the famous Preface to *The Nigger of the Narcissus:*

> My task which I am trying to achieve is, by the power of the written word, to make you hear, to make you feel,—it is, before all, to make you *see*. That—and no more, and it is everything. If I succeed, you shall find there according to your deserts: encouragement, consolation, fear, charm—all you demand and, perhaps, also that glimpse of truth for which you have forgotten to ask.

This very detachment, with his devotion to a purely esthetic ideal, helps to explain Conrad's rather curious status in modern fiction. One of the greater writers of this age, he was also in some important respects always a stranger to it. Its special interests were not his interests; his genius does not bear a clear imprint of its peculiar pressure. In time he takes his place among the Edwardian novelists, in his technique he joins the Georgian pioneers, but in spirit he belongs to neither. Hence he disturbs those critics who are unhappy until they have classified all that comes before them as fish or fowl.

In the first place, Conrad is obviously not the conventional realist. He was not like Bennett a close observer of everyday life (Mrs. Conrad tells of his exclamation of surprise when first looking at his baby son: "Why! It's just like a human being!"—an inaccurate observation at that) and he did not systematically document or analyze. Neither did he draw so literally from his own unusual experience as is often supposed: this experience underwent a wonderful sea change before it appeared in his fictions. And although these fictions were like himself invincibly romantic, he was yet not a shallow romantic seeking in fantasy an escape from the commonplace. Flaubert himself did not struggle with more terrifying earnestness to render the exact truth of human experience as he saw it; certainly few realists have felt so ascetic a responsibility to their visions. Various critics have accordingly attempted to define his "romantic realism" or "realistic romance"—and succeeded only in illustrating once more the inadequacy of these labels, the similarity in the basic material and final effect of all great fiction.

If label there must be, "impressionist" is the most suitable for Conrad. The appeal of a novel, he wrote, "must be an impression conveyed through the senses." This impression, however, could never be conveyed through the most complete inventory of details; it is an intuitive whole and must be rendered so, instantaneously. Thus he approached life as if it were a wonderfully skittish and chameleon-like animal that is as dead as a stuffed owl once it has been caught and photographed in a frozen attitude. "The meaning of an episode is not inside like a kernel but outside enveloping it," his spokesman Marlow declared; and the object of all Conrad's agonized effort was to evoke this enveloping atmosphere, to render the shimmer and shadowiness that were to him the essence of reality. Hence his concern with point of view and tone, his habit of telling his story at several removes, his avoidance of generalized narrative, his disregard of chronology and of other conventionalizations of perception. Hence too the mysteriousness and shadowiness that blur the edges of all his scenes and characters. It is not the mere vagueness that Sherwood

Anderson often mistakes for profundity; it is the mysteriousness of all experience that is completely *felt*—the mysteriousness of the eternal gap between sensation and thought.

As Dr. Welsey Carroll points out in his subtle thesis on Conrad, Conrad's entire career as novelist strangely but strikingly resembles that of Marcel Proust. The romantic sea captain and the neurasthenic esthete both retired from the active world to recover from their consciousness all of enduring worth, and they had the same conception of their task: not a logical analysis of their memories, with the object of filing them according to some neat index, but a "complete realization of anterior experience through the recovery of actual sensory impressions." They both freely exercised intellect as an aid in elucidating their impressions, but in Conrad particularly the intellectual content is all held in suspension. His commentary is a speculative supplement or tangential hypothesis; when most illuminating it still does not dissolve the mystery or transfix the characters. The essence of Conrad is pure sensory impression, at his best rendered with extraordinary vividness and immediacy.

In all this Conrad is in line with one of the important movements in modern fiction. Yet his subject matter remains strikingly different. He seldom entered either the drawing room or the market place of his society; neither did he withdraw to its fashionable retreats. He remained entirely aloof from the industrial world, and he showed no interest in the paler, attenuated emotions or the complicated maladjustments or any of the special problems and peculiar attitudes of a sophisticated society. When he approached European civilization at all, as he did in *The Secret Agent* and *Under Western Eyes,* it was to deal with revolutionists and anarchists—in short with its most lawless, least civilized elements. But his best and most characteristic work treats of simple seafaring men in remote, primitive countries, and its drama of primal emotions is set against the background of elemental nature.

"An Elizabethan gentleman" is one of Ford Madox Ford's descriptions of his friend Conrad, and Conrad's novels do indeed suggest, more than any of our time, the tragedies of Shakespeare. He had the Elizabethan fondness for exciting incident and exotic setting, violent conflict and gorgeous pageantry. Though his heroes are not of noble rank, they are typically of large dimensions—in their own world imposing, statuesque figures. Like Shakespeare's heroes they grapple with external forces often objectified in the shape of villains; like them too they are still lustrous in defeat and death. His tragedy has in general much the same pomp and stir, passion and glow. Conrad recaptured the glamor that many sober contemporaries believe to have permanently departed our literature, or at most to survive only in the tawdry trappings of popular romance.

2

With these sober contemporaries Conrad has nevertheless strong blood ties. His tragedy is not an atavistic performance; it does not, like *Cyrano de Bergerac,* provide simply a glorious romantic spree. For its philosophical basis is an invincible pessimism that again raises the peculiar issues of modern literature. However dark and deadly, the world of Shakespeare appears to be governed by a moral order, or at least has a definitely moral complexion. Conrad's world is utterly soulless, unintelligible from any rational point of view. All he could make out was a "mysterious arrangement of merciless logic for a futile purpose." Even his many villains do not imply a disturbance of the natural order. Ordinarily they are simply grotesque, like so much else in Conrad's primitive society; but when, like the spectral Mr. Jones of *Victory* or the vicious Brown of *Lord Jim,* they become the concentrated essence of malevolence, they appear to be, in Conrad's own words, blind accomplices of the Dark Powers. From first to last he carried with him a conviction of the "immense indifference of things"—an indifference so callous that it often seems, as in Hardy, downright malignancy. "The sea and the earth are unfaithful to their children; a truth, a faith, a generation of men goes—and is forgotten, and it does not matter." Noble and ignoble are destroyed with a fine impartiality. Almayer, Willems, and Verloc are miserably weak and ineffectual; Captain Whalley is ruined because of his very nobility. Of them all Conrad appears to say what he said of the characters of Alphonse Daudet: they "*marchent à la mort*—and they are very near the truth of our common destiny; their fate is poignant, it is intensely interesting, and of not the slightest consequence."

This vision of life is plainly not, strictly speaking, a philosophy. Although it was recently dignified by being made the subject of a philosophical exercise for Ph.D. purposes (*Joseph Conrad: His Philosophy of Life,* by W. W. Bancroft), the author did all the heavy work. Conrad had no genuine philosophical interests, and even distrusted such interests ("Nothing humanly great . . . has come from reflection"). Unlike Hardy, he never systematized his prejudices. In his letters he occasionally liked to call life a machine, and as he played with this figure he indeed suggests *The Dynasts:* "And the most withering thought is that the infamous thing has made itself: made itself without thought, without conscience, without foresight, without eyes, without heart. It is tragic accident. . . ." He adds, characteristically, "and nothing matters." Such statements, however, are only expressions of a fancy or mood. They present not a philosophy but a feeling.

Yet it is a well defined, impersonal feeling that colors almost every page Conrad wrote. The main scheme of his novels is accordingly as simple as it is persistent. His heroes are always engaged in hopelessly unequal conflicts with the Dark Powers; if they escape absolute destruction, it is only to carry away an ineradicable memory of the inscrutable, implacable, uncompassionate masters of their destiny. Still worse, the Powers appear to be grim practical jokers. "It is to be remarked," says Marlow, "that a good many people are born curiously unfitted for the fate awaiting them on this earth." From these people Conrad chooses his heroes; he is forever thrusting them into impossible situations that by nature and training they are ludicrously unprepared to meet. Heyst, Lingard, Nostromo, Decoud, Verloc, and many others could testify to the freakishness of celestial whims, but Willems of

An Outcast of the Islands will do for an example. He is rushed headlong to infamy and death by a passion that he himself realized to be wholly unreasonable, doomed from its outset to a miserable end. For he and Aissa "had nothing in common—not a thought, not a feeling; he could not make clear to her the simplest motive of any act of his . . . and he could not live without her." The dreary futility of the entire drama is emphasized in the last scene: a maudlin conversation between a tipsy traveler and the sulky, irritable Almayer. Almayer shakes his fist at the grave of Willems and voices the pious hope that his soul has found no mercy; and we learn that Aissa is grown a hag. Such, as Conrad sees them, are the workings of Providence.

It is a tribute to the subtlety and intensity of Conrad's art that an irony so insistent as this rarely seems labored and arbitrary. Like the irony of Hardy it is a prejudice, a violent wrenching of common experience; but where Hardy baldly states, Conrad evokes and suggests. His attitude is less externalized in invented incident than it is diffused in the clinging atmosphere that gives his stories, separately and as a body, their profound unity. Also pervasive and still more fundamental in Conrad's art, however, is a withering sense of solitariness. "We live as we dream—alone," says Marlow; and Conrad is obsessed with this inescapable, desolating condition of experience. Lord Jim, Emilia Gould, Nostromo, Lingard, Verloc, Captain Whalley, Heyst and Lena—all are alone in their struggles, all feel the "tremendous fact of our isolation, of the indestructible loneliness that surrounds, envelops, clothes every human soul from the cradle to the grave, and, perhaps, beyond." There is only Marlow to understand, and even he sees as through a veil, dimly.

One explanation of this obsession is Conrad's untiring search for the secret inner truth that explains all surface phenomena, his endless concern with the strange, private, mysterious essence of the individual's soul that distinguishes and also isolates it from every other soul. Few writers, in fact, have managed to convey so deep a sense of the strangeness underlying the familiarity of the world of ordinary appearance. But in *The Polish Heritage of*

Joseph Conrad, Gustav Morf suggests another explanation: Conrad was simply projecting his own fate as an expatriate. After he had transplanted himself in England, he liked to consider himself thoroughly English in sympathies, and had, indeed, a characteristically romantic devotion to English traditions and ideals, especially those that inspired the merchant marine. Actually, however, he remained very much a Pole—an alien at heart to the end of his days. Certainly he was not rooted, like Hardy, in the English soil, nor like Galsworthy in English society. Although his short story "Amy Foster" is the most thinly disguised expression of his loneliness in a strange land, almost all his heroes are like himself outcasts, melancholy and aloof.

It would seem, then, that Conrad's world is a pretty chill and comfortless one. Somber, sinister, inscrutable, unfathomable, inexorable—these are among his favorite adjectives, and he is lavish in his use of them. This obsession with impotence and frustration, chorused by heavenly mockery and keyed by human loneliness, indubitably narrows his art. Although he explicitly rejected, with the "fettering dogmas" of the romantic or naturalistic creeds, the conventional philosophical attitudes, pointing out that what is "so hopelessly barren in declared pessimism is just its arrogance," clearly he was himself often guilty of this arrogance; and his imaginative powers were to that extent fettered. The unvarying formula of his tragedy results in a kind of monotony. His heroes are characteristically serious-minded men who rarely smile and never laugh, and he introduces few simple people to shade his pictures. He almost never descends to the level of ordinary human life, with its blessed trivialities and absurdities; he seems blind to the ordinary man's acceptance of life as a toilsome, perhaps wearisome and perplexing, but not necessarily desperate business. And occasionally he writes a story like "Freya of the Seven Isles," in which suffering is so outrageously unjust and evil so completely dominant that the tragedy is merely painful.

Many readers are accordingly repelled by what they deem the unmitigated cheerlessness of Conrad's world. They object, moreover, to his apparent coldness. He seems to watch his men go down to defeat with as much unconcern as the gods themselves; his own comment would appear to be, "It does not matter." Some of his remarks, to be sure, are inconsistent. "Ah, Davidson, woe to the man whose heart has not learned while young to hope, to love—and to put its trust in life!"—these are the last words of Heyst, and plainly they are Conrad's own commentary on the story of *Victory*. But why, one wonders, should one trust a life that has been so harsh to Heyst and Lena—not to mention the long list of his disenchanted heroes? And why, then, does Conrad himself remain so aloof?

If this question of the sources of consolation is by now all too familiar, at least the answer in Conrad is somewhat different. He had not the profound compassion that distinguishes much modern tragedy. Although his treatment of Lord Jim and some of his sea captains is obviously tender, he was too consistently detached and ironic to display openly much love of man. He often prided himself, in fact, upon an Olympian isolation. "The attitude of cold unconcern is the only reasonable one," he once wrote to a friend; and he accordingly professed a dislike for "The End of the Tether," perhaps the most pathetic of his tales, because it seemed to him unrestrained and therefore sentimental.

Yet Conrad was far less unconcerned than at times he liked to think. We have his own words in the Familiar Preface to *A Personal Record*. He was resigned, yes—

> But resignation is not indifference. I would not like to be left standing as a mere spectator on the bank of the great stream carrying onward so many lives. I would fain claim for myself the faculty of so much insight as can be expressed in a voice of sympathy and compassion.

Even in his bitterest visions he was heartened by an "invincible conviction of solidarity"; "the recognition of the hard facts of existence shared with the rest of mankind becomes a point of view from which the very shadows of life appear endowed with an internal glow." That he "forgets to strew paper roses over the tombs" is not to say that he lacks sympathy. The point is simply that he is wary of extravagant emotional displays. In these the writer is likely to become a victim of his own exaggeration, "losing the exact notion of sincerity, and in the end coming to despise truth itself as something too cold, too blunt for his purpose. . . . From laughter and tears the descent is easy to sniveling and giggles." For if human affairs deserve pity, they are worthy of respect too:

> And he is not insensible who pays them the undemonstrative tribute of a sigh which is not a sob, and of a smile which is not a grin. Resignation, not mystic, not detached, but resignation open-eyed, conscious, and informed by love, is the only one of our feelings for which it is impossible to become a sham.

This is an austere artistic code, and it is largely because of Conrad's scrupulous fidelity to it that he has been misjudged. He remained "always faithful to that sobriety wherein there is power and truth and peace." Underneath his sobriety, however, the discerning reader will perceive a genuine sympathy. But even the undiscerning reader should find as well a source of positive exhilaration; and this is Conrad's immense, unwearying zest for life. Unlike Hardy, he did not despair because of his assumptions about life. He not only accepted a destiny "of not the slightest consequence," but delighted in life simply as a spectacle. "I have come to suspect," he wrote in *A Personal Record,* "that the aim of creation cannot be ethical at all. I would fondly believe that its object is purely spectacular: a spectacle for awe, love, adoration, or hate, if you like, but in this view—and in this view alone—never for despair!" Thus he stood before life endlessly fascinated, a thrall to "the visible wonder, the haunting terror, the infinite passion, and the illimitable serenity; to the supreme law and the abiding mystery of the sublime spectacle." His whole attitude is summed up in his attitude toward the sea, to which no writer has paid more radiant tribute. Early in his career his eyes were opened by an experience with a shipwrecked crew, and he lost his youthful awed reverence for the sea. Now he could look coolly at the life of his choice; and he wrote, "The ocean has no compassion, no faith, no law, no memory . . . nothing can touch the bitterness of its heart." Yet when his illusions were gone his fascination remained. "Its cruelty was redeemed by the charm of its inscrutable mystery, by the immensity of its promise, by the supreme witchery of its possible favor. Strong men with childlike hearts were faithful to it, were content to live by its grace—to die by its will."

And so was Conrad content. In the introduction to *Chance,* in which the controlling powers seem most wanton and soulless, he signs his testament: "The history of man on this earth since the beginning of ages may be resumed in one phrase of infinite poignancy: They were born, they suffered, they died. . . . Yet it is a great tale!" A great tale!—this poet's cry echoes up and down the novels. Even when his heroes are weak and contemptible, he gives their tragedy glamor by getting into it the sense of the immense, the mysterious, the awful—the sublime. He does not refer the reader merely to the puny endeavors of man; he leads him insensibly into a vaster world that, however terrible, is never mean. Thus even the sordid drama of Almayer takes on a kind of solemnity because of the dark magnificence of the background against which it is enacted.

This perpetual wonder at the strangeness of life and this love for its pageantry, together with his tireless pursuit of the essential truth beneath its appearances, give Conrad's novels their depth and universality. His characters are seldom familiar types with whom we can readily identify ourselves. They are instead highly original figures, involved in strange actions, dwelling in a shadowy world peculiarly their own. But Conrad is able to make us feel at home in this world. Behind his scenes, as Hugh Walpole writes, is a "lyrical impulse that unites them with all the emotion and beauty in the history of the world." In the consciousness of his lonely heroes is to be found the consciousness of the race, and in the story of their thwarted lives "the 'ideal' value of things" that was always his primary concern.

More specifically, however, the chief source of this ideal value, of the ideal pleasure in Conrad's tragedy, lies in his display of the resplendence of the human spirit. No other modern novelist has created so many large, vital characters who can powerfully stir and capture the imagination—simple but splendid fellows like Lingard, old Giorgio, Captain Whalley, Captain Anthony, Lord Jim. Facing a massive indifference, they are never themselves indifferent; marching to certain destruction, they are not merely resigned. In defeat they lose none of their force and stature. However futile, their struggles are accordingly not meaningless, for in death they still affirm an idealism that is the triumph of life.

This magnificent vitality of Conrad's greater characters distinguishes them from most of their fellows in modern fiction, who have to contribute something of their substance to some kind of deterministic view. All are in his view at the mercy of "unprovoked malevolence"; but they choose their own ground and they fight their own battle. For they are not the products of their social environment, living as they do in a relatively uncivilized and unregulated world, and they are not at the mercy of an industrial organization. Similarly they are free from the less external determinism implicit in the psychoanalytical approach. Although Conrad's researches into the human soul are remarkably subtle and penetrating, they are carried on intuitively, impressionistically, without the apparatus of the ordinary psychological investigator that makes the hero seem more like a patient than an agent; and he does not enter the field of the definitely abnormal, where the individual is enslaved by complexes beyond his understanding or control. In short, his emphasis is finally less upon the implacable might of the Dark Powers than upon the integrity, gallantry, and fortitude of man that make him a worthy antagonist, and his defeat no occasion for abject despair.

3

If Conrad's approach to life is pessimistic, it is clearly, then, also romantic and idealistic. His whole adventurous career testifies to a romanticism as incurable as that of his own Lord Jim; and he was never more adventurous than when, his youth past, he deliberately forsook the life he knew and embarked upon a literary career in a foreign land, and a strange, difficult tongue. This romanticism explains, indeed, why his reputation suffers at this day a partial eclipse. His repeated references to the Point of Honor have an archaic sound to a generation preoccupied with the intricacies of the gold standard, the relations of Capital and Labor, the laws of supply and demand in all fields of activity. He appears remote, naïve, hopelessly out of touch. No less strange is the simplicity of his faith in an age mistrustful of simplicities and oppressed by a conviction of infinite complexity. For however unintelligible to Conrad the cosmic scheme, however mysterious and elusive the inner life of man, his world is fundamentally not complex. Man's activities are directed by but a few simple principles, a few humble truths. "Those who read me," he writes in the Familiar Preface, "know my conviction that the world, the temporal world, that is, rests on a very few simple ideas, so simple that they must be as old as the hills. It rests notably, among others, on the idea of Fidelity."

The "idea" of fidelity, he declares; but it was to him again a pure feeling—a feeling got from his life at sea, not a conviction arrived at through ratiocination. This feeling, however, shaped all his characters and themes. His heroes are typically simple men; those he admires are gallant, eminently trustworthy fellows, so honest and straightforward that they may appear "stupidly guileless." He extols their elemental virtues, above all "that manful simplicity which alone can bear men unscathed in mind and body" through an encounter with the sea. This was what enabled Captain MacWhirr of *Typhoon* to pass through the nightmare of the elements untouched; and though Conrad is aware of the bewildered, unimaginative, almost doltish gallantry of the man, of the irony in his total incomprehension of the titanic forces attempting to accomplish his destruction, he has nevertheless a genuine affection for him and puts his faith in just such devotion, however stupefied, to an ideal of duty. In this love of simple people and trust in the humble virtues Conrad is again like Hardy—even to the extent of sharing his distrust of sophisticated society. He was less provincial than Hardy, wider in the range of his understanding and more detached in his observation; but he felt really at home only in the world of ships and their men. His least successful novels are generally those in which he dealt more with sophisticated, self-conscious people, whose conduct is less clearly governed by a "few very simple ideas," and in whom he accordingly could not so whole-heartedly believe. He appears to have looked up somewhat wistfully to Henry James, the "historian of fine consciences."

Among his sturdy sea captains there often strays, to be sure, a pronounced intellectual like Martin Decoud, and it is instructive to see what Conrad makes of him. Decoud is melancholy, skeptical, ironic, aloof. So too are his fellow intellectuals in Conrad's pages: Heyst, Mills, Stein, Kennedy, and above all the "discreet" and gifted Marlow. Yet they too illustrate Conrad's values; when their disenchantment leads to complete detachment and loss of faith in human nature itself, then, like Heyst and Decoud, they are destroyed with those they distrust or despise. In fact they are all, with slight variations, editions of Conrad himself—the intellectual Conrad, that is. They are a sign of the double vision that, as Virginia Woolf has remarked, enabled him to celebrate seafaring life as romantically and fervently as Marryat and at the same time to subject it to a cool, subtle, almost fastidious analysis. Hence even his simple characters remain a little mysterious and elusive, and are not merely romantic types. They are built up gradually, as if by a process of discovery; they are moved by obscure impulses, undefined emotions never quite clearly perceived; they are still a little shadowy at the end. Lord Jim "passes away under a cloud, inscrutable at heart"—and so do Conrad's other heroes. Yet they are not really complex. What impressed Conrad was just the strangeness of the human soul—the strangeness of the simplest sensation, and its resistance to definition or analysis. Whatever impression of complexity he leaves, his heroes are typically compounded of but a few elements, and guided in their conduct by but a few principles.

In keeping with such views is Conrad's predilection for barbarous scenes and violent action. He used almost exclusively the baldest and crudest materials—native uprisings, revolutions, anarchistic outrages, and the like. For one thing he was simply writing of the kind of life with which he was most familiar, from both his heritage of a romantic ancestry and his own experience. More significant, however, is that in this life he could most effectively illustrate the working of his "few simple ideas." In a more crowded, complicated society he could not so plainly make out his values; what seemed to him the fundamental issues are obscured by the confusion of transient interests and superficial forms. "'He steered with care,' coming at the end of a storm, carried in it a whole morality," observes Virginia Woolf; in the modern world such terse statements have less rich or clear significance. The essential stuff in man is buried underneath the refinements of civilization, and is perhaps never put to the test of simple Fidelity. Hence Conrad stripped off these refinements, isolated the individual among the elemental realities of nature, and thrust him almost brutally into some crisis in which he must rely on his own resources.

This is plainly an arbitrary practice, and in this day one dangerous to recommend. When the individual is perforce a cog in an immense, intricate machine and must constantly make the peculiar adjustments demanded by this embarrassing position, it lays Conrad open to the charge of irrelevance. Certainly social and economic problems are today fundamental, and difficult for the responsible artist to ignore. But certainly too they are not the necessary subject matter of all artists. What finally matters most is the spirit that dictates the artist's choice of materials; and Conrad's spirit was not that of evasion or mere wishful fantasy. He did not, like Stevenson, aim to provide an "escape" from the actual—nothing irked him more than to be known merely as a writer of sea stories. The escape he offers is, in his own words, from "perishable activity into the light of imperishable consciousness." He ignored the forms of contemporary life only to isolate more plainly the basic patterns of experience. Although his values are inadequate, or at least in need of translation into the terms of contemporary experience, they are not irrelevant. Something is to be said for going directly to the bedrock of human nature, if only to rediscover what is there.

In employing the stock in trade of the sensational novelist, Conrad was at any rate not himself striving for the sensational. His primary concern was that of all great novelists: desire and emotion, the conflict between aspiration and actuality. It was not shocking action for its own sake, but the soul of man under the stress of such action. In his exciting tales he often passed hurriedly over or merely suggested the most obviously exciting incidents—in *The Arrow of Gold,* for example, they take place off stage. He was interested less in effects than in causes, less in actions than in states of mind; and to this extent, at least, he was a typical modern. In short, though he was obviously fond of barbarous and exotic scenes, of violent and spectacular conflicts, his concern as an artist was primarily with the truths about human character and experience that they would yield, and this concern makes his often shopworn, apparently cheap materials glow with a profoundly new and fascinating significance. His novels do not merely startle, and they never descend to mere melodrama. They remain on the level of high tragedy; they generate the reflective emotions that are the end of such tragedy.

4

Of Conrad's novels separately little more need be said. All reflect the same vision of life, affirm the same values. His early novels grew more directly out of reminiscence, and are marked by a tenderness and lyricism that in time were chastened; he became less prodigal with adjectives and epithets. In his later novels there is also some falling off in power, and some suggestion of concession to popular taste—as perhaps in the greater prominence given to woman and love (his world was naturally a predominantly masculine one), and in the occasional consolation of a subdued happy ending. But as a tragic poet there was in his career no significant development.

His most popular work is apparently *Lord Jim*. This is not surprising; it is the most tender, romantic, clearly triumphant of his tragic stories. As it contains the quintessence of his personality, it is also prized by most lovers of Conrad—whose enthusiasm, like that of most devotees, is kindled less by the author's greatness than by his peculiar personal charm. It is of added interest because of Gustav Morf's plausible suggestion that Lord Jim is Conrad himself, and the story of his splendid rehabilitation the sublimation of Conrad's secret fear that in leaving Poland for the sea, at a time when it was struggling for its freedom, he had been guilty of dishonor. He was manifestly romantic enough to consider his departure a desertion, and neurotic enough to brood over it.

Yet to at least one reader who has come under the spell of his charm, Conrad's masterpiece is *Nostromo*. Of all his tales it is certainly the widest in scope. In the largeness of its canvas, the sweep of its action, the stature of its actors, the intensity and universality of its passions, it has the quality of the epic. As one of the great novels of modern times, it deserves especial comment; but it is as well a virtually complete statement of the art and philosophy of Conrad.

Nostromo is in the first place unmistakably a complete statement of Conrad's pessimism. Even the minor characters bear the message of the terrible impotence of man and the "irremediable joylessness of human condition." Linda and Don José Avellanos fail in the passionate quest that has given life meaning to them; the superb Antonia Avellanos is left to mourn in barrenness the deaths of a father and a lover; old Giorgio's wife dies in the bitter conviction that the hope that has been the passion of her last days is to be unfulfilled; the trader Hirsch, a prey to the abjectest fears for his safety, meets through these fears the most grotesque and miserable end of all. In the fates of the more important characters, however, this sense of frustration becomes almost overpowering. Emilia Gould, "all alone in the Treasure House of the World," loses in her struggle to preserve the love and comradeship of her husband and prevent his enslavement by "material interests"; we leave her hopelessly resigned, like a "good fairy, weary with a long career of well-doing, touched by the withering suspicion of the uselessness of her labors, the powerlessness of magic." Martin Decoud kills himself, a "victim of the disillusioned weariness which is the retribution meted out to intellectual audacity." And Nostromo himself—the "magnificent capataz de cargadores" whose first appearances on the stage were an unbroken series of triumphs—dies, after terrible suffering, in a hospital bed, a "victim of the disenchanted vanity which is the reward of audacious action." Each is swallowed up in the "immense indifference," leaving behind an unanswered and unanswerable question. For all this frustration, the fantastic and sordid futility of the national life of Costaguana forms an appropriate background.

Worked into this tragic pattern is Conrad's most characteristic theme: the searing loneliness of all these unfortunates. They are engaged in a common struggle, but their motives, aspirations, and whole inner lives are so unlike that each lives in a mournful world of his own. There is none to understand the passion of Linda or her mother, none to pity the miserable Hirsch, none except his daughter to share the exaltation and despair of Don José. Nostromo must bear alone the crushing weight of his bondage to the stolen treasure. Martin Decoud, in spirit always detached from the extravagant tragi-comedy being enacted about him, at length finds himself alone in fact on a deserted island, and is driven to suicide by a tense, unbroken silence in which his utter lack of faith in himself and others sinks into a doubt of the reality of his own existence. And Emilia Gould is perhaps the most pathetic victim of all: "wealthy beyond great dreams of wealth, considered, loved, respected, honoured, and as solitary as any human being had ever been, perhaps, on this earth."

In short, in none of Conrad's novels does human life appear more hopeless. Yet it is a grandly stirring, not a depressing book. Again Conrad's stress is finally upon his ideal values, the greatness of the human spirit. Again there is triumph in defeat: triumph in the fervid, self-effacing devotion of Dr. Monygham, in the fortitude of Doña Antonia, in the passionate idealism of Don José Avellanos, in the sheer beauty of soul of Emilia Gould—in the gallantry of man amid all the futility of his endeavor and the certainty of his defeat. There is above all the dark splendor of Nostromo himself. It clings to him even after the foundation of his colossal vanity has been swept away, and he lies dying miserably on a hospital cot. Upon his death, Linda cries out passionately from the lighthouse tower; and "in that true cry of love and grief that seemed to ring aloud from Punta Mala to Azuera and away to the bright line of the horizon, overhung by a big white cloud shining like a mass of solid silver, the genius of the magnificent capataz de cargadores dominated the dark gulf containing his conquests of treasure and love." Behind the immense sadness at the end one hears Conrad's characteristic cry: "A spectacle . . . never for despair!"

At the end, too, Conrad touches upon a theme that has since engrossed many contemporaries. Sulaco is saved from the bestial rapacity of its comic-opera revolutionists—only to be delivered to the tyranny of "material interests." In other words, it has got in its mouth the sour taste of Big Business. But this is an incidental irony, not an important theme. Essentially *Nostromo* is built up on the principles that underlie all Conrad's work. In this day they may seem, once more, outmoded and inadequate. Yet one should remember that in basing his art on "a few simple ideas: so simple that they must be as old as the hills," Conrad takes his stand with most of the great creative artists of the past. Like them he still has something pertinent to say; like them he says it with a pitiless and passionate sincerity. For the very reason that he does not scratch the peculiar itches of this generation, and is by it therefore somewhat overlooked, he is in time likely to take an assured place among the great. Meanwhile *Nostromo* is an example of the monumental work that can yet be produced by the modern pessimistic spirit.

XV

D. H. LAWRENCE

I

I HAVE so far been paddling in relatively limpid and quiet waters. Although the novelists I have treated still disturb ultra-conservative readers, none was so daringly original or ventured so far that the plain reader is unable to follow. One may disapprove, but one can easily understand and appraise their purposes and methods. They are ranged like weather-beaten statues in the background; when the contemporary raises his eyes from the noisy, swirling confusion about him, he can make them out plainly—somewhat remote, perhaps, and in attitudes antiquated and stiff, but solid and stable. And with a fine sense of propriety, like gentlemen of the old school, they retired almost in a body. Hardy, Conrad, Bennett, Moore, Galsworthy—all died within a decade, leaving the field to a new and very different generation.

As one approaches this generation, he faces a plunge into much muddier, if not deeper waters. The broad currents I have so far been following now begin to swirl and eddy and run off into widely diverging channels. Writers are shooting a dozen different rapids. Or they are like Stephen Leacock's hero who leaped madly to horse and dashed madly off in all directions. They have introduced a period of experimentation such as the novel has never before known. They have adventured into new and strange worlds, developed subtler and more intricate methods of communication, made new and more difficult demands. They scarcely stand still long enough for the critic to take their measurements, much less to arrange a group picture.

Now, to hark back to an earlier chapter, the recent developments in fiction are up to a point a logical extension of the realistic spirit, not a romantic revulsion against it. Realism is not necessarily earthbound and pedestrian. Dostoyevsky wanted to tell the whole truth, and conveys in fact an extraordinarily vivid and immediate impression of the actual; but he also leaves a deep impression of the mystical. Thomas Mann begins with concrete detail of everyday life—and ends in the clouds of metaphysics: his mountain is at once solid and magical. D. H. Lawrence, seeking to extend our understanding to the farthest and darkest recesses of the mind, presently sets up his everlasting rest (or unrest) in a realm so unfamiliar that it seems as unreal as Heaven or Hades—it is difficult even to decide which it is. And many others wander as far afield in the interest of a more exact or complete rendering of a reality more complex and elusive than had yet been dreamed of.

The specific findings of science have naturally given an impetus to these tendencies that are in intention usually centripetal, in effect clearly centrifugal. I have already discussed the conspicuous influence of the new psychology. All the diverse experimenters tend to discredit the traditional patterns of character and explanations of behavior; most of them tend to make consciousness more fluid and complex, and personality an elusive whole whose analytically dissociated elements are either meaningless in themselves (*Gestalt*) or else seemingly incongruous (psychoanalysis). In all fields, however, scientific thought has come to play more and more with the immaterial, or at least to break up the relatively simple concepts into which the material had been neatly stuffed. The artist might be unhappy in the positivistic, mechanistic world of the nineteenth century, but at least he could read all the signs and find his way around. Today he lives in an "exploding universe" in which it appears that his common-sense notions of time and space, cause and effect, are but illusions, and that all he knows and needs to know is the twin principle of relativity and discontinuity. One has but to contrast the systems of Darwin, Comte, and Spencer with those of Einstein, Whitehead, and Jeans, the psychology of Hartley and Wundt with that of Koffka and Freud, to understand why few today write like Zola and Dreiser. The ordinary novelist has seldom, indeed, been initiated into these mysteries, but they cast a large shadow. He is likely to regard them with something of the simple awe of the man on the street and take them on faith; he is at any rate less likely to put his trust in an orderly catalogue of externals or a patient dissection of mind or any of the simpler methods of conventional realism.

Finally, the self-conscious and critical spirit characteristic of the whole modern age has in the last generation been greatly intensified, as men have come to realize more fully the consequences of the new views and conditions of life. It has even turned on its parent, Science: the anguished protests of the pious and the nostalgic have been given some logical content by critics as cool and objective as the scientists themselves. Everywhere one sees men gnawing at their own vitals, chopping off their own heads. This biologically so unnatural spectacle is the natural climax of the evolutionary process over the last century; but its immediate cause was the post-war disintegration of the old order, the spiritual and intellectual chaos that followed the collapse of collective ideals. On the lower levels disillusionment expressed itself in such crystallizations of wit and wisdom as "Oh yeah?" "So what?" and "So's your old man"; but the most sober, balanced men had inevitably to take stock and often to seek a new mooring. No sensitive man could pass through such a holocaust untouched. The older novelists might finally continue in the ways in which they had become settled, if perhaps with a weary resignation. Younger and more impressionable writers felt naturally a restless desire for a new deal.

A dispassionate judgment of the original, often intoxicating, and extremely diverse literature of this period is a considerable feat, demanding unusual agility as well as sureness. The critic walks a tight-rope, before a partizan audience who breathlessly hope for the worst, and who will be noisily discontent whether he gets across or tumbles into the wrong lap. Of my own exhibition I should say only that I have made a reasonably patient attempt to penetrate the many brilliant and exciting surfaces; to discover what the novelist is trying to do and why he does it; and then, never condemning him merely because he is not doing something else, to appraise both his aim and his accomplishment —to weigh his meanings and values for both their timeliness and their timelessness. For the central problem of modern literature remains no less acute today, when the post-war fever of disillusionment has passed out of its worst phase, and many of the erstwhile patients have become doctors and clamorously peddle their cures.

2

"I always say, my motto is 'Art for my sake,'" D. H. Lawrence once wrote to a friend. "One sheds one's sicknesses in books. . . ." Here is the key to an understanding of an intensely personal, idiosyncratic artist, and also the reason why he still defies a complete understanding. That he was indeed sick—and if anything, got sicker after each shedding—is plain enough; but the cause and the exact nature of his illness are still somewhat obscure. His art was bound up inextricably with his personality, but we cannot be sure that we have penetrated to the springs of that personality. Although he touched his age at a number of important points, his relationship seems at times almost accidental; so far as he consciously felt the influence of his contemporaries it was ordinarily to react violently against it. Even when they are most familiar, his symptoms seem peculiar to himself. He was, in short, one of the wild birds: the unique, erratic, and homeless geniuses who appear in all ages and cannot be satisfactorily explained by reference to them. Comet-like he flashed across the horizon, where he glowed with a singular brilliance. How long the glow will survive his death it is hard to say; but meanwhile he is by the sheer force of his originality and his passion a significant figure in an age of transition.

The genius of Lawrence is undeniable. It impressed all who came in contact with him—hardly had he drawn his last tortured breath when his friends were squabbling over his remains and setting to work on memoirs. It lights up all but the most casual of his fascinating letters. It inflames his most crippled as his most violent work—if none of his novels is clearly great, all were written greatly. Thus even John Strachey, who as a Marxist would not be disposed to overpraise Lawrence, calls him "the one copious and vital writer which England has produced since the war; the one man who still wrote as if he knew that it was worth while to write." His impassioned force, moreover, did not shatter itself against the walls of a blind alley, nor did his wings beat furiously in a void. Despite his unique gifts and his peculiar irritations, his forlorn and perhaps futile excursions into a world really known only to himself, Lawrence does stand in a vital relation to the contemporary world. Simply by the vehemence of his protest he helps, like most great rebels, to define and to some extent shape the spirit of his times. Whatever road the future takes, one feels that he will cast some light upon it.

Unlike most of his predecessors and many of his contemporaries, Lawrence had indeed no economic or political interests, no social program. Others have found much to condemn in modern society, but their novels are so many documentary records of its activities or so many studies of its special problems. He attempted simply to flee it as something unclean, fatal to accept and impossible to reform. Yet he always came back. He recognized how deep-rooted is the "primeval societal instinct." He felt above all the supreme importance of "real human relationships." Mere individuality, his own or others', wearied him; he was not of those who sought and celebrated a private salvation. He could not, like Proust, retire behind sound-proof walls—he expressed a hatred of Proust and his whole way of life. Neither was he able ever to adjust himself—his profound, devastating sense of frustration was the matrix of his art. But he continued to address his contemporaries, directly and eloquently, even when he seemed beside the point.

The terms of Lawrence's protest are far more radical than those of most rebels today. He had a passionate hatred, not only of science, but also of critical philosophy and all exaltation of conscious knowledge over unconscious instinct. The unholy of unholies is in short Intellect, of whose aborted offspring science is but the most monstrous and today the most spoiled. He insists upon the superiority of the physical, instinctive, emotional life over the conscious, mental, wilful life. He insists that an excess of knowledge is a downright blight: it lessens the sense of wonder, it blunts sensitivity, above all it deadens the natural instincts that are the source of all beauty and gladness and truth.

> My great religion [he writes in his letters] is a belief in the blood, the flesh, as being wiser than intellect. We can go wrong in our minds. But what our blood feels and believes and says, is always true. . . . I conceive a man's body as a kind of flame, like a candle flame, forever upright and yet flowing: and the intellect is just the light that is shed on to the things around. And I am not so much concerned with the things around—which is really mind—but with the mystery of the flame forever flowing, coming God knows how from out of practically nowhere, and being *itself,* whatever there is around it, that it lights up.

Here, then, is Lawrence's grievance with the modern world: it has gone whoring after the bitch-goddess Intellect and continues to sacrifice what miserable goats it can still breed. Intellect has through science created our machine-governed industrialism, with all its oppressive standardization and appalling ugliness—the "coal-blasted countryside" in which he himself grew up. Above all, it has stunted man's glorious instincts, stifled the voice of the blood. The great masses are made up of half-men, in whom the spontaneous, intuitive side is dead; the so-called upper classes are equally deformed and are bloated as well with a false spirituality. All have a bat-like concern for the two hundred or two thousand objects lit up by the candle. All forget the candle, the flame itself—and the outer darkness, the mystery out of which we have our being.

Here too is the reason for Lawrence's preoccupation with sex. It is the chief instrument of "adjustment in consciousness to the basic physical realities," of communication with what Aldous

Huxley calls the "divine otherness," beyond the boundaries of the conscious mind, that was Lawrence's natural home. By sex, however, he meant neither the self-conscious sensual activity celebrated in so much modern fiction nor the disembodied, ethereal love endorsed by Plato, Shelley, Dostoyevsky, and other conspicuously "spiritual" writers. His conception is a mystical one, difficult for the uninitiated to grasp, in which flesh is frankly and reverently accepted but is also transfigured. Sex is the symbol of and gateway to the outer "darkness," to use again Lawrence's favorite word. It is the one force that can most surely take us out of our little conscious selves, merge us with the vital principle of all life, unite for a moment our jet of flame with the immortal flame forever flowing. "Phallic consciousness" is the term Lawrence finally settled on to describe this blessed state. "Phallic unconsciousness" would perhaps be more apt, for this transfiguration is as blind as it is involuntary and spontaneous.

Such ideas Lawrence pleaded vehemently, powerfully, bitterly —and, it would seem, futilely. Despite his furious tilting, the windmills still stand. It is sufficiently ironical that his chief apologist, the one important novelist who was for a time influenced by his ideals and not merely blinded by the glare of his genius, is Aldous Huxley—who is conspicuous for the intellectuality Lawrence despised. Women swooned at the sight of him, and recovered to struggle desperately with other women for possession of his soul, alive or dead; outside this clawing little circle the world moved on, oblivious of the angry prophet. Restlessly Lawrence sought to materialize his ideal. For a time he dreamed of founding a self-sufficient colony of congenial spirits in—of all sites for Utopia—the real estate of Florida. He wandered the earth, to Ceylon, to Australia, to Taos, to Mexico, always in search of the ideal primitive society, the noble savage whose natural goodness was to be phallic, not—like Rousseau's —merely moral. But always he returned to Europe, driven by a sense of responsibility and the need of fulfilling his "primeval societal instinct" that he believed went even "deeper than sex instinct." As he found himself unable either to accept or to escape the world into which he was born, he cultivated more and more exclusively his unique gifts, concentrating still more upon "unknown modes of being," plunging still deeper into the secret passional places of the soul, the dark unconscious, the "divine otherness." At the same time he drafted his gifts into the service of more and more direct preachment and prophecy. Finally he wrote in *Lady Chatterley's Lover* what Huxley aptly calls "the epilogue to his travels," giving a complete, explicit statement of his doctrine of the phallic consciousness, "the source of all real beauty, and all real gentleness," that alone can restore "the good natural glow of life."

3

An excellent point of departure for an analysis of Lawrence's original contribution to modern fiction is the greatest, but also the least characteristic, of his novels: *Sons and Lovers.* It was written early in his career, before his unique genius had completely asserted itself and his exasperation come to a head, and its more solid, familiar virtues provide a useful ballast for judgment. But in the course of this novel Lawrence took off on the flight into the strange world where he was henceforth to dwell. The critic may accordingly follow him from not too great a distance behind, and have a clearer idea of how he got there. Once there himself, the critic is also in less danger of being simply dazzled by the novelty of his surroundings, for he has come trailing familiar clouds and still has fresh memories of life on earth.

Sons and Lovers runs much of its course within the traditions of the English realistic novel. It is a straightforward biographical novel, it is liberally documented with grim detail, and it presents the tragedy of a life worn down by attrition. Yet this realistic tragedy strikes some new notes that anticipate the strange harmonies and discords of Lawrence's later work. Its often sordid detail is shot through with the wild, exotic poetry that is the soul of all his work. More especially, it introduces elements and attitudes that are peculiarly modern, and in their extreme form peculiar to Lawrence. It begins in a recognizable country and in daylight; it ends in the outer darkness.

In the first place, Lawrence was here one of the pioneers who were opening up the new world of abnormal psychology. Paul Morel, the hero of the novel, is so closely bound to his mother, so dependent upon her for the stability and meaningfulness of his life, that he is unable to establish satisfactory relations with other women. When finally she dies, he loses his hold on life and simply disintegrates. At the end he is like a perverse child on his way to destruction, who yet perversely refuses to put out the spark within him, even though perceiving how tiny it is and how immense the impenetrable darkness that on all sides presses in on it; the last we hear of him is a piteous whimper: "Mother! Mother!" In short, his love for her is definitely a perversion—one of the complexes dear to this generation and since popularized as "mother-fixation."

It is characteristically inconsistent of Lawrence that despite his hatred of science he should owe a debt to modern psychology. It is also characteristic that his treatise written while under its spell, *The Fantasia of the Unconscious,* is more poetical than scientific, and that he finally rejected its machinery. Psychoanalysis was for him too intellectual; it was only another form of mechanization that would quench the vital instincts, finish us as living beings. "They can only help you more competently *to make your own feelings,"* he said, washing his hands of psychologists. "They can never let you *have* any real feelings." Hence, though he helped to popularize Freudian psychology and was for a time the darling of its devotees, this contribution was only incidental.

Much more significant is Lawrence's departure from the methods of conventional realism and his invention of an impressionistic technique better adapted to his special interests. *Sons and Lovers* begins, once more, in broad daylight: objects stand out sharp and clear, characters have steady and familiar outlines, and both are projected by a precise notation of externals. But by the end of the novel these outlines have dissolved in the flutter and glimmer of a highly charged atmosphere. "It's more shimmery," Paul explains of one of his sketches, "as if I'd painted the shimmering protoplasm in the leaves and everywhere, and not the stiffness of the shape. . . . Only this shimmeriness is the real living. The shape is a dead crust. The shimmer is inside really." And inside Lawrence himself has now got, almost oblivious of the surface and seldom to return. He is now trying to render life *directly* as he himself experiences it, not as it is interpreted by the intellect or as it appears to the informed eye. He has scrapped the apparatus of introspective analysis, for analysis is a rationalization and therefore a falsification of experience—it loses the honey while preserving the wax. He does not dissect or explain sensation but tries to render it whole and pure, immediately, intuitively. He tries to give the actual *feel* of life, the flame forever flowing rather than the composition of the candle or the light it casts.

Hence the change that comes over character toward the end of *Sons and Lovers,* and baffles the simple reader who had thought himself in familiar company. In the beginning he had felt at home among domesticated types posed in fairly simple group pictures. A few of these plain folk, notably Paul's father, comfort him by their presence until the end. But Paul himself, and the companions of his young manhood, become increasingly queer and disturbing. Their motives and impulses are often obscure, their emotions seemingly unreasonable, the patterns of their relationships wavering and blurred. They seem to have no clear outlines; it is difficult to take their picture or their pulse. In short, they are somehow strangely alive without being what is ordinarily regarded as lifelike.

What causes this uncomfortable state of affairs is not merely that Lawrence's characterization has become less formal and explicit. It is rather his plunge into the dark, subterranean world of the unconscious, to whose modes he was so peculiarly sensitive, and his refusal to represent these modes in the language of the conscious world, to provide the traveler with a Baedeker. His characters appear to be made up of incompatible elements because he is emphasizing chiefly the obscure impulses and emotions that underlie intellect and will, and are often in conflict with conscious intentions. In this underground world his characters have a kind of mysterious awareness of one another; their relations are governed not by simple logic but by subtle affinities and repulsions—by an interchange that Lawrence likes to describe as electrical. Hence the curious attraction for Paul of Baxter Dawes, whom by the logic of ordinary life he ought to hate. Hence the feverish alternation in Paul of rushes of love and hate for Miriam and then for Clara—and all the violent loving and hating that goes on in this as in all Lawrence's novels. This perpetual battle of the sexes, recalling Strindberg, strikes a discordant note in Lawrence's hymn to communion with the "divine otherness": even those of his heroes who most clearly represent his ideals have a reluctance to be absorbed, a desire to dominate, that seems inconsistent with his protest against mere individuality, his worship of the dark life force that flows through all egos. But this inconsistency is at least more understandable when one remembers that Lawrence locates this force in the unconscious, and is in all his dramas simply objectifying its mysterious, irrational modes.

Lawrence's characters have, indeed, many cousins in modern fiction; but he went further than any other novelist in his utter repudiation of traditional patterns of character as relics of a false way of life. "You mustn't look in my novel," he wrote, "for the old stable ego of the character." Conventional character, Catherine Carswell explains for him, is amusing and interesting, and will no doubt persist. But it is a static, a *made,* not a spontaneous thing. It is a purely intellectual convention that can provide a merely intellectual excitement. "Given *a, b,* and *c* acting upon each other and being acted upon by circumstance, what will be the result? All of which *seems* to have a lot to do with life, all of which is, indeed, so much the appearance of life that it is easy to mistake it for life itself. But it is not life." Lawrence's main interest was in what the person *is* beneath the conventional pattern of thoughts and feelings: the essential unconscious being, the jet of undifferentiated life energy. It was in the life force itself, not the shapes it happened to assume or the rationalizations it happened to inspire.

Lawrence's later characters are accordingly mere bundles of instincts with no shape to speak of. They are so utterly children of Nature that one almost forgets that nominally they represent human nature. Each is a kind of central station, receiving and radiating waves of electrical energy, and differing from the others chiefly in its wave length. Similarly their stories have no definite plot structure, no dramatic action with conflicts resolved and issues settled. They are but a series of electrical interchanges, a tangle of conflicting instincts, a convulsion of subterranean forces. Such changes as appear on the surface are unimportant; such dramatic moments as occur seem as incidental as the joy or sorrow that accompanies them. Lawrence's final concern is neither the drama nor its individual actors but the life force that passes through them. Although the consequences of this passing are usually sobering, one seldom at once recalls, in any given novel, precisely what they were.

In this lofty disdain of plot interest Lawrence again resembles many modern novelists. Probably he gave an impetus to the widespread revolt against plot. Yet the most indefatigable seeker of "influences" cannot explain his practice by reference to what his contemporaries were doing. Neither was he himself deliberately experimenting. His novels were the natural, almost unconscious fulfilment of his feelings; he simply let his "demon" have its way. "It's like a novel in a foreign language I don't know very well," he wrote during his labor pains with *Women in Love;* "I can only just make out what it is about." No novelist provides a clearer example of technique at every point determined by a central vision of life.

In his last work, to be sure, Lawrence gave us back our everyday world—and with a vengeance. He returned to the familiar shapes and modes of conscious activity. But this return was no concession to his critics, or admission of error. It was simply the destination to which he had been slowly but inexorably driven by the circumstances of his life and temperament. He had been growing steadily more angry at the world's opposition to his novels and the way of life represented in them. He had wandered the earth in search of the ideal society, only to find his quest vain and his feeling of responsibility to his own society more imperious. His letters grew more impassioned, his books filled with more explicit and bitter comment. Finally he returned to Europe wearing the robes of a prophet, burning with the holy fire of a mission. He was almost happy as he wrote *Lady Chatterley's Lover* and preached his gospel of the "phallic consciousness" that can be the only salvation of the modern world. This gospel had been implicit in all his later work, but now he states it baldly, in terms plain to the most thick-witted. He had once tried merely to render sensation; now he interprets it with rhapsodical comment. His characters had once seemed almost oblivious of the world about them; now they talk incessantly about their relations to it—and if they escape it, they escape deliberately, almost insolently. They had once had their being almost entirely in the regions of the unconscious, and been driven almost despite themselves into their sexual relationships; now they plunge wholeheartedly into these relationships and lose their self-consciousness only during the raptures that are their reward. Here was an experience that Lawrence's shell-shocked generation could understand, even if they missed some of its sublimity and were themselves incapable of its ecstasy. But it was only a translation, into the simplified English of more conventional fiction, of the experience of his other novels; a rationalization of the philosophy behind them all.

4

Now, it is easy to ridicule the whole philosophy of Lawrence, not to mention some of his specific illustrations of man in rapture as he merges his little flame with that of the Eternal Candle. Yet it deserves sober consideration—even apart from the humility that should guard the ordinary mortal against being merely supercilious in the presence of so much passion when it bears the stamp of genius. Even when most fantastic, his exhortations are never wholly irrelevant, his course is never wholly erratic. The drift of his criticism of modern life is indeed in the general direction of that of many distinguished contemporaries. In his revolt against the dominion of intellect, for example, he joins the large, if diverse, company that includes Conrad, Proust, Yeats, Gide, and Hemingway; in his interest in the primitive he is another expression of the spirit that drove Rimbaud into exile, Gide into the Congo, Anderson and Van Vechten to the American negro, and that has filled a hundred galleries with examples of African art, a hundred concert halls with the music of negro spirituals. At his strangest, he is still a significant symptom of his age.

Lawrence's work is at least no longer dismissed as merely indecent or sensational. "They ought to censor eggs," he stormed during one of his many battles with Mrs. Grundy, "as revealing the intimate relations of cock and hen"; today all except *Lady Chatterley's Lover* of his novels seem innocuous. Unmistakably he was the "passionately religious man" he often insisted he was, and what most impresses us now is the terrific passion that kept him struggling to have his say when violent abuse was relieved chiefly by sympathetic incomprehension. Only on the shifting grounds of taste can he be condemned, but he himself admitted the fallibility of his taste: "My Cockneyism and commonness are only when the deep feeling doesn't find its way out, and a sort of jeer comes instead, and sentimentality, and purplism."

Similarly one cannot hold him responsible for the cult of which he became willy-nilly the symbol—the cult of the healthy and happy animal. "To the preacher of a new way of life," Aldous Huxley remarks, "the most depressing thing that can happen is, surely, success." What happened to Christ happened to Lawrence: the ardor of the disciples is matched only by their misunderstanding. As the problem of many tormented spirits is partly a matter of physiology or hygiene, his doctrines have been perverted into a glorification of gross sensuality, a worship of Orgasm. Actually, however, Lawrence was nauseated by anything like prurience or promiscuity; he was simply shocked by a Casanova or a Don Juan. Mabel Dodge paints an unforgettable picture of his amazed and angry presence on a steamer from the South Seas, amid the reckless, carefree love-making of a Hollywood crowd. All his intimates agree that he was not only prudish in behavior but puritanical in attitude; and even the casual reader should see that *Lady Chatterley's Lover* could have been written by only such a man as this.

Yet there remain obvious and serious objections to Lawrence's creed. The most enthusiastic disciple must presently be troubled, for example, by its vagueness. Sex, once more, is only a symbol of the good life, the means to a glorious end; but Lawrence is always preoccupied with this means and never clearly pictures the end. He never shows us the heaven where we shall dwell once we have acquired the proper attitude and mastered the proper technique. Presumably Lady Chatterley's gamekeeper dwells there, but he demonstrates chiefly how to get there; in the moments between raptures he appears to be thinking chiefly of the next one to come, and what else he does with all the spare time that even so lusty an animal as he has on his hands is not quite clear. Similarly one wonders what is the exact function of intellect. We have a mind and cannot simply drop it in the nearest wastebasket, but Lawrence never tells us precisely what to do with it. And one who has tried conscientiously to listen to the voice of his blood still does not know how to distinguish it from a dozen conflicting voices and recognize its commands. In short, like so many violent preachers, Lawrence is at the critical moments of his dispensation hazy and obscure, blown from his moorings by his own eloquence.

Even when most sober and lucid, however, his program is still inadequate. He leaves out too much. Like most prophets of one principle, he seeks to ignore all others—to deny by a mere effort of will the very necessities of his being. In *The Contemporary and His Soul,* Irwin Edman aptly states the fundamental inconsistencies in his way of life: "He wishes to be a sturdy, true child of nature and a poet appreciating the sturdy child of nature. . . . He wishes to be the bull breeding and the mystic celebrant of sex." But one cannot be an animal and have as well this ecstatic self-consciousness: "No really carnal person could be quite so lyrical as D. H. Lawrence on the subject of physical love." Briefly, he forgets that only simple people can live simple lives, and only God can make a gamekeeper.

Like countless poets and philosophers, Lawrence succumbed to the black magic of words, and mistook names for things. "The most opposite things," writes Santayana, "may become miraculously equivalent, if they arouse the same invisible quality of emotion"; with Lawrence emotional identity instantly became logical identity. He set ideas on their heads, and then asserted that this was their only natural position. Scientists declare that sunshine makes the crops grow; Lawrence corrected this half-truth by declaring that growing crops make the sun shine—and in the act of statement was convinced that his teleological metaphor was the whole, absolute truth. Because he found mystical states of mind valuable, he gave his intuitive perceptions the strategic name of "knowledge"; because this "knowledge" is obviously different from common experience, it must naturally be "superior"; and presently it became the only "true" knowledge. Constantly he confused different functions of thought and language, hypostatized first his ideas and then his favorite words. He rang bells when he thought he was conveying ideas; his philosophical exercises became a kind of verbal onanism. And this refusal to call things by their right names not only makes his language ambiguous and misleading, but muddies the springs of his thought.

In this view one can better understand the "violent monotony and intense indistinctness" of Lawrence's novels that Aldous Huxley complained of, and that makes them, despite their strange richness and beauty, such difficult reading. "Tell Arnold Bennett," Lawrence once wrote in defense of his unorthodox technique, "that all rules of construction hold good only for novels which are copies of other novels. A book which is not a copy of other books has its own construction, and what he calls faults, he being an old imitator, I call characteristics." This is an irrefutable argument, and the ultimate wisdom concerning the subject of technique. But it also lays Lawrence open to far more serious criticism. It follows that what makes his novels finally unsatisfying is not a fault simply of structure or method, but a fault primarily of the vision of life that shaped them.

One may doubt in the first place that Lawrence's genius was suited to the art of drama or fiction (like Hardy, he is one of a number of modern novelists who in an earlier age would almost certainly have written only poetry): he was unwilling to adapt his essentially poetical or mystical "characteristics" to his medium, which for all its freedom makes certain demands. One may complain that in effect he dissolved character, split it up into elemental units that do not then cohere into a personality, resolved it into "psychological atoms" as unreal to ordinary men as the agglomeration of electrons and protons into which the scientist resolves a table. One may add that his "demon" often wears the agonized expression that came of its desperate struggles to find its way out. Ultimately what one is saying, however, is that Lawrence's vision was warped, strained, hyperopic. If his concept of experience as an indivisible totality has close parallels in modern psychology (William James, the *Gestaltists*), in practice he did not present a whole, for he was too antagonistic to the intellectual and consciously wilful operations that are an inseparable part of it. He attempted to represent the life energy almost as if it could be dissociated from the shapes and modes it assumes in the external world, and by which alone it is known—it is as if he had tried to take a picture of electricity. In his preoccupation with the unconscious he failed to return to the surface of the conscious, which is no less "real" and to the world at large certainly important. Many critics have pointed out that he never achieved a complete character; with his bias it was impossible that he should.

Hence the implications of Lawrence's fiction are definitely restricted even when least distorted. He not only deliberately ignored the main concerns of contemporary society; by reason of his scorn of intellect and what commonly passes for spirit he perforce left out of his account at least half of the significant activities of man in any civilized society. The tragedy he wrote is the tragedy primarily of frustration of instinct. The struggle is almost entirely subterranean. Society enters into it not at all, conscious will and intellect very little. Edwin Muir sums it up admirably: "It is a tragedy almost purely of nature rather than of human nature; it might befall a lion caged or a tree mutilated as easily as a human being thwarted in his unconscious desires. It is new in literature, it is sometimes very beautiful, but it has not the full significance of human tragedy."

This criticism is equally pertinent to Lawrence's last work, where he more concretely objectified his philosophy. *Lady Chatterley's Lover* is in many ways an impressive as well as original novel. Its characterization is on the whole more vivid than in all but his early novels, its passion and poetry are often as strangely beautiful as in his best passages. Its intention, moreover, is noble; Lawrence is again as moral as he is lyrical. He sought to throw a white light on the secret, hitherto ignored passional places of the soul, to give a more sensitive and sympathetic awareness of one of man's major experiences, in short to clarify, cleanse, and refresh as only great art can. Yet here again he falls short of his lofty intention. He not only gets mired in an excess of argument; he is held down by the very conditions of this argument.

Lawrence incidentally stumbles over the vocabulary that is only part of his unaffected purpose: the Anglo-Saxon four-letter words that many readers have mistaken as the whole reason for the book. These words have for centuries kept unfortunate company, and so have inescapably ludicrous connotations; when the lovers rhapsodize in them, it seems simply funny. Throughout the whole stage business of these rhapsodies Lawrence's lyricism periodically collapses, falling in awkward folds about the frame of a poor, naked, forked animal; and the same irreverent impulse to laugh ruins the climax of *The Man Who Died,* the loveliest poetic-prose statement of Lawrence's creed. What finally robs

Lawrence's message of much of its force, however, is not this humorlessness of an impassioned preacher. It is the insufficiency of his message, of which these lapses into the ludicrous are but one obvious sign. Although he strives for an organic view of man, he is actually celebrating only one organ, only one province of human activity; and as in his prophetic books he magnifies his one value and fiercely attacks where he had once merely ignored all others, we see the more clearly that this way of life cannot suffice, even for those temperamentally and physically equipped for it. If it is good mental hygiene, it is still only one phase of an adequate therapeutic program; an adjustment to the physical realities but prepares one to face the many still more difficult problems. Even if there were enough ladies and gamekeepers to go around, and each with a secluded cottage in the woods, civilized man cannot be happy simply in prostrating himself before the Genital Godhead—as Lawrence himself was not happy.

5

We are back, then, at the first and final question about Lawrence: the question of the source of his obsessions, his incessant conflict with his society, and hence his devastating torment. I do not pretend to have the whole answer. One can never entirely explain genius and its ways; one is particularly hard-pressed to explain a genius like Lawrence, who drew so little directly from the thought of his age, so much from his unconscious—"the mysterious, irrational source of power within him," to dress up his inexorable "demon" in the words of Aldous Huxley. Yet even a tentative inquiry will help to make clear the real value and significance of his work which for too many critics are obscured by its obvious limitations, for it leads back to the major issues of modern literature. At his most erratic, Lawrence was never a complete stranger, and at his most fanatical never a narrow partizan. He never haggled or patched or tinkered. While others quarrel like jealous specialists over diagnosis of specific symptoms, he sought to get at the roots of the sickness of the age and proposed a whole new way of life.

Lawrence is in the first place not to be explained as one of the Father Times sired by modern pessimism; among his woes was no lack of faith. The distresses he saw he considered remediable, and what particularly exasperated him was man's folly in not remedying them. "I hate Bennett's resignation," he wrote. "Tragedy ought really to be a great kick at misery." In another letter he asked, "But why this giving in before you start, that pervades all Conrad and such folks—the Writers among the Ruins. I can't forgive Conrad for being so sad and for giving in." Certainly Lawrence himself never gave in. He never even asked the questions these others did, nor got around to brooding over the designs of the gods; he was too busy dealing with the immediate realities of this earthly sphere. Although his passionate faith has indeed little reference to the ultimate meaning of human life and the transcendental scheme into which it may fit, it was to him all-sufficient. He was content with the flame forever flowing, and did not bother with the questions of why, whence, and to what end.

Similarly one must discount the simpler physiological explanations: the thesis that Lawrence was impotent, or Middleton Murry's more seductive thesis that he suffered from the mother-fixation that destroyed his own Paul Morel. Frieda and his intimate friends deny both. For Murry's case there is indeed the plain evidence of *Sons and Lovers,* which is almost literal autobiography. "I had a devil of a time getting a bit weaned from my mother, at the age of 22," Lawrence wrote to a friend; Frieda has added that she had a devil of a time for weeks when he was writing the scenes of his mother's death; and there is the very honest and moving personal record of E. T., the unfortunate original of Miriam. Yet this sickness at least he seems definitely to have shed in his books—as his rich life with Frieda and his productive career suggest. The explanation is in any event chiefly paraphrase; among the many artists now thought to have suffered from mother-fixation Lawrence still remains unique.

More provocative is John Strachey's Marxist interpretation in *The Coming Struggle for Power.* In taking up "what literary people call literature," he attempts to explain why Lawrence alone of our problem children has such unquenchable vitality—and he finds the answer, naturally, in a deep though unconscious interest in class and class relationships. By origin a worker, Lawrence rose out of his world like the bourgeois Proust to view the upper crust; and he too came back to report that there was nothing there. Although he never actually identified himself with the proletariat, "in a kind of semi-conscious way he had faith in the victory of the workers." Hence the theme that recurs in *Aaron's Rod, The Man Who Died,* and *Lady Chatterley's Lover:* the theme of the salvation by the vigorous proletarian of the lovely lady at the top—"myths of the young worker revivifying society: as, truly, the workers alone can do." Unfortunately, however, this never quite came into consciousness; "and Lawrence, instead of standing outside of capitalist society and drawing strength and assurance from its decline, became himself inextricably involved in that decline." Hence his agony: "the terrible sense of frustration which sometimes overshadows even his incomparable passion."

This is an ingenious explanation—that he exacted from Strachey his fanciest display of legerdemain is another tribute to Lawrence. It is also difficult to refute in downright language. Once the critic drags in the unconscious (as with Lawrence he must), all pretense of finality must be dropped: the unconscious is a happy hunting ground where all can sight the game they are looking for, and wave away all the other animals (as Lawrence himself would have done) as delusions of the conscious mind. Yet even Strachey's carefully selected hares do not fit his description. In *The Man Who Died* it is the proletarian hero himself—the resurrected Christ—who is revivified; and what revivifies him is the discovery of functions shared by workers and capitalists alike, the awakening of the "phallic consciousness" that Lawrence claimed as the birthright of all men. In *Lady Chatterley's Lover,* moreover, Lawrence specifically includes the workers in his indictment of a mechanized, mind-ridden, devitalized world. The whole emphasis upon political reform—not to mention the Communist dream of a paradise fitted up by Science and the Machine—is irrelevant or even fatal to what he most cherished. The only issues that seemed to him vital have no real relation to the class struggle, are obscured by it, and would continue to plague a classless society. He appears, indeed, to have been always conscious of his humble origins; but when Strachey declares that "class relationships obsessed him," that "his novels get their incomparable vitality from this theme" of the vigorous young proletarian revivifying capitalism, he is simply refusing to speak Lawrence's language. He is not merely brushing aside Lawrence's whole conscious philosophy, as it is incessantly expressed in his letters and published work; he is failing to recognize the one thing that would seem clear in Lawrence: that this philosophy, however distorted, is a complete rationalization of his deepest feelings and a natural fulfilment of his unique gifts.

I have labored this objection to the narrow Marxist interpretation of Lawrence because only by a clear perception of how completely it misses the point can one appreciate the actual significance of his work. As an unconscious champion of the proletariat Lawrence would still be a significant enough figure. Even as the mere teacher of sex hygiene or the amateur psychoanalyst that others make of him he would still be pertinent. Actually, however, he comes closer to the fundamental issues of modern life than do most of his critics. Like Strachey, he seeks to cut through the heterogeneity and confusion of the age and find a basis for solidarity, a scheme of integration. But he cuts even deeper than the Marxists. He undermines the whole rationale of science that for the most part they accept. He redefines the whole situation. He reintroduces the animistic principle and employs the poetic and religious metaphors, he restores the primacy of the oldest emotional needs of the race, he emphasizes the deeply human as opposed to the impersonal or knowledgeable—in general he sets modern experience in an entirely new perspective by focusing its oldest elements. The Marxist philosophy may indeed be a more practicable program, a more solid base for vigorous collective action; but the very radicalness of Lawrence's attack that makes it vulnerable to criticism is also what makes it valuable. He forces a return to first principles as Strachey does not. Strachey is scornful of those who would temporize and tinker in a world hell-bent for destruction; from Lawrence's point of view he is himself a creature of expediency, a dabbler in salves and ointments.

In defiance of human history, men naturally tend to accept as inevitable, self-evident, and immutable the basic schemata of their age. "The common inherited scheme of conception which is all around us," writes F. M. Cornford in *From Religion to Philosophy,* "and comes to us as naturally and unobjectionably as our native air, is none the less imposed upon us, and limits our intellectual movements in countless ways—all the more surely and irresistibly because, being inherent in the very language we must use to express the simplest meaning, it is adopted and assimilated before we can so much as begin to think for ourselves at all." Hence any really significant criticism of this scheme must reexamine its premises—the premises, today, of science and industrialism—and use a strange vocabulary; and herein lies the significance of Lawrence. As a practical reformer he made little mark—he ignored the conditions under which the reformer must work, simply waving away with an angry gesture an industrialism impossible to scrap. As a prophet he was as vague as he was violent—our present chaos will seem cosmic when one pictures a society in which everyone adopted literally his design for living. But he at least had his finger on the pulse of his society and felt in his own blood its sickness; he drove back to fundamentals in search of a remedy; and hence even amid the immense concourse of spiritual doctors who are in consultation over the patient his impassioned voice carries authority. Like the great mystics, he turned the world upside down and set accepted meanings in a new light—a light in which the Marxists themselves would do well occasionally to contemplate them, so as to be able to see around them. That he was plainly a reactionary in an age in which *reactionary* is one of the most horrid words does not lessen his importance. As Nietzsche remarked of Schopenhauer, the value of the reactionary genius is that for a time he forces back our feeling into the great old ways of viewing man and the world; and in this regression is also the germ of progress, a new and fresh development. Lawrence seems to mark a relapse precisely as, to civilized antiquity, the early Christians must have seemed to do. Despite his extravagances, the drift of Lawrence's criticism is in the necessary direction: the direction of humanizing the rationale of science and industry, subordinating it to "real human relationships."

In this perspective one can also perceive more clearly the sources of Lawrence's frustration, implicit as it was in the very terms of his genius. There was in the first place a painful disharmony in his own soul. "He is rarely really gay," a friend wrote discerningly to Mabel Dodge; "he is truly the somber Anglo-Saxon, which he hates with a bitter hatred." He was also at heart a Puritan. His native temperament seldom permitted him to feel the "good natural glow" that he passionately proclaimed as man's birthright—hence his frequent exasperation with Frieda, who was instinctively and without effort what he strove desperately to be. Moreover, his cardinal principle of sex could not unlock for him the innermost shrine in the holy temple of life, even apart from his secret resentment that women are its priestesses, a masculine reluctance to depend on them or be absorbed by them. ("For the great mergers," he once wrote, "woman at last becomes inadequate.") But still deeper than this obvious inability satisfactorily to live his own doctrines and be himself a gamekeeper was the torment caused by the flat opposition of a predominantly intellectual, scientific age to his own peculiar intuitive gifts, his extraordinary sensitiveness to the instinctive, involuntary, spontaneous life of man. In the modern industrial world this opposition is especially pronounced—and to page Strachey again, would be still more pronounced in the Russia of today. At the same time it is implicit in the conditions of any society we please to call civilized. D. H. Lawrence was a highly imaginative and articulate savage, too civilized to speak meaningfully to savages, too primitive to live on easy terms with sophisticates. He could have been entirely happy in neither daylight nor darkness. His heaven carried within it its own hell.

In this light the limitations of Lawrence are again only too obvious. But in this light too his kind of greatness shines more brightly. He was utterly loyal to the mysterious urge within him; passionately he clung to his birthright. As F. R. Leavis has said, "He had the same gift [as Blake] of knowing what he was interested in, the same power of distinguishing his own feelings and emotions from conventional sentiment, the same 'terrifying honesty.'" These emotions, moreover, were not forced or facile. "Your people," Lawrence wrote of American poets, "have such little pressure: their safety valve goes off at the high scream when the pressure is still so low"; there is no mistaking the immense pressure in Lawrence, the terrific force that racked his frail body and drove it, like a crazy little skiff, through perpetually high seas.

Most important finally, however, is that the force in Lawrence was not merely self-destructive, nor its direction merely unfortunate. It shattered itself in a lost cause, but his was a pertinent as well as a gallant and high endeavor. Despite the strangeness of his utterance, he was stating a very simple and very old truth: the truth of the beauty and power of the instinctive life that civilized man is prone to forget. "His chief title to greatness," Edwin Muir concludes, "is that he has brought a new mode of seeing into contemporary literature, a new beauty which is also one of the oldest things in the world. . . . Life has come to him fresh from the minting at a time when it seemed to everyone either soiled or banal." He returned to the roots of life while others gazed wanly at its sickly flowers. If he strove vainly to deny the claims of intellect, he gave a wonderfully vivid and compelling account of a way of life that is not simply illusory, irrelevant, or alien. If he sacrificed his own keen intelligence (and incidentally his contentment), it was to the talent that was death to hide and that made possible his unique contribution.

Lawrence lived, indeed, in a world not only brighter and intenser but essentially different from ours. He seemed to be in constant touch with the dark life force from which the rest of us are removed by layers of experience thickly crusted with habitual and mechanical responses, and to participate directly in the processes of nature. His novels transport us to the very borders of human experience. It is a bewildering and finally a fatiguing journey: we return with a feeling of relief to the familiar conscious world in which we have spent, and must continue to spend, most of our lives. But it is also an exciting journey, lit by many vivid flashes that reveal unrealized or forgotten but significant experience. One who cannot accept the half-truth of Lawrence's creed still cannot afford to reject these many specific revelations. To the reader fresh from this journey, as to one just come from the equally strange world of Dostoyevsky, other novelists are likely to seem tame, shallow, and artificial.

Lawrence thus has something to say to those seeking a richer way of life; much of his criticism of a machine-ridden, science-worshiping society is valid. Yet it is finally the sheer lyricism of his novels that makes him so conspicuous a figure in modern fiction. All his critics agree that he was more poet than novelist. Hence *Sons and Lovers* is much more than a study in pathology. One may forget its literal realism, its pioneering exploration of dim and murky recesses—forget all that made it of especial interest to its audience; one cannot forget the lovely imagery, the wild and immense poetry, the vivid sense of man's relations with things elemental and eternal. And when in his later work Lawrence seems most blind and perverse, lost in a world of his own, he is still an impassioned poet, flooding his stories with a strange beauty that blurs his jagged theories and illumines, intensifies, and enriches our experience of life. His arguments may be as shallow and quixotic as at times Shelley's are—Lawrence had the same intense, childlike innocence; like Shelley he still often manages by the sheer force of lyrical emotion to voice the deepest aspirations and sorrows of the human spirit.

XVI

JAMES JOYCE

I

ALTHOUGH there are official guides with keys to unlock the thousand doors of the temple of James Joyce, they usually perform their duties with a simple reverence that takes their occupation for granted: his central aims and methods they accept without question at his own valuation. Moreover they have the habit of swooning once they have got us to the inmost shrine, the holy of holies. We are thus left to judge pretty much for ourselves what is really there; and sober judgment has been made difficult by the very elaborateness of our initiation. The astounding virtuosity of Joyce is in the end bound up with his comment upon life, but it is often simply a distraction. Many readers become so rapt in following the wondrous maze of his methods that they forget what he is saying—as at times Joyce himself appears to forget. And the more intent explorers come back with widely different reports. *Ulysses* is an immense cesspool—or it is an "emancipating comic vision." It is the apotheosis of absolute negation—or it is an affirmation of life as hearty as Molly Bloom's. It is the prank of an incorrigible Irishman—or it is the serene final statement of genius. It is a beginning or it is an ending, sometimes of Joyce himself, sometimes of the whole modern world.

Fortunately there is in *A Portrait of the Artist as a Young Man* a simple, direct approach that leads through more or less familiar country. This short novel is a preface to *Ulysses* and presents the early life of Stephen Dedalus, one of its two central figures. As confessed autobiography, it separates some of the threads spun into the complex genius of Joyce: the family heritage and the Irish background, the scholastic education, the profound religious experience, the awakening and growth of the artist, the final repudiation of his society and flight to the Continent and freedom. It contains both the lyric poet of *Chamber Music* and the naturalist of *Dubliners,* and it anticipates the later innovations in style and method, notably the use of the stream of consciousness. It announces the basic principles of his esthetic creed—got largely from St. Thomas Aquinas. And all this it does plainly, if strangely, so that even the uninitiated may understand.

By itself, however, *A Portrait of the Artist as a Young Man* does not seem to me the great novel it is often considered. Its various elements, remarkable in themselves, are not clearly focused by a dramatic idea or fused in an artistic whole; its various scenes are strung out like so many beads on the thread of Stephen's personality. The story does not really move and gather strength as it develops, but simply expands about a number of arbitrary fixed points. Its merits are the merits of its individual scenes, and the sum of these is distinctly greater than the whole. In short, it makes clear what the vastness and brilliance of *Ulysses* obscure: that Joyce is apparently incapable of carrying out a dramatic action, of gaining the cumulative effect that should come with length, and is in a sense not primarily a novelist at all.

The *Portrait* has, moreover, the limitations of most studies of adolescence. Although the modern novelist makes a more realistic study of youth than did the Victorian story-tellers, he has come to substitute a design no less familiar. The sensitive and misunderstood child, the awkwardness of adolescence, the first stirrings of love, the collision between ideals and reality, the painful shedding of illusions—these elements recur with a somewhat monotonous regularity, in Joyce as in Butler, Maugham, Lawrence, and more recently Floyd Dell, Rosamond Lehmann, and innumerable others. This is not indeed to be wondered at. The course of youth, especially of sensitive youth, is everywhere pretty much the same; always there is the gradual discovery of the shocking "facts of life," always the more or less difficult problem of adjustment. Yet if one cannot rightly quarrel with this underlying sameness, one may at least point out that growing pains cannot be made the subject of really great drama. Deserving as they are of sympathetic understanding, they are necessarily of limited significance to the mature man, for they touch only indirectly the vital issues of his own life. They are but a prologue to the actual drama.

Even when Stephen Dedalus has stormed into manhood, however, the reference of the *Portrait* is narrower than that of the other autobiographical novels I have mentioned. Butler and Maugham stressed the philosophical implications of their stories and attempted to universalize them; even Lawrence thought he was writing "the tragedy of thousands of young men in England." Joyce's main interest was intensely personal. The problems of Stephen Dedalus are finally the very special problems of an Irish artist of strange genius. We are interested in him as we are interested in all genius; although we are not flattered by his complete indifference to us and our own concerns, and might wish that he were not so snarling, unattractive a fellow, we recognize that genius naturally has different ways. But we return to the sober business of living neither emancipated nor purged by a solution that consists simply of a deliberate rejection of society, a repudiation of its interests and responsibilities, in order to embrace a way of life impossible to men at large.

2

"I go to encounter for the millionth time the reality of experience and to forge in the smithy of my soul the uncreated conscience of my race"—with these ringing words Stephen Dedalus took flight into freedom. *Ulysses* is what he forged. As all the sophisticated world now knows, it embraces the events of a single day, June 16, 1904, chiefly as they are refracted through the minds of Stephen and one Leopold Bloom. It is a very ordinary but comprehensive day, with a funeral, a birth, an adultery, and even—glory of the commonplace—a parade. Stephen (who has passed a year in Paris since we last saw him) gets up in the morning, walks the beach, teaches a class, delivers an article to a newspaper office, propounds to literary friends an ingenious theory about *Hamlet,* gets drunk with some medical students in a lying-in hospital, and winds up brawling in a brothel, where Mr. Bloom rescues him, dusts him off, feeds him coffee and cocoa, and sends him home. Mr. Bloom gets up, potters about the house, potters about the streets while pursuing his prudent commercial and amorous interests and fulfilling his decent human duties, gets innocently involved in a tavern brawl, is attracted and finally embarrassed by the antics of an ingenuously lecherous maiden on the beach, meets Stephen and his friends in the hospital and follows them to the brothel, and after caring for Stephen and incidentally parading before him his fond intellectual interests, crawls into bed. Here he awakens his wife Molly, magnificent daughter of earth; and the last chapter is the famous earth-swell of her very specific thoughts about her life and loves.

The framework of this narrative is realistic. With the modern impulse to tell all, Joyce throws in a host of minor characters, all carefully individualized, and has by the end re-created the city of Dublin, with a frankness, minuteness, and thoroughness of detail never before approached in fiction; Zola and Bennett now seem fastidious dabblers, dilettantes of realism. Similarly by the use of the interior monologue he completely renders the minds of Dedalus and Bloom. In the *Portrait* Joyce had employed only occasionally and then selectively the stream-of-consciousness method; he himself was still present, filtering the thought stream, imposing some order, occasionally halting it by references to externals ("The train went on and on"). Now he withdraws entirely and allows the stream to flow, as it were, by itself. The result is a minute, thorough realization of character also hitherto unapproached (unless perhaps by Dorothy Richardson). Joyce once remarked to Frank Budgen that in all fiction there was not one *whole* man; in Leopold Bloom he conscientiously remedied this deficiency. Bloom defies tidy summary or category. As critics have admiringly observed, it takes precisely the whole of *Ulysses* to present him.

Although it still dazzles many students and writers, the stream-of-consciousness method is an obvious enough affair: a natural outcome of the new interest in the mind, and the new notions about it. It is also a logical culmination of the efforts of novelists like Conrad and James to dramatize consciousness, or of the efforts of the impressionists at an immediate and pure rendering of experience. But it is finally—and this is apparently what means most to Joyce—a realization of the ideal of complete impersonality. In the *Portrait* he states his concept of the evolutionary progress in art from the lyrical form, "wherein the artist presents his image in immediate relation to himself," to the dramatic form, "wherein he presents his image in immediate relation to others." In the dramatic form "the personality of the artist . . . finally refines itself out of existence, impersonalizes itself, so to speak." Here is an esthetician's statement of Flaubert's ideal—but an ideal that for all his fastidious aloofness Flaubert himself never quite realized, nor Zola after him. In his careful selection and disposition of detail and above all in his ironic manner he constantly reveals his sympathies and judgments. Hence Joyce will not obviously select and shape; he empties out the whole mind of each character. Hence he will avoid even style; he simply reproduces the thought stream, without analysis or comment, remaining himself entirely out of the picture. As the creator of this whole world he is everywhere, but at any given moment he is nowhere. He achieves an unparalleled degree of self-effacement. He achieves a paradox that climaxes and almost summarizes the chief developments in modern fiction: the paradox of attaining at once the height of subjectivity in material and the height of objectivity in method.

Implicit in the thoroughness of this method is the "indecency" that has attracted as many readers as it has repelled—the casual use of all the unmentionable words. These words pass unbidden through the minds of even the chastest of us—and Joyce's characters are not conspicuously chaste; he draws no line but reproduces everything. Implicit also is the obscurity that makes *Ulysses* such difficult reading, for he explains or interprets nothing. The mind of Stephen Dedalus is a medley of leaping fancies, unbridged associations, telescoped memories of his esoteric reading and chaotic experience—all of these pellmell, and most of them wearing the motley of metaphor. And if the more prosaic thoughts of Leopold Bloom are easier to follow, they are as jumbled and fragmentary: a crazy-quilt of his commercial, scientific, and amorous interests—the appalling miscellany that clutters up the mind of the modern man—threaded with a hundred trivial concerns. He unbuttons his vest to rub his finger over his belly and experiment with the sense of touch, and then forgets to button it; one has to pick up that button a couple hundred pages later from a puddle of thoughts as trifling. In the minds of both Stephen and Bloom, moreover, the significant thought is likely to enter as casually and drop out as incomplete as the most wayward fancy—especially since each has the habit of running away in panic from his most troublesome concerns. Bloom refuses to mention even to himself the name of Blazes Boylan, who he knows is carrying on an affair with his wife; Stephen's mind swirls still more dizzily whenever there enters the thought of his mother, whose dying request that he kneel by her bedside and pray for her soul he had refused to grant.

All this, however, is but the beginning of the difficulty, the groundwork of Joyce's intention. To its first readers *Ulysses* seemed an appalling chaos; Stuart Gilbert has made clear, with his indispensable Baedeker, that it is instead the most formal, elaborate, and systematic structure the novel has ever known or is ever likely to know. "Rhythm," declares Stephen in the *Portrait,* "is the first formal esthetic relation of part to part in any esthetic whole or of an esthetic whole to its part or parts or of any part to the esthetic whole of which it is a part." It is a statement to make one a little dizzy; but *Ulysses* is a vast complex of such rhythms. Motifs recur throughout the novel as a whole—for example, the metempsychosis, the omphalos, the father-son motifs—and each chapter has as well a number of internal rhythms. Already in the *Portrait* Joyce varied his style and technique in each chapter, adapting them to the kind of experience he was representing; now, with the remorseless thoroughness and amazing resources of genius, he carries this principle to its logical extreme.

Ulysses is divided into eighteen episodes, each a distinct unit with a severe development of a number of esoteric themes having no direct relation either to development of plot or to motivation of character. Each scene has, besides a definite time and place, a title corresponding to a person or episode in the *Odyssey,* an association with a given Organ, a relation to a given Art, an appropriate Symbol and Technic, and often—with reference to Catholic liturgy—an appropriate Color. Thus, in the name of the art of Rhetoric, as well as the organ Lungs, Joyce in one chapter illustrates every known rhetorical device—Gilbert lists a hundred-odd. In the interests of Botany, he buries in another chapter the names of I forget how many hundred flowers. And in the scene in the lying-in hospital, whose organ is Womb and whose symbol Mothers, he invents the appropriate technic of Embryonic development: telling his story in an unbroken series of literary parodies, beginning in the chaos of medieval prose and ending in the pandemonium of modern slang, paralleling the growth of the embryo in the mother's womb until it emerges as a squalling infant.

The following of these labyrinthine ramifications is a fascinating business. It is not, however, the business of this chapter; Stuart Gilbert has already done it with discouraging thoroughness. Yet there are important implications in Joyce's methods, and especially in his specific Technics. The episode of the Sirens he narrates by "fuga per canonem": it contains overlapping parts corresponding to the themes of a fugue. (To appreciate this, Gilbert casually remarks, the reader must listen to all parts at once and not follow them separately—he must listen vertically as well as horizontally.) Across the episode of the newspaper office he throws bands of bold type, grotesquely vulgar and blatant headlines: SOPHIST WALLOPS HAUGHTY HELEN SQUARE

ON PROBOSCIS. SPARTANS GNASH MOLARS. ITHACANS VOW PEN IS CHAMP. By such devices as these Joyce is seeking to put a still greater distance between himself and his story, remove the last traces of a personal style or of any one manner that might be suspected as his own, project his esthetic image in still purer dramatic form so that he may achieve the ideal of utterly impersonal, divinely mysterious creation stated in the *Portrait:* "the artist, like the God of the creation, remains within or behind or beyond or above his handiwork, invisible, refined out of existence, indifferent, paring his fingernails." But what Joyce is also doing here has been clearly pointed out by Professor Beach: he is employing the principles of abstract composition exemplified in the various brands of expressionistic painting and drama. He is not merely distorting surface reality but conventionalizing it. He is presenting the essential idea of his scene, a blend of the time and place and minds of his characters with all his incidental themes, in the form of an abstract symbol that corresponds to no fact in nature. He is adding a kind of Einsteinian fourth dimension. Hence he has in the same novel carried the realistic method further and departed from it more radically than any other novelist.

More important, however, is the whole intention of Joyce, the idea behind all the Organs, Arts, Symbols, and Colors. And this seems in general clear enough. He has attempted to encompass the whole of human experience. His thorough realism will explore the whole living surface of the external world and the mind of man; his Organs will together compose the whole body and symbolize a living organism; his Arts and Symbols will embrace the whole content of human knowledge and human history; his Technics will synthetize all these relationships and intensify the ideal reality beneath them. Hence he will present not merely the entire modern world, but the Present with the entire Past summed up in it and the Future implicit in it. In the very ordinary day of a befuddled poet and a maundering canvasser he will present a miniature of the universe and a symbol of the history of mankind.

3

This is a vast and magnificent conception, and makes one pause for breath. There is nothing in the literature of the ages quite like it. Even *War and Peace* is less ambitious; and if the *Divine Comedy* and *Paradise Lost* are loftier enterprises, they are less comprehensive, even less daring, for the glorious transcendental scheme that presented a challenge to Dante and Milton also simplified their intellectual and imaginative problem, and gave them an obvious initial advantage. "Language grows limp" as one attempts to do justice to the erudition and the versatility demanded to body out this teeming microcosm; to the intellect that marshaled all this material and firmly commanded it, at once in its entirety and in its intricacy; to the powers of expression that never fall short of the most diverse and severe demands; to the imaginative resources equal to the innumerable daring feats demanded by the whole design. Joyce's gifts for observation and insight into character, for parody and satire, for shimmering poetry and robust comedy, for hewing out a colossus and carving a cherry stone—separately they may be surpassed, but in combination they are unique. There can be no doubt, I believe, that he is the most amazing genius of this age, and one of the greatest of all ages.

Joyce's achievement is not, moreover, an isolated and merely outlandish performance. It is a significant product of the modern age, and has had a powerful impact upon it. As almost all critics now recognize, *Ulysses* is rich in beginnings. Innumerable streams in contemporary fiction have their springs in it—so many and so divergent that their common source is already lost sight of. Although the work as a whole is by no means a model for future novelists, and indeed effectually defies imitation, many of Joyce's specific innovations have proved fertile. Most important novelists now writing display some indebtedness to him—I name at random Virginia Woolf, John Dos Passos, William Faulkner, Conrad Aiken, Thomas Wolfe; and it is doubtful that many important novelists of the future will write as if Joyce had not written.

For he has not merely invented some fancy accessories or literary gadgets. He has made a serious effort to find new forms and symbols for the new modes of perception and new patterns of experience; and his effort is impressive if only because he has worked on a scale at once so gigantic and so minute.

Yet with this said, one must again pause for breath—for a more pedestrian exercise. All these superlatives have not resolved the deepest issues of Joyce's work: the final issues of the quality of the vision of life served by such extraordinary gifts, the adequacy of the comment upon life expressed with such extraordinary virtuosity, in short the positive values and the final meaning of this whole extraordinary creation.

Simply as a realist, in the first place, Joyce has few superiors. His observation is unerring, his insight almost uncanny; even the many layers of artifice cannot smother the vitality of his concrete representations of experience. They may not be representative or complete, but one accepts almost unthinkingly the truth of specific motives, emotions, or actions. Joyce's characters have a kind of inevitable reality, as if they had been set before us by Jehovah himself; Mr. Bloom *is,* and there's an end on it. And this achievement is the more striking because so much of *Ulysses* is invention. Most generators of streams of consciousness have, like Dorothy Richardson or Conrad Aiken, obviously reproduced their own consciousness, or that of minds very like their own; as one listens to their intimate revelations, he has at times the uncomfortable feeling that comes with unwanted confidences. In Stephen Dedalus Joyce is plainly making similar revelations —and doing what up to a point any bright schoolboy can do (and too often does in themes entitled "On Writing a Theme"). But in Leopold and Molly Bloom he has performed the remarkable imaginative feat of reproducing convincingly the whole consciousness of minds fundamentally unlike his own.

Wyndham Lewis, it is true, has entered a serious objection. Bloom, he declares, is but a projection of another facet of Joyce's personality, and like Dedalus a wholly conventional figure. One is the misunderstood Poet, the other the stage Jew; Joyce's conception of the first is as sentimental as of the second it is shallow. It is indeed difficult warmly to defend Stephen Dedalus; he is both less interesting and less significant than I suspect his creator intended him to be. Yet if he is a too familiar type, he is also individualized with a wealth of brilliant detail; above all, he is objectively rendered, and his voice is by no means the voice of Joyce. Joyce does not bid us simply to weep at the plight of the sensitive artist in a crass world, but makes Stephen as befuddled as talented; he has neither the serenity nor the clarity and force of purpose that made possible the writing of *Ulysses.* To Leopold Bloom, however, Lewis is completely unjust. There is no proving the glory of Mr. Bloom, but I cannot understand how any reader can see in him only the traditional caricature of the Jew. Although he has certain racial characteristics, he also has characteristics that make him an almost perfect symbol of that statistical abstraction: the Average Man; and all are bodied out in the flesh and blood of an individual with an independent, quivering, and unique existence.

A far more familiar objection to *Ulysses,* however, is that it is an enormous sink, a Cloaca Maxima, an Inferno, a monstrous inventory of the ugliest, most depraved and perverted elements in human life. Paul Elmer More, for instance, was simply appalled by it; he saw in it "the ultimate principle of evil evoked as the very enemy of truth." Others, like George Russell, were able to overcome their queasiness only because of the pious hope that having belched this out of his system, Joyce would settle down to nobly constructive work. Such distress is understandable—there is much in *Ulysses* to try even tough minds and strong stomachs. It is also unfortunate, for it misses the features for the pimples. Joyce's obscenity is like that of Aristophanes and Rabelais. It is at once hearty and intellectual, and it is dignified by being subordinated to a universal comic intention—an intention that Professor More failed to see.

To his great comedy, Edwin Muir has noted, Joyce gives the last and crowning touch "by a running contrast between the vast symbols invented by man and his simple earthly reactions, between the extravagance of belief and the simplicity of fact, the decency of civilized life and the unseemliness of instinct." Hence if only for the sake of this contrast Joyce had to include in his design the spiritual element that even Muir seems to have missed; and if he subordinates this element, it was simply because he was writing a comedy, not a heroic epic. Even so, he presents from this point of view a more or less adequate picture, with the elements that go to make up the mixed and flowing substance of human nature represented in something like their true relation and their true proportion—and always with enormous gusto and humor. If it is scarcely a flattering likeness, it is still a likeness. In his maudlin confusion Stephen Dedalus nevertheless expresses some of the loftiest aspirations of the human spirit. In her rich earthiness Molly Bloom has the naturalness and health of the Wife of Bath. And Leopold Bloom, once more, is the Whole Man, at once stronger and weaker than the incarnation of ethereal imagination in Stephen, the quintessence of lusty flesh in Molly. He is an admirable symbol of ordinary decent humanity, with its utterly human blend of flesh and spirit, of noble and ignoble in dream and action alike.

Hence *Ulysses* is not clearly the statement of absolute pessimism and misanthropy, the sheerly destructive work, that it would be almost comforting to regard it. Frank Budgen, an intimate of Joyce, in fact believes that he affirms the world with a Yea as positive as Molly Bloom's—and the gusto of the book would seem to bear him out. But in the end one cannot positively commit Joyce to any philosophy of life. The very essence of his manner is his refusal to commit himself. *Ulysses* is specifically neither moral nor immoral, optimistic nor pessimistic. In his complete detachment Joyce neither praises nor blames, affirms nor denies; he simply records. In short, he has achieved something like the miracle of impersonal creation that he strove for: like the Lord of Creation he remains serene, inscrutable, invisible, imperturbable, "paring his fingernails"; and about his handiwork there is accordingly as violent disagreement as there is about Jehovah's.

Yet he is finally perhaps not so inscrutable and invisible after all. The accomplishment of the miracle is in itself revealing. André Gide has remarked that the greatest novelists and dramatists have always, like Dostoyevsky, found a way of being impartial toward their characters while yet passionately committing themselves. This way Joyce obviously did not even seek. He is as remote as the aggregate of mathematical formulas and symbols that Professor Whitehead calls God. This Olympian attitude has made his great work possible; at the same time it explains why we admire this work but are never deeply moved by it, why we read him with awe but never with love. It suggests finally an indifference or an actual coldness—no artist who felt deeply about the joys and sorrows of man could be quite so serenely objective. Similarly Joyce is no more able than any other artist to escape the implications in the selection and emphasis of his materials—for he has *not* told everything. The point of the *Ulysses* parallel, for example, is clearly ironic; this inglorious day in Dublin is the modern version of the majestic epics of the past, the squatting figure of Leopold Bloom the modern substitute for the ancient heroes. But what Joyce omits from his universal comedy is especially significant—and points to the limitations that make *Ulysses* finally so unsatisfying a masterpiece.

In this view the familiar complaints about the excessive difficulty of *Ulysses* are not merely incidental. The extremely intricate design suggests that Joyce is more concerned with manner than substance. Even one who does not resent the need of a key may feel that Joyce wastes much of his force in what comes to seem mere trickery. His many devices more often obscure than clarify and intensify his underlying meaning. The parodies, flowers, organs, rhetorical devices, and all the stunts provide a fascinating game, like a jigsaw puzzle, but it is a distracting game that must be forgotten if one is to get at his meaning and find out what is going on among his characters. In general Joyce sacrifices too much to the logical symmetry of an artificial design—not to mention his determination to write a masterpiece at all costs. The deliberate insertion, for example, of a tangle of misleading clues to symbolize the Wandering Rocks of the *Odyssey* is purely a work of supererogation. Even if one quickly gets the point of his devices, one has to sit through the whole elaborate, often dull demonstration. The scene in the cabman's shelter is purposely but insufferably tedious, and it takes up fifty solid pages—only to be followed by a still more exhaustingly monotonous catechism in which is laid bare the whole fusty skeleton of pseudo-science. In short, Joyce subjects the reader to more downright tedium than any great novelist since Richardson; at least part of the satisfaction of one who has read carefully every word of *Ulysses* is the melancholy distinction felt by the reader of the unabridged *Clarissa Harlowe.*

These demands upon the reader's patience and ingenuity at length seem, moreover, excuses for Joyce's inability to perform one of the primary jobs of the novelist. There is no real movement or dramatic development in *Ulysses;* it is simply an agglomeration. Its episodes do not follow with any inevitability or culminate in a clear impression of finality or completeness; they simply pile up. On a much greater scale it is what the *Portrait* is: a miscellany of remarkable scenes; and because these scenes are packed into a much smaller unit of time and contain so much more diverse material, *Ulysses* seems even more static, more lacking in vital unity. What grows on the reader is chiefly amaze at successive revelations of Joyce's versatile genius, not a cumulative emotion generated by a dynamic work of art.

Some readers take it that the point of this account of a day in the modern world is precisely that there is no point: that nothing of consequence happens or can happen, that life today is viewless, meaningless, valueless. If so, *Ulysses* would indeed be a work of absolute negation—and one would have better reason to deplore the expenditure of so much effort, the display of so great genius, for purposes both so simple and so chill. Yet this is not clearly Joyce's point. The impression of a mere miscellany, without organic unity or development, does not seem the result of deliberate intention; some of his many devices were apparently designed to correct it. And the trouble is that they only create a demand for more keys. The *Odyssey* parallel, for example, is an ingenious but an external framework, superimposed upon the sprawling material, that lends an added significance but does not impress one as the animating principle of the book; except for the clue in the title the reader would miss it entirely. Similarly the father-son motif is in effect less consequential than Edmund Wilson and other interpreters have made it out. Whatever Joyce's intention here, I cannot feel that Stephen's quest of a father, Bloom's quest of a son, is their ruling passion, or that their meeting has seriously influenced their lives. This meeting seems only another arbitrary and incidental episode, not a dramatic climax. Stephen stumbles out into the darkness—not until ten years later to begin *Ulysses,* the great work he has in mind. Bloom crawls into bed—for all one knows to get up the next day to put on a similar performance. And Molly thinks of them both in terms of her designs on the whole male part of creation.

What we have here is something far more serious than a fault in technique. It is the key to the insufficiency of Joyce's representation of life. One may point out many significant issues that he does not embrace in his microcosm—problems political, economic, and philosophical that might seem more important than the flowers, organs, symbols, and all the wealth of medieval and Oriental erudition. The reader of *Ulysses* would scarcely suspect, for example, that a terrible war was presently to engulf the world of Stephen Dedalus and Leopold Bloom, or that even on June 16, 1904, forces were at work that were to shake their society to its foundations. But underlying all these specific omissions is Joyce's failure to provide a central dramatic issue to bring his material to a head and deepen its meaning. He shows us with a wonderful vividness and precision the dark, shaggy, tangled undergrowth of the human mind; he does not show us the final flowering of this rank growth into conscious and significant action. Since George Eliot, English novelists have become steadily more interested in analysis of consciousness, and since Henry James more inclined to dwell lovingly on given moments, exhausting every sensation that passes through them, but this business has not been an end in itself; they have subordinated these studies to some dramatic intention, pointed them to some criticism of human behavior. So too have Lawrence, Anderson, Virginia Woolf, and others who have minimized or almost eliminated plot; their wavering or unfinished actions are brought within the focus of a vital issue. But, as Professor Beach points out, Joyce does not finally relate impulse and emotion to behavior. He does not explore the souls of Dedalus and Bloom to explain their actions; in effect he presents the incessant flux of sensation for its own sake.

What explains the sharp disagreement among critics about Joyce's essential criticism of life is not, then, merely his impersonality, his refusal to commit himself. It is his failure to present an action that would provide a basis for such criticism. Although his world gives the impression of immense and endless busyness, he does not really set it in motion; it is a still picture. Although Dedalus and Bloom appear to be swamped by sights and sounds, they live for all practical purposes in a void. Although we know them inside out, we have little more real, intimate relationship with them than they have with one another or the people about them. They shut themselves in with their fantasies and their phantoms; they strut and fret before a mirror; they resolve nothing, do nothing—and nothing significant happens to them. In short, we have the raw material for a world such as fiction before Joyce has never given us, but it has yet to be fashioned and energized. As Edwin Muir says, Joyce has magnificently objectified his world, "but it is not a world in which we could live, and to him that is, indeed, a matter of no concern."

This unconcern deepens the obvious objections to the stream-of-consciousness method. Some astute Frenchman has remarked that Joyce greatly oversimplifies our mental experience by presenting it on a single level; actually we have several thought streams flowing simultaneously at different levels, with periodic irruptions of the lower into the upper. The ordinary reader will forgive Joyce this one simplification. But he finds it harder to forgive the inevitable triviality, repetitiousness, and incoherence of much of the experience thus rendered. In *Blue Voyage,* Conrad Aiken skirts these yawning pits of inconsequence by employing the method only at a crisis when his hero has to make an all-important decision; Demarest's disconnected thoughts are focused by his anguished uncertainty and despair, they are strung on the black thread of Misery, and so they are made dramatic and meaningful. Joyce too weaves various themes into his patterns of consciousness; but some of these are esoteric, others inchoate, and none finally resolved in decision and action. Although the most important—the ghost of his mother that haunts Dedalus, the frustration as husband and father that haunts Bloom—are brought to a head and dramatized in the grandly conceived *Walpurgisnacht* scene in the brothel, this lurid glare suddenly fades into the dismal gray of the cabman's shelter and then the pure blackness of the scientific catechism, leaving Hamlet Dedalus and Everyman Bloom precisely where they were, the one to whirl and the other to potter among his fantasies, and their attendant ghosts to call wanly from far off-stage.

The negation in Joyce is thus, to repeat, not in his downright denial of specific values; it is in his failure to present a significant action in which values would be implicit. With an infinite capacity for taking pains he lays out a vast playing field and elaborates a thousand ingenious rules; but then he refuses to play ball. In cutting himself loose from the shambles of Irish politics he also cut himself loose from most of the responsible activities of modern man. What he forged in the smithy of his soul is not, as some still think, mere forgery; at the same time, one need not listen to the indignant voices of his countrymen to realize that it is not the uncreated conscience of his race. Despite the pertinence and value of many of its specific elements, *Ulysses* accordingly remains a kind of monstrosity—a monstrosity even among embryos. It is the product of unmistakable genius; it contains many passages that recall the greatest names in literary history, and other passages of a kind of greatness hitherto unexampled; it will be read at least in parts until men have become the angels or robots that the prophets foresee, and meanwhile it has been read with profit by many artists in a still imperfect, unregulated society; but as a *whole* work of art it is likely to take its place in literary history among the great curiosities, like the *Anatomy of Melancholy*.

4

In his latest performance, *Work in Progress*, Joyce withdraws still further from the world of affairs and its dilemmas and makes still less effort at cooperation. He has diverted his splendid intellectual and imaginative gifts to the invention of a still more private and elaborate game. A number of sections have already appeared—*Anna Livia Plurabelle, Tales Told of Shem and Shaun, Haveth Childers Everywhere,* etc.—but as the work grows, it becomes less rather than more intelligible. I do not pretend to have read all these fragments, or to have understood those I have read. I am too preoccupied with meanings to get more than occasional whiffs of the new fragrance that Joyce is distilling. His more devout interpreters indeed make this work sound exciting —though they are again vague about its central purpose, and take its necessity and its significance for granted. All by myself I at times feel this excitement; if he can induce a kind of hypnotic trance in which his inquiring intellect is put to sleep, the most insensitive reader can appreciate some of the rich humor and the magical music of Joyce's latest prose. One should with practice learn to get at least the same kind of pleasure that "Kubla Khan" affords. Especially when one hears Joyce himself read this prose (there is a phonograph recording of the end of *Anna Livia Plurabelle*) one is carried away by the lovely noise it makes. One even catches glimpses of its meaning, or at least falls into the mood in which this meaning can by itself somehow ease its way into the background of consciousness; many of the words that on the printed page look merely queer and baffling come to life and reveal their associations and origins, take on elusive connotations. It is possible that when the work is finally completed and provided with the indispensable keys, it will appear as significant as *Ulysses*. Meanwhile I for one can only guess—and comment on only its more obvious implications.

It appears, however, that Joyce is attempting to do for night and the dreaming state what in *Ulysses* he did for day and the waking state. Some postman is sleeping, and some kind of psychological drama is being worked out inside his mind. As the subconscious has no language of its own, Joyce has accordingly felt obliged to invent one—again to realize his ideal of pure projection. But it is probable too that he is answering some of the subtler criticisms of his methods in *Ulysses*. The stream of consciousness is after all only another convention, not—as some still appear to think—the precise and whole truth of mental experience; with the old-fashioned method of analysis, interpretation, and comment, Proust gives a fundamentally truer impression. For instance, Joyce had perforce verbalized the stream, whereas most of our mental experience is not explicitly verbal. *Work in Progress* is accordingly an attempt to render *wordless* states of mind by a necessarily new and strange language, made up of hybrids, compounds, and pure inventions, all with tentative and tangled associations, none with the logical references of everyday speech.

Needless to say, Joyce brings to the performance of this difficult task an amazing ingenuity and resource. Almost as needless to add, however, this is the simplest part of his intention: there are many elaborate sub-designs. He who is patient and adept may disentangle, for example, the names of some of the five hundred rivers that Joyce has woven into *Anna Livia Plurabelle*. *Work in Progress* has, in fact, an intricacy of design that makes *Ulysses* seem mere child's play. Where there was in *Ulysses* one, there is here a whole set of parallels: Adam and Eve, Tristan and Isolde, Michael and Lucifer, Cain and Abel, Swift and Vanessa, Napoleon and Wellington. *The Ondt and the Gracehoper,* Michael Stuart tells us, is "a mosaic of seventeen or more tongues," of which English is only the basic element: "Names of insects and insect-members, references to Egyptian religious symbolism, and to the four principles of the development of human society as laid down by the Italian jurist, Vico, are the material from which the author creates his fable." And C. K. Ogden suggests solemnly that to adjust oneself to this high endeavor one ought first to learn Eskimo.

All this I have perforce taken on faith. Even the central meaning of the drama that is being played out I must take similarly. The most owl-like critics have admitted some difficulty in catching this meaning; and to read the various things they have caught is to feel that this modesty is in order. From Joyce himself the most we have is the smiling assurance he gave Max Eastman, that in the end he will give us back our language—though in return for this handsome concession he demands that we spend a lifetime on his works.

Now, despite Joyce's expressed resentment at those who believe him to be writing with his tongue in his cheek, it is difficult to take seriously all his mystifications. One must cock an eyebrow at his remark, for instance, that one motive for planting the names of five hundred rivers was the thought of the pleasure he might give to some bright youngster in Tibet who would unearth that of his native stream. One grows suspicious of his earnestness when he spends so much time and energy on devices and displays of erudition that appear to have no vital connection with his main purpose, and that are at best decorative, at worst distracting. One wonders why he must draw upon Scandinavian, Gaelic, and so many other languages, when practically all readers are bound to miss the associations he wishes to be gathered. It is of course presumptuous to question the ways of genius, especially in one who admits uncertainty about the whole intention and import of Joyce's work; at the same time one cannot help feeling that Joyce has played by himself for so long that he simply does not have his eye on the ball.

Even after one discounts Joyce's excess baggage, however, troublesome questions remain. Like many modern poets, he is extending our poetic experience, making a provocative attempt to *render* modes of experience hitherto only suggested or described. Yet once the poet discards the language of logical reference and calculable emotive effects, once he deliberately avoids symbols whose weightings are more or less uniform, it is doubtful whether his poetry can have either a solid core of meaning or a controllable evocative force. The very care with which Joyce breeds and builds his words would seem to be wasted; the associations and connotations he so ingeniously weaves are peculiarly his *own,* they are conditioned by his peculiar experience, learning, and temperament, and there is no telling what their effect on different readers will be. But above all one wonders of the relative value of this experience: whether Joyce's latest work is worth the whole attention of so great a genius. And then one feels that as in *Ulysses* Joyce is magnificently rendering relatively insignificant experience. Like so many contemporaries he is bedazzled, and naïvely bedazzled, by the subconscious. To the moderns is the glory of the discovery and exploration of this New World. For some years now, novelists have been pointing to the irrelevance, incoherence, incongruity, and irrationality of much of our mental experience. But if it is well to take this truth into account, mature readers no longer demand so elaborate and repeated demonstration of it. If the unconscious is primal, it is not finally the most interesting and important world for responsible men. Intellect and will, decision and planned action, all that men are pleased to consider conscious, if not always rational, behavior, that appears in the great crises, leads to the great achievements as to the great failures, and is the source and measure of our values —all these results of perhaps unconscious drives, with their attendant problems for both the individual and the race, are in the end of far more significance; and this end Joyce no longer approaches. He has become, as Desmond MacCarthy declares, "the most pertinacious explorer of blind psychological alleys."

Hence there arises the question all-important to thoughtful contemporaries: What in this age has caused Joyce to withdraw and virtually repudiate its vital interests? Why, if his thought is as simple as he himself declares it is, does he feel obliged to embroider it so fantastically, bury it under so many layers of esoteric material that apparently only a gifted Eskimo can find it? It is indeed easy to make merry over *Work in Progress,* and it is relatively good clean fun; but the fun should give way to sobering reflections. What we have here is the spectacle of the greatest genius of our time spinning himself into a cocoon, squandering his extraordinary gifts in what amounts to an almost private transaction with his artistic conscience. Although the ways of genius are always mysterious, they are seldom as heathen as this.

This problem is not to be resolved by the conventional opposition between "expression" and "communication," and the easy assumption of many critics that modern poets are for some reason content merely with "expression." In no work of art can these purposes be clearly dissociated, and to assume that they are opposite poles is only to obscure the processes of poetry and confuse its issues today. The only pure self-expression is the yell when the winning touchdown is scored or the howl when a tooth is yanked; the artist is always trying to make others feel and see as he does—to communicate, to justify, to convince. Thus even Joyce appeals to the youngster in Tibet; and though the Dadaists proclaimed that "Art has no meaning!" they issued their proclamation in a *manifesto*. The mere act of publication is a manifesto, an avowal that the artist's "self-expression" should have meaning for others. Not only does he always have, however obscurely, some audience in mind while shaping his expression; his very experiences are conditioned by the society of his fellows, and modified from their inception by the age-old habit of communication.

Hence the obscurity of much modern poetry is not to be explained simply as unlicensed self-expression. To preserve his self-respect, the bewildered critic often asserts that our poets are merely babbling to themselves, chasing their own tails; the only intelligent approach to them is through a recognition that they have chosen to communicate different meanings and by different means. They are reflecting new concepts of reality, attempting to render different modes of experience. Their practice may indeed be extreme and ill-advised, and certainly it is difficult; it may harden into mere mannerism, the *rigor mortis* of most conscious innovation; but their central purposes are ordinarily both serious and intelligent. There is no mistaking the earnestness of most members of the so-called "cult of unintelligibility"—of Hart Crane and T. S. Eliot, in more recent times of Auden, Spender, and Lewis. Far from being indifferent to their audience, they have an excess of the evangelical ardor behind all art. They make an intensely, even a desperately serious comment upon life. If what they live for is not clear, they give the impression of being ready to die for it. And precisely here Joyce parts company with this earnest group. His mystifications often seem to be an end in themselves; when they are more clearly a concomitant of his materials, these materials in turn fail to suggest a deeply significant purpose, to embody vital meanings and values. He is intent upon saying something—obviously he is not writing just for his own amusement—but what he is saying grows not only more esoteric but seemingly more incidental. And so again the question arises: what has caused Joyce to turn his back on his society—on not only the present scheme of values, but on all efforts at revaluation?

One may in the first place point to a few obvious influences on his work. By education and by temperament Joyce has affinities with the medieval schoolmen; his nostrils still quiver at the faintest whiff of what Lynch in the *Portrait* calls the "true scholastic stink." Like T. S. Eliot he has affinities with the seventeenth-century metaphysical poets—abstruseness and obscurity are by no means the exclusive property of modern artists. More significant, however, is the weak eyesight that made the Dublin of *Ulysses* a city of voices and sounds rather than of sights, and that has since steadily failed. As early as the *Portrait* Joyce shows a bat-like interest in words for their own sake, and himself remarks that, partly because of his dim sight, "he drew less pleasure from the reflection of the glowing sensible world through the prism of a language many-coloured and richly storied than from the contemplation of an inner world of individual emotions mirrored perfectly in a lucid supple periodic prose."

Frank Budgen tells us of Joyce's satisfaction in the product of a whole day's labor on *Ulysses:* two sentences. Nor was he seeking, like Flaubert, the *mot juste,* for he had the words to begin with; all he sought was the perfect order. (For those who wonder whether they were worth such pains, these are the sentences:

"Perfume of embraces all him assailed. With hungered flesh obscurely, he mutely craved to adore.") Hence it is not strange that Joyce finally came, like Gertrude Stein, to have an almost mystic regard for words as having a mysterious life and will of their own. Writers are always prone to love and worship words in themselves—for the same reason that a hunter fondles his gun, a scholar his books, a craftsman his tools, and mankind generally the instruments of its welfare—machinery, education, the ballot. It is a natural and pious instinct. It is also a dangerous one, likely to lead to a confusion of means with ends. Thus both Joyce and Gertrude Stein forget that however enchanting their colors and rhythms, words are by mankind at large inevitably associated with meanings; that language is finally not a toy to play with but man's chief instrument of communication and cooperation.

Kenneth Burke suggests that Joyce's blindness is the *result,* not the cause, of his heretical accomplishments. Joyce has so ruthlessly analyzed and reclassified his earliest, deepest pieties that one might expect to find physical counterparts of this spiritual disintegration; thus his eyesight has failed sympathetically with the outraging of all the perceptions of his youth. This is a curious restatement of what in earlier, more reverent ages might have been interpreted as the vengeance of an angry deity. But if the idea is difficult to accept even in this fashionable version, it at least points to another important element in the complex genius of Joyce: the hangover from the intense religious experience of his youth pictured in the *Portrait.* Thus T. S. Eliot has remarked that his work is "penetrated with Christian feeling," and that he is the "most ethically orthodox" of eminent modern writers. Others perceive an adolescent desire to shock and disgust, a preoccupation with physical love as evil and exciting, an overpowering sense of sin, that would indicate that Stephen Dedalus never really recovered from the effects of the sermon on hell-fire and has still a vivid fear of the Devil. Desmond MacCarthy locates the genesis of *Ulysses* in "hag-ridden horror," Stephen Spender sees chiefly a nightmare of "endless sin and no salvation"; both leave the book with the taste of dust and ashes in their mouths.

The *Walpurgisnacht* scene indeed bears out this interpretation of *Ulysses:* here is a nightmare of sin, a ghastly picture of hell-fire burning men's souls, more horribly vivid than even the old Puritan divines ever conjured for the edification of their flock. But the *Walpurgisnacht* is not the end of the book. It is immediately toned down; the book ends with Molly—and in the magnificent rendering of Molly there is certainly no squeamish horror or disgust with flesh. If *Ulysses* contains many dusty pages, it also contains many of a Rabelaisian gusto. And this suggests that although there is undoubtedly still a strong Catholic element in Joyce, he has nevertheless been able to dissociate it, view it with the remarkable detachment that made his masterpiece possible, subject it to the same merciless analysis and fit it into the same formal design as he did with other experience. The religious hang-over explains, moreover, only some of his matter; it does not adequately explain his manner, his whole vast and intricate scheme.

Edwin Muir indeed attempts to explain all of *Ulysses* so—though he has Joyce suffering from more than the torments of a Catholic conscience. "A writer whose sufferings were so great and so conscious," he writes in *Transitions,* "needed a more elaborate technique than most writers do, as much to put a distance between himself and his sufferings as to express them." What oppresses Joyce is finally the mediocrity of his age, the "miasmal mist" of modern life. "It is a weight of second-rate sentiment and thought, and the time comes when the only thing to be done is to clear it away." Hence *Ulysses* is a purge, an immense catharsis—and the still more elaborate technique of *Work in Progress* the result presumably of acquired habit. But one doubts that Joyce is indeed so hypersensitive to the crudities and vulgarities of modern life—he portrays them, once more, with too much gusto. One doubts even more that really intense suffering would find surcease in laboring a day on the perfect rhythmic ordering of two sentences. Certainly Joyce's intimates give no such account of a bruised and tortured spirit; what chiefly impresses an observer is the serenity with which he goes his way in the face of both extravagant praise and violent abuse. And when Muir writes,

"One feels again and again in *Ulysses* that the uproariousness of the farce, the recklessness of the blasphemy, is wildest where the suffering of the artist has been most intense," I can say only that I feel nothing of the kind. If one did feel this, he would be more deeply moved than most readers of *Ulysses* are.

That Joyce suffers from his age is certain; but what he suffers from, finally, is less its mediocrity than its chaos—the chaos underlying not merely Irish politics, or even capitalist politics, but all fields of thought and activity. His most profound linkage, if not his most immediate, is with the Symbolists. These poets, as Edmund Wilson says, made it their whole business "to communicate unique personal feelings." Every sensation was to them private, special, singular: never to be conveyed by bald statement, always to be intimated through a series of images or symbols—"a complicated association of ideas represented by a medley of metaphors." And Joyce, as in various ways Proust, Yeats, Valéry, Gertrude Stein, and Eliot, has but amplified this refined and private business, extending it into new fields and further developing its esoteric implications.

In its beginnings, Symbolism was that familiar literary phenomenon: the swing of the pendulum. Wilson explains it as the second romantic movement of the nineteenth century, a reaction more specifically against science and its literary counterpart, naturalism; in this view the highly suggestive, personal style of the Symbolist poets is a reaction against the purely conceptual, denotative style of the scientist, the endless naming of things by the naturalist. Yet even in its beginnings Symbolism had still deeper implications. In the rapidly growing confusion of modern life, the whole poetic medium was beginning to break down. The scientist conveys information through a universal language of symbols whose references are precise and unmistakable; the poet, seeking to move his readers and convey a state of mind, must use a vocabulary loaded with emotional associations, secondary meanings, implications of value, and can be effective only when this vocabulary evokes a more or less uniform, predictable response. The scientist could thus still address his whole society; the poet could not. The Symbolists accordingly gave up trying to address mankind. They were content to address a small group of chosen spirits as exquisitely sensitive as themselves.

If this is reading too much into the earlier Symbolists, in their spiritual children the movement has plainly taken on philosophical implications and broadened out into something far more significant than a merely literary reaction or a new and fancy fashion of writing. Mallarmé may have cultivated his subtle, fleeting, unique sensations chiefly in protest against the broad, heavy strokes of naturalism; Proust exploited similar material because it seemed to him the only material available, the only source of truth. What explains Proust's work is accordingly not mere snobbishness, or perverse whim, or calculated eccentricity. It is the blurring of objective reality and the dissolution of certainties in all fields of thought. It is the resultant dearth of authoritative values, the collapse of lines of communication. New perspectives and new causes are suggested daily, but no choice has clear validity or meets with universal approval. Lesser writers have been content to live from hand to mouth on fashion; greater writers have often sought some integrating social principle—Lawrence in a phallic consciousness, Mann in a reconstructed humanism, Wassermann in a Christian brotherhood, more and more today in Communism. But it is not surprising that others have faced inward, retreated to the only reality they felt that they could know: their own immediate consciousness. This retreat can be followed step by step in the career of Gertrude Stein, from the tender simplicity of *Three Lives* through *The Making of an American* to the confirmed unintelligibility of her latest manner. It is equally plain and steady in the career of James Joyce, from *Dubliners* through the *Portrait* and *Ulysses* to *Work in Progress*. He took off from the world of familiar, objective reality; he has landed in the remote, exclusive world of his own individuality.

Hence both the glory and the impotence of Symbolism, early and late. It has attracted some of the greatest talents of our era. They have opened up exciting new possibilities, introduced methods and materials for a brilliant new art. But in being driven back upon themselves, they came to make their poetry and fiction a too narrowly personal affair. All lost touch with, or even curiosity about, the external world, which is the more real and urgent as it becomes more confusing. All have suffered the fate that awaits the extreme introvert, and lapsed into some form of morbidity or absurdity, some of them into sheer unintelligibility. It is not enough, once more, merely to call them names, stigmatize them as "defeatists" or "escapists"—the adjustment to reality of all artists commonly involves some denial of the present, some revolt against things as they are. Yet one may fairly protest that the adjustment of these artists provides relatively little of substantial and universal significance, that the states of mind they induce usually have little vital connection with the serious problems of living, that in general their values are too rarefied and idiosyncratic. The logical culmination of their art was the pure freakishness of the Dadaists, who denied logic, morality, principle, and all possibility of universal meaning, and who did not even pretend always to understand their own work.

In none of these writers is the resultant waste as deplorable as in James Joyce. Only Proust can rival him in bold and brilliant originality and in mastery of his materials; but only Gertrude Stein rivals him in the distance he has put between himself and his readers. "Poets talking to themselves," Max Eastman calls this assorted company, and what particularly exasperates many readers is that they can manage to overhear so little of the talk. The linguistic difficulties that Joyce presents are by themselves, however, relatively unimportant. Readers may in time become adjusted to them, as through the ages they have learned to accustom themselves to strange, original modes of expression—to Blake, to Wagner, to Cézanne. But when they have learned to read Joyce fluently, and no longer congratulate themselves on their accomplishment, they are likely to feel that this is what it is: an elegant accomplishment. Joyce's indifference to the demands he makes upon his readers is but a symptom of a deeper indifference: a refusal to cooperate with his fellow men, to address their deepest needs, to enter the world of their conscious and responsible activities. Although art need not give explicit instructions for an art of living, a great art always has some vital relation to it. Joyce has indicated exhilarating possibilities for such an art, and pointed to ways of orientation in a new world; but instead of himself realizing these possibilities he has steadily retreated. He has provided an appropriate vocabulary but not an ideology. Perhaps he has written in the only way possible for him to write; he has in any event given us so lavishly, especially in *Ulysses,* that it may seem churlish to ask for more; yet as it now stands, his is primarily a performer's art. Extraordinarily skilful as it is, and fascinating to observe, it is an art finally in which only a few specialists in the audience can really participate. It is more an exhibition than an experience.

XVII

VIRGINIA WOOLF, AND FEMININE FICTION

I

THE novels of Virginia Woolf, supplemented by her numerous critical essays, make an excellent primer for the study of the advanced technique of modern fiction. Her early novels, *The Voyage Out* (1915) and especially *Night and Day* (1919), were more or less conventional in form; *Jacob's Room* (1922) made a bold departure that has been confirmed and extended by all her later work, and rationalized in an explicit, consistent creed. She protests in the first place against the materialism of the great Edwardians (Bennett, Galsworthy, Wells)—the sea of *things* in which their characters are drowned. But with their detail she rejects their methods and their whole conception of the art of fiction: the externalized description and analysis, the tight, symmetrical plots, the trim patterns of character—in sum the solidity and rigidity of life as they portray it. Life is not a "series of gig lamps" but a "luminous halo"; and this halo cannot be rendered by mere inventory or analysis. In "Mr. Bennett and Mrs. Brown" she admitted that enlightened contemporaries have themselves not yet created a great character, but she is confident that in time they will catch the elusive Mrs. Brown. Then will begin "one of the most important, the most illustrious, the most epoch-making" chapters in the history of the novel.

For this glorious cause Virginia Woolf has accordingly done her bit, with as great conscientiousness as modesty. She has made it her whole business to reproduce in purer form the actual sensation of living: to render immediately the essence of experience by subtle intimation and not by analysis or comment, by the evocation of atmosphere and not by formal narrative, by innumerable quick snapshots and not by set pictures of studio poses. In short, she is one of the most thoroughgoing impressionists. The Edwardians, she declares, give "a vast sense of things in general, but a very vague one of things in particular"; and life does not necessarily exist more fully in apparently big than in apparently small things. "Let us record the atoms as they fall upon the mind in the order in which they fall, let us trace the pattern, however disconnected and incoherent in appearance, which each sight and incident scores upon consciousness."

Hence the minimizing of plot in her novels, as in so much modern fiction. Matthew Josephson once announced that the novel is approaching the saturation point because of the limited number of "situations" available, the sameness of most story material (the statisticians of criticism have reduced the number of basic plots to a distressingly low figure); he finds the chief significance of Mrs. Woolf, Joyce, and others in that they are confronting the problem of "how to write a novel without telling a story." This is a new version of a complaint as old as Horace. But Josephson not only overlooks the endless possibilities of variation and combination; he forgets that the same objection might be made to life itself—yet people go on living, and apparently find life on the whole as strange and exciting as ever. The invincible popularity of the risqué anecdote is in itself enough to make nonsense of the notion that we have grown weary of familiar situations. The real reasons for the contemporary's exaggerated distrust of "story," his sophisticated contempt for "mere story-tellers," are rather those implied by Virginia Woolf: an interest in states of mind more than in actions, an impression of enormous complexity impossible to fit into simple molds, above all a feeling that neither the deeper truths nor the actual *feel* of life can be adequately rendered by tidy narratives with a definite beginning, middle, and end. It is an insistence, once more, that life itself does not narrate. Plot has gone the way of the other trappings of conventional realism, and for similar reasons; all have come to be regarded as superficial, artificial, or *unreal.*

This central intention explains all the striking characteristics of Mrs. Woolf's methods: the myriad sensory impressions, the stream of consciousness, the deliberate discontinuity and the liberties with chronology, what Professor Beach calls the composite picture or Gide the "breadthwise cutting" of the slice of life; and all have many parallels in modern fiction. She is especially indebted to James Joyce, most obviously in her use of the interior monologue. She differs from Joyce in that she filters and canalizes the stream of consciousness, selecting, distilling, and then projecting by a very personal style a blend of sensations and conscious and subconscious thoughts that gives a vivid illusion of mental experience without being a literal picture of it; but like him she is interested in the endless flux of consciousness, and presents the outside world only as refracted through it. She remains almost entirely within the minds of her characters. In *The Waves,* indeed, she never gets out.

All this is best illustrated in *Mrs. Dalloway,* the most successful of her novels. Like *Ulysses,* it is the record of a single day, a day in London; and like Joyce, Virginia Woolf introduces unconnected characters and incidents, and develops a number of themes whose relation is primarily symphonic. She gives as vivid an impression of a dense cross-section, and a distinctly more vivid impression of the flow of time, the passing of a day. Many readers have admired the subtle, continuous interpenetration of consciousness and background—London at every moment suffusing the minds of her characters until it becomes a living presence. In a sense Clarissa Dalloway presides over this scene. She is on the forefront of the stage most of the time, thinking about her old lover and the party she is to give. Her relations with Peter establish a kind of dramatic conflict, her party finally winds up the day. Yet there is no real dénouement, no real plot, for nothing is resolved. These more prominent characters provide a focus and a point of view, but they are not Mrs. Woolf's whole interest. Nor does she, like Joyce, introduce purely artificial devices to unify her scattered material. She apparently has more confidence in the legitimacy of her intention and is free from his uneasy feeling that without such devices he could not convey a whole and single impression. She is content simply to give the full sensation of living during her day; and without all his organs, her novel is more clearly organic and has a more distinct configuration. She succeeds in establishing a subtle kind of unity and completeness that satisfies all readers but those who must have a full stop to their symphony, a resounding chord that leaves no doubt as to the propriety of clapping and reaching for their hats.

2

As I am not an ardent admirer of the work of Virginia Woolf, simple justice demands a prefatory tribute to her many admirable qualities. Almost all readers are impressed by her exquisite artistry. It is revealed immediately in a prose style that has few equals in modern fiction. Always delicate, supple, shimmering, cadenced, it is at once lovely in itself and splendidly expressive. Inevitably one speaks of "nuances," the precision with which she renders the elusive shades of thought and feeling, sight and sound. With so fine an instrument at her command, Mrs. Woolf hence achieves brilliantly the end she set for herself: the imaginative re-creation rather than the formal dissection of human experience.

By her highly selective art, moreover, she manages to skirt the more obvious dangers implicit in her methods and materials. She gains all the intimacy and immediacy of the mental soliloquy at the minimum cost of triviality, incoherence, irrelevance, or mere messiness. Above all, she does not explore consciousness and record sensation for its own sake. If she presents no dramatic struggle, she always refers the sensations of her leading characters to fundamental problems of conduct: the joy and the sorrow, the mystery of the meaning of life with which they are all intensely preoccupied.

Finally, one should be grateful for the mellowness of Mrs. Woolf—a mellowness, unlike that of some of her British contemporaries, neither self-conscious nor premature. She is one of the few important literary personalities of this age that seem in no way maimed or poisoned by it. Her art is no sublimation of her private woes or compensation for her private frustration; it offers no excuse to call in the psychoanalyst lurking around the corner. Although contemporary novelists are less prone to a cold hate of their characters than they are reputed to be, none remains on more affable terms with his characters while yet keeping so clear of them. She has all the easy familiarity of the great Victorians without their habit of taking liberties with it. In short, her fiction like her criticism consistently displays a spirit serene, tolerant, humane, civilized.

So much, at least, must be granted Virginia Woolf. She is on one of the forefronts of modern fiction; she is one of the most distinguished of living women writers. Yet this very eminence sharpens a somewhat embarrassing issue. What finally impresses me in her fiction is its insubstantiality. This exquisite art somehow runs thin, this "luminous halo" somehow grows wraithlike. Her novels have nothing of the elemental force of Dostoyevsky, Hardy, or Dreiser; among their own impressionistic kind they have little of the intensity and glow of Conrad, Proust, or Lawrence. Behind all their subtlety and vividness is no real passion or energy. With her unfailing acuteness Mrs. Woolf has stated exactly the limitations of the art of Arnold Bennett; Bennett was himself as just when he remarked, with masculine bluntness, that her novels "seriously lack vitality."

This deficiency is in part the price of her method and creed. To "record the atoms as they fall," to "trace the pattern . . . which each sight and incident scores upon consciousness," is inevitably to give disproportionate emphasis to separate moments, and hence likely to leave an effect of inconsequence. Mrs. Woolf flits about her subject, throws a flashing light from many angles, darts in to capture bright bits of truth; but by the very nature of this method she never comes to grips with a situation. She does not confront steadily a deep emotion or really plunge into it. A brilliant butterfly, swift in flight, she settles unerringly on the choicest flowers and extracts their choicest essence; but she never gets to the roots. Hence even the lovely style—dipping, sparkling, rippling, at any given moment a marvel of expressiveness—ultimately palls. The constant flutter and glimmer becomes monotonous; at the end it suggests preciosity or mere fussiness.

Similarly Mrs. Woolf pays the penalty of her too constant immersion in the inner life—which is not the whole of life. In reacting against the excesses of laborious documentation, she has contracted a kind of horror of externals—which are after all *real.* Too often we are straining our eyes at a mist. In actual experience, the halo that is her constant concern surrounds a solid, earthy substance; but of this substance she gives us only fleeting, sidelong glimpses. Hence, as Elizabeth Drew remarks, "we feel rather as if we were trying to construct the plot of a Greek play from nothing but the remarks of the chorus." Fragile and anemic to begin with, her characters come finally to seem disembodied spirits—wispy, evanescent, despite their spiritual essence perishable. One has only to set the fragile Clarissa Dalloway beside Mrs. Morel of *Sons and Lovers* to perceive the difference between characterization that is subtle and sharp and characterization that is also solid. And this refining away of the solid substance of character becomes even more fastidious in the later novels of Mrs. Woolf. *Mrs. Dalloway* is set against the living background of London; in *The Waves* the outside world fades into a backdrop, leaving six minds quivering in a sensitized vacuum, six characters in search of an author: an author to give them flesh, blood, dress, a home, a world—anything to clothe their precious spirits.

What sucks the blood out of Virginia Woolf's novels is not entirely, however, this ultra-refined technique. Even her early, more conventional novels, written before she had arrived in this rarefied realm where material circumstance is a kind of vulgar illusion, are wanting in vitality. They are less memorable, in fact, than her later novels, and plainly suggest that her later manner is more natural and becoming to her. And so one must look into her temperament, her whole equipment as a novelist, to discover the final explanation of her limitations.

In reviewing *To the Lighthouse,* Conrad Aiken paid a poet's tribute to the old-fashioned fragrance of Mrs. Woolf's spirit, the odor of old lavender that comes off her work despite the ultra-modernity of her technique and her insight. Her characters are all gentle folk framed in a beautiful little picture in a cloistered gallery; and this tightly circumscribed scene is what gives her novels "their odd and delicious air of parochialism, as of some small village-world, as bright and vivid and perfect in its tininess as a miniature: a small complete world which time has somehow missed." Here is the charm of her work—and it is much the charm of Mrs. Gaskell's *Cranford*. Here is also the reason why it is little more than charming. As creatures of shelter, her characters are too delicate to participate in a really big or intense drama. They never have to worry about vulgar necessity or the intrusion of rude, elemental emotion. They hear only as off-stage rumbles and rumors the great, terrifying, destructive forces of the outside world—as Clarissa Dalloway experiences the World War, a very horrid thing for a lady to have to think about. "I am all fiber. All tremors shake me," declares one of the six soliloquists of *The Waves*. "I dance. I ripple. I am thrown over you like a net of light," says another. "Now," exclaims less fortunate phantom No. 3, "I will wrap my agony inside my pocket-handkerchief." This is an almost complete summary of the perfected art of Virginia Woolf. These are indeed children speaking, but when they are grown up as ladies and gentlemen their accents are as highly mannered, their responses as tremulous, their feelings as refined. None has an emotion that cannot be wrapped up in a pocket-handkerchief.

This is not to say that Mrs. Woolf is herself tender-minded and merely genteel—she clearly sees through her Mrs. Dalloway. Neither is it to deny her the right to her materials—the world is infested with Mrs. Dalloways. Yet one may fairly comment that out of such material at most only minor classics can be woven. In the world she has chosen to create, neither robust comedy nor deeply moving tragedy is possible. And what clearly defines her limitations is that this is apparently the only kind of world she is able to create. In *Mrs. Dalloway,* to be sure, she introduces one

Septimus Smith, a shell-shocked veteran, to supplement the narrowness of Clarissa's range of experience. His madness and suicide would appear to symbolize the brutal realities of the outside world, set Clarissa's party in its right perspective, provide the complement necessary for a whole picture of London. But even this madness has been toned down, purged of all terrifying elements. It is a very gentle, tender, wistful madness, nothing like that represented by Shakespeare and Dostoyevsky. It is merely touching, at worst disturbing. It is indeed almost pretty.

To this extent at least Mrs. Woolf shares the frailty of her characters: like them she never surrenders herself to life. She is seemingly as afraid to pull out all the stops and let go. The penalty of her culture and refinement is a too highly self-conscious art, an almost fearful aloofness, in Aiken's words a "dexterous holding of the raw stuff of life at arm's length." Conrad was equally concerned with the "semi-transparent envelope" about human experience, but he strove to penetrate it, sink his teeth in the solid emotional experience from which it emanates; she gives us simply the envelope. She shies away from any experience so uncouth that it cannot be reduced to the tidy proportions of her drawing-room world, so powerful that it might break through the gossamer web of her art. It is, once more, a brilliantly woven web; but it is too finespun to contain any big emotion, any violent conflict, any profound or tumultuous experience.

3

In *A Room of One's Own* Virginia Woolf wrote a notable preamble to a kind of feminine Declaration of Independence. She asked that women writers be granted the same freedom as men, the same right to follow their calling in retirement without being asked to perform more mundane duties. Although her very well-mannered plea scarcely created a furor, it was still a challenge; and no doubt it helped to secure a privilege already more generally taken for granted. Mrs. Woolf now has a room of her own. But what does she do in it? She sits and embroiders. She does water colors in pastel shades. She plays minor chords with the soft pedal down. In short, her room might as well be the drawing-room of a parsonage, and she serving tea to the ladies of the parish. Essentially, she writes like that busy housewife, mother, and soft-eyed model of Victorian womanhood, Mrs. Elizabeth Cleghorn Gaskell.

Now, this is a quite legitimate occupation, today as before. I would not join the rude pack howling outside her window and demand of Mrs. Woolf that she go out and rub elbows with the workers, give us a strike with bloody riots, hail the coming Revolution. Yet one wonders at the persistence of this fragile femininity. One wonders why so many other women novelists in rooms of their own write in the same key, and why their works are greeted so rapturously by other emancipated women critics. One is finally tempted to generalize the contribution of women to modern fiction, to group them in a single chapter as the Society of the Daughters of Henry James.

The first of the nine volumes of Dorothy Richardson's *Pilgrimage,* a continuous record of the atoms that fell upon the consciousness of one Miriam Henderson, was greeted with some enthusiasm; the discontinuance of this record saddened few readers—was in fact scarcely noticed. At first attracted by the novelty of the method—a mere association of sensations and ideas without dramatic issue and social or philosophical theme—most readers had all they wanted of Miriam and her sensitive impressions long before the ninth volume. In *The House of Mirth* Edith Wharton made what in its day (1905) seemed a daringly realistic study of high society, and in *Ethan Frome* she wrote a poignant, if too perfectly chiseled and "artistic," tragedy of New England life; but the bulk of her work concerns the doings of pallid gentlefolk and soon acquires the mustiness that has already sent *The House of Mirth* to the attic. In her early work, especially *My Antonia,* Willa Cather wrote simply, robustly, almost grandly the epic of the Mid-Western pioneers; she has since withdrawn into a kind of nunnery to give herself up to wistful reminiscence, and now employs her beautiful prose in the embroidery of such wispy stuff as *Shadows on the Rock* and *Lucy Gayheart.* Ellen Glasgow has still a vein of iron and irony; but the author of the starkly realistic *Barren Ground* recently gave way to a rather petulant outburst against the school of novelists that has been portraying the cruder, harsher realities of Southern life, and now seems more at home among the refined emotions of the decayed gentility in *The Sheltered Life.* Similarly one could tick off the names and generalize the achievements of Anne Sedgwick, Rosamond Lehmann, Dorothy Canfield Fisher, and innumerable lesser practitioners of this delicate art. At their worst they seem simply remote, hovering fussily over the fringes of modern life. At their best they have a rare sensitiveness, they write beautifully, they render with nice precision the subtle gradations of perception and sensation—but in this delicious banquet the mere man still yearns for a little red beef and port wine.

There are, of course, many significant exceptions to this generalization. In an earlier age, George Eliot's work has a quality that men are pleased to call masculine; *Wuthering Heights* seethes with an unladylike passion. Among contemporaries, Sigrid Undset writes in a major key; Pearl Buck's *The Good Earth* has a simple strength, as do the novels of Henry Handel Richardson; Evelyn Scott is, if not first-rate, at least not fluttery; and a number have caught fire from the class war. Yet most of the more conspicuous women novelists are like Virginia Woolf still specialists in the wistful, fragile, filmy, dainty. They are Mrs. Gaskells in modern dress. Even the sophisticates, like Tess Slesinger in *The Unpossessed,* do not penetrate to the roots of the dilemma of the disenchanted, and they display in their cynicism a quality that a Victorian would instantly recognize as feminine.

The simplest explanation of this quality is that women have for centuries been insulated against the larger, more abstract problems, conditioned to a more direct dependence upon their immediate human environment; and ingrained attitudes cannot be changed overnight by new fashions or even by new legislation. Probably, too, women are biologically adapted to different modes of experience. In his fascinating studies of child psychology, Jean

Piaget observed that little girls have no single game with as many rules as the little boys themselves have elaborated for marbles, no game with "as fine and consistent an organization and codification." Their ingenuity in hopscotch, for example, is displayed chiefly in the invention of new figures; rules they revise freely, having less regard for their authority and less interest in general concepts. At any rate the fact as we now have it is that women writers concern themselves primarily with the more concrete and intimate problems of human relationships, less with large issues or ultimate meanings. As Elizabeth Drew remarks, it is difficult to imagine a woman writing a novel like *Lord Jim, The Brothers Karamazov,* or *Arrowsmith,* based on the hero's necessity of harmonizing his soul with some ideal concept apart from the practical problems of everyday living. And as Edwin Muir admits after a eulogy of Virginia Woolf, "The one important quality of the critic which she lacks is the power of wide and illuminating generalization." In short, the explanation of their work in the novel is also the explanation of why there are women columnists but few philosophers, of why there are women singers and musicians but few composers, of why—though for centuries they have been trained to paint—there are few great women painters. They reproduce with consummate sensitiveness; they seldom create on a large scale or in the light of a large ideal concept.

I repeat—and not out of chivalry—that all this by no means justifies a contemptuous attitude toward the women novelists. Their province is a legitimate one in the midst of whatever crises or revolutions; and if it is difficult, in the face of *Remembrance of Things Past* or *Death in Venice,* to continue romantically to attribute to them a delicacy and sensitiveness beyond the experience of men, it is foolish to scorn the charm of their work or deny its validity within their range. If they seldom produce more than minor classics, only the portentously solemn reader would spend all his time among masterpieces. Moreover, they have generally a sureness and directness, a balance and poise, that are restful in a restless age. If at times they settle into a superficial and depressing "soundness"—as in the Maine school recently become popular—at best they have the sanity that comes from a clear perception of the simple realities and simple values of ordinary existence. Precisely because they are chiefly concerned with immediate realities, the women writers are less likely to be distracted or thwarted by the profound uncertainties of this era. Yet for this same reason they are less significant for the purposes of this study. The deeper issues of modern literature and life have no doubt given to many men a sickly and oppressive self-consciousness; but they are nevertheless urgent, they must somehow be met. Virginia Woolf and her sisters contribute little but their incidental refinements of method and manner.

XVIII

MARCEL PROUST

I

LIKE James Joyce today, Marcel Proust became something of a myth even before he died. His asthma, his cork-lined room, his overcoats, his owl-like excursions into the world from which he had withdrawn—these and other elements mysterious and fantastic were woven into legends that swelled the esoteric reputation of his great work. Readers still approach *Remembrance of Things Past* with the preternaturally solemn, expectant hush of one about to be initiated into holy mysteries, distinguished from the generality of men. To him who has read *Ulysses,* however, the ceremony proves relatively simple. One needs no keys or guides, but only patience and perseverance. If he is at first bewildered, overwhelmed, he at length finds, in the last volume, a complete explanation of Proust's intention, an explicit statement of his whole philosophy of fiction. But long before he has reached *The Past Recaptured* he should have recognized that despite his originality, Proust has many linkages with contemporary novelists, and as many with the old-fashioned novelists of the nineteenth century. His remarkable novel is as much a culmination as a pioneering expedition.

As is commonly remarked, Proust's whole world comes out of a teacup—the teacup into which he dipped the famous madeleine. His novel is the epic of involuntary memory: the memory that comes unbidden, is perhaps unrecognized, but brings the pure emotion of the original experience. He insists that the conscious, voluntary memory summoned by intellect is colorless, undistinguishing, essentially false. It is an arbitrary selection from a file of mental thesis slips, a blunt generalization of past experience that does not contain its living essence; like all the abstractions of the intellect, it is merely convenient for practical dealings. Involuntary memory, however, recaptures "a fragment of time in its pure state":

> But let a sound already heard or an odour caught in bygone years be sensed anew, simultaneously in the present and the past, real without being of the present moment, ideal but not abstract, and immediately the permanent essence of things, usually concealed, is set free and our true self, which had long seemed dead but was not dead in other ways, awakes, takes on fresh life as it receives the celestial nourishment brought to it.*

Hence Proust belongs with the large group who are protesting against the dominion of intellect, and more specifically with the impressionists. "The ideas formed by pure intellect," he declares, "have only a logical truth, a potential truth." Far more profound are the ideas that life communicates to us, without our knowledge, in the form of sensory impressions. The mere engraving of these impressions upon our minds is always the guaranty of their indispensable truth. "Only the subjective impression, however inferior the material may seem to be and however improbable the outline, is a criterion of truth"; it is for the artist "what experimentation is for the scientist," for though it comes through the senses, the mind can discern its inner meaning.

Now, in making such invidious contrasts of different mental functions, substituting *versus* where the reasonable connective would seem to be a simple *and,* Proust falls into the familiar fallacy of hypostatizing verbal symbols—mistaking his printing press money for minted gold. Certainly he is prodigal with such counters as *truth, reality,* and *essence,* which have a fine ring but an almost illegible inscription; certainly he does not clarify our picture of the mind by using the symbols of logic and science to disparage logic and science and to magnify the value of a different

* These and subsequent quotations are reprinted from F. A. Blossom's translation of *The Past Recaptured,* with the permission of Random House.

kind of experience. Although he seeks a vital synthesis, he approaches it through artificial dualisms, abstractions as arbitrary as those he rejects. Yet his philosophy is at least the real core of his novel, not a mere appendage. It actually explains his practice, and gives it both dignity and consistency. His retirement from the active world was in this view no flight from reality; it was a flight *into* reality. He consecrated himself to the study of the true nature of things, the extraction of the essential meaning and value of his impressions (throughout this exposition I repeat his admittedly loose references to "truth"); and the only way he could study these impressions was "to try to know them more completely at the spot where they were to be found, namely, within myself." He had to dismiss the present in order to recapture the past, for his imagination could not function freely until the object that inspired it was absent; only after impressions have settled in our consciousness can we distill their essence, perceive their whole significance. Hence Proust's joy at the realization that his whole misspent life up to the time he began to write had been an unconscious Vocation. In the midst of his frivolous pleasures he had unwittingly been storing up the materials for his great work. Life, like a beneficent mother, had steadily been implanting impressions on the mind of its heedless child. Now in a spirit of filial gratitude he would make use of this bounty.

No less joyous to Proust was the realization that he need not be disturbed by all the conflicting literary theories about subject matter and method: he had his only possible materials at hand, and his method was implicit in them. Above all he could escape the dreary bondage to the false gods of Realism. The "miserable listing of lines and surfaces" is precisely the art farthest removed from reality; for reality is hidden beneath all the details the realist so painstakingly notes, all the layers of formal knowledge he substitutes for it. The essence Proust sought lay in a greater intimacy not with things but with self, a more complete realization of our total response to these things. It was to be found "not in the outward appearance of the subject, but in the extent to which this impression had penetrated to a depth where that appearance was of little importance." In short, realism is but another of the abstractions or conventions of intellect.

At the same time—and here he differs radically from Lawrence—Proust was far from scorning the intellect. It is useful in developing the "negatives" in our memory. It throws some light of its own, helps to pierce with understanding the impressions life has stored. If nothing else, its grosser perceptions provide a medium in which can be held in suspension the precious essences "too rare for the work of art to be composed wholly of them." "I felt surging within me," he writes, "a multitude of truths concerning passions, characters and customs which might well serve in that manner." A multitude indeed! *Remembrance of Things Past* is so packed with comment that it makes Thackeray or Meredith seem shy and reticent. Proust's stream of sensations is constantly swollen by the products and processes of cerebration; even his hymns to involuntary memory are accompanied by a chorus of reflections. In fact, he carries the nineteenth-century novel of analysis to a point undreamed of by the most enthusiastic intellectuals. No reader of Proust need be told of the extraordinary subtlety and precision with which he defines the most fleeting or delicate sensations, the extraordinary nervous sensitiveness that extends into the remotest regions of the mind and quickens all its processes. Ramon Fernandez has praised Conrad for his "thinking mastery of the unthinkable"; Proust's mastery in this kind is unrivaled by Conrad or any other novelist.

Similarly the management of his whole immense and complicated design is a triumph of directing intelligence. The principle of composition of his novel is from one point of view primarily musical. It is a Symphony of Time, with themes stated, developed, and resolved in the manner of a composer rather than a narrator; the episode of "Swann in Love," for example, has little plot connection with the hero's life but is simply a leit-motif, a preliminary statement of the main theme of the novel. In still another aspect more intimately related to Proust's main intention, *Remembrance of Things Past* is an immense "dream-novel," and its principle of development the involuntary association of ideas. Like the novels of Conrad and Dostoyevsky, it has an indefinable psychological movement rather than a chronological narrative sequence; it grows as an experience grows in the mind, it records impressions in much the disorderly way life makes them—its harmony and logic are in short the harmony and logic of the unconscious. Yet all this is conscious, the result of deliberate intention. From whatever point of view one chooses to regard Proust's discontinuous presentation of incident and character, his work is clearly not aimless or formless; although he is one of the least tidy of novelists, the least in a hurry to get on with his story, ultimately he manages an admirable balance between the broad and the minute, and his work emerges as a magnificently integrated whole. Upon completing it, one has only to reread *Swann's Way* to appreciate both the care and the skill with which Proust has unobtrusively introduced, in this overture, every important character and theme, and presented his whole novel in miniature.

If the intellectual element of Proust's work is thus more prominent than he admitted or perhaps realized, he is nevertheless fundamentally consistent. In the end *Remembrance of Things Past* is what he intended it to be: a monument to sensory impressions as recalled by involuntary memory and distilled by imagination. He never leaves the province of his own sensations; he employs his intellect simply to decipher these sensations and wring out their whole significance. Only when he is most prolix does his commentary seem an excrescence. His constant presence in his story is one of the reversions to the outmoded past that make Proust's masterpiece difficult to classify, his originality difficult to define; but his free use of the resources of a remarkably keen intelligence is one of its chief glories. It enabled him to project a comprehensive, organic view of mental experience in defiance of the artificial antitheses he set up.

2

Although, as an impressionist, Proust has obvious affinities with many modern novelists and takes a conspicuous place in the recent reaction against the assumptions and the methods of literal realism, he also has many linkages with the past. Saint-Simon, Chateaubriand, and Baudelaire left their mark on him plain to see. Balzac helped to indicate his self-appointed rôle as social historian. Flaubert taught him precision and thoroughness. Stendhal contributed to the notions of love and jealousy that govern his work—the perpetual see-saw that provides the chief action of both *Remembrance of Things Past* and *The Red and the Black*. Among English writers he learned from Dickens, George Eliot, and above all Ruskin, whom he translated; the stern moralist gave the young dandy a new vision—not indeed his specific ideas about art, but a love of the Middle Ages, an attitude of appreciativeness, a reverence for the beautiful. And no less curious at first glance is Proust's admiration, shared as curiously by André Gide, for Dostoyevsky. "Instead of presenting things in their logical sequence," he writes of Dostoyevsky, "that is to say beginning with the cause, he shows us first of all the effect, the illusion that strikes us." This describes precisely one of the most striking and characteristic methods of *Remembrance of Things Past*.

More important among the direct literary influences, however, is the work of Mallarmé and his followers, which is a highly specialized form of impressionism. Proust was absorbed in the same unique, private, fleeting sensations, and he employed similar methods to communicate these sensations. As Edmund Wilson points out, he was the first important writer to apply the principles of Symbolism to the novel. The shifting images of Symbolist poetry are the recurrent patterns of character and situation, the various "themes" of his novel. Although he worked on an immeasurably larger scale, he often worked to much the same purpose; *Remembrance of Things Past* is by all odds Mallarmé's greatest work.

Still more significant is Proust's relation to Bergson. He indeed denied any indebtedness (he also tried to maintain the melancholy pretense of young writers that everything in his book was "fictitious"), but it makes little difference whether he was telling the truth, or whether the influence was direct or indirect. His philosophy of fiction is essentially the philosophy of Bergson. Bergson's doctrines that *knowing* reality is different from *explaining* it, and that the chief instrument of understanding is not Intellect but Intuition; that life is a never-static creative process which the logical faculty can only break up into arbitrary concepts that make practical dealings more convenient but do not actually *represent* life or reveal its true nature; that we know most things only relatively in terms of other things, but that we can know directly by intuition our own personality in the continuous stream of time; that our true selves are not the aggregations of differentiated and externalized parts we habitually conceive, but fluid wholes that at every moment sum up the past and presage the future; that as progress consists in bringing the past to bear on the present, in order to participate more fully in the creative evolutionary process, Memory is the primary spiritual principle—these ideas are at the very heart of *Remembrance of Things Past.* If Bergson has reason to be piqued by Proust's refusal to acknowledge indebtedness, he has much more reason to be grateful that his philosophy has provided not only the skeletal framework but the living essence of a great work of art, as have few other systematic philosophies before him. The best proof of the living quality of his thought is indeed that it permits this transformation. One can scarcely imagine a miracle that could similarly transform the metaphysics of some other philosophers.

Yet the final explanation of Proust's work lies in his neurasthenic temperament. Bergson, Mallarmé, and many others helped to shape *Remembrance of Things Past;* the death of his mother appears to have been the chief reason for its being. She had accepted all his whims, anticipated and satisfied all his wants, cushioned him against all cares—and for years he had done nothing but diddle and dabble. With her death he was rudely ejected from this placental paradise. He could find no other woman to give him the endless sympathy and attention he demanded, to relieve him of the responsibilities of social intercourse. Hypersensitive, precious, extravagantly tender, he felt unequal to the coarse demands of life; nor did he even attempt to adjust himself. The very asthma from which he constantly suffered was plainly self-induced as a defense mechanism, an excuse to evade all distasteful duties. He lovingly cultivated his complaint, feasted on his symptoms; at least one doctor refused to attack them, recognizing that if he managed to cure them, Proust would simply develop another set. Hence, when his mother died, he shut himself up in his cork-lined room for the remainder of his life, to emerge, swathed in overcoats, only for occasional brief expeditions; and he set about writing his novel in an effort to find a satisfactory substitute for the normal human relationships he was unable to enjoy. It is a strange spectacle, in which the stern moralist, the hypochondriac, and the pampered darling can alike find comfort. The ordinary man finds it difficult to dissociate the cowardice from the courage, the morbidity from the integrity—the weakness that caused Proust to flee his fellows from the strength that enabled him to submit to a discipline of unsurpassed rigor, and to continue working feverishly until almost the moment of his death, of which he had always had a diseased horror.

In this light one may easily set forth the limitations of *Remembrance of Things Past.* It is, I believe, a very great novel. Like *Ulysses,* it continues to dazzle even after one has said the worst; unlike *Ulysses,* it remains as a whole work of art definitely superior to its serious limitations. But its greatness is best established by first going down the long list of Proust's sins.

Among the more irritating, though less important, of these is his excessive straining of the reader's attention. One must wade through pages of unbroken prose without the usual aids of logical punctuation and paragraphing. Interminable sentences meander with a mazy motion through interminable paragraphs of interminable chapters. If one's attention flags for but an instant, he finds himself lost in a forest of dependent phrases and must return to the remote beginning of the trail in order to find his way through them. The fugitive sentiments with which Proust is dealing, as well as the associative method of reverie, partially justify these involved sentences. One must also admire their beautiful cadences and the skill with which he finally disentangles himself—he may appear himself lost, but he almost always emerges with a period in his mouth. Yet he raises unnecessary difficulties. Although his own laments of his technical unfitness are exaggerated, it is unfortunate that with his anxiety to salt the tail of every last sensation he had not the discipline of long experience with the problems of communication.

One may as reasonably complain of the prolixity of Proust, the monotony of incessant repetition. The hundred and fifty pages of "Swann in Love" contain as elaborate a study of jealousy as fiction had yet known; but this is only a sketchy preface to the loves of Marcel, first with Gilberte, and then over whole volumes with Albertine. One's pleasure even in the brilliant pages of "Swann in Love" may be qualified by a doubt that this experience deserves such extended treatment; when Proust makes so interminable a pother over Marcel's affair with Albertine—an affair that he himself knows is morbid, transitory, mean—one becomes at times simply exasperated and feels like kicking the precious hero in the pants. Even when Proust is making an objective study of the fashionable world about him, he takes far too long to make his point. Here he has not the excuse of evocation of the elusive, for the sum of all these pages is broad satire. What he is saying, in his intricate, elaborate way, is fundamentally obvious. This is indeed often true of Proust's delicate analyses; one is surprised, upon penetrating to his holy of holies, to find enshrined there a platitude.

At his subtlest Proust still pays, moreover, the penalties of his method. Under this tirelessly close scrutiny, experience may become tenuous and at length simply disintegrate. The emotion itself is refined away, leaving only an intellectual pleasure in the study of its complicated origin and ramifications. Hence one reads coldly of the death of Albertine. One's chief emotion, whether it be a bright interest or a fortified patience, arises from the perception that now a new stream of sensations will flood the hero's consciousness, and that the processes of forgetfulness will probably be as tortuous as the processes of jealousy.

This objection is deepened by the nature of Proust's materials.

What we are straining our eyes at over some thousands of pages is the sensations of the neurasthenic narrator. This prolonged immersion in subjective experience results, indeed, in a clearer view of certain truths hitherto inadequately represented in fiction—the truth, especially, of the relativity of human relationships. Proust presents his characters in a succession of aspects corresponding to the hero's impressions at different stages in his acquaintance with them, and as he peels off layer after layer of appearance the effect is striking; in thus re-creating a whole world on the basis of the theory of relativity, "he has supplied for the first time in literature," Edmund Wilson remarks, "an equivalent on the full scale for the new theory of modern physics." At the same time the characters are occasionally too blurred by the rank mists in Marcel's mind—his loves especially have too little life of their own. There is an excessive vagueness and confusion about dates, ages, and all material circumstances. In general Proust sacrifices too much of the solid substance of life, he is too afraid to touch the trees to see if they are there.

And after all they are there. If all men must ultimately fall back upon subjective impressions, in practical experience they constantly supplement and check these impressions by reference to external reality. Hence the relativity in human relationships is by no means so extreme as Proust makes it, nor the subjectivity of our deeper experience so tragic. Endlessly he insists that a man loves a woman in his own and not in her image, that there is always a wide gap between the beloved object and the idea in the lover's mind. His lovers—Marcel, Swann, St. Loup, Charlus—are accordingly always miserable; the possibility of a happy love was to him unthinkable. And this invariable misery is contrary to common experience; the gap is not inevitably so wide as Proust would have it. Somehow people often manage to bridge it; and they succeed if only because their subjective impressions often do correspond closely with actuality—do have, in short, the kind of truth that in his larger view he ascribes to them.

What narrows and distorts Proust's fiction is accordingly not so much his central philosophy as the mirror that reflected it. The subjective impressions upon which he leaned so heavily were the impressions of a morbid, frustrate spirit. Thus the misery of all his lovers is clearly a reflection of his own unfitness for amorous adventure. Similarly his animadversions against friendship as wholly a delusion, destructive of the spiritual life and even of intellectual integrity, are only another rationalization of his inability to find the solid, lasting satisfaction that more normal men get from their relations with their fellows. Proust was in other words the extreme introvert, who finds too little reality outside himself, too little happiness in the present moment; who enjoys his mistress only when she is asleep and his friends only when they are absent. Hence his absorption in the processes of his sick soul, his anxious obsession with his neuroses, his loving notation of every detail of his anguish, for example, upon entering a new room. This conviction of the immense importance of every detail of his experience is clearly unhealthy, poisoning his subtlety at its source. But it is also naïve—as naïve as Dreiser shows himself in *Dawn*.

Proust has said many noble things about art and its idealism. It alone, he repeats ecstatically, is outside time; it alone can give the precious essence of life. But if art is the best way of communing with reality, it is still Proust's serious limitation that in his intense self-consciousness he could commune in no other way. His thought was not proved by living, his experience was not whole. As Ramon Fernandez observes in *Messages,* his was a "lazy interpretation of life"; his passivity facilitated his analysis, but it did not enrich it; and that he had to "relax and stretch" in order to apprehend life, that his imagination and will were powerless while his sensibility was active, was not the necessary sign of the artistic temperament but only another symptom of his peculiar spiritual weakness. Similarly Proust has written eloquently of the value of grief in developing the powers of the mind, supplying the artist with both subject matter and incentive, and he dwells on his own sufferings as the animating principle of his work. Yet if one cannot say of any man's sufferings that they are purely imaginary, one is perforce suspicious of a grief so carefully cultivated and complacently exploited as Proust's. It brought him too little understanding and sympathy for others; it came to be simply an end in itself. He becomes faintly ludicrous when, after asserting the necessity of repeated sorrows, he solemnly assures the writer that he may embark upon a long work without apprehension: "Let the intelligence but begin its task and there will come up along the way sorrows in plenty which will undertake to complete it." Then he adds, with characteristic malaise, "As for happiness, it has hardly more than one useful quality, namely to make unhappiness possible."

The natural culmination of such views was a comprehensive misanthropy, a catholicity of disgust, that steadily darkens the pages of *Remembrance of Things Past* and plunges its last volume into what would be utter blackness were it not for its vivid horrors. Like an awful avenging spirit Proust follows his creatures into a ghastly old age, and subjects them to a refinement of persecution that makes Jude Fawley's fate seem merciful and Hardy's treatment gentle. Except for the sections in which the narrator rhapsodizes over the discovery of his mission, *The Past Recaptured* is perhaps the most macabre and the ashiest book ever written. Proust stages a final reception in the Faubourg Saint-Germain in order to assemble all his characters, and at this feast he places a death's-head in every chair. All these people have aged horribly; none has a trace of the peace and dignity that can come with old age. They are simply putrescent before they have had the decency to die. And over this scene presides the Baron de Charlus, like a hideously senile faun, conducting the last rites with a gruesome joy:

> It was with an almost triumphant callousness that he kept repeating in a monotonous tone of voice, stammering slightly and speaking with a thick, sepulchral resonance, "Hannibal de Bréauté, dead! Antoine de Mouchy, dead! Charles Swann, dead! Adalbert de Montmorency, dead! Baron de Talleyrand, dead! Sosthène de Doudeauville, dead!" And each time that word "dead" seemed to fall like a shovelful of dirt, thrown heavily by a grave-digger anxious to rivet them more securely in their graves.

In this nightmare, the emphasis upon sexual perversion that distresses or offends many readers comes to seem but an incidental horror. His preoccupation with the abnormal is nevertheless another of the serious limitations of Proust's work. He was justly proud of being one of the first to introduce this important subject into fiction, and of his impartial treatment of it. He recognized, too, the neurotic element in modern homosexuality—the deliberate, self-conscious cultivation of a wayward impulse, which is quite different from the love celebrated by Plato. But he did not realize that the potential value of such materials is necessarily limited. Above all, his emphasis is disproportionate. He presents a distorted picture while insisting that it is representative. After a number of premonitory hints, he suddenly announces his theme, boldly underscores it, and proceeds to ring all the changes. *Cities of the Plain* is an elaborately orchestrated symphony of the abnormal. Most of the male characters turn out to be homosexuals, and the Baron de Charlus, who has been hovering in the wings, now takes the spotlight in the center of the stage. It is indeed a magnificent performance; but after incessant repetition the fascination wears off, and the reader recognizes what at bottom it is: the almost hysterical reaction of a frustrate, hypersensitive spirit, another extravagant expression of the misanthropy resulting from Proust's inability to enter the world of men and find normal satisfaction.

Hence the mark of decadence is plainly on this immense work. We feel, Edmund Wilson rightly says, "as if we were reading about the end of something"—the end of a world over which Proust is conducting the last rites. Wilson goes on to call him "perhaps the last great historian of the loves, the society, the intelligence, the diplomacy, the literature and the art of the Heartbreak House of capitalistic culture." Proust would appear, indeed, to offer an ideal text for the strict Marxist thesis. Yet I think that the decadence in him is not to be included among the many sins of capitalism. He presents only one segment of society, and that more a relic of feudalism than a product of capitalism; his is the fashionable world that is in most ages shallow and effete. His study, moreover, is highly specialized; the reader feels a strange surprise when an airplane flies over Proust's world, or when he refers to H. G. Wells or hints of industrial unrest or introduces any familiar, everyday concerns—it is as if we had suddenly come down from Mars. And though his disease was no doubt aggravated by the decadent society in which he lived, it was at bottom a very private affair. As Wilson himself points out, *Les Plaisirs et les Jours* reveals that Proust's temperament was already formed by 1890—when he was just entering the society he was later to analyze so mercilessly, and when, according to John Strachey, capitalism was in its heyday. What makes his misanthropy depressing is precisely that, like Flaubert's, it never appears to have been earned by painful experience, or to have any necessary connection with an imperfect society. In short, Proust is plainly a case for Freud rather than for Marx.

3

This constitutes, indeed, a formidable indictment of the work of Proust. Plainly he belongs among the many thwart, disnatur'd spirits of this chaotic age. Yet *Remembrance of Things Past* is more than a great curiosity, more too than an elaborate case history of Proust or his society. Once its novelty and its clinical interest have worn off, it should stir an even deeper interest. Proust is not only a remarkable specialist who has contributed something new to fiction; he is by virtue of both imaginative and intellectual strength the creator of a whole world, a world that despite its apparently restricted locale in time and space is finally outside both.

In their anxiety over certain of his doctrines, too many readers forget that Proust was first and foremost a creative *artist;* like Paul Elmer More, they treat him as if he were writing, not a novel, but a manual or morality play. One should be able to appreciate the unique poetry and insights of Proust without endorsing all his conclusions, to accept his whole world in the same spirit in which one accepts life, without necessarily approving such of Jehovah's intentions as one may think he perceives. Similarly, when John Strachey calls *Remembrance of Things Past* the "odyssey of snobbery," "the final proof of the absolutely necessary and praiseworthy character of snobbery in a class society," he is missing the whole point of Proust's intention as it is endlessly restated in *The Past Recaptured*. He fails to see that Proust's intense concern was with his consciousness, not his individuality or worldly achievement; that the fascination for him of the Faubourg Saint-Germain was primarily poetic, in keeping with his romantic fondness for everything old, and that his celebration of its glamor soon gives way to a ferocious satire—the most devastating exposure of the shallowness, stupidity, hypocrisy, and vulgarity of fashionable society ever recorded; and that he employed his own experience in this society, not because he had smug notions of its intrinsic value, but simply because in accordance with his philosophy of fiction it was the only material available to him—his chief defense of it was a constant insistence "that the subject is a matter of indifference and that the mind can put anything into it."

All the familiar charges of "escape" are as much beside the point. Granted that Proust retired from the world of men to evade normal responsibilities, the reader's final concern should be simply with the consequences of this retirement; and it proved to be no mere flight into fantasy or prettiness. In the end one should be impressed by the high resolution and courage demanded by Proust's enterprise—the courage to submit to a rigorous mental discipline, and under pitiless introspection to surrender many of his fondest illusions—but impressed above all by his integrity, an ascetic fidelity to his vision comparable to that of Conrad and his sea captains. Given his neurotic sensibility, what other kind of work could he have written? Certainly no stirring contribution to the struggle of the workers or to any immediate cause whatever. His greatness is inextricably tied up with his limitations, his especial contribution grows out of his very disease. Had he been a healthier spirit he might well have written a still greater work, but it would have been a different one; and hypothetical contrast is an idle speculation. Meanwhile we have God's plenty.

One of the elementary signs of greatness in Proust, so obvious that it is often overlooked, is the indestructible vitality of most of his characters. Despite his constant nervous pawing and prying, they maintain a vigorous life of their own. Each has his characteristic manner, his unmistakable accent, his peculiar *Gestalt*—all the signs, both intangible and minutely particular, of an individual existence. Proust clearly fulfils the first and essential obligation of the novelist. He fulfils it, in fact, with the prodigality that is the hallmark of the greatest geniuses in fiction. No contemporary has so immense a fertility; one never touches bottom in him, but feels that like Tolstoy, Balzac, and the great Victorians he could go on creating indefinitely. And this elemental fecundity is the more remarkable in view of his wide learning. Few writers with great creative powers have had so rich a culture, few have drawn so heavily upon the artists before them without sacrifice of their own unique quality.

The range of Proust's understanding, moreover, is much wider than many think. In dwelling on his specialty, critics are likely to overlook his broad humor and his shrewd understanding of common people—such as the immortal Françoise. At any moment the tortuous, morbid workings of the hero's mind may be interrupted by the entrance of a servant or a tradesman, and the procession of subtleties be halted by a pure belly laugh. Similarly most critics have noted, only to forget, his extravagantly satirical, almost melodramatic presentation of the social world, and his gift for grotesque caricature. His grandaunts, the Verdurins and their circle, and a number of the elegant residents of the Faubourg Saint-Germain would be thoroughly at home in the world of Dickens. As a matter of fact they do not really belong in Proust's world of subjective impressions. They are out of keeping with his delicate analyses, they make nonsense of his elaborate theory of fiction; the neurasthenic narrator should logically be incapable of perceiving and rendering them so. It is thus a tribute to the vitality of Proust's characterization that only upon second thought are we aware of the incongruity of their existence, and that instinctively we accept them without question as we accept the impossible Mr. Micawber. And at the other end of the scale this diseased spirit that follows so anxiously every last twist of its own squirmings and writhings can sound simply and strongly the major chords of human emotion, as he does at the death of his grandmother. This is one of the most poignant and beautiful scenes in world fiction.

Proust's genius presents so many facets that one cannot talk easily of a "double vision"; but the essence of this genius is a union of analytical and poetic powers that separately are remarkable, in fusion unique. Stendhal has been called the first modern man, the first to unite the sentimental and the scientific interests of the eighteenth century and study the human mind with at once imaginative enthusiasm and cold objectivity. This enthusiasm I for one have failed to catch. I am impressed chiefly by the coldness of *The Red and the Black,* the utterly desiccated analysis, the lack of passion or gusto; I am unmoved by its most dramatic scenes. But Proust did achieve this vital synthesis. He saw his characters at once from within and from without, his attitude was at once romantic and objective. The scientific analyst worked on the materials provided by the romantic poet, the poet was in turn stimulated by the analyst's findings; but if one or the other dominates a given passage, *Remembrance of Things Past* as a whole is the product of a perfect union.

Most obvious, and most generally praised as the source of his special contribution, are Proust's analytical gifts. "I don't think that there ever has been in the whole of literature such an example of the power of analysis," wrote Joseph Conrad, "and I feel pretty safe in saying that there will never be another." Proust's work makes the investigations of George Eliot and Meredith seem amateurish, those even of Henry James blunt and superficial. Like Lawrence and Virginia Woolf, he rendered the most delicate and difficult sensations; unlike other impressionists, he then squeezed the last drop of significance from his impressions, exhausting their whole intellectual and emotional content. When a sensation dropped into the pool of his mind he followed to the shore every ripple. Prolix, often tedious in their thoroughness, his analyses are wonderfully sensitive and precise; and they are often highly original. He introduced into fiction truths never before really apprehended. To set *Swann's Way* beside other studies of jealousy and other studies of adolescence is enough; but perhaps most striking is his complete rendering of the processes of forgetfulness, as the painful memory of Albertine gradually fades in Marcel's consciousness until it becomes a negative that he can pick up with no other emotion than surprise at his lack of emotion.

At the same time Proust was a poet whose imagination responded instantly to the faintest stimulus, thrilled to experiences that the ordinary novelist passes by as dull matters of fact. Hence his lovely cadences and vivid imagery, and whole shimmering passages, such as the evocations of Venice, of Combray and the "ways," of Balbec and the frieze of girls; but his poetry envelops luminously the entire experience of the hero, glowing even in the most analytical passages. In his last volumes there is indeed less appeal to the senses, and a dryer intellectual quality. Possibly the arteries of Proust's imagination were finally hardening with age; the simpler explanation is that he died before he had time to revise these volumes and clothe their skeletal framework. But this noticeable difference only emphasizes the wonderful synthesis and harmony in the work as a whole.

From another point of view this synthesis might be described as a rare combination of youthful enthusiasm and mature judgment. Proust had the intense, unspoiled eagerness of the child—the gift cherished by Arnold Bennett of seeing life like a baby, who lives each moment for itself. His mind remained a virgin soil apparently never covered by layers of accumulated experience. His perceptions and responses seem to have been never dulled or standardized by habit; each experience was fresh, discrete, unique. Yet he completely assimilated all this experience, penetrated it to the core, dominated it. His cool mastery extended to its most intimate and shameful elements. Proust was a spoiled child, a dandy and dilettante, a hypochondriac, a neurotic misanthrope, possibly even a pervert; but he was also the captain of his scrofulous soul as few "normal" artists ever have been. He could dissociate the various elements of his personality, view them dispassionately, analyze them acutely, finally subordinate them. Hence the morbidity of his hero is not the whole essence of his story. If it is too great a part, it is still only a part.

Here we approach the central issue of Proust's work: the substantiality and depth of its meanings, the richness and pertinence of its values—in a word the measure of its universality. What does it contribute to a satisfying art of living beyond its magnificence as the re-creation of the life of one highly exceptional individual?

Proust's own testimony about his intentions is conflicting. He often writes, especially in the earlier volumes, as if he were merely symbolizing his private experience, objectifying his private world, which he recognized to be morbid and exceptional. Once he even apologizes (though most readers will quickly forgive him) for all he has perforce omitted from his many volumes: he has had "to whittle down the facts and to be a liar" because he has presented only one universe, whereas there are almost as many millions as there are people. His very insistence upon subjective impressions might appear to deny the possibility of objective, universal truth. Yet all along, his generalizing intellect was delightedly busying itself in revealing similarity beneath apparent diversity—in the pursuit of analogy that is the essence of man's pursuit of truth; and as he goes on, he talks more and more of the great universal laws of human life that he hopes to discover. In the last volume he endlessly protests that he has not been grubbing for petty details, that he has been studying life through a telescope, not a microscope. His hero feels his love, tragically subjective as it has been, "merge into a vaster reality"; the private sicknesses with which he has been obsessed have led him to a perception of "the true nature of things." "People foolishly imagine," Proust writes in defense of his limited subject matter and point of view, "that the vast dimensions of social phenomena afford them an excellent opportunity to penetrate farther into the human soul; they ought, on the contrary, to realize that it is by plumbing the depths of a single personality that they might have a chance of understanding those phenomena." In short, at the end Proust clearly believed that he had symbolized the general experience of mankind.

This is indeed the natural conclusion for an artist who has dedicated his life to one crowning work. The artist normally wishes to address his fellow men, convince them of the pertinence of what he is doing if only to vindicate himself in his own eyes; he is seldom, if ever, really content with the flimsy, self-hypnotic justification of art-for-art's-sake. At any rate Proust's conscious intentions do not settle the issue; constantly men build better or worse than they know. Yet in his actual performance it seems to me that he did achieve, within the limits of the immeasurable and unknowable imposed upon all art, a surprisingly rich and full representation of universally significant experience. His way is not, as he implies in the quotation above, the only way. Still, it is one way; and if the single personality who is plumbed has wide possibilities and is of sufficient sensitiveness and depth, it is a fruitful one. Hamlet has for centuries been a compelling spokesman for all thoughtful men; Proust's spokesman qualifies by the same test. If the sensations upon which Proust built his work are less pregnant with immortal essences and absolute truths than he believed, they are nevertheless the immediate materials of artists through the ages; and he supplemented them on a much larger scale than do most artists who reject both his intuitivistic philosophy and his impressionistic methods.

Many of his enthusiastic admirers indeed deny Proust universality. In the view of Conrad, for example, Proust did not reproduce the general experience of mankind but brought to it something hitherto unrecorded. The "hitherto unrecorded" elements are unmistakable: there is nothing in literature, once more, like many of his passages or his work as a whole. Yet he is more than a specialist and he does more than enrich our experience with novelties. He illumines and intensifies it generally. His world, peculiar as it is, overlaps that of the ordinary man in many important provinces. The most militantly normal and "sane" readers should find what Proust himself proudly declared: that his work is an optical instrument, "a sort of magnifying glass" by which they can read themselves. Such discrepancies as they might find he believed should be laid largely to their own fault. I should say that these discrepancies are not so wide and numerous as is commonly imagined, and that the fault is by no means entirely Proust's. Although he was too ready to believe that "the subject is a matter of indifference," and hence dwelt too often and too fondly on abnormal experience, I should still insist that a world containing Bergotte and Berma, Françoise and the Verdurins, St. Loup and the Duchesse de Guermantes, Marcel's mother and grandmother—to mention but a few of its countless citizens—is not a remote or alien world; that even Proust's monsters are at bottom recognizably, pitiably human; that the neurasthenic hero can isolate and calmly analyze his own disease, thus making it only part of his experience; that many of his insights are as profoundly true as they are strikingly new; that, in short, only to the most shallow, incurable extravert, or the most fanatical partizan of an immediate cause, will this immense experience really be foreign, irrelevant, or incidental. The force of *Remembrance of Things Past,* unlike the force of *Ulysses,* is often brought to bear on the major emotions, decisions, and actions that organize human life.

The shallowest of the many widely circulated charges against Proust's work is that it is unmoral, or even immoral. Although his treatment of homosexuality, for example, is admirably unsensational—he deals with it simply as a fact, neither more nor less important than it is—he finally does not succeed in achieving anything like the serene impartiality of James Joyce. Those who demand moral indignation with their art can find plenty of it in his work, if they can only recognize it outside of a professional sermon. A number of critics have noted the Hebraic quality of Proust, the gloomy prophet and implacable judge who lays about him with a fierceness the more intense because he dare not be explicit. This quality appears in the lucid, pitiless analysis of his own weaknesses—the "fiendish, self-torturing delight" with which he lays bare, for example, his lack of will-power; it appears above all in the dustiness and bitterness of *The Past Recaptured,* the lamentations of a modern Jeremiah. Only with this in mind can one understand Proust's admiration for George Eliot, his enthusiasm for Ruskin, his assertion that the most important influences upon his work were English. He had the same moral bias that especially distinguishes English literature.

Despite his misanthropy, moreover, Proust's characters are not simply ignoble. The beautiful unselfishness of his mother and the lofty idealism of his grandmother provide a solid background of spiritual values. Even his damned souls, however, are not uniformly contemptible. Albertine is at least pitiable; St. Loup is definitely ennobled before his death. But the triumph of the book is the Baron de Charlus. Feeble-minded, depraved, ghastly, horrible—he has still at the end something of dignity and grandeur, like a rotten old oak. The creation of this monstrous figure is the monument to Proust's disgust with all that is vile in the human animal. It is also a perhaps unconscious tribute to the compelling force of this animal even in its degradation and decay.

There remains, finally, the essential spirituality of Proust. Ramon Fernandez has acutely defined his chief limitation in this aspect: that there is no hierarchy of values, no spiritual progress in him. Instead of relating his flights of sensibility to a living, growing, striving personality, he identifies the ego with particular experiences and so cuts it up into pieces; the accesses of involuntary memory that he treasured are not only intermittent but parallel, discrete, self-contained. In this view soul becomes a kind of miscellany, not a dynamic, purposeful unit; there can be no real guaranty of our acts and sentiments, no clear spiritual development, no surpassing oneself. But granted that Proust's is a "lazy interpretation" of life, that he fails sufficiently to energize his values and integrate them in a satisfying scheme, he still points to positive spiritual values. In his conviction that the meaning of life is to be found in idealities, he approaches the Platonists.

"It is not possible," he writes, "that a piece of sculpture, a piece of music which gives us an emotion which we feel to be more exalted, more pure, more true, does not correspond to some definite spiritual reality." This attitude brings art back to its origins as a fundamentally religious exercise, an expression of the communal striving for the immortal ideal; and it was not in Proust merely the posturing of an esthete, a sophisticated version of the art-for-art's-sake evasion of responsibility. It was a deep piety, which inspired the exalted scene of the death of Bergotte, another of the great moments in fiction. It was carried over into the ethical sphere as the intense idealism of his grandmother, which continues to provide a point of reference long after her death. It lends a deeper significance even to scenes whose initial impulse is morbid. The origins of Proust's work are pathological; its end is not.

Proust is accordingly not to be identified, as Paul Elmer More identified him, with the frequent horror of his materials. He was not only always sensitive and discriminating, never coarse, in his treatment of such material; he did not finally mistake it for his meaning. Although he has outraged the susceptibilities of tender readers, he is at bottom with Bishop Berkeley, Shelley, and company on the side of the angels. One may disagree with his specific ideas, perhaps reject his entire idealistic philosophy as misty moonshine; but at least this approach gives perspective to his work and proportion to its many unpleasant elements. His way of life is as a whole inadequate; it nevertheless embraces valuable attitudes—attitudes especially valuable in a fact-ridden, dehumanized world.

The whole issue of universality is in much critical controversy greatly oversimplified. Who is to say offhand that a healthy, broadly humane, and by general consent "universal" novelist like Fielding, with his caricature and artifice, his simplifications and omissions, his avoidance of the heights and depths for the common-sense middle-of-the-way, is closer to "truth" or gives a more veracious impression of life than the neurotic Proust? There are different kinds as well as degrees of universality. Some writers, like Shakespeare and Tolstoy, give at least the impression of reproducing the *whole* general experience of mankind. Others, like Arnold Bennett, give the essence of *average* experience. Still others, like Dostoyevsky and Conrad, command a definitely limited but nevertheless substantial realm of universally significant experience. In this last class belongs Proust. In reading him one must therefore make important reservations—but one makes similar reservations when reading *Ecclesiastes,* Æschylus, Dante, Milton, Dickens. If of all the plays of Shakespeare only *King Lear* had come down to us, we would scarcely be identifying him with Nature. *King Lear* is plainly not only a heightened but a distorted picture of human life, dominated by monsters of good and evil, with the most painful emotions of man writ so large that it seems nightmarish. By itself it might be regarded as a companion piece to *The Brothers Karamazov.* Yet it is the mightiest of Shakespeare's plays, the most overwhelming proof of his genius. In itself it is a great work—and for all its distortions rich in universal meanings. In the same spirit one should be able to accept *Remembrance of Things Past.* That Proust was incapable of supplementing it with a *Tempest* or a *King Henry IV* sets a limit to his genius, reveals that he was not a Shakespeare; but it does not invalidate what he did achieve, nor take away from the large measure of the only kind of "truth" literature can offer which is to be found in his masterpiece.

XIX

ANDRÉ GIDE

I

"I WRITE to be reread," André Gide has remarked with characteristic bravado; and much of his strange work deserves and demands rereading. "I am quite certain," he has told André Breton, "to be the man who will exert the greatest influence fifty years from now"—but of this there is some question. It is doubtful that he is so far in advance of his age, or that they are moving in the same direction. Still, even apart from his fascinating personality and his reputation as the leading man of letters of France today, he handsomely repays study. His protean, many-faceted spirit has caught and reflected innumerable rays of modern thought—Flaubert, Nietzsche, Dostoyevsky, Mallarmé, Wilde, and Conrad are but a few of the sources of his art. His work raises important issues, if not always the issues he is himself proud of. And he is especially interesting because to many he is the symbol of all that is most rotten in modern letters. Even emancipated readers, who have learned from Mencken to scorn morals in literature and to detect the smell of a Baptist or Rotarian a mile away, often dismiss Gide as a mere pervert or monster. He is one of the plainest examples of the havoc wrought in criticism by stock responses: automatic judgments based on ingrained habits rather than on an intelligent inquiry into what a writer is trying to do and why he is doing it.

A few years ago the chameleon Gide turned Red, and so again confounded his audience. His conversion to Communism caused skyrockets to be set off in Moscow; Soviet critics like Ivan Anissomov hailed him as "the glory of our epoch," and explained the inner conflict and the "evil" in his previous work as the result of infection by the decaying bourgeois culture. But although it should not surprise one to find Gide writing a proletarian novel (even now, when his "glory" has been tarnished by unorthodox criticism of the Soviet), it is difficult to conceive of his doing so. Despite his versatility, all his fictions have been written from an altogether different perspective. Meanwhile it is safe to generalize his contribution on the basis of his masterpiece, *The Counterfeiters,* for it is a virtually complete statement of his art and philosophy. While writing this novel, he sought to pour out without reserve everything that was in him, to persuade himself that it was the last book he would ever write. In a sense it is, in fact, what he calls it: his only novel.

With the Journal that Gide kept while working on it, *The Counterfeiters* makes an excellent textbook on technique. He has something wise to say about almost all the problems of the art of fiction as conceived by modern novelists, and in his practice exemplifies most of the new methods of telling a story. He takes as great pains with point of view as Henry James, and has as exquisite a concern with light and shadow. Like Dostoyevsky and Conrad he builds up his characters gradually and dramatically, and like Proust he gains startling effects by successive revelations, peeling off layers to uncover unsuspected qualities. Like the impressionists generally, he seeks to render rather than relate, re-create rather than analyze, eschewing direct exposition and all obvious suggestion of the omniscient author. Like Huxley, Dos Passos, and Wassermann he cuts the slice of life breadthwise and depthwise as well as lengthwise in the direction of time; and like Huxley and Proust more particularly he introduces the principles of musical composition, developing his themes contrapuntally. At every moment, moreover, he is conscious of what he is doing, and of its difficulties and dangers. In the Journal he expresses his intention of departing the practice of most artists and critics by navigating for days out of sight of land instead of safely hugging the shore.

Gide's methods appear to be dictated in part by a concept of the "pure novel." With the Frenchman's instinct for form and order, he proposes to purge the novel of all unnecessary, irrelevant elements. As to precisely what constitutes "purity," however, and specifically what elements do not belong to the novel, he is pretty vague. When he says that Stendhal is the purest of all novelists and Balzac, despite his greatness, the least pure, I think I know what he is talking about; but when he adds that Defoe, Richardson, Fielding, and most English novelists have considerable purity, I am frankly puzzled. Whatever they are, Gide's standards are apparently artificial and arbitrary, and lead one to suspect that he has fallen into the hoary fallacy of confusing means with ends.

In the last analysis, however, Gide's experiments in technique involve much more than notions of formal chasteness. They derive from new concepts of experience and are in line with the reaction against conventional realism. What Gide aimed at in *The Counterfeiters* was in general comprehensiveness: the whole intricate truth of human experience. He did not want to cut the slice at all; he wanted to include all of life in its complexity and fluidity, its inconsistency and inconclusiveness. He objects to the excessive neatness, logic, continuity, and formal consistency of the old masters of fiction. They bathe their scenes in too clear and steady a light; their simplified, symmetrical patterns leave out too much; in general they give as little true impression of experience as an eighteenth-century garden does of nature. Character is much more incongruous than they represent it, experience much more surprising, elusive, blurred, illogical. And to point his idea, Gide makes his "deep, underlying subject" not the facts or events themselves, but the novelist's effort to make a book out of them. He writes a novel about a novelist writing a novel for the same reason that Proust does; his Edouard stands at the very center of *The Counterfeiters* and is not, like Huxley's Philip Quarles in *Point Counterpoint,* merely an excuse for writing essays.

Edouard accordingly represents Gide himself. He incidentally is a homosexual; he is grappling with the same problems of art; he obviously expresses Gide's main ideas. Yet he is not to be identified with Gide at every point. Despite his conscientious and sympathetic observation, Edouard is always left behind the march of events; while life piles up rich concrete facts, he loses himself in a cloud of abstract ideas. For he is dismayed by reality and resents its illogic. When reality presents him specifically with the fact of the suicide of Boris, he refuses to make use of it, because it will fit into no tidy pattern. As he himself fears, he will never be able to write his novel; and his failure emphasizes Gide's central doctrine.

Now, Gide's own experiment is far from an unqualified success. His practice is like his theory, now inconsistent, now extreme. It is difficult to reconcile his objection to the neat, formal patterns of Flaubert and James with his admiration for Sophocles and Racine; and though he proclaims his rebellion against all convention and artifice, actually he does not eliminate them. He merely substitutes a different, if subtler kind; his pretense of perfect naturalness becomes flimsier with each insistence. One is often aware of contrivance in the novel, one does not believe his repeated exclamations of surprise at what is happening or of perplexity about what is going to happen next. In his deliberate indifference to conventional verisimilitude, on the other hand, Gide is at times extreme. He introduces too many fantastic coincidences, and pushes illogic and inconsistency to the point where he endangers the general truth he aims at—as in the dreadful precocity of his schoolboys. He has an exaggerated fear of externals and particulars, forgetting that they are important in our most intimate experience as in our immediate perceptions. In general he pays the penalty of his intense self-consciousness. "Everything which is created by the intelligence alone is false," he asserts, proclaiming the superiority of intuition as an avenue to truth; his keen and sleepless intelligence is nevertheless the most conspicuous element in his endowment as a novelist. His "deep, underlying subject" is too explicit, intellectualized, detachable. "A good novel is written more simply than that," Bernard tells Edouard; but that Gide is characteristically aware of the valid objections to his work does not destroy their validity.

Yet if *The Counterfeiters* is too much a curiosity, a tour de force, a novelist's novel, it is also a serious, intelligent effort to provide new symbols and patterns appropriate to new modes of perception, and it is significant for precisely the qualities that Gide well knew would be the major source of irritation to most readers. Nor does one have to take his purposes and meanings on faith. He does not write merely a novel of ideas. The ideas he leaves largely to Edouard; he himself goes on to establish them concretely, immediately, in a large gallery of living characters and moving scenes. For the most part he actually renders his vision of life, projects it in drama and not merely in talk. His novel is an extraordinary *mélange,* a wild symphony of jumbled themes and broken melodies and unresolved chords; but it hangs together somehow, it builds up, it has an intangible unity and completeness. It does convey remarkably the impression of life that Gide wished: of life incongruous, intricate, inconclusive, unpredictable, intractable, yet whole. "The author has dropped a stone into these still waters," writes Professor Beach, "and the circles keep widening out, to infinity." It is a haunting book, of a strange beauty and truth. Many dislike it; few forget it.

2

Gide's reckless disregard of the conventions of decent story-telling has troubled many readers. What really outrages them, however, is the repulsiveness of his materials. They cannot forgive him for presenting, with apparent relish, perhaps the most monstrous characters and abominable scenes in modern fiction. His early novels are steeped in a Baudelairean atmosphere of lush sinfulness and decay; in his later novels he treats crime and perversion with a cool, casual complacence that is even more shocking. Where the Dostoyevsky he revered depicted monsters primarily to emphasize their essential, pitiable humanity, Gide appears to introduce them for the sake of their monstrosity. In *The Vatican Swindle* ("Les Caves du Vatican") his hero murders a harmless stranger simply out of curiosity, for the pleasure of performing a wholly free and gratuitous act—and Gide looks on and makes no sound. Worse yet, when he does make a sound it is only to condone or approve. In *The Immoralist* he appears to accept sexual vagary as proudly as does his Nietzschean hero; in *Corydon* he definitely defends homosexuality; in his autobiography, *If It Die,* he spreads his scandalous practices before the world. In short, many readers can make of him only a "demon," the apostle of evil, the quintessence of corruption—the perfect symbol of the spiritual disintegration of the modern world.

This distress is easy to understand—Gide's pleasantries are often "un peu forte." It is even justified by certain elements in his personality and philosophy. Some of his earlier work has the "rotten elegance" prized by the esthetes of its time; in his later work he still plainly delights in shocking his public. He has a fondness for black magic, even something like a belief in demonology—he remarks in his Journal that he would like the Devil to travel through his book incognito, affirming his reality the more as one believed in him less. He prides himself upon a Mephistophelian quality. Above all, his whole ethics is up to a point anarchically individualistic. He makes constant war on all forms of constraint, all taboos, all traditional standards that in any way restrict the full and easy development of the individual's possibilities; and so his attitude toward even his vilest characters is often defiantly indulgent. Yet to regard Gide as simply a damned soul, or even as a rotten sophisticate, is to be naïvely taken in by his bravado, his pose. It is to refuse the challenge of one of the most complex, fascinating personalities of our time. Most unfortunate, it is to miss the whole point and force of his significant work.

The monsters in Gide can be explained in ways not at all terrifying even to pious spirits. One is his resolute indifference, as a matter of esthetic principle, to verisimilitude; like Shakespeare in *King Lear,* he presents the pure essence of good and evil. Another is his fondness for violent contrasts. The compositional scheme of *The Counterfeiters* is in this aspect quite simple; a scene of inhuman frightfulness or ugliness is almost invariably followed by one of love and unselfishness—again like the storm scenes on the heath in *King Lear.* If the pious will count, moreover, they will discover that in this crowning work the decent characters outnumber the vicious. But even without such numerical demonstrations it should be plain that Gide is finally neither cynical nor unmoral. Despite his cool, objective manner, his judgment is often clearly implied. There can be no doubt of his disapproval of such horrible characters as Gheridanisol and Passavant in *The Counterfeiters;* as for the crimes of Lafcadio in *The Vatican Swindle,* they are not to be taken too seriously, embedded as they are in lusty farce, and at that Gide indicates that the thrill of murdering is unsatisfying—at the very least suggesting, let us say, the superiority of the pleasures of philosophical contemplation over those of gross action. Like all of Gide's offensive heroes, Lafcadio is undoubtedly based on his creator's own personality, but like all the others he objectifies only one aspect of this kaleidoscopic personality. He not only lacks the good sense that, as Gide remarks, prevents his own indulgence in folly; he lacks above all Gide's moral earnestness, his concern for spiritual rather than intellectual values. For this seeming immoralist has a definite moral code, however strange and unorthodox. When he attacks conventional morality, it is at bottom always in the name of what he conceives to be a truer and loftier morality. As Marcel Arland has said, "from his first book to his last, Gide claims to deliver and enrich mankind"; and to this exalted purpose he finally bends his most appalling materials.

The most obvious objection to this view of Gide's work is his treatment of homosexuality. He not only admits perversion into his ethical scheme; he frankly glorifies it—notably in his novelist Edouard. This is a difficult and delicate subject. The healthy, red-blooded male's habit of either punching or laughing at homosexuals is plainly a crude and arbitrary handling of the problem, but even one who regards them as guiltless unfortunates cannot really understand them. They are a problem for specialists; the layman can be downright only in insisting that their mode of life be recognized as vagary and not as norm. Yet those who condemn Gide's attitude should at least note the delicacy with which he expresses it in *The Counterfeiters.* No eighteenth-century swain ever conceived a more spiritual love for his nymph than Edouard for Olivier; so idyllic are their relations that many simple readers do not recognize them for what they are. If this book is to go on the Index, then many of Plato's dialogues must go with it. This same Platonic spirit explains Gide's obvious animus against his Passavant, whose vice is purely carnal—the cultivated, sophisticated, decadent brand of homosexuality treated by Proust, the corruption that has brought it into especial disrepute. The really serious objection to Gide's treatment of the whole subject is indeed its sentimentality. He perhaps acquiesces too easily in his perversion; he idealizes it as a special sign of divine grace; he makes a precious virtue of an unfortunate necessity.

Gide's attitude is at any rate consistent with the doctrine of ethical relativity behind all his later work (it is stated most clearly in *The Return of the Prodigal Son*), and is indeed the source of this doctrine. His peculiar experience more than his reading in Nietzsche explains his rebellion against orthodox morality. Society officially condemns what after a long period of shame and torment he came to accept as the law of his nature; hence he insists that there can be no one moral law for all men, and that each must discover his own principle of morality. "The belief that becomes truth for me," says Bernard in *The Counterfeiters,* "is that which allows me the best use of my strength, the best means of putting my virtues into action." Gide attacks all moral strait-jackets that prevent the individual from realizing his peculiar strength and exercising his peculiar virtues.

This may be a dangerous ethic. It may give insufficient emphasis to the values of discipline and sacrifice; it may encourage unsocial or even anti-social behavior. It does not at any rate greatly aid one in selecting wisely from the host of conflicting impulses. But it cannot be dismissed as simple evil or error. Above all, it does not automatically condemn Gide himself or his work. He has not only recognized the practical necessity of social conventions and himself made compromises that his heroes may not make; in the end he has not made his doctrine an excuse for sloppy self-indulgence. It has been for him a challenge and even a discipline. Whatever its distortions, it reflects a fundamentally humanistic attitude, which led him at the age of sixty to turn to Goethe and Montaigne. It is based on a naturally pious conviction of the value of the human spirit. And this conviction, which is at the heart of all great literature, is far more important than the artist's specific moral ideas.

As a matter of fact, there is even a strong religious tendency in Gide. His constant interest in the Bible, his intermittent attacks of conscience, his belief in demons, his revulsion against carnal love, his reverence for Dostoyevsky, his tormented self-questioning, his recent conversion to Communism—all testify to the religious bias that was ingrained during his youth, when by day he dedicated himself to God and by night slept on planks to mortify his flesh, and that persists after his violent reaction against it. Gide is at heart more of a Calvinist than his sternest critics. He has after all *not* acquiesced in his perversion. Hence his "frightful honesty"; the inexorable moralist in him must atone for his sins by summoning his private demons and telling the world the whole appalling truth about himself. His autobiography (which, incidentally, disappointed his enemies by being less vile than they had hoped) is not only a fascinating work in itself, far more honest than the exhibitionist *Confessions* of Rousseau; it is the logical culmination of a series of works that have been essentially confessional. "I know as well the mistake that I make in telling this and what is to follow," he writes; "I foresee the arguments that can be drawn from it against me. But my narrative has no other reason for being than truth. Let us say that it is out of penitence that I write it."

In this light one can better understand Gide's addiction to extremes: the violent contradictions in his personality and career; the curious *mélange* of satire and poetry, of classic style and romantic subject, of impersonal manner and intensely personal matter; and the curious succession of mutually repellent novelettes. His *Treatise on Narcissism* is a youthful apology for Symbolism; *Paludes* is a pitiless satire on the Symbolist mania for introspection and love of the Ivory Tower. *The Immoralist* is not only Nietzschean but Rousseauian—it proudly affirms the good of the natural, sensual life; *Straight Is the Way* satirizes the excesses of ascetic zeal but also satirizes the immoralist's way of life. *The Vatican Swindle* is the "literary cocktail of our age," but beneath its sparkling wit and robust farce lurk misanthropic implications; *The Pastoral Symphony* is a mournful but beautiful idyll that could have been written only by a reverent spirit. A single glance makes plain that these could not be the works of the same man—and a second glance reveals that they unmistakably are. Gide himself does little to reconcile these contradictions and fit them into a cozier pattern. One reason, again, is that he enjoys the rôle of *enfant terrible*. Another, he explains in his Journal, is his excessive sympathy; in writing he forgets himself entirely to *become* one of his characters, just as in life he quickly abandons his own point of view to take on the thought and emotion of another—and to make matters more confusing, is most attracted by what differs from him. Here the self-conscious Gide appears to be preening himself before an audience, posturing before posterity; at the same time he is as usual speaking at least partial truth. But behind all the paradoxes of Gide, the impossible combination of elements angelic and demoniac, lies the conflict between the Puritan and the emancipated modern, between an old-fashioned, inflexible conscience and a subtle, protean intelligence—a conflict intensified by an ingrained abnormality he can neither accept nor deny. The disharmony in his soul may be sublimated in a faith like that of Communism, which can appeal at once to his religious instinct and to his quick intelligence; or it may simply be softened by the mellowness of old age. It would be rash, despite the increasingly religious tone of his latest work, to rejoice in his renunciation of his early "errors" or to predict his future course. Safer are the words with which M. Souday concludes his study: "With him, one never knows."

Yet if the explanation of Gide's work is in part simply physiological, it also leads one to the spiritual confusion of an age in which nothing is certain or fixed—except perhaps the law of relativity. He is as unstable as this age, and in his own person almost as heterogeneous. He has accordingly left some striking records of the mind of his time; his narratives are interesting primarily for their immediate moral and psychological significance. At the same time he has made a definite contribution to contemporary consciousness, leaving more than mere documentary evidence, for he has not surrendered to the confusion and uncertainty about him. By his intelligence and his daring he has enlarged our moral experience. By the essential seriousness underlying his bravado he has made his work important simply in the questions it raises. In a period of transvaluation he has driven down to fundamentals.

Gide is not, to be sure, a great novelist. He pays the full penalty that may be exacted by sophistication and self-awareness. The great objection to the Symbolists, he remarked, is their lack of curiosity about life; of him it might be said that he has too much mere curiosity. To compare *The Counterfeiters* with *The Magic Mountain* is to perceive the difference between a shrewd observer and a brooding philosopher and poet. Nor can he, like the Dostoyevsky he reveres, whole-heartedly and passionately commit himself; for the same reason that he always keeps his head he misses the greatest effects of art. Yet he is not the unfeeling monster with whom the orthodox frighten their spiritual children. Although his values may not be our values, he does a service in forcing us to reexamine our values, and his sincere concern for spiritual meanings gives his work general significance. "It is not," as Marcel Arland says in summary, "the work of a pure spirit, nor of a pure sensualist, nor even the work of an extremely sensitive man, but one always finds in it a soul."

XX

THOMAS MANN

I

LIKE many modern novelists, Thomas Mann began his literary career by following the sinking star of naturalism. His early stories and sketches deal grimly, though sympathetically, with life among the poor. From these the step was short to *Buddenbrooks,* a conventional sociological chronicle. *Buddenbrooks* is indeed a distinguished novel, more solid and profound than *The Forsyte Saga,* and deserving of more attention than it will receive here. But Mann himself was not content to stop with this kind of performance; a highly self-critical artist, he continued to grow. He was profoundly concerned with the need of justifying his seemingly remote and unworldly activity. In a number of stories, culminating in *Death in Venice,* he wrestled with the peculiar problem of the artist: menaced by his very love of beauty, the artist is always prone to forget his responsibility to himself, his kind, above all his society. Such arduous soul-searching grew out of the incertitudes of the modern era, to which Mann was sensitive even before the World War; with the appalling catastrophe of the war, however, it became a desperate business, the very condition of his survival. For some years he was as artist completely paralyzed. In a long series of treatises and essays he painfully examined his conscience, groped toward enlightenment. And of this spiritual travail *The Magic Mountain* is the magnificent summation and the epilogue. Here he finally exorcised his demons, sublimated his distress, converted the confusion and the din into imperishable beauty. It is, I believe, one of the indubitably great novels of the world.

Commentators have already appeared with keys for the many entrances to *The Magic Mountain;* * for if it is immediately impressive, it is also bewildering. At first glance it might be taken simply as a realistic account of a young man's experience in a sanatorium—an experience Mann himself had had. It is always leisurely and solid; Mann carefully individualizes every character, minutely annotates every experience. In his Foreword he announces that he is going to tell his story at length, in detail: "We do not fear being called meticulous, inclining as we do to the view that only the exhaustive can be truly interesting." Or again *The Magic Mountain* might be considered a psychological novel, a Freudian excursion into the subconscious. It is among other things a brilliant study of disease and its effects—a subject that has always fascinated Mann. Those who have lived in a tuberculosis sanatorium testify to the truth of his study; those who have not can at least feel its power. Many readers remark the uneasy feeling that they themselves are getting the disease simply by reading, succumbing to the power of suggestion even as did his hero, Hans Castorp.

Yet realism, psychology, are plainly not the whole of Mann's intention. The simplest reader recognizes *The Magic Mountain* as a philosophical novel, highly charged with meanings not visible on the surface. When it is most concrete it still carries with it a haunting suggestion of allegory and mystical meaning; the very sharpness of the contours of the characters makes their shadows stand out more boldly. The title itself carries a plain suggestion of symbolism—this is the Magic Mountain of the *Siebenschläfer*—and Mann throws out many similar suggestions. He plays, for example, on the mystic number 7: after a seven weeks' stay Hans Castorp submits to the X-ray examination that settles his fate, and then he remains for seven years; for seven minutes at a time he keeps his thermometer in his mouth and listens to his blood; he sits in turn at the seven tables in the dining room; his

* *Thomas Mann's Novel "Der Zauberberg,"* by Professor H. J. Wiegand, is the most exhaustive study yet to appear in English, and one to which I am greatly indebted.

enchantress, Clavdia Chauchat, occupies room # 7—Professor Wiegand gives a long list of such details. The greatness of Mann's novel lies finally in just this wealth of implication, the many layers of meaning under its vivid surface.

One of the more obvious of his deeper purposes is spiritual autobiography. Hans Castorp represents, in his most significant traits and concerns, Thomas Mann himself. Hans seeks to integrate his whole experience, to find the meaning of life; and he goes about this exalted metaphysical business in a manner at once phlegmatic and impassioned that is typical of his author. Many readers are misled by Mann's Olympian irony, an irony that turns in on itself, smiles at its own image, gives the impression of lightness and mockery when he is in holiest earnest. Thus he constantly calls Hans "mediocre" and has him blunder ludicrously. Hans is indeed a naïve fellow, never more naïve than when most solemn. Yet his "mediocrity," Mann is careful to point out, is finally an affliction caused by his age: a restless, viewless, chaotic age that vouchsafed him no "reasonably satisfying explanation of the meaning and purpose of man's life." In the end, moreover, Hans proves to be *not* mediocre. His simplicity is noble as well as amusing. He is clearly a better man than either of the brilliant dialecticians, Settembrini and Naphta, and unassumingly finds his own way between them. Finally he comes closer to the truth than all the apparently superior men who fight over his simple, honest soul. "You must have more in you than we thought," writes his creator in an affectionate farewell. Hans wins our respect as well as our affection; for "Life's delicate child" has proved to be a "genius in the realm of experience," a hero worthy of even so heroic an adventure as that of *The Magic Mountain*.

This adventure is not, however, a purely personal one. As spiritual autobiography, *The Magic Mountain* is like *Wilhelm Meister* and the *Confessions* of Tolstoy, much vaster in scope than *The Way of All Flesh, Sons and Lovers,* or *A Portrait of the Artist as a Young Man*. Mann is not seeking a way of salvation for himself alone, or for a few superior spirits like him. He is seeking to express the consciousness of the race, to synthetize and integrate the whole experience of modern man.

Hence the setting of his novel. The International Sanatorium Berghof incidentally provides an opportunity for an interesting pathological study; its tubercular patients may incidentally symbolize, as some critics think, the sickness of bourgeois society; but it is essential to Mann's whole epical intention. In the first place, the rarefied atmosphere of the mountain accelerates the metabolism of Hans Castorp and thus prepares him for his adventures—with his habitual irony, Mann takes pleasure in pointing out this simple physiological basis of lofty endeavor. More important, this is the *International* Sanatorium, located in Switzerland, most cosmopolitan of European countries. Mann is thus able to assemble representatives of all nationalities, to submit for synthesis many different points of view, and so more clearly to universalize his story. He is also able to put Hans Castorp beyond Time itself. Time ceases to exist for the patients of the Berghof; Time is one of the dominant themes of *The Magic Mountain* as of *Remembrance of Things Past,* and Mann seeks as earnestly as Proust to escape its tyranny. But above all, in the isolation of this setting the simple nature of Hans can be distilled and redistilled until nothing remains but its pure essence. He is cut free from all the snarls and tangles of the contemporary world. He is placed against the background of Nature, the elemental created Universe. Undistracted by the shifting appearances and ceaseless pressure of the world of practical affairs, he can grapple directly with problems metaphysical. If accordingly Mann pays little attention to immediate political or social problems, it is only to go behind them to the last and absolute issues of human life.

Hence the failure of Hans Castorp to return to the "flat-land," his succumbing to the dangerous lure of the sanatorium, is not to be considered mere weakness, nor the whole novel interpreted—as many readers interpret it—as an "epic of disease," a fatal spell or morbid dream from which the hero is awakened only by the World War. Mann plainly does not, like the common-sense

Shaw, regard disease as an unmitigated evil. Although in Frau Stöhr and most of the patients of the Berghof he displays its dehumanizing and stultifying effects, he joins Dostoyevsky, Proust, and the German romantics in regarding it as an ennobling principle too, and in Hans Castorp he displays its possible value. Death and disease have indeed an unhealthy fascination for Hans, but he presently resists their more dangerous charms. He returns to the flat-land unmistakably a better man for his prolonged stay on the Magic Mountain. His refusal to leave proves to have been no flabby self-indulgence but an obscure devotion to the law of his own nature. It enabled him to "take stock" once and for all, made possible his exciting and fruitful adventure.

When one begins, however, to examine more closely the fruits of this adventure, to inquire specifically what Hans found out after seven years of taking stock, one discovers a whole new range of meanings, a whole new set of symbols. Upon the outbreak of the World War, Mann felt a profound obligation to assume the rôle of spokesman for spiritual Germany, and over some years he labored unhappily in a series of political treatises; *The Magic Mountain* triumphantly discharges this responsibility. Hans Castorp is the representative, not only of Mann, but of the German nation, and his story is an elaborate symbolical statement of the ideal rôle Mann wishes it to play. If the present régime in Germany makes this intention appear grotesque, Professor Wiegand nevertheless shows how it governs both the conception of character and the invention of incident down almost to the last detail of the novel. Unlike the *Odyssey* motif in Joyce's *Ulysses,* it is foundation, not superstructure; a vital animating principle, not an incidental overlay. Its main outlines stand out boldly, and its significance to a German is attested by the otherwise surprising popularity of *The Magic Mountain* in Central Europe.

Mann adopted for this purpose the traditional national view (of Adam Müller, Nietzsche, and others) that he had outlined in his *Reflections of a Non-Political Man:* Germany is the mediator between Western and Eastern civilization, more particularly between French rationalism and Russian mysticism—"das Volk der Mitte." Accordingly the two most persistent influences to which he subjects his obviously Teutonic hero are the eloquent Settembrini, symbol of the Western enlightenment, and the slovenly, alluring Clavdia Chauchat, symbol of the mysticism of the East. Hans is vastly impressed by Settembrini and learns much from him—his thinking grows more precise, his speech more fluent; his simple nature is also deepened and enriched by his passion for Clavdia. Yet he succumbs to neither; in the end he goes his own way, following the laws of his own nature. Symbolically he achieves an ideal synthesis of the opposing cultures while retaining his peculiar native genius. He fulfils the lofty destiny of the German people: "the race," as Mann declares in his essay "Goethe and Tolstoy," "that practises a sly and ironic reserve toward both sides, that moves between extremes, easily, with non-committal benevolence; with the morality, no, the simplicity of that elusive 'betweenness' of theirs." Yet this pretty wish-fulfilment is also a challenge. Like Nietzsche, Mann combats the excesses of the German romantics and calls for more rationality, more devotion to logic and the habit of analysis. Germany must complement its splendid romanticism, qualify its peculiar genius. And Mann is himself, more clearly than the Nietzsche he admires, the embodiment of his ideal: he has blended the native genius of music with a logical, analytical prose. Hence his growing cosmopolitanism, which has made him, while still deeply and reverently a German, the foremost man of letters of the world. Hence his love of Switzerland: in this land French and German have met and combined.

These meanings, unmistakable and important though they are, the unaided English reader is likely to miss entirely. He can even afford to miss them. For they are but part of still larger and more universal intentions. Mann's very conception of the ideal destiny of Germany demands that he transcend the specifically German. The "mediocre" Hans Castorp, "Life's delicate child," proves great enough and robust enough to represent not only Thomas Mann and Germany but all inquiring, aspiring mankind. His spiritual adventures carry him beyond the borders not merely of self but of nation; he "takes stock" as *Homo Dei.*

Hence what in the final analysis governs the pattern of *The Magic Mountain* is the principle of synthesis, the effort at an all-inclusive understanding. Themes and characters are arranged in pairs. Settembrini is balanced by Naphta, Clavdia by Joachim. Behrens represents the physiological, Krokowski the psychological approach to the problem of disease and finally to the principle of life. The metaphysical speculations of Hans are supplemented by his intensive scientific studies. In this welter of opposites only a few elemental forces stand out singly: the force of pure, inarticulate feeling in the magnificent personality of Mynheer Peeperkorn; the force of Nature, a sublime and abiding presence; and always at the center the force of Hans Castorp himself: an absurd and appealing little figure busying itself on a vast stage, a piping voice in a confused uproar, a pin-point of flickering but unquenchable light in the illimitable darkness—the human spirit on its forlorn, gallant, and preposterous adventure among the immensities.

2

The spirit that conceived and broods over every page of *The Magic Mountain* is in the deepest sense of the word humanistic. In an age of cultural specialization and violent partizanship, Mann is conspicuous for his catholicity and tolerance, the range and depth of his understanding and sympathy. He has suggested that the two most significant experiences of the nineteenth century were the experiences of Nietzsche and of the Russian soul: Nietzsche is a symbol of pride and freedom, Dostoyevsky of humility and reverence. Like his own Hans Castorp, Mann has succeeded in reconciling and fusing these experiences; and because both are natural to him, his synthesis yet does not seem synthetic. He has the piety of the great Russian writers, their deep conviction of the dignity and worth of the human spirit even in degradation; despite his unfailing irony he always pities, respects, and loves his people. At the same time his spirit is not that of resignation or meek submission; he has Nietzsche's love of reckless spiritual challenge and adventure, his willingness to risk his soul in hazardous inquiry. He is at once tender and austere, mild and lofty, ironical and earnest. And this attitude leads him to break down all rigid dualisms, the analytical abstractions that separate men from the living truth of experience. Love and lust, flesh and spirit, mind and matter, reason and emotion—to insist upon these as absolute categories is not "genial"; it is even, he permits himself to say, "inept." Mann is fundamentally idealistic, he is primarily concerned with spiritual essences and values, but these he would draw from the totality of man's relations to the universe, his entire integrated experience. They are both flower and root, not merely choice distillations.

To state these meanings and values more specifically, however, is not easy. Many readers leave *The Magic Mountain* perplexed. Mann raises innumerable questions and indicates their urgency —but he does not answer them. The novel ends, in fact, on a question. Hans Castorp goes to war, presumably to his death: "Out of this universal feast of death, out of this extremity of fever, kindling the rain-washed evening sky to a fiery glow, may it be that Love one day shall mount?" Mann does not say. He refuses to intervene and state preferences, refuses to be stampeded into judgment, refuses to set up as a messiah. "I am neither learned nor a teacher, rather a dreamer and a doubter who is hard put to it to save and justify his own life." And the uneasy reader is further distracted by Mann's sovereign irony, which plays over his holiest concerns and makes him always appear to be saying less than he is.

This skepticism and this irony nevertheless are not simply a refuge. In his essay "Thomas Mann and André Gide" Kenneth Burke asks, "Are not these men trying to make us at home in indecision, are they not trying to humanize the state of doubt?" In a sense they are—and it is a humane vocation. It is also a realistic one; for as Burke adds, becoming certain too quickly is perhaps an evasion, a shirking of responsibility. Yet this proposition is likely to give a false impression, at least of the work of Mann. With him, skepticism is included within a larger frame and serves chiefly as a means to an end. Although he does not hope to attain absolute truth, he earnestly seeks some measure of certainty, some path out of the contemporary wilderness. Suspended judgment is for the present particularly needful; but if it is not to become sheer evasion, it must be accompanied by a feeling of responsibility and a deep concern for values. A confirmed and complacent skeptic would not have suffered the travail of Thomas Mann during the war years, nor could he have written *The Magic Mountain*.

Hence, if one is forced to depend upon implications, these are not tenuous or wholly uncertain. One can find a wealth of meanings in Mann's novel; one cannot find whatever he wants. The limitations, for instance, of the fiery pedagogues—Settembrini and Naphta—are obvious enough. Settembrini blows too hard on "the penny pipe of reason"; he gets intoxicated on his own eloquence, blown from his moorings by his own windy rhetoric. His idealism is noble, but it is also vague, shallow, ultimately illiberal—Woodrow Wilson was a tragic example of both its insolence and its insufficiency. The whole confusion and inconsistency of his thought is brilliantly demonstrated by Naphta, who clearly states Mann's negative criticism. But Naphta, through whom Mann indulges (somewhat excessively) his love of dialectics, himself illustrates the absurdity of the logical extreme. He is too often merely negative—his suicide is symbolical; his only positive affirmation is an inhumanly rigorous dualism that justifies Settembrini's criticism: "His form is logic, but his essence is confusion." Even before the entrance of Mynheer Peeperkorn Hans Castorp has rejected them both, found his own way "between two intolerable positions, between bombastic humanism and analphabetic barbarism." With the coming of the magnificent Dutchman, however, Settembrini and Naphta are made to seem mere wrangling schoolboys. Inarticulate, incoherent, beyond the reach of the most eloquent rhetoric or the most incisive argument, Peeperkorn is the embodiment of pure feeling—feeling that makes possible the "roused and intoxicated life" in which man appears godlike. By the sheer force of personality, simple, elemental, unanalyzable, he overshadows their most brilliant talk, dwarfs them into insignificance. He does on a mighty scale what Zuleika Dobson's maid did on a small one: he makes chaos cosmic.

Why, then, does Peeperkorn kill himself? Because, says one commentator, the principle of Life could not exist in this sickly atmosphere. But a deeper reason is the inadequacy even of his sublimely simple way of life. As an old man, he could no longer live it. He is indeed still majestic in death; his suicide is no token of futility or despair but an act of devotion to the ideal for which he had lived. "He was built on such a grand scale," Hans explains reverently, "that he considered it a blasphemy, a cosmic catastrophe, to be found wanting in feeling." Yet a complete, harmonious way of life should not demand such martyrdom. Simple feeling, however godlike, is not enough. Mynheer Peeperkorn failed to see that the rational faculty must also play a part in the ideal life, and is also a sign of divinity.

It is thus left to the unassuming, undistinguished, unheroic Hans Castorp, the plastic pupil of a dozen tutors, to correct all their distortions and point the way to truth. Lost on the mountain during a snowstorm, he achieves, if only for a moment, what none of the others was able to achieve: a vital, all-inclusive synthesis, a view of life in which all the faculties of man, rational and irrational, are divinely fused. This scene is plainly the spiritual climax of the novel, and the quintessence of Mann's message. Here Hans harmonizes all that he has learned, and most clearly sees through and beyond his teachers. Here he escapes the orbit of disease and triumphs over death. In this transport he affirms life once and for all:

> There is both rhyme and reason in what I say: I have made a dream poem of humanity. I will cling to it. I will be good. I will let death have no mastery over my thoughts. For therein lies goodness and love of humankind, and in nothing else. . . . It is love, not reason, that is stronger than death. Only love, not reason, gives sweet thoughts. And from love and sweetness alone

> can form come: form and civilization, friendly, enlightened, beautiful human intercourse. . . . *For the sake of goodness and love, man shall let death have no sovereignty over his thoughts.**

The vision fades—but it leaves a residue. Henceforth Hans is consistently a better man. "I will remember," he promises himself in his ecstasy; and he does remember. This one moment has justified his long stay on the Magic Mountain.

Despite his habit of skepticism and irony, then, Mann is not merely a skeptic, and certainly not a defeatist. This scene is a lyrical affirmation of life, and its echoes linger as overtones throughout the rest of the novel. It gives even the question at the end a positive implication. This remains, significantly and fittingly, a question; but in the light of the experience of Hans Castorp in the snowstorm it is a sign of hope, not of despair.

It is also clear, despite Mann's discreetness, that with all his intellectual interests and remarkable powers of thought he has strong mystical leanings. Elsewhere in the novel he suggests that the dark tracts of the human soul known as subconsciousness are perhaps better called superconsciousness, "since from them sometimes emanates a knowingness beyond anything of which the conscious intelligence is capable . . . giving rise to the hypothesis that there may subsist connections and associations between the lowest and least illumined regions of the individual soul and a wholly knowing All-Soul." During his vision Hans Castorp is aware of a mystic bond of unity between himself and the universe, a kind of communion with this All-Soul, and this communion takes place through the channels of intuitive sympathy, not of reason. In a similar spirit Mann writes his many disquisitions on Time; but throughout his novel he displays a readiness to leave the "saner, chaster realms of thought" and embark upon "highly questionable" speculations, such as those on spiritualism in the strange scene of the séance.

Yet Mann does not join in the crusade against, or flight from,

* Reprinted from *The Magic Mountain,* by permission of and special arrangement with Alfred A. Knopf, Inc., authorized publishers.

intellect. Hans Castorp does not scorn the rational faculty; he indulges it freely, with great pleasure, pride, and profit. Mann's essential attitude is most clearly stated in his essay "Freud's Position in the History of Modern Thought." Freud was among the first modern thinkers to emphasize the primacy of the instinctive and affective, to point out "the powerlessness of mind and reason by contrast with the forces marshaled in the death of the soul, with the dynamic of passion, the irrational, the unconscious." Many converts then proceeded to grovel before the throne of the dark powers. As part of the ritual of worship they poured scorn on intellect. Instead of pitying this poor power and trying to protect it in its weakness, they despised it as a base illusion, gloated over its defeats, kicked it and flogged it, performed a witch dance about its remains. Paradoxically, they came even to fear it—while proclaiming its powerlessness, they yet pointed to it as a menace. But Freud does not join in these obscene rites that his researches helped to instigate; he does not himself glorify the affective at the *expense* of the intellectual. His own summation is this:

> We may emphasize as often as we like the fact that intellect is powerless compared with impulse in human life—we shall be right. But after all there is something peculiar about this weakness; the voice of the intellect is low, but it rests not till it gets a hearing. In the end, after countless repulses, it gets one after all.

And this is essentially the view of Mann himself. He recommends an attitude of research "in which feeling, intuition, spiritual implications reassert their right, and art secures its position as a genuine instrument of knowledge." But he also clings to the "large and trusting and enduring conviction" that the power of reason, which has played so great and honorable a rôle in historical enlightenment, will continue to do so. He stresses the need of "conscious possession . . . the culture of men developed to complete self-consciousness. The name of revolution belongs only to the will that leads futurewards by the path of consciousness and resolution."

The humanism of Mann is accordingly an effort to embrace

all the faculties of man, integrate all that is valuable in his new knowledge and experience, in the hope of fully realizing his potentialities. He seeks to reconcile the many conflicting claims of specialists and partizans, to order the many overlapping and tangential perspectives. In the disorder of the present, when the immense accumulations of scientific investigation have been incorporated neither in the practical administration of society nor in the emotional and spiritual attitudes of the individual, he recognizes the necessity of reexamining and redefining the whole humanistic tradition. But he wishes above all to preserve the essential values of this tradition. In his essay "Goethe and Tolstoy" he declares that "it is time for us to lay all possible stress upon our great humane inheritance and to cultivate it with all the means at our command." He praises Goethe particularly for his reverence for the past and his strong communal spirit in the face of an increasingly anarchical individualism: his call for piety, discipline, conformity of the ego within a noble and estimable community. Goethe's "conception of humanity and human dignity, culture and civilization, is so consonant with solemn regulation and gradation, with such a pronounced sense of reverence, of traditions, symbols, mysteries, and rhythm, with such a symmetrical, almost choreographic restraint in its freedom, that I may be permitted to call it statesmanlike in the best and finest sense, by way of pointing the contrast to Tolstoy's 'letting the children out of the benches.' "

The emancipated modern may regard this as hocus-pocus. Yet he has only to appeal to his own gods, the psychologists, to be told its truth: still stronger than man's desire for freedom is his instinctive desire to conform, to follow worshipfully, like the child with his marbles, the rules of the game. To those who would dismiss the cultivation of "our great humane inheritance" as mere irrelevance, or as a luxury that the contemporary cannot afford while practical problems are so urgent, Mann answers that modern socialism, for example, "has all too long allowed its spiritual life to languish in the shallows of a crude economic materialism," and has no greater need than to find access to this inheritance. His criticism is pertinent simply because from his elevation he does not lose sight of immediate realities. He maintains an admirable balance between the old and the new, the heritage of the past and the needs of the present. With as pious a devotion to the humanistic tradition as that of the New Humanists, Mann nevertheless refuses to isolate it and make it the exclusive property of a few gentlemanly scholars. He recognizes that it is an organic growth, an ennobling and not a repudiation of nature; he is unafraid to reinterpret it, as it has constantly been reinterpreted in the past, in the terms of new knowledge and a new cultural context; he seeks above all to relate it to the special interests and inescapable conditions of modern life, in the faith that it is still noble and valid even when working men have the ballot and ride in Ford cars, and when even gentlemen are conditioned by reflexes and complexes. But at the same time Mann respects the methods and accepts the findings of modern scientific thought without swallowing them whole. He embraces many perspectives—Freudian, Marxist, behavioristic—but he recognizes them for what they are: illuminating perspectives, not exclusive avenues to truth. He perceives that the rationale of science is a splendid means but not a sufficient end, that it is not even the only and inevitable means, and that the disposition to accept it unquestioningly is but the latest evidence of the age-old tyranny of "climate of opinion."

This whole attitude may seem pretty vague and tentative—and necessarily it is. The humanistic tradition has never supplied specific weights and measures or elaborate blueprints for a spiritual home; to sign on the dotted line of Thomas Mann is not to achieve a fearless personality and wisdom and success within a thirty-day or even a thirty-year trial period. He himself pays the penalty of his breadth, his freedom from partizanship, his habit of doubt and humble inquiry. At times he takes almost too cool and abstracted a view of the exigencies of the moment; in the interests of his Olympian pursuits he seemed for a time too willing to compromise with such temporal monstrosities as Hitlerism. At best, tolerance is a beautiful but not a dynamic virtue. It is not the way to get things done; active measures, for better or worse, are taken care of by the zealots, the one-idea men. We have on our hands imperious problems, and wars and depressions are not dispelled by the loftiest thinking. Yet Mann has not lost touch with his age, nor is his thought ever irrelevant. If there is always a need for the practical reformer, there is always a need too for the man who detaches himself from the immediate present in order to gain perspective, to return to first principles, to grapple with final issues—to clarify meanings and establish values to which the reformer can appeal in the course of his more "practical" activity. Marxists have the habit of appropriating the "long view" for themselves; Mann's is clearly a still longer view.

3

At the very least, the philosophy of Thomas Mann is an excellent one for the artist, whose primary duty is not specifically to settle problems; it not only gives him an exalted function, but does not cramp him in the fulfilment of this function. Here one comes back to where all discussion of Mann ought to end: his own work as an artist. Although *The Magic Mountain* makes all too plain that he is a brilliant dialectician, he has himself pointed out that "all mere pronouncements are relative and vulnerable, regardless of the pretensions to absoluteness and finality with which they may be felt and uttered," and that "only the shapes of esthetic creation are impervious to the ravages of time"; the precious advantage of the work of art lies precisely "in its protean vitality, its non-committal independence, its spiritual freedom." If Mann's thought is still provisional and occasionally too misty, it has nevertheless inspired great fictions; and if it in time loses something in pertinence, its position in a majestic compositional scheme gives it, like the thought in *Hamlet,* an indestructible vitality.

Mann's most important work since *The Magic Mountain* is his Biblical trilogy, of which as yet only two volumes have appeared: *Joseph and His Brethren* and *The Young Joseph.* It is a somewhat bewildering work, and no doubt will remain so even when the final volume has appeared and his whole intention is manifest. It is also somewhat disappointing, and makes plainer the dangers in Mann's attitude. He exploits too freely the ironical possibilities of his material, at times suggesting the easy sophisticated fun of Anatole France or even John Erskine; he is too superior to his characters and has too explicitly the attitude of Olympian Jove; he is long-winded and at times super-subtle, too readily using his simple story as a springboard from which to dive into the sea of metaphysics and esthetics; in general he makes his materials almost oppressively pregnant with meaning. Yet the novel grows more impressive as one reads on. It widens and deepens, not only in its thought but in its simple humanity. And it is thoroughly characteristic of Mann. The Biblical setting serves the same purpose as the sanatorium on the Magic Mountain: it enables him to escape the confusion and distraction of contemporaneity, and more clearly to disengage his timeless values and reveal the timeless laws of human life. More specifically, Joseph is another symbol of the problem that has always concerned him: the menace of beauty, the abyss surrounding the artistic temperament, the relation of the artist to his society. What Joseph learned from his experience has yet to be revealed, but the well into which he is cast is obviously symbolical.

Meanwhile *The Magic Mountain* is its author's masterpiece. It is not only a vast record, packed with man's deepest experience; it is a magnificent work of art that constantly suggests even more than it expresses. It is not only wide, solid, and deep, but resonant, rich in the overtones of great poetry. It carries an enormous weight of fact and thought and carries it lightly, without seeming either a treatise or a tour de force. Despite his seeming artlessness and his old-fashioned intimacy with his characters and his reader, Mann is a self-conscious, highly sensitive craftsman who has learned much from the masters of technique, and who carefully selects, arranges, and excludes without giving the effect of artifice or exclusion. To return to *Buddenbrooks,* where he constantly writes expository essays and introduces his characters complete with an inventory and a label, is to appreciate the unobtrusive skill with which in *The Magic Mountain* he dramatizes his exposition, chooses the point of view from which light and shadow will fall appropriately, disposes his wealth of material about the central figure of Hans Castorp, and, in general, leads Hans through his high adventure without seeming like a professional guide. And although most readers appreciate, even in translation, Mann's musical and beautifully expressive prose, few are aware of the many subtleties of suggestion, the symbols and leitmotifs, woven into its texture. He has shaped his immense intention in a work of art whose wonderful intricacy is yet compatible with clarity and order. He has again reconciled the French and German antitheses: the French concern for form with the German concern for substance, the French genius of lucid, logical analysis with the German genius of pure poetry and music.

The chief source of Mann's greatness is thus not merely that he makes the novel hold more than all but a very few writers have attempted, but that his novel holds it in solution. As in *Remembrance of Things Past* and *The Counterfeiters,* we have here the fusion of creation and criticism, "self-consciousness playing with its own content"; but Mann manages this dangerous business more successfully than either Proust or Gide. Some of the philosophical disputations are excess baggage, exercises in dialectics for its own sake; except for these the whole content of *The Magic Mountain* is vividly dramatized, concretely objectified in the story, carried in its blood. Unlike Butler, Huxley, and most markedly intellectual novelists, Mann sacrifices none of the primary demands of fiction to his deeper purposes. His novel is an organism, not an omnibus. The knowledge that Hans Castorp absorbs becomes part of his live tissue, his personality. His thought and emotion are perfectly fused, his spiritual adventures made real and exciting.

The Magic Mountain is indeed of especial interest as a splendid climax to the development of the realistic method, a splendid triumph over its obvious dangers and difficulties. The foundation of the novel is solidly realistic. Yet its detail is highly charged.

It never exists for its own or history's sake, but is always vitally related to the central problems of Hans Castorp. His cigars—the dignified *Maria Mancinis;* the family baptismal bowl, symbol of continuity and natural piety; the checkered trousers, the threadbare coat, and the waving mustaches of the "organ-grinder," Settembrini; the chewed fingernails, the slouch, and the door-slamming habit of Clavdia—these and innumerable other details are as expressive as the famous hat of Charles Bovary. Particularly significant, however, is Mann's deliberate emphasis upon certain machine products, like the thermometer, the pencil, the phonograph, the watch, and the X-ray machine and its pictures. Through these symbols, unprepossessing in themselves, he conveys the deepest experience of Hans. He succeeds, in short, in endowing with spiritual significance the forms of modern life, making the homely thermometer serve the timeless purposes once served by the nightingale and the daffodil. In his creative activity if not in his thought, he makes good the prophecy of Wordsworth and achieves the synthesis of poetry and science.

To have written such a novel among the angry polemics and the profound incertitudes of these scrambled times is a sufficiently notable achievement. Yet if *The Magic Mountain* is timeless, incommensurable, it is also clearly a product of the twentieth century. Mann's concern for values has been forced upon him by the anarchy of his age; he has had to ask questions that never troubled earlier artists. And unable to be content with a merely personal salvation, or the hand-to-mouth solutions by which even serious artists have managed to live, he has faced squarely the central problem of modern life. He has sought to order a system of values, to restore communal ideals, to establish unobstructed lines of communication both with the past and between the many isolated outposts of the present. He has sought to provide a whole scheme of reorientation, and then to vitalize it in the enduring shapes of art. In short, he has sought to be both the poet and the philosopher of his age, and do for it what St. Thomas Aquinas and Dante together did for theirs.

It is an enormously difficult task. It demands not only great imaginative but great intellectual powers—powers such as we do not expect of the geniuses of the past, or find in any but a very few of them. So ambitious an artist must today embrace an immense profusion of perspectives, an immense range, diversity, and complexity of specialized thought and experience; and unlike the artist of the past he can take nothing for granted but must work out all his assumptions. In this view the importance of Mann lies in that he is not only better equipped for this task than any other contemporary writer, but less oppressed by its necessity, less appalled by its conditions. Like Lenin in another sphere, he is the great man called forth by the great moment. It is interesting to speculate upon what he might have accomplished in a simpler, stabler, more homogeneous age; meanwhile he appears to express himself as completely in this one, make as full use of his special gifts, as did Dante in his.

The Magic Mountain is not, to be sure, the final and positive solution of the problems of the age, or even of Thomas Mann himself. He is one of the few important writers today who continue to grow, to shoot arrows at a farther shore. He is still an inquirer, a self-questioner, and still follows the path of the middle, the path of irony. He is still wary, perhaps too wary, of anything like finality; as he wrote some years ago, "In matters of humanity every decision may prove premature." He is convinced only of the dignity of man, the worth of man's aspirations and possibilities. If he is not a witch doctor or wonder-worker, we can get along with this one absence from the host we already have. Through both his profoundest convictions and his profoundest doubts he carries himself with absolute integrity; and if he offers no dogmatic assurances, at least he points steadily, austerely, to a way.

XXI

APOSTLES OF THE LOST GENERATION: HUXLEY, HEMINGWAY

I

THE "lost generation" that came out of the World War now has a further reason for melancholy: it has been crowded into the background, relegated to the attic, consigned to the museum of antiques where wander the ghosts of eminent Victorians. Its woes were for a time the object of universal concern and regarded as premonitory rumbles of the crack of doom. Now they are commonly diagnosed as the febrile hangover with which men usually awaken after a disastrous war. In the last few years the literary atmosphere has unmistakably changed, if scarcely cleared. A younger generation has emerged, fired by new hopes and oppressed by new fears. They contemplate somberly the approach of another war, which can be expected to produce a still more violent headache. They grapple with more tangible monsters, like Fascism and Depression, and do battle on political and economic fronts. They have found causes to live and die for. But hopeful or fearful, almost all view the distresses of their elders as a little quaint and faddish, like the megrims indulged in by fashionable ladies of the eighteenth century.

Yet the post-war period is important in modern literary history. Many of the spokesmen of the lost generation are still doing a lively business at the old stands. Their cynical manner still influences younger writers, they still make converts—one of the latest is John O'Hara, author of *Appointment in Samara* and *Butterfield 8*. They produced, moreover, a literature that at its best is interesting in its own right and likely to leave some mark upon the literature of the future. And their disillusionment, finally, was not merely faddish or synthetic. "To have to take it all," wrote the appalled Henry James at the outbreak of the war, "for what the treacherous years were all the while really making for and *meaning,* is too tragic for any words." This generation had to take it so, they had to work out the whole bloody meaning, and they had then to endure the mockery of Victory, play out the farce of Peace. If their violent reaction for a time confused or obscured the deeper issues of modern life, it also intensified them, so that now, from a distance, they can be perceived more clearly.

In America the disenchanted were perhaps most noisy and extravagant. France had its Dadaists, to be sure, but they were taken seriously by only a few; the echoes of their catcalls soon died away. The urgent problems of reconstruction left Europe little time for a spree. Its writers—especially in England—were further restrained by a long, aristocratic tradition. But America had suffered relatively little, materially, and had at once plenty of time to contemplate the ruins and less occasion for releasing its explosive energy in riot and revolution. It had marched into war with the most inflated ideals and fantastic hopes—with all the luxury and pomp of a holy Cause. As children of a vigorous young nation just come into its own, its writers were less given to decorum, less curbed by the discipline of tradition. And so it was here, and in American colonies abroad, that debunking had its rankest growth, the jazz and cocktail era its loudest fanfare.

The master of ceremonies at the opening of this era was no doubt F. Scott Fitzgerald. He is so completely identified with it that when recently he broke silence and published another novel (*Tender Is the Night*) he sounded like a hollow echo—a "ghostly cricket, creaking where a house was burned." A quite ordinary novel, it suggests, moreover, that with the passing of this era his subject matter is gone. Yet if much of his work is as ephemeral as its material, the best of it outlives its period. Although *The Great Gatsby,* for example, is tinged with the flippancy, hard-boiled sentimentality, and cock-eyed idealism of this period, it is on the whole honestly, soberly, brilliantly done. Similar in technique to the novels of Conrad, it leaves a similarly haunting impression of its strange and pitiable hero.

The most significant representatives of the post-war period, however, are Aldous Huxley and Ernest Hemingway. Both have brilliantly recorded its ways and expressed its mood, and from their work its deeper implications can be clearly disengaged. Hemingway became, in America at least, the most popular spokesman for the lost souls, less because he writes so well than because he gave so congenial expression to their spiritual attitudes. And though Huxley was less closely identified with his contemporaries and made it a point to remain aloof, he nevertheless represented much the same attitudes—from the point of view of the seasick intellectual—and most clearly connected them with the whole modern dilemma. *The Sun Also Rises* and *Point Counterpoint* are excellent companion pieces, and together almost sum up an era.

2

One of the more exciting of recent literary events was the publication of *Eyeless in Gaza*. It is by no means a great novel, nor even so good a one as others of Huxley: it is still talkier, and the talk is less sparkling. But the outcome of all this talk is the thing. At the end the hero, Anthony Beavis, sallies forth to address a pacifist meeting, despite threats of physical violence: "Dispassionately, and with a serene lucidity, he thought of what was in store for him. Whatever it might be, he knew now that all would be well." One doubts that all will be well. What is in store for Anthony is probably either a riot or the dismal futility of telling a group of earnest ladies what they already believe and wagging a finger in the face of dictators. Yet this is a unique ending in Huxley's fiction, and significant for students of modern literature.

A review of his previous work will make plain this significance. It is an easy review: *Point Counterpoint* is a complete statement of Huxley's art and philosophy before this recent development.

His earlier novels, particularly *Antic Hay,* are still very readable, and perhaps realize more perfectly their more modest intention; but *Point Counterpoint* is a synthesis of all their elements of thought and emotion, with several new elements added. It seemed at the time like his last will and testament.

It is in the first place interesting as an example of the latest modes in technique, and as such immediately recalls *The Counterfeiters.* Both are novels of ideas; both have at the center a novelist, in whose notebook the author can discuss the problems of his art; both are composite pictures; both are constructed according to principles of musical composition, their contrapuntal plots having little formal narrative connection but developing as modulations and variations on central themes. And Huxley's experiments, like Gide's, are an integral part of his central intention, a direct consequence of his vision of life. His music has the cacophony of modern music, with its discords, broken rhythms, and unresolved chords; more especially, his contrapuntal themes emphasize his conception of the relativity of truth. There is contiguity but little real contact between the various worlds he presents: what one sees depends upon where one stands. Above all, Huxley vividly represents by these means the heterogeneity of modern society. "The essence of the new way of looking is multiplicity," declares Philip Quarles, his mouthpiece. "Multiplicity of eyes and multiplicity of aspects." A novel that contains all these at once will be "a very queer picture indeed"—but it can't be too queer, Philip adds. It can never be queer enough to do justice to the facts. "That's what I want to get in this book—the astonishingness of the most obvious things."

Huxley's equipment for this task consists primarily of a fine yet fluid intelligence—"that quick, comprehensive, ubiquitous intelligence," as he writes of Philip Quarles, "that could understand everything, including the emotions it could not feel and the instincts it took care not to be moved by." It appears not only in the ideas with which the novel is packed, the many witty or incisive comments, but in the large and brilliantly illuminated gallery of characters. Huxley commands a wider range of experience than he is commonly given credit for, and his observation is shrewd and penetrating. Although he makes his people up out of his head and has no intuitive command of them, they are so brightly and sharply conceived that they have much of the animation of Dickens's puppets. They may not haunt, but they stick in the mind. And they are the more successful because their creator's cool understanding extends to himself as well. Huxley never gets outside his range, but cultivates his particular plot of ground for all it is worth.

To say that Huxley is clearly aware of his limitations, however, is to point to these limitations. One may add to the list of his virtues a graceful style equal to all the demands he makes of it, and one may pay tribute again to his wit, his sophistication, his often stimulating thought; but all these virtues can be easily and exactly defined. When one has done listing them, nothing is left over—nothing of the mysterious and unanalyzable that veils all great art. Huxley is himself never taken by surprise, and so his reader never is. He never rises to unexpected heights, never snatches a grace beyond the reach of art; he has glitter but no glamor. *Point Counterpoint* is in his own words "a made-up affair," and like all his work it shows the signs of manufacture. Unlike *The Counterfeiters,* it has all the defects of the novel of ideas. Where Gide begins with men and then expresses his ideas through them, Huxley builds his characters upon an idea and expresses them through this idea. Instead of dramatizing his material he talks about it. And he talks down from too great a height. He has the Victorian habit of perpetual comment, but unlike the Victorians he never comes down and really mingles with his people. Gide points out the value of a gradual, suggestive revelation of character and event in which the reader collaborates with the author (as in Conrad), discovering things for himself, piecing together, filling in gaps, perhaps even correcting the author; Huxley has too obvious and pronounced a superiority over both his characters and his readers. He explains everything, leaves no shadows. Everything is bathed in a blinding light and stands out hard, sharp, excessively neat and bright. Hence he does not really explain everything, his oppressive omniscience is yet not omniscient. He misses the shadowiness and elusiveness of personality, the strange undercurrents of thought and feeling, the wild darkness from which they flow and into which they disappear. He misses the very queerness and "astonishingness" of life that he hoped to convey.

Hence, too, the coldness and dryness of *Point Counterpoint.* Huxley performs interesting experiments upon his characters and brilliantly analyzes the results, but the reader always perceives him, scalpel and notebook in hand. His characters have no real life of their own, never take the story into their own hands. And all this he knows and admits. "In art," he observes, "there are simplicities more difficult than the most serried complications." His Philip Quarles could manage the complications as well as anyone. "But when it came to the simplicities, he lacked the talent—that talent which is of the heart, no less than of the head, of the feelings, the sympathies, the intuitions, no less than of the analytical understanding." All Huxley's novels are wide, fluid, animated; none is solid or deep.

In thus laboring the obvious I am not indulging the simple pleasure of beating a straw man. The very limitations of Huxley help to explain his popularity with the post-war generation—a generation that preferred literary cocktails to literary port, and liked to think of itself as having the same super-awareness as he had. *Point Counterpoint* is a virtually complete expression of its mood. "We're headed for hell," says one of the characters. There are a number of ways of getting there, however, and all these Huxley explores. He analyzes, too, the various fashionable drugs: the drug of violent pleasures, of sensuality, of extraverted activity, of religion, of scientific research. Some produce an agreeable stupor, others chiefly hangovers; none is a satisfactory substitute for deeply human relationships. Huxley's whole society is futile or damned. His Mark Rampion, who rails against all its monstrosities, never gets beyond incessant protests; "I don't care!" he cries as he watches the parade to hell—but he does care. His Philip Quarles, who remains the aloof, disinterested spectator, never solves and never can solve the problem of transforming his "detached intellectual skepticism into a way of harmonious all-round living." The one really happy man amid all this frustration is the slimy Burlap. The novel ends with Burlap in the bathtub with the aging virgin he had seduced: "Of such is the Kingdom of Heaven."

It is an appalling spectacle. Yet it does not arouse the emotions of great tragedy. It does not deeply move; it inspires pity but nothing like awe. The final impression left by the novel, even without its cynical ending, is simply of dreariness, futility, despair. There is little dignity in its suffering, there is no splendor or triumph in its defeat. "A great artist," declares Burlap, "is a man who synthesizes all experience. The cynic sets out by denying half the facts—the fact of the soul, the fact of ideals," spiritual facts of whose existence we are aware "as directly and indubitably as we're aware of physical facts." It is depressing to have one's sentiments echoed by the ineffable Burlap, but through Quarles Huxley himself endorses them—and by implication, then, censures his own work. His synthesis is incomplete, and what he fails to represent adequately is precisely the nobler elements of character, the more valuable elements of experience.

Now, this is not to make of the author of *Point Counterpoint* the misanthrope that many saw in him. Huxley made an effort to understand and not merely to expose—his account of Margery Bidlake's gradual slide into an oozy religiosity is one of the most deeply human studies he has made. He plainly did have spiritual values—the Quarleses and the Rampions provide a frame of reference. The very disgust and the cold hate apparent in his treatment of most of his characters betrayed the moralist, the earnest reformer he is at heart. As an intellectual and sophisticate he tried to think that he did not care, but as plainly as Rampion he *did* care. His grim jesting, his savage cynicism, the downright horror of some of his scenes—all sprang from a desire to shock as he himself had been shocked. But the point is that he succeeds in shocking, and does little else. Most of his characters are monsters, their fates of relatively little moment, and those who are sympathetic or who embody positive values are involved in no significant action. Rampion simply talks; Quarles simply looks on and takes notes; his wife Elinor, the most beautiful and pitiable character in the novel, is chiefly passive—horrible things simply happen to her.

In short, Huxley had his full share of the weariness, disillusionment, and despair of the society he was picturing, was himself bogged in its futility. He had sufficient detachment to understand but not to keep clear. He had not mastered his own difficulties, achieved a catharsis in his own soul. He was unable to participate deeply in any communal enterprise, to surrender himself to any natural piety, to make any kind of satisfactory peace. Although he was obviously attracted by the philosophy of Lawrence, which he expounds sympathetically through Rampion, the most vital character in his novel, he doubted its practicability and was as obviously unable to live it—not for so pronounced an intellectual as he the life of the Natural Man, the voice of the Blood. Edwin Muir remarked the complete impersonality in the relations of his characters, who confess to one another with the utmost freedom but only because they mean nothing to one another; who can say what they like because finally it makes no difference. In Huxley himself there was as little real communication or cooperation.

In short, Huxley displayed in this novel all the familiar symptoms of shell-shock. Yet the World War was not the whole cause of his disillusionment. It only brought to a head the fundamental conflict in his soul, aggravated a torment that was in this century his by birthright. For as a pronounced intellectual he has clearly perceived the disintegrating forces of the modern world; and as, despite his air of entire sophistication, one of its more tender-minded citizens, he has keenly felt their pressure. He provides perhaps the plainest case history of modernity.

Huxley has in the first place found disagreeable the new knowledge of human nature—the unlovely origins of human emotions. "Our attitudes and impulses are being compelled to become self-supporting," writes I. A. Richards; "they are being driven back upon their biological justification, made once again sufficient to themselves. And the only impulses which seem strong enough to continue unflagging are commonly so crude that, to more finely developed individuals, they hardly seem worth having." Hence when Aldous Huxley contemplates two lovers, he perceives them "quietly sweating, palm to palm." When he ponders the miracle of birth, he visualizes the "blob of jelly" in the mother's womb, the "kind of fish" or "parasite worm" that would presently invent a god and worship, dispute good and evil, express grandiose sentiments in rhyme. When he listens to immortal chamber music, he remembers that rosined horsehair is being drawn across the stretched intestines of lambs. This kind of cynicism and irony is of course part of his professional smartness, and not always to be taken seriously; yet that it should be his stock in trade is significant. Huxley's work is often shallow and flashy. Often his brilliance is meretricious, his irony too obvious, his fun too easy. *Brave New World,* his burlesque Utopia, is a cheap professional performance, ingenious and amusing at first, but presently as dull as a prolonged vaudeville skit whose point one has caught; Huxley could not have worked up a sweat dashing this off. As usual, he is himself aware of this defect: Philip Quarles notes that his books would be better if he did not have an itch to be always amusing. That Huxley nevertheless continued to indulge his facile wit in defiance of his artistic conscience suggests that his uncomfortable notions about human nature had sapped his faith even in himself.

This conflict in him between acquired knowledge and inherited ideals has been waged along the whole intellectual front. John Strachey, Granville Hicks, and others have accordingly made him a prize exhibit in the chamber of capitalistic horrors. With his political and sociological interests and his pictures of the crawling rottenness of the upper classes with whom he identifies himself, Huxley indeed fits snugly into the Marxist thesis. Yet these critics fail to see that the terms of his protest and the source of his despair are even more fundamental, that his sickness might not be cured by even such strong medicine as the proletarian revolution, and that, in fact, like the fastidious Proust and the fanatical Lawrence he might be revolted by the conditions of the mechanized classless society. What have been eating into his soul are the "acids of modernity" that Walter Lippmann analyzed in *A Preface to Morals*—the acids that have corroded established meanings and values all along the line but especially in religion and ethics. Despite all his flippancy, Huxley misses the Absolute more than any other emancipated modern. *Point Counterpoint* made sufficiently clear that he could not be content with the rôle of detached observer, could not wave away the world as a vulgar or amusing illusion. He had to justify his activities, he had to improve the illusion, he had to assume solemn responsibilities, he had to participate deeply and harmoniously in some kind of communal life. He needed, in short, a simple faith that would provide a way of living as well as a way of writing.

Here, then, is the significance of *Eyeless in Gaza*. It not only reasserts Huxley's integrity as a responsible artist; it expresses such a faith. Like Philip Quarles, his new spokesman, Anthony Beavis, finds personal relations "disagreeable and laborious," and instinctively shirks their responsibilities; unlike Quarles, Beavis surrenders his empty freedom and solves his problem. Huxley now definitely rejects, on the one hand, the philosophy of Lawrence: "How could one be content with the namelessness of mere energy, with the less than individuality of a power, that for all its mysterious divineness, was yet unconscious, beneath good and evil?" Lawrence, he remarks wryly, had never examined biological energy through a microscope—never seen the "appalling, the awful unconsciousness of that unconquerable, crawling desire," the "violent and impersonal egotism" of spermatozoa in process of fertilizing an ovum. Even more definitely, on the other hand, he rejects the Communist program: violent means beget brutal ends, the individual is ruthlessly sacrificed to an inhuman abstraction. He preaches instead the gospel of love and goodness. "Love is the best policy"—love of "goodness and the potentialities for goodness in all human beings." Love and peace make for unity, the ruling principle of the universe; pride, anger, and hatred make for division, whose metaphysical counterpart is the dualism Huxley has always attacked. And his translation of this message into more practical terms is a Pacifist program: after a hard struggle with his reluctance to commit himself, Beavis at length actively works for the cause. Although orthodox religion or any transcendent faith is still impossible for Huxley, the humility he exalts is essentially Christian. He displays, indeed, an almost Tolstoyan rigor in his demand that we turn the other cheek.

Now, honest and hard-earned as Huxley's faith is, it is obviously an easy target to pepper with ridicule. The wildest shots from the Left-wingers, for instance, can scarcely miss it. It is unmistakably intended as a practical social program—Huxley-Quarles was a novelist concerned with his art and his private salvation, but Huxley-Beavis is a sociologist worried about Communism and Fascism—and as such it is a pretty weak stick to beat dictators with, a pretty mild salve to apply to the grievous sores of the contemporary world. Even sympathetic critics, conscientious liberals like himself, will find much to embarrass them. Not only is Huxley's talk of goodness at times stuffy, but his concrete representations of it—especially his hero—are uninspiring, even unconvincing. (One does not quite know, incidentally, what to make of his Mrs. Foxe; an oppressive type who would have been annihilated in his earlier novels, she now seems to have his approval.) His message has a cultish flavor and occasionally comes uncomfortably close to Buchmanism. He trims his goodness with vegetarianism and hygiene; he has Beavis go through spiritual setting-up exercises that might have been prescribed by a popular faith-healer; in general he appears not a little soft and naïve, a likely customer for patent nostrums. Yet he also has wise and noble things to say. In the long view his words are not irrelevant, and even in the turmoil of immediate problems they deserve attention. Above all, he has affirmed values that can sustain the artist in the midst of this turmoil. Although Anthony

Beavis is not going to save the world, he appears to be in a fair way of saving his own soul; and that accomplishment sets him apart from all Huxley's other heroes.

It is unfortunate, therefore, that one cannot honestly report that Huxley's hard-won victory over doubt and despair has already made him a better artist. *Eyeless in Gaza* is as a matter of fact distinctly inferior to *Point Counterpoint*. His change of heart has not made him a less purely intellectual novelist, nor even eradicated the habits of the professional sophisticate. He is still unnecessarily clever; he still introduces more lusciously erotic scenes than his serious purposes warrant; he still dwells on naughty or shocking physiological detail just for the fun and the hell of it. His method of telling his story—the shuttling back and forth in time—further weakens his aim; although it makes possible some striking dramatic or ironic effects, he could have brought out the development in his characters and ideas much more clearly and solidly had he been humble enough to stoop to the conventional chronological narrative. And at the same time his earnest purposes have cast a pall over his novel, made it at once softer and heavier. *Eyeless in Gaza* has less sparkle and bite than *Point Counterpoint,* and above all nothing like the sharp, vivid characterization; only a few of its characters and scenes are memorable. But the explanation of all this is simple: Huxley's faith is still highly self-conscious. It is a "made-up affair," an attitude not yet really assimilated, an idea still ill at ease in his mind. His gospel of love is much like the vision of Hans Castorp in the spiritual climax of *The Magic Mountain,* but Mann's attitude has behind it much more thought and emotion; it is organic and not synthetic. Where, accordingly, Mann's tone is deep and resonant, Huxley's is thin and a little squeaky. Where one richly orchestrates, the other plays a few anxious variations. Where one swells into lyrical affirmation, the other jots more notes in a notebook.

Yet what is finally most significant, once more, is that Huxley has found a way out of his dilemma—a way "to be simultaneously dispassionate and not indifferent." He is no longer of the lost generation. One can now look forward with fresh interest to his future work and expect more than a brilliant picture of purgatory. Whether Huxley's faith in the power of love and forbearance will be able to withstand the brutal shocks that the world's rulers appear determined to give it, whether it will actually sustain him as citizen and artist, is as uncertain as the fate of our civilization. Meanwhile, however, he provides another encouraging example of man's stubborn habit of wrenching values from chaos, the pertinacious idealism that makes modern literature more than a swan song.

3

As I have said, the reason for Ernest Hemingway's popularity with the lost generation is not merely that he happens to be its most brilliant and original artist. It is rather, as Clifton Fadiman has said, that he provides a violent romanticism for the lost souls, he "makes lostness picturesque, beautiful, or dramatic"—even dazzling. He enabled his forlorn fellows to be sentimental while feeling very hard-boiled. He enabled them to cry into their beer while feeling very virile and noble and tragic.

Fadiman also suggests an illuminating comparison of Hemingway and Byron. However unlike their work, its impact on their contemporaries was much the same. Both became suddenly famous. Both are muscular and athletic, exalting action, violence, and the simple, manly virtues. Both defy conventional morality, using the naughty words and treating the naughtier aspects of sex—the one flamboyantly, the other with a premeditated casualness. Both are torn between cynicism and romanticism, and in the conflict become semi-mystical—the one about Greece, the other about bull-fighting. Both suffer from "the need of fatality"—"a kind of splendid, often very beautiful, disease of the imagination noticeable during periods of social decay"—perhaps most marked in Robinson Jeffers, with his courting of violence, darkness, and death. And neither is a great thinker, nor much interested in rational analysis. In short, both reflect a post-war disillusionment, a spiritual breakdown and consequent shift in values.

The essentials of Hemingway's manner—the complete objectivity, the habit of understatement, the extreme simplicity of both his diction and his sentence structure—are familiar enough. They are also strikingly effective. The straightforward, first-person narrative, with a minimum of formal exposition, analysis, or comment, is admirably adapted to the simple kind of story he chooses to tell and to his simple conception of character. In his understatement he gets the full force of suppression—the last sentence of *A Farewell to Arms* is already famous. But the chief source of his strength is his prose style. Like the great painter, he makes one see as never before—really see, as if for the first time, so homely a sight as a lunch-counter, or a woman sweeping a sidewalk in the morning. His characters are neither original nor remarkable; as Henry Seidel Canby has said, "It isn't *what* they are but *how* they are that seems important"—they have so vivid an existence that one forgets how shallow it often is. In short, if in view of the early work of Gertrude Stein his style cannot be considered an entirely original creation, it is nevertheless individual and remarkably successful. Theoretically, it ought to become monotonous and barren, as it does in the hands of Hemingway's innumerable imitators. Actually, it proves to be almost as flexible as it is graphic and precise.

More important, however, is the reason for this creation. Simplicity is a deceptive quality, and perhaps the most difficult to analyze. The style of the Old Testament is simple. So is that of Addison, of Sherwood Anderson, of a schoolboy—and all are different from Hemingway's. Simplicity is not necessarily naturalness or ingenuousness. It takes many forms; it may be, as in Hemingway it obviously is, self-conscious and highly mannered. One can be sure that he sweat blood over these seemingly artless sentences. Similarly his dialogue is conventionalized. Some critics have praised him, ludicrously enough, for catching "the very accent of everyday speech"; Ring Lardner did that—and he who skims may read the difference. The conversation of Hemingway's characters is always clipped, athletic, pointed; the conversation of everyday life is above all things wordy and loose. The ordinary man does not say, "Why do that?" He says, "What the hell are you doing that for?" His negative is a "Well, I don't think so" or a "Not on your life"; Hemingway's people say "No."

Now, one can point to specific literary influences upon Hemingway. He undoubtedly learned much about writing from Sherwood Anderson and Gertrude Stein. His fiction is perhaps a literary reaction against the excesses of introspection, the craze for subtlety, the absorption in the mysterious intricacies of consciousness—against the whole fashion of Proust, Lawrence, Dorothy Richardson, Virginia Woolf, etc. Probably, too, he owes some debt to the naturalists—Zola, Maupassant, Dreiser, the Joyce of *Dubliners;* during his youth their frankness and objectivity, their refusal to moralize or edify, were the ideals about which rallied young America. Yet his resemblances to these and other writers finally seem incidental, for his motives and aims are essentially different. Both his subject matter and his style are dictated by a special view of life, and this is the view of the lost generation: the generation that felt that the war had knocked the bottom out, and that to try to put it in again was futile.

Hence Hemingway's refusal to moralize or philosophize is not primarily an esthetic principle. Such exalted business would seem to him a hollow or even obscene pretense. Similarly he makes a habit of understatement, not merely because it is artistically effective, but because he is fearful of rhetoric, of again being taken in. Lieutenant Henry, the hero of *A Farewell to Arms,* could stand to hear only the simple names of things. "Abstract words such as glory, honor, courage, or hallow were obscene beside the concrete names of villages, the numbers of roads, the names of rivers, the numbers of regiments and the dates." Hemingway accordingly uses few abstract nouns, few adjectives of ideal or rational connotation. Eating, sleeping, drinking, making love—his characters find these equally "nice," at best "fine." "Feeling fine" is all they ask of life.

This attitude has behind it essentially the same impulse as Dadaism. Hemingway and his heroes simply turn their backs on a sick society and all efforts to cure it. They will have none of the sociological, the metaphysical, the spiritual—the World

War had made a ghastly farce of all such pretentious activity. They fall back on the Hindenburg line of primal instincts and emotions, reducing life to its simplest elements: physical sensations. "I was not made to think," says Lieutenant Henry. "I was made to eat. My God, yes. Eat and drink and sleep with Catherine." Thus in his short stories Hemingway writes typically of peasants, bull-fighters, boxers, gangsters, and similar uncomplicated types; and the more civilized characters of his novels seek to live on the same level. They are not ingenuous or insensitive but deliberately primitive and non-intellectual, sophisticatedly simple. They have reduced their needs for happiness to a good meal, a bottle of wine, and a wide bed; when these needs are satisfied, they "feel fine." Their answer to such doubts and difficulties and complexities as still obtrude is invariably, "Well, don't think about it."

And they don't think about it. Hence Hemingway's simple, objective, externalized story, and the complete absence of analysis. There is nothing to analyze. His characters avoid thought and do not investigate their emotions. Similarly Hemingway reduces prose to its simplest elements, stripping it of all but its bare essentials. He writes no involved, complex sentences simply because he has no involved, complex ideas to express. "And" is his invariable connective for the same reason that it is in the Old Testament. The early Hebrews had not yet reached the stage in mental development where men begin to analyze, correlate, systematize; their thought was a simple sequence of sensations and perceptions. Hemingway deliberately reverts to their intellectual level.

This "cult of the simple" appears in various forms in the modern world: the "hard-boiled school," the movement back to the farm, the interest in primitive people, the craze for primitive art. It is usually a symptom of surface restlessness, a craving for novelty or thrill—the popularity among sophisticated readers of novelists like Dashiell Hammett is more a fad than a portent. But it also represents a serious effort by some intellectuals to find happiness in the mere being or doing of the great mass of common people; and as a means of salvation, a cult, its futility is obvious. The introvert, Irwin Edman points out, cannot become an extravert by a mere effort of the will: thought may be a disease, but it is also part of his necessity. Even if the individual succeeds in putting away thought, blinking all social and philosophical problems, society as a whole cannot afford a prolonged spree in the simple life. The widest bed cannot serve as its foundation, nor the headiest wine as its life's blood; somebody has finally to do the heavy work and pay the bills. And those, like the Southern agrarians, who do not seek a merely individual salvation but wish to simplify the whole structure of society, have as yet offered no concrete, practicable program to realize their wistful ideal.

Meanwhile, however, it is interesting to see what Hemingway and his heroes manage to wring out of their way of life. In *The Sun Also Rises,* as the Scriptural title indicates, they get little enough. Like *Point Counterpoint,* this novel is simply a record of a sick and lost generation. Its characters have a moral code, a drunken fellowship and gallantry, but they have no faith, no purpose or force to give meaning to their existence. Despite their appearance of violent activity they are really inert, drugged, empty of will. They drink cocktails up and down France and Spain, but in cocktails is no surcease of sorrow. To their spiritual is added a perpetual physical hangover; for meanings they substitute pick-ups. They merely thumb their noses at life, and though this flippant gesture gives them some satisfaction, it also heightens their self-pity, intensifies their disenchantment, deepens their futility. Like most of Hemingway's work, *The Sun Also Rises* is brilliantly written; like *Point Counterpoint,* it is ultimately sterile.

A Farewell to Arms, however, is a very different matter. Although superficially it may appear to be a companion piece, actually it embodies a simple faith that can nourish the lost souls. The novel grows, indeed, out of a rigorous, apparently intolerable pessimism:

> If people bring so much courage to this world the world has to kill them to break them, so of course it kills them. The world breaks every one and afterward many are strong at the broken places. But those that will not break it kills. It kills the

> very good and the very gentle and the very brave impartially. If you are none of these you can be sure it will kill you too but there will be no special hurry."

Yet this pessimism does not result in a sour indifferentism or barren despair. It leads Hemingway to celebrate certain sustaining values: the value of kindliness and decency, exemplified by the inn-keeper and the priest; the value of courage ("Nothing ever happens to the brave"); the value above all of love, for which the lovers are glad to live and die. And these values are not merely talked about, as through Rampion and Quarles Huxley talks of possibly satisfactory ways of living. They are objectified in a vivid, dramatic, and compelling action. None more squeamish than Hemingway about employing the conventional vocabulary of idealism or the trappings of high tragedy—but no contemporary novelist comes closer to the romantic tragedy of the past. *A Farewell to Arms* is the nearest modern equivalent to *Romeo and Juliet.* It is based on the same unquestioning acceptance of love as a glorious good, even the highest good. Despite the sophistication of its manner, it has much the same simplicity and purity of feeling. Despite the frequent horror of its incidental detail, it has much the same beauty and even splendor. And so despite its harrowing ending, with its gruesome obstetrics, it is more than harrowing and gives much the same lift.

Romeo and Juliet is of course not the expression of Shakespeare's mature genius; and *A Farewell to Arms* is similarly a youthful work. Like Conrad's Lord Jim, Hemingway is "excessively romantic." He has not written a masterpiece, nor has he supplied the answer to the dilemma of the modern man—the way of life of Lieutenant Henry and Catherine Barkley cannot be the way of most. His meanings are inadequate. But they are not anachronistic. They correspond to deep, age-old, universal emotions. His values can be carried over into other spheres of activity, they can inspire even the revolutionaries who are prone to regard such a theme as adolescent or atavistic. By putting his faith, like Conrad, in a few simple ideas, a few simple virtues, Hemingway at least succeeded in putting a bottom in his world and escaping sheer futility. Such a faith makes possible great art —an art that may also deal more inclusively and pertinently with modern life. If meanwhile the scope of *A Farewell to Arms* is narrow, its theme of love against the background of war is certainly big enough for a single novel; and it remains a memorable novel.

Hemingway's subsequent work, however, is disappointing—at least to those who had hoped that he would continue to grow and make still better use of his remarkable gifts. Although he has thrown off some of the worst symptoms, he still suffers from the malady contracted from the war. For the most part he continues to write superbly (aside from some cheap and slovenly contributions to *Esquire*); he also continues to repeat himself, rework his formula. The few excellent stories in the collection characteristically entitled *Winner Take Nothing* add nothing to the stature he gained with *In Our Time* and *Men Without Women*. His longer works not only confirm his habit of posturing in public, flexing his muscles and throwing out his chest, but reveal more clearly his subtler maladies. Thus *Death in the Afternoon,* his monument to bull-fighting, is simply a rationalization of violent pleasures, a boyish glorification of blood and death, at bottom an adolescent and sentimental performance. It is perhaps the last word in the fashion—to quote Max Eastman's devastating phrase —of wearing false hair on the chest. In *Green Hills of Africa* (The Rover Boy in the Congo) he hunts big game in the same spirit, making of a primitive sport a holy rite—though his petulant flings at the critics, the "lice of literature," suggest a strangely sensitive skin on the so hairy chest. No doubt there are enough wild animals to last him the rest of his life; but their slaughter, even though it puts a sparkle in one's eye and a healthy glow in one's cheek, is scarcely a significant activity for a mature man or a responsible artist. Hemingway's exploits have little meaning for his contemporaries, no vital relation to their deeper needs and interests.

Yet with him as with Huxley a postscript is necessary: recently he has been fired by the cause of the Workers' Front in Spain.

This parallel with Byron's Grecian episode neatly completes Fadiman's analogy. It also gives reason to hope that he too may finally throw off the sickness of his generation.

4

The "hard-boiled school" as such deserves only brief notice. Their most conspicuous accomplishment is a large breach in the dam of the unmentionable and unprintable. They are a peculiarly American product; although James Hanley's *The Furys* belongs on the same shelf with them, other English novelists continue to follow the aristocratic tradition, which permits gross or violent materials but demands a gentlemanly style. They are also a diverse company, including Dos Passos, Hammett, Burnett, Caldwell, O'Hara, and many lesser men who have little in common except the plainness of their speech, and their offensiveness to gentle readers. And although Hemingway is commonly associated with them, he is not their prophet or parent. Undoubtedly he has inspired much of this prognathous prose. A more important influence, however, is that of the proletarian writers, who have given the whole tendency toward the hard-boiled manner not only a new impetus but a new direction.

This tendency is in fact interesting chiefly because of its sources. It is in part an extension of naturalism, which from the beginning subordinated style to matter. It is in part, too, an expression of the post-war mood, with its distrust of rhetoric—of all the pretensions and prettinesses of writers before the deluge; amid the frightful realities of the war and its aftermath, an ornate or polite style seemed to many an indecent affectation. But it involves the whole complex tissue of modern literature and life, and is to be regarded finally as another sign of disintegration and revaluation, another attack upon the underlying problem of communication. Although plain writing is weighted with the emotive implications of ordinary speech and does not actually have the neutrality of the language of science, it *is* plain. Its matter-of-factness gives at least the illusion of firm ground. It cuts through heterogeneity and complexity and reduces life to its simplest elements. Hence it is attractive both to sophisticates attempting to flee the confusion of their society and to earnest advocates of some principle of solidarity.

In this view, however, the common objections to the fashion of plain writing are deepened. It reflects the disorganization of the age and serves chiefly as a stop-gap; it rejects too many of the resources of language to satisfy the literary artist indefinitely. Hemingway's lean prose is brilliantly evocative—it is a genuine style, and one of the finest instruments in modern fiction. The leanness of too many contemporaries is mere bareness. As a whole, the hard-boiled school has simply swollen the flood of slovenly, downright bad writing on the market today.

XXII

MEDLEY OF CONTEMPORANEA: THOMAS WOLFE

I

IN the *Nation,* a year or so ago, two ladies amused themselves by sticking pins in a number of swollen critical reputations. They bedeviled eminent critics by summoning the ghosts of their pronouncements of not many years back—pronouncements in which they hailed as a masterpiece an already forgotten novel, saw genius in some pleasing talent, mistook perspiration for inspiration. The fun was easy, and not altogether clean. It consisted simply of proclaiming the obvious as the scandalous. Although some readers appeared surprised at the revelation that William Lyon Phelps is not alone in his capacity for simple enthusiasm and wonder, or that Harry Hansen is more Polonius than Plato, such surprise is itself naïve. Apart from the fallibility of human judgment and the especial difficulty of retaining perspective in the welter of contemporaneity, the professional reviewer has to contend with an enormous weight of third-rate fiction. When he encounters the clearly second-rate, he is accordingly likely to froth with superlatives. A merely touching novel like Hans Fallada's *Little Man, What Now?* becomes high tragedy; an ambitious novel like Evelyn Scott's *The Wave* becomes *ipso facto* an epic; a delicately wrought novel like Thornton Wilder's *The Bridge of San Luis Rey* becomes a great work of art; and a Hervey Allen bestrides this narrow world like a Colossus. But the judicious reader soon learns to discount these raptures, and expects to find in the latest novel to inspire them no more than another honest, intelligent, interesting, but far from great novel

—as Samuel Johnson might say, a good novel but not one to invite a man to.

This is not to sneer at the large company of the second-rate. If posterity will forget them while reading excitedly its own minor novelists, posterity is not the sole concern of the thoughtful contemporary. Their work is often valuable because of its pertinent comment on the world in which we perforce live. To the critic it is further interesting as illustration and portent. It gives form and substance to the "tendencies," and often provides a better basis for significant generalization than work clearly superior. It amplifies and even corrects the work of genius. At the very least it provides a background against which genius can more profitably be studied.

At the same time a few names stand out: names associated with strong, original talent and promise of really distinguished work. In America one that demands at least passing comment is William Faulkner. *The Sound and the Fury* and *As I Lay Dying* excited a small number of readers, and not merely because of Faulkner's use of the still novel stream-of-consciousness method; *Sanctuary* widely extended this excitement. *Sanctuary* is indeed a curious vehicle to fame—that it was the vehicle Faulkner rode is another example of the disorder in the whole contemporary system of communication, as a result of which only the striking or sensational is likely to leap the gap between the artist and his conglomerate audience. It appears to have been written in a spirit of bravado, and it is at times almost a burlesque of Faulkner's habitual manner; he stresses the grotesque and horrible to the point where they become simply ludicrous. Even so, *Sanctuary* deserved the attention it received, for it clearly revealed the brilliant and peculiar gifts of its author. He has a splendid technical mastery of his materials: a narrative sense that keeps his story moving steadily, gathering force, even when he is looping backwards into the past, retelling an episode from a different point of view, or employing any of the sophisticated devices that to other contemporaries have become ends in themselves. He has a remarkable ability to project highly original characters; upon reflection one may not believe in his people, but while one reads it is impossible not to believe. He has a penetrating insight into the dark recesses of the soul, which apparently owes little to fashionable psychological theory—at least he does not give us the crude, diagrammatic simplifications of *Mourning Becomes Electra.* And at his best he can write superbly, in a manner not Hemingway's or Joyce's but his own. In short, Faulkner's is one of the most striking talents in America today.

Light in August, his next novel, should accordingly have created a greater stir than it did. Most reviewers treated it as simply another Faulknerian exercise in the macabre, dusting off the adjectives they had used on his earlier work; but here he began more fully to realize his potentialities, or at least to curb his extravagance. It is still not a great novel. Faulkner still depended for power too much on the strength of his raw materials; he still showed a youthful or morbid fondness for the lurid, the violent, the horrible, the simply painful; he was still interested primarily in the pathological. At the same time he exercised more restraint, showed less desire to shock, gave more signs of maturity. He introduced more normal circumstance and emotion, and more significant character. With no sacrifice of his strange power, he moved nearer to the constants of experience. He raised strong hopes that his next novel might be still closer to the center, "the main march of human affections."

These hopes have been disappointed, however, in Faulkner's subsequent novels, *Pylon* and *Absalom, Absalom!* Here he does business at his original stand and with his original wares. He deals again almost exclusively with the aberrant and fantastic, the waifs and strays of human emotion. Like all his work, these novels provide an intense, unforgettable experience; but it is also an experience of limited value: one that, like a Grand Guignol melodrama, does little to sensitize and organize the normal responses to life, and that powerfully stimulates the imagination without greatly refining or enriching it, making it a more efficient instrument in controlling experience. Even Faulkner's style is hardening into strained, grotesque mannerism. And so he must for the present, despite his brilliant achievement, be placed among the curiosities. It may be that he is content to repeat a successful formula. More probably, he is at home only in this murky, demonic world.

Meanwhile, however, a new and still brighter star has risen on the horizon. The publication of *Look Homeward, Angel* started a considerable buzz about the name of Thomas Wolfe; when after a long interval he finally published *Of Time and the River,* the buzz became an uproar. The most jaded reviewer felt the need of supplementing his customary set of adjectives. Wolfe is the one living American writer, indeed, who deserves the extravagance with which he is both praised and condemned. His work can evoke any kind of reaction except a tepid one. And in the face of the examples ghoulishly set forth by the ladies in the *Nation,* I join the cheerers. Although Wolfe is young and just started on his career, he has already given reason to hope that here at last is the Great American Novelist for whom critics have been crying these many years.

2

To unsympathetic or satirically-minded critics, Wolfe offers, indeed, a target impossible to miss. The most random critical shot will find a bull's-eye, the bluntest shaft of irony or wit will stick in the soft stuff of some section of his sprawling novel. All that should discourage those who would make merry over his sins, in fact, is that in his worst passages he has done his own burlesque more fantastically than they can hope to do it—and perhaps that in *The Story of a Novel,* one of the simplest, most honest and unpretentious records of an intense artistic experience, he has himself pointed out these sins with no trace of false humility or false contrition.

It is well at the outset, however, to read out the bill of charges, not merely to keep the record straight, but finally to establish the virtues that are tied up so closely with Wolfe's faults. These faults are summed up in a relentless excess: an excess in both his materials and his treatment of them. His novels contain whole acres of verbiage that should have been ploughed under. Wolfe suffers from what he describes as "an almost insane hunger to devour the entire body of human experience, to attempt to include more, experience more, than the measure of one life can hold, or than the limits of a single work of art can well describe." The insanity of this hunger, moreover, is reflected less in the quantity than in the strength of the food it demands—less in the extent than in the intensity of his experience. His story is explosive with overcharged emotion, his language is a remorseless blaze of adjectives and epithets. No sensation so fleeting but he charges it with ineffable meaning; no emotion so casual but he tears it to tatters; no reflection so simple but he makes it pregnant with the whole Mystery of Life. His experience is constantly writ double its size, and then put in boldface, underscored, and repeated.

In other words, Thomas Wolfe is still young, still drunk with life and art. Everything that has happened to him seems tremendously important; his experience is still so close to him that he is only beginning to recollect it in tranquillity, to sublimate and subdue it. Hence, like most young novelists, he not only writes obvious autobiography but writes it often with a literal verisimilitude and a naked intensity that shock the neighbors and the hometown folk. Hence he pours out a flood in which the obvious and the rare, the ephemeral and the profound, the idiosyncratic and the universal, all assume an equal importance, and their attendant emotions boil at the same temperature. And hence the weakest character in his novel, the focus of his worst writing, is precisely his hero—himself. All the thought and emotion of Eugene Gant are Homeric. He never reads a book but tears its guts out, he never smiles but roars with laughter, he never shudders but writhes in agony; and as sensitive youth remembers chiefly its shocks, Eugene is chiefly writhing. He goes through life excruciatingly tense, bristling with nerve ends, almost demanding hurt. Even as a baby he is represented as a little hotbed of passion, seething with resentment at an uncomprehending world. He grows up simply to become more articulate in his fury and frenzy, his shame and despair. As a young man he is habitually "white with constricted rage" or "frantic with horror"; he is forever "bellowing madly" or "howling in anguish"; when he isn't battering his head against a wall it is usually because no wall is handy. In short, Wolfe's portrait of the artist as a young man could scarcely be caricatured. He makes Byron himself seem prosaic and stolid.

Now, one does not need the testimony of Wolfe's early friends to realize that as a young man he did not blaze with so unremittingly, intolerably fierce a light. Obviously he enjoyed many a simple pleasure, experienced many a tame emotion, indulged in many a casual thought, looked calmly at many a wall. No less obviously, however, his novel has grown out of genuinely profound and intense experience. If it is intemperately romantic, it is not merely mannered or maudlin; if it is fantastically overwritten, it still has a core of truth. Wolfe is not the poseur that Byron was. His "almost insane hunger" for life arises from a Gargantuan appetite, and all his extravagances from a superabundance of vitality and enthusiasm. The critic may deplore these extravagances, but he should at least temper his dismay as he does at those of Marlowe, Shelley, Whitman, or the immortal Shakespeare himself. They are never attempts to be sensational, to pass off spurious coin for the King's gold; rather they spring from a too teeming memory and too heated imagination, a too impassioned zest and desire, a too lusty and fertile creative gift. In the full flow of creation Wolfe is swept off his feet, intoxicated by dazzling vistas, overwhelmed by a host of images; and so he shouts drunkenly and flings his arms about where a Flaubert or a Henry James would fastidiously shape his more orderly inspiration.

"Genius is not enough," announced Bernard DeVoto in a devastating review of Wolfe's sins. I should say that nothing can take its place—not the sharp observation or the honest reporting or the skilful craftsmanship or the intelligence, sincerity, sensitiveness, and sympathy of dozens of contemporary novelists for whom DeVoto, like most reviewers, has had little but praise. To welcome these modest talents so benignly and then to reserve so much fire and thunder for one of the few writers of our time who display actual genius is to be simply churlish. (And who would attribute genius to, for example, Dos Passos?) The faults that excite DeVoto are plain enough, and they are serious; but his protest that "we could do with a lot less genius, if we got a little more artist," his celebration of shape in preference to size, his emphasis upon "inescapable form"—such talk, in the face of all the sprawling masterpieces in the history of fiction, is a little silly. One thinks of the acknowledged great, like Scott, Dickens, Thackeray, Dostoyevsky, Tolstoy—or even among the French, the masters of form, of Rabelais, Balzac, Hugo, Zola, Proust. Wolfe's prime impulse, like theirs, has been the healthy impulse to write rather than to cut. Exquisite workmanship seldom accompanies a powerful creative gift; few great novelists have been perfectionists. And although Wolfe's sins are indeed greater in that he is more addicted to sheer rant, and magnifies above all his ego and all the labor pains of creation—still, he is young, inexperienced, and in process of self-discovery.

All this would be a feeble apology, however, were it not for the genius of Wolfe that even his detractors admit. This genius, moreover, expresses itself primarily in the proper business of the novelist, not in mere rhetoric. DeVoto to the contrary, Wolfe does not simply assert and declaim, does not present chiefly disembodied emotion. He performs admirably, in the first place, the duty to which Conrad devoted so much energy: to make the reader *see*. "The quality of my memory," Wolfe writes, "is characterized, I believe, in a more than ordinary degree by the intensity of its sense impressions, its power to evoke and bring back the odors, sounds, colors, shapes, and feel of things with concrete vividness." This is a modest statement of the power that has created the "blazing pageantry" of *Look Homeward, Angel* and *Of Time and the River*. The look of a small town at night as seen from a passing train, the sound of the train itself, the rich smell of earth in the spring, the feel of a great city—hundreds of such familiar sensations he renders at once precisely and suggestively, evoking all the magic and mystery of the homely and commonplace. He spreads before us the vast, swarming surface of America, in all its tawdriness and ugliness, its mightiness and glamor; and because he never merely catalogues, like Conrad he makes us *realize* as well as comprehend. He is the poet of American life, as sensitive, lyrical, and robust as Whitman, and in his symbols still more concrete.

No less remarkable are Wolfe's powers of characterization. Eugene Gant, once more, never becomes a real personality; he is simply a random assortment of nerves and howls. His bellows make more sound than sense, his rages and agonies give off more heat than light—one is aware chiefly of a great noise and a great blaze, and is deafened and blinded to little point. When Eugene is left alone, it is a kindness to Wolfe to leave him alone, and skip to the passage where he next comes out to join his fellows. But all the people Eugene jostles spring into full-blooded, vivid life. His father and mother, his brothers and sisters, his uncle Bascom, and the whole Gant family are only the more conspicuous figures in an unforgettable crowd. Wolfe's people are distinctively modern, complex in their psychology; they are typically bundles of incongruities, tangles of obscure and conflicting impulses. Yet like the great characters of the past they are creations rather than demonstrations; they are projected whole, with no elaborate machinery of explanation. The reader instantly gets an imaginative grasp of them, and need not be led by the hand through the winding corridors and into the dark recesses of their minds. And that they are almost all drawn from life makes no difference, for Wolfe has made them his own. He gives us a teeming, throbbing world; the sources of this world are as unimportant as the sources of Shakespeare's plays.

In their bedazzlement, reviewers have recalled such illustrious names as Dickens and Dostoyevsky. Wolfe largely justifies these flattering comparisons. He has Dickens's gift of endowing with astonishing vitality the most grotesque types—the whole Gant family is Dickensesque. At the same time he seldom contents himself with caricature or flat surface, however striking. He turns his people around and views them from different angles, he adds a third dimension, he gives them the substance as well as the appearance of life. Like Dostoyevsky, he emphasizes the profoundly human in the seemingly monstrous. Old Gant is at once as fantastic and as understandable as old Karamazov, as impossible and as intensely real.

Wolfe's rendering of the basic elements of personality, the primal emotions, is most impressive when he deals with the great crises. He is one of the very few living writers who can do something like a big Shakespearian scene, striking surely and strongly the major chords of emotion and opening up before us the whole vista of life and death. Although the conceptions of O'Neill, for example, are often majestic, he seldom attains the eloquence they demand; Wolfe can not only grandly conceive but grandly execute. The death of Eugene's father is one instance of magnificent drama; the death of his brother Ben is the best. This is one of the great scenes in American fiction: with its tableau of the Gant family, terrible, pitiable, grotesque, and sublime, its members drawn together "below all the splintered wreckage of their lives . . . in a superb communion of love and valiance," dominated at this moment by the strange splendor of the spirit of Ben; and with its picture of Ben himself, who, "casting the fierce sword of his glance with utter and final comprehension upon the room haunted with its gray pageantry of cheap loves and dull consciences and on all those uncertain mummers of waste and confusion . . . passed instantly, scornful and unafraid, as he had lived, into the shades of death." Many American novelists today can strike single notes powerfully, but none can strike chords as vibrant, resonant, many-toned and deep-toned, as can Thomas Wolfe.

3

Especially significant for his contemporaries, however, are the deeper purposes of which Wolfe only gradually became conscious —and among which he is still groping. Although he has already written well over a million words and is now in the dangerous process of rationalizing them, one cannot be sure what will finally emerge; but in general he is striving to write the epic of the modern man in the ageless quest of salvation. In his own words, his central theme is "man's search to find a father, not merely the father of his flesh, not merely the lost father of his youth, but the image of a strength and wisdom external to his need and superior to his hunger, to which the belief and power of his own life could be united." And this larger subject disengages itself even from the bathos that periodically floods the soul of Eugene Gant.

From another point of view Time is the central subject of Wolfe's novel: Time and the River, the river of human life darkly and endlessly flowing. What cost him most anguish and almost defeated him, he tells us, was the management of this element, the problem of integrating the three aspects of time: time as the palpable present, moving toward an immediate future; time as "the cumulative impact of man's experience," every moment being conditioned by the whole past history of the individual and of the race; and time as immutable, "the time of rivers, mountains, oceans, and the earth; a kind of eternal and unchanging universe of time against which would be projected the transience of man's life, the bitter briefness of his day." This is of course no sophisticated or scientific concept. Neither is it the mystical concept of Proust or Mann, in which time becomes a kind of illusion. It is primarily a common-sense attitude. Wolfe deals with time precisely as it enters the emotional experience of the ordinary man, as it has been apostrophized and brooded over by poets through the ages, as it is felt by Hamlet and Macbeth. And though he occasionally maunders, loses himself in the ephemera of modern life or the trivia of Eugene Gant's adolescence, at his best he does convey powerfully this sense of the immutable universe of time, the present with the whole past summed up in it and the haunting mystery of the future implicit in it.

From still another point of view Wolfe is attempting to recreate a period of American civilization, to write the epic specifically of America. Hence the gigantic scale of his book. After writing furiously for some time and piling up most of the million words, he realized that "what I had to deal with was material which covered almost 150 years in history, demanded the action of more than 2,000 characters, and would in its final design include almost every racial type and social class of American life." The experience of Eugene Gant will accordingly provide only a nucleus, a point of reference, for this vast chronicle.

Now, even in these several aspects Wolfe's project is scarcely an unprecedented one. Fiction from the time of Balzac on provides innumerable models for it. One can point as well to influences absorbed from his voracious reading. Doubtless he has profited by the work of the American realists before him—Dreiser, Anderson, Lewis; certainly he has borrowed specifically, for example, from Joyce—tricks of style, the stream-of-consciousness method, the deliberate discontinuity of the Wandering Rocks episode in *Ulysses,* all particularly noticeable in the long account of the train ride that opens *Of Time and the River*. Yet his work is only at times obviously imitative. Most of his materials he has made thoroughly his own; his work is finally as original as is all great fiction, however conventional or unconventional its form.

Far more pertinent, then, than criticism of Wolfe's incidental borrowings is John Chamberlain's suggestion that he still lacks "an intellectual idea to work on"—"a controlling idea, a frame of reference" for his epic of Time and America. Undoubtedly his work so far has suffered from such a lack. He is still groping, and his struggles have involved a great deal of waste, confusion, useless anguish and tumult. Even one who has been deeply impressed by the flood of experience rendered in *Of Time and the River* is likely to lay the book down with a question: Whither? To what end? Wolfe does not yet clearly indicate. But at least he is himself asking this question, he does not himself locate value merely in the density of his slice of life, the vastness of his panorama, or the intensity of his experience. He seeks "the image of a strength and wisdom" outside himself, an image to which he can unite "the belief and power" of his life. Apparently he has some notion of this spiritual destination—the next to the last of his series of novels, he tells us, is to be entitled *The Death of the Enemy*. Precisely what his image will prove to be, precisely who is the enemy doomed to defeat, is still a matter of speculation; but there is at least good reason to believe that his huge work will finally fall into a frame, assume a shape.

Meanwhile, however, Wolfe's work is rich in values; and these are in general the values of the humanistic attitude, a welcome of all the rich possibilities of experience. One doubts that his image will prove to be a transcendental one, a religious faith that would satisfy the orthodox. One doubts that it will be a political doctrine that would satisfy the extreme Marxists. One doubts that it will be any rigid or cramping dogma. One may, in fact, discount in advance such *specific* conclusions as Wolfe may append. The vitality like the values of his work springs from a kind of faith that is more instinctive than intellectual, a vital animating spirit more than a formal philosophy. Wolfe has a natural respect for the possibilities of the human spirit, a natural enthusiasm for life and art, a natural conviction that the story of man is a great story and the telling of it its own glorious justification. However youthful this faith, moreover, it is not blind or shallow. Although he appears incorrigibly romantic, he has a strong sense of fact: his lyrical celebration of America soars from no roseate picture of American life. Although he may disappoint the crusader by failing explicitly to champion the cause of the oppressed, he is aware of the appalling miseries and injustices of this civilization: his whole sensory and creative equipment reached its highest degree of sharpness during the years of the depression, and his vision of American life has been deepened and darkened by the "scenes of suffering, violence, oppression, hunger, cold, and filth and poverty going on unheeded in a world in which the rich were still rotten with their wealth." In general Wolfe is despite his exuberance a naturally somber man who has a strong sense of mortality softened by no notions of divinity—who is to many readers, in fact, a symbol of the especial gloominess of modern fiction. Yet his work remains an impassioned affirmation of life, a lyrical Yea-saying that should invigorate all but those who demand that their flesh or spirit be pure, or who have some specific formula for salvation.

Hence the "controlling idea" that Wolfe settles on will be useful chiefly as it gives more point and pungency to this affirmation, more form, sureness, completeness, and finality to a work of art still too scattered and diffuse. Even in its present amorphous state, however, this work is significant simply because he is not only working on an extremely ambitious project, but working with boundless energy and gusto in the face of the very great difficulties that he himself clearly perceives. His statement of these difficulties in *The Story of a Novel* cuts cleanly through all the distracting side issues, goes straight to the heart of the problem. He dismisses the sentimental assumption of the early crusaders that the American artist stands alone in a land of Puritans and Babbitts, and that the chief condition of his greatness is their slaughter. He goes beyond the more real handicap of the lack of a solid body of tradition. He speaks, "in the concrete terms of the artist's actual experience," of the vast proportions of the physical task confronting the American writer: the task of creating a cosmos from "the enormous space and energy of American life" and discovering a complete language for it. "Out of the billion forms of America, out of the savage violence and the dense complexity of all its swarming life; from the unique and single substance of this land and life of ours, must we draw the power and energy of our own life, the articulation of our speech, the substance of our art."

Such words an American can read without the flush of shame brought by the loud cheers that greet all the loose talk about "American art." With the authority of Wolfe's own work behind them, they describe an art that is genuinely native without being insular or provincial. They encourage the hope that he may write the long-awaited Great American Novel, do for the nation what Walt Whitman attempted but only half succeeded in doing, and what today a hundred regional writers provide only the raw materials for. Yet if he speaks here for the American writer particularly, he defines as well the problem that confronts the responsible artist in all lands: the problem, once more, of reorganizing and revaluating modern experience and creating appropriate forms and symbols for its expression, of pouring into new bottles the ageless wine of great art, of finding in a shifting world "the tongue, the language, and the conscience that as men and artists we have got to have."

"All that I know," Wolfe's publisher and mentor assured him when *Look Homeward, Angel* was about to appear, "is that they cannot let it go, they cannot ignore it. The book will find its way." It was an excellent judgment, if it demanded no unusual prophetic gifts. One feels safe in predicting that Wolfe's subsequent volumes will not be ignored either. Their promise has indeed recently become even more exciting. It at first appeared that his faults were an inseparable element of his peculiar greatness. One heard picturesque anecdotes of manuscripts being sent to him for cutting, and returning with 40,000 additional words. One felt that discipline and restraint were perhaps incompatible with his special quality of zest and abundance, and that one must accept the bad for the sake of the good in the same spirit that one accepted the extravagances of the Elizabethans, of Byron and Hugo, of Dickens and Dostoyevsky. *The Story of a Novel,* however, has been a revelation in its surprisingly dispassionate review of his work. It is the story of a romantic, intense artist, and accordingly it has many all too familiar notes; but it strikes them modestly, temperately, surely, and without the familiar flourishes. One learns that Wolfe not only realizes the need of ruthless condensation but has already cut out tens of thousands of words. It has been for him a monstrously unnatural operation—his soul quivers at the "bloody carnage," the "carnage of so many lovely things"—and he has rescued far too many of his darlings; but he has nevertheless cut, often reducing whole sections to a quarter of their original size. Although one can scarcely hope to see Wolfe emerge from this ordeal as a finished artist in complete command of his immense materials, one can reasonably expect to see him shorn of his shaggier extravagances and looking less like a wild man.

Moreover, the material of his last volumes is of a kind less likely to tempt him to purplish orgies. He has discovered that his whole work falls naturally into two cycles. The first, comprised in the two volumes already published, describes "the period of wandering and hunger in a man's youth"; the second, which will occupy the remaining volumes, is to describe the period of "greater certitude" and is to be "dominated by the unity of a single passion." This announcement has a faintly ominous sound; and certainly Wolfe's enterprise is still fraught with danger. At the same time John Chamberlain can expect to find the "frame of reference" he rightly misses. The lovers of "inescapable form" can expect to find a clearer design, a more beautiful shape. All of us can expect to listen to fewer yawps from Eugene Gant. In general, one can look forward to enjoying the magnificent memories and creations of Thomas Wolfe at less cost of patience and tolerance.

Part Four

CONCLUSION

XXIII

THE CASE FOR THE MODERN NOVEL

I

"WE fight," writes T. S. Eliot, "rather to keep something alive than in the expectation that anything will triumph." Certainly there has been no clear triumph for any one principle or cause in modern literature. Yet much has been kept alive, if under a different appearance, and by artists who do not feel with Eliot that they are vestal virgins tending, in a secluded temple, the sacred flame of culture. Much, too, has been discovered—new worlds opened up and new hopes born. The last word about a literature so often impressive and original is appropriately, I believe, one of respect.

We live in a dim light, and whether of dawn or of twilight our many prophets do not agree; but they are at least agreed that this is a period of transition. I should insist in the first place that it is no mere interlude, and all its vigorous experimentation no mere hubbub in byways and blind alleys. It has discovered fruitful methods and materials, brought into consciousness possibilities of experience hitherto obscurely realized if realized at all. To rehearse all the specific contributions indicated in this study would be tedious; suffice it that one may be confident that if there is a future, its fiction will be greatly indebted to the work of Joyce, Proust, Lawrence, Conrad, Gide, Mann, Dos Passos, and others.

Perhaps most remarkable, however, is the magnitude of much of the work produced by this febrile, supposedly frustrate and sterile age. Working under grave difficulties, modern novelists have nevertheless made themselves conspicuous by the immense scope of their operations. The fiction of Zola, Joyce, Proust, Mann, Romains, and Wolfe would be impressive if only because they have worked on so gigantic a scale; and almost as ambitious is the work of Rolland, Undset, Gorky, Wassermann, Dos Passos, Werfel, and others. Whatever else these writers may be, they are not mediocre, they are not wanting in vitality. All have responded boldly to the challenge of a chaotic age. Though their novels are often diffuse, their art somewhat discouragingly long when time is fleeting, they have a better excuse for diffuseness than do most of the Victorians. Seldom, moreover, do they get lost in cloudy visions. Ordinarily they body out their visions with a wealth of concrete detail, and can be as minute as they can be enormous.

These mighty enterprises are not really surprising. The more socially minded artist, like Thomas Mann, will naturally feel the need of a big subject, in order to create cosmos out of chaos; but even the intensely subjective artist, who shares the sickness of his age and hence suffers from some obscure sense of guilt, will naturally be impelled in the same direction. He must solemnize his stigma, make it the cornerstone of a holy edifice; if he has force or anything like genius, he is likely to move so far in his search of materials, his efforts to order and convince, that his final reference will be much wider than his initial purpose—and perhaps very different. He may, and frequently he does, create a whole world. Proust is only the most striking of the many modern examples of this pious impulse to system as well as form: beginning with an anxious microscopic scrutiny of his private neurosis, he was at the end looking through a telescope, talking through an amplifier of the "universal laws" he had discovered.

Plain as is the fact and serious as are the consequences of the pronounced subjectivity in modern literature, most critics greatly oversimplify this issue. Both social and egocentric impulses are evident in the artist type everywhere and always, and are never in complete harmony—in *Art and Artist* Otto Rank makes a profound study of their interaction through the art of the ages.

The creative impulse is an assertion of self; even when the artist expresses the collective spirit of his society he also expresses his individual will to immortality, and must somehow be in conflict with the collective spirit before he can make it deeply his own. On the other end of the scale, the most subjective artist feels the need to communicate and win social approval; moreover, the creative impulse is an impulse to form, and form is impersonal. Hence the eternal conflict and compromise—"a balance," Rank writes, "which is difficult, impermanent, and in all circumstances painful." It is especially painful today. It has been growing more painful ever since the Renaissance, with the weakening of the collective faith of Christianity, the growth of individualism, the new "religion of genius"; and the pain has within the last century been intensified by the artist's natural opposition to the prevailing technical-scientific ideology and by all the profound discrepancies in his society. But the essential problem is not peculiar to the modern artist.

In Rank's terms, the difficulty of the artist today is that "the old art-ideology is no longer, and the new personality-idea not yet, strong enough" to admit a generally satisfying solution of his age-old dilemma. Even this statement implies, however, too sharp a demarcation and too flat an opposition between the alternatives. Some modern writers, like the proletarians, are definitely returning to a form of the old collective art-ideology, while others, like Proust, cultivate the personality idea for all it is worth; their final references nevertheless overlap and are a blend of the collective-individual. Many writers, however, are attempting to do what Thomas Mann does most consciously, consistently, and comprehensively: effect a reconciliation between the two extremes, fit the individual into some kind of "estimable community." An anarchical individualism is not the natural state of man. As Jean Piaget's study of children reveals, the ideal of cooperation is not something imposed by brute force upon a recalcitrant animal; the very young child judges lies simply by their "size" and immediate tangible consequences, but an interiorized understanding and more successful application of the principles of morality develop naturally, unconsciously, from his relations with his fellows—not because but in spite of parental teaching. And so men, having thrown off the yoke of their spiritual parents and had a holiday from spiritual school, are in diverse ways striving to establish once more a scheme of conformity.

None of these efforts has been entirely successful or satisfying—this is, to repeat, a period of transition, and no one can be sure to what. But the effort remains, and it has resulted in much valuable work. The distress of those readers who perceive only aimlessness, negation, or waste in modern literature is caused chiefly by their nostalgic preference for old symbols and by their inability to recognize their values in new forms, to accommodate themselves—as throughout the history of art men have had to accommodate themselves—to the new terms imposed by a different cultural context. And those, on the other hand, who impatiently reject all solutions but their own fail to see that every statement in art has as logical a counterstatement; for life is an interpenetration of opposites, a complex of forces and manifestations in which no one can be elected as the source and guarantor of all the others, a sliding scale on which high and low depend upon a point of reference arbitrarily chosen—a vast phantasmagoria in which men can know only relatives, never absolutes, and in which the mere fact of existence is as unthinkable as it is unquestionable.

2

Immensity and originality of achievement are of course not to be confused with its quality: they indicate vigor and boldness, but they do not insure value. Despite its staggering scope, *Ulysses,* for example, has serious deficiencies; and so do most of the greater modern novels. This is not an age for wholeness and sureness. But with all its vagaries and uncertainties and contradictions it has nevertheless produced much work of impressive quality. "We would almost accept it as metaphysical evidence for the goodness of a thing," writes Thomas Mann, "if a capital piece of writing were done in its name." At the outset I asked whether modern novelists can satisfy the deeper needs that ancient tragedy served so gloriously. The answer is that the best of them can and do; and I see nothing in the conditions of modern life and knowledge *necessarily* fatal to the essential values of tragedy. The fundamental differences between modern fiction and ancient poetry may be traced to two main sources: the growth of the scientific and realistic spirit, with its predisposition to analysis and its preoccupation with homely, familiar, unheroic life; and the resultant decay of faith, appearing specifically in the loss of belief in a divine scheme and actual immortality, but generally in the corrosion of old idealisms along the whole spiritual front. Both trends have plainly often threatened the tragic spirit. Neither is irreconcilably hostile to it.

That the tragedy of humble lives is superficially less glamorous than the tragedy of royal lives is obvious enough; the downfall of Edipus is more striking than the downfall of Jude Fawley simply because he falls from a greater height. But the proper measure of tragedy is not the estate of its actors nor the momentousness of its issues nor the magnitude of its catastrophe. It is rather the magnitude of the personalities and emotions represented: the celebration of the power of impassioned man to aspire and suffer greatly. Dostoyevsky, Hardy, Hauptmann, Dreiser, O'Neill, Mann, Malraux—none endow their unpretentious heroes with the sheer magnificence of the ancient heroes; but all give them a dignity and force that make them superior to their material circumstances, greater than their fate. All proclaim that man has great possibilities, for both good and evil, and that in the grip of passion he is a grandly compelling figure.

In itself, then, realism has nothing to do with the matter. It is too often confused with its occasional defects: an absorption in the temporal and particular, a failure to supplement documentation and analysis, an identification of material with meaning and of verisimilitude with value. In their eager interest in all forms of reality, too many novelists seem equally and indiscriminately interested in everything, and thus minimize the qualitative differences that are the source of values; too many become engrossed in the trivial, abnormal, or ignoble almost to the exclusion of the experiences that give human life its significance and worth. Yet realism does not necessarily imply a smothering of imagination or a loss of perspective or a surrender of values. Especially as it has been refined and amplified in recent years, it is recognized more clearly for what at bottom it is: not an exciting end in itself but a technique, not a vision of life but a way of projecting a vision.

Hence the crux of the matter is the pessimism of the moderns, their vision itself—the attitudes conditioned by the new knowledge and new ways of life, the values emerging from the terrific onslaught on the unquestioned ideas and ideals of the past. The more obvious consolations of ancient tragedy are clearly not for us. No divinity shapes our ends, no flights of angels sing us to our rest; the specific faiths of the Greeks and the Elizabethans are to us only grandiose illusions, heroic strains from the fading distance. More artists today than in any previous generation suffer from a kind of fear of life. They have the timeless impulse to immortalize, but they cannot believe in an actual immortality or in any divine scheme that would give a transcendent meaning to their work; and if they set about eternalizing the ideal forms of their society, they are still often hag-ridden by the fear that in a shifting world these forms may soon be dissolved, or even swept away in a universal cataclysm. Hence some are simply gnawing at their own vitals, others have fled to the past or sought some secluded sanctuary, and still others have taken to the easy luxury of cynicism—a cynicism that mocks all values and ideals, that considers the world not strange and splendid and terrible but dreary and mean, that finds comfort chiefly in a narcissistic contemplation of its own virility and perspicacity.

Such cynicism, however, is really natural only to the sophomore who has discovered that there is no God. It is not the necessary consequence of pessimism, and it is not the hallmark of modern fiction. Pessimism can mean a bracing challenge—the mere expression of it *is* a challenge. Conceivably it may lead to a strengthening of collective bonds, thus restoring a larger good that today many not-so-rugged individuals obviously feel a need for; shipwrecked men are likely to pool their resources. Conceivably it may fortify the spiritual element in man, which, in the absence of a heavenly scheme, he must cling to all the more tenaciously in order to fulfil his profound immortality-urge. "Is there a pessimism of *strength?*" asked Nietzsche. "An intellectual predilection for what is hard, awful, evil, problematical in existence, owing to well-being, to exuberant health, to *fulness* of existence?" And he gave a triumphant answer in his doctrine of *"highest affirmation,* born of fulness and overfulness, a yea-saying without reserve to suffering's self, to guilt's self, to all that is questionable and strange in existence itself. This final, cheerfulest, exuberantly mad-and-merriest Yea to life is not only the highest insight, it is also the *deepest."*

Few today sing so lusty—and youthful—a goat song. Yet most of the greater modern novelists are united in a faith in human nature and a reverence for its possibilities, a more or less robust acceptance of life on its own terms and within this earthly sphere. They are in varying degrees bewildered, dismayed, appalled; they have nevertheless wrenched from a seemingly unethical universe some form of idealism that outlives death. This idealism is plain enough in relatively old-fashioned writers like Hardy, Conrad, Galsworthy, Bennett, Wassermann, and Mann; but in a different guise it is no less plain in more recent writers like O'Neill, Werfel, Wolfe, Malraux, Sholokhov, and many of the proletarian novelists, and it appears even in such sophisticates as Hemingway and Huxley. Whether their faith is invested in some specific cause, like the building of a new society, or in the simple virtues and ideals that grace and dignify human life in any society, they have pointed to some larger good that makes life more than a poor sordid prelude to death. They have rooted their art in humanistic values that are essentially the values of most great writers of the past. They have, in short, achieved a catharsis.

Potentially, indeed, a robust pessimism can provide an esthetic experience still richer than that of ancient tragedy. One may reasonably object to the religious consolations of the Greeks and to the obvious compensations at least suggested by Shakespeare—to the introduction of all such notions as the punishment of Evil, the hope of Heaven, the vindication of divine Justice or Rationality. These comforts not only expose the whole experience to the assault of critical intellect and thus make for a less stable composure; they restrict the experience itself by simplifying the emotions to be ordered. If they are not actually distracting, they are at least too easy, and suggest the obvious subterfuges and crude responses of ordinary men. Milton's *Samson Agonistes* is the clearest example of the loss resulting from a too explicit reconciliation with suffering, a too complete confidence in divine justice; his triumph is too absolute, his "Nothing is here for tears" too literally true, and so he misses the deepest tragic effect. We have today no poet of Milton's stature—few ages do; but if we had, such a poet could conceivably achieve a harmony still richer and subtler, a composure still more stable, a synthesis still more comprehensive. Shakespeare is the greatest tragic poet of the past if only because he made fewer compromises with grim reality and reconciled more of the opposing elements of experience.

Some will protest that it is impossible for man to endure a life stripped bare of illusion. This issue is unreal. As man can never attain complete knowledge or absolute truth, he has always to make metaphorical assumptions, state arbitrary preferences; and he can be trusted to poetize these new "illusions" as he did the old. If the immensities that science is now dealing with make a chill substitute for the gods, he can still have faith in his own potentialities, still employ such metaphors as Nietzsche's "tragic dignity" of history, still idealize the immediate possibilities offered by his amazing technological resources and the remote possibilities suggested by evolution. Here, indeed, is the problem actually confronting the contemporary artist: the problem of integrating the values of humanism with scientific knowledge, relating them more concretely to the scheme of modern life, harmonizing the discrepancies within himself. It is an exceedingly difficult problem, and still far from solution. It is, in fact, impossible of wholly satisfactory solution, except in Utopia. But throughout their history men have managed to live this side of Utopia.

Although in the face of the immediate and very grave difficulties confronting the modern world these may seem absurdly simple or abstract terms to summarize in, they are nevertheless fundamental in art, and even underlie the concrete problems in political economics. All larger purposes are rooted in some philosophy, however unconscious. From any point of view, however, to refer to this as simply a devaluated age is to miss its most significant activity. The processes of devaluation are still in full swing, and causing much anguish; but more vigorous today are the processes of *revaluation*—the widespread efforts to reconcile, synthesize, and simplify. With these in mind one can better appreciate the significance and possible value of seemingly remote or anarchical writers like Proust, Lawrence, and Gide. One can also better understand the susceptibility of this knowing age to quacks of all kinds, and such phenomena, in the so-called practical world, as Hitlerism. One can scarcely count all these developments a clear gain. Yet at least the decay of old faiths has not resulted in the dispirited, dismal surrender that some critics still consider its inevitable consequence. In the face of a universe that they now consider soulless, purposeless, most writers still cling to the essential faith of high tragedy. "I'll tell you what the world's like," says the hero of Robinson Jeffers' *Thurso's Landing:*

> Like a stone for no reason falling in the night from a cliff in the hills, that makes a lonely
> Noise and a spark in the hollow darkness, and nobody sees and nobody cares. There's nothing good in it
> Except the courage in us not to be beaten.

But such courage he has; and to this melancholy comment on human destiny Jeffers adds this comment on human nature:

> It is rather ignoble in its quiet times, mean in its pleasures,
> Slavish in the mass; but at stricken moments it can shine
> terribly against the dark magnificence of things.

In these words of the most somber and violent of modern poets is still the source of the ideal tragic pleasure.

3

Under the most auspicious conditions, prophecy is a dangerous business. I am not one of "God's spies"; I do not know what the novel of the future is going to be like, and I do not propose to indulge in wishful speculation. All I should venture confidently is the innocuous statement that all kinds of novels will be written—as they are today, when one can match every type written in the past. Clearly, in view of the freedom and scope of the form itself, and the variety in indubitably great fiction, one must admit the validity of different ways of writing and cannot prescribe for the genius yet unborn. Maupassant, who as a critic performed that most unusual feat of recognizing the obvious, declared that since an exact view of life is impossible, the most conscientious scientific realist is only an "illusionist." The novelist communicates his personal vision, which is colored by his experience and temperament—the thousand distinguishing differences in perception that separate the wisest and most clear-sighted of men; the great artists are accordingly "those who impose on humanity their particular illusion." Only the most invincibly illusioned of the present will predict the illusions of the future.

At the same time, one can make out strong drifts in the fiction of this century, and so hazard broad guesses. Thus naturalism in the strict sense—or any kind of realism based on a mechanistic, materialistic philosophy—appears to be on the decline, despite its recent impetus from the proletarian writers. The latest developments in the physical sciences are undermining its basis, psychology and the social sciences are tending to question or discard its assumptions, the weight of the best critical thought and creative practice is against it—and there is always the plain objection that it does not serve the deepest needs of man. The realistic method will no doubt continue in use, but more as it has been modified or supplemented by Conrad, Lawrence, Joyce, Proust, Gide, Mann, Dos Passos, Wolfe, and indeed the great majority of the important novelists of today; drama seems likely to swing still further in the direction of expressionism, symbolism, or poetry. Although a great deal of novel or shocking fact and theory remains to be exploited, and spurious history, science, or economics will always masquerade as fiction, it is unthinkable that great atists could indefinitely content themselves with an activity so foreign to their fundamental impulses—Zola himself grew discontent. In general I believe that there is likely to be more emphasis upon the oldest emotional needs rather than the latest intellectual interests, upon the broadly humanistic rather than the merely scientific—upon the basic elements of experience that have been slighted in the scientific rationale and industrial organization of this age. It is significant, once more, that disciples are now proclaiming that Marx was essentially a humanist, and recommending Communism as the most practicable method of incorporating humanistic values in the structure of society.

Hence only superficially inconsistent is another, more pronounced and definable tendency: the growth of a strong feeling of social responsibility, and the subordination of the individual. Hardy, Ibsen, Gissing, Wells, Shaw, and other early students of social problems were interested primarily in superior or unusual individuals who suffered from the rigid conventions or manifest inequities of the social scheme; Society was typically the villain of the piece. Many contemporary novelists and dramatists are interested rather in the whole group, or a large class within the group, and introduce the individual primarily as the symbol or agent of a much greater drama. This attitude dominates the literature of Russia today, and is gathering strength in France, America, and even England. Many critics accordingly believe that the age of individualism is passing, and that Society and its welfare will presently replace the Individual and his destiny as the ruling concept of creative literature. This is a plausible forecast. In modern society, with its immensely intricate interrelationships, the individual has much less independence than he had in the relatively simple, predominantly agricultural society of the past; whatever his political freedom and economic opportunities, his material and spiritual welfare is tied up more closely and obviously with that of the group. Wars and depressions are like science and art now cosmopolitan: a strike in a Southern mill town has repercussions in Europe, a civil war in Spain makes the whole world grave and fearful. Neither individuals nor nations can solve their problems or settle their differences in their private backyards. Naturally, then, the artist is likely to concern himself directly with the forces that so vitally and manifestly condition his experience, and that at the present moment threaten his very existence.

Some good humanists seem troubled by this socializing of literature. Their anguish is futile. If this is the drift, no mere critic can stop it; literature is inevitably an expression of the time-spirit, a reflection of what life has come to mean and be, and the large forces that shape a whole civilization are beyond the control of dictators in the literary as in the political world. But their anguish is unnecessary as well. The subordination of the individual would in fact be a return to former conditions of literary greatness. The long age of individualism has after all occupied but a few centuries, a brief hour in the history of civilization; the great bulk of the world's art—primitive, Hebrew, classical, Oriental, and early Christian, down through the age of chivalry until the full flower of the Renaissance—has been inspired and governed by a strong collective ideology. Moreover, the rise of the Society-concept need not mean the scrapping of the whole tradition of individualism. Fiction will inevitably present individuals; the artist is himself an assertive individual never in complete sympathy with the collective spirit; and even apart from the certain continuance of idiosyncratic and unorthodox work, of swirls and eddies within the main stream of art and of currents separate from it, one can expect to find this main stream carrying much of the achievement of recent centuries. One can imagine, indeed, a great art, incorporating the best elements of the tradition of individualism and having also a social resonance that modern literature too often lacks. In any event the humanist will still have his place, and plenty of work to do. At present he has before him a rank growth of social fiction in which the individual is often a mere economic fraction, without inwardness or spiritual potentiality, who hardly seems worth the fuss being made over his numerator. In an age dominated by the Society-concept the critic's function would be to refine the social ideals and keep them worthy of living and dying for, to ensure that they engage the best of the individual's personality and permit a full, harmonious development of his possibilities, in general to align them with the values of a humanistic culture. If humanism rose with *laissez faire,* it need not fall with it.

There remain, finally, the common fears that the machine, and the materialism and regimentation of a scientific, machine civilization, are killing the Poet in man, developing a race of robots. Such fears, however, are simply an extension of the old pathetic fallacy. The ugly consequences of this kind of civilization are plain and depressing enough—our machinery often seems but an immense amplifier for all the banality, vulgarity, and downright infamy of which the human animal is capable. But culture has never meant universal sweetness and constant light; the citizenry of all ages has preferred mediocrity to genius. The growth of culture, moreover, has not been a steady refinement; many of its signs have been unprepossessing in themselves—the custom of human sacrifice, for example, embodies spiritual concepts beyond the reach of the most primitive men, and is viewed by anthropologists as a sign of incipient civilization. And civilization today presents such a multiplicity of aspects, such a welter of symptoms, that one can easily set any argument on its head. Thus Kenneth Burke remarks that this so materialistic society has constructed the most elaborate system of abstractions that man has ever known, and from this point of view may be considered not materialistic enough. We live in a world of paper money, stocks and bonds, bookkeeping figures, statistics—a "great plethora of symbolizations"; we look down on the man who actually gets his hands on his work. The manipulation of such huge, complicated symbols as factories and corporations is in itself a kind of poetry, an exercise of creative imagination; and many artists are more specifically poetizing the forms of modern civilization.

Inevitably men do so. "The remotest discoveries of the chemist, the botanist, or mineralogist," Wordsworth wrote, "will be as proper objects of the poet's art as any upon which it can be employed, if the time should ever come when these things shall be familiar to us, and the relations under which they are contemplated by the followers of these respective sciences shall be manifestly and palpably material to us as enjoying and suffering beings." Though one may prefer a feudal castle to a skyscraper, an eagle to an airplane, the older symbols are not *intrinsically* more poetic. The sources of inspiration, the objects of dream and desire, change through the centuries; the creative impulse itself, the will to form and the needs it serves, is invincible to change. Critics are constantly confusing appearances with essences, means with ends. And they are constantly assuming that current attitudes are an inevitable and permanent consequence of science and industrialism.

I may appear to be romping too blithely through very grave issues and dismissing too airily very grave objections. Certainly I do not wish to minimize the difficulties that beset the modern artist, or to scout the various forms of sterility and futility into which he is often diverted; and over all discussion of culture today falls the shadow of impending war. But what leads me to discount the unhealthy developments in modern literature and the gloomy estimates of its future is not merely the appearance of more promising developments and estimates. It is finally the immutability of human nature itself. I fall back, in short, on a platitude. Life remains as dramatic as ever, and its drama as spectacular. Those who pronounce poetry dead and tragedy dead and fiction already moribund set too much store by merely intellectual convictions, too little by the instinctive procreative processes of life itself. They forget that all the new thoughts and gadgets of man have not altered his physiological structure and biological function, or the basic patterns of his experience. For though it casts something of a blight on this or any other discussion of ideas, the simple truth is that men do not live by their ideas as much as they like to think.

"Why," asks Hauptmann's Michael Kramer, "why do we cry our cries of joy into the immense incertitude—we mites abandoned in the infinite?" Why, indeed. But men do—and will continue to cry their cries in whatever kind of society they fashion. They will continue to aspire and suffer and wonder, to no more reasonable end. They will continue to make metaphors, and create forms, and shroud "with a veil of beauty the vulgar horror of actual fact."

BIBLIOGRAPHICAL NOTE

An exhaustive bibliography is unnecessary in a work not aiming at exhaustiveness, and is at any rate impossible. One could scarcely begin to list the works valuable for anyone interested in a thorough study of a study so broad and many-sided; my own first feeling of pride in the comprehensiveness of my materials is immediately swallowed by the thought of all I have not read and am ignorant of. In my text, moreover, I have referred to most of the writers who have contributed appreciably to either the general critical background of this study or the analyses of individual novelists.

It might be helpful, however, to list a few works dealing specifically with the modern novel. The many suggestive studies of technique, notably those by James, Lubbock, Muir, Forster, and Ford, do not properly belong here; but I should mention Joseph Warren Beach's *The Twentieth Century Novel* (1932) as not only the most comprehensive of them but a work invaluable to students of modern fiction from whatever point of view. Among the better general studies are *The Modern Novel,* by Wilson Follett (1918); *Contemporary American Novelists,* by Carl Van Doren (1922); *The Modern English Novel,* by Abel Chevalley (1921; American edition 1925); *The Modern Novel,* by Elizabeth A. Drew (1926); and the later chapters of *The History of the Novel in England,* by Robert Morss Lovett and Helen Sard Hughes (1932).

Among the more stimulating specialized studies are *Transitions,* by Edwin Muir (1926); *The Later Realism,* by Walter L. Myers (1927); *Axel's Castle,* by Edmund Wilson (1931), particularly the brilliant introductory chapter and the chapters on Joyce and Proust; and *Messages,* by Ramon Fernandez (1927), particularly the acute discussions of Conrad and Proust. Finally, mention should be made again of the more illuminating discussions by the novelists themselves, as in the letters of Flaubert and Lawrence, the Journals of Hardy, Gide, and Bennett, Zola's *The Experimental Novel,* Virginia Woolf's essays in *The Common Reader,* Ford Madox Ford's memoir of Conrad, and the essays of Thomas Mann.

INDEX

The following index contains, besides references to individual writers and works, a number of important general terms—such as Symbolism, Communism, and Impressionism—that are not adequately indicated by either the Table of Contents or the names of individuals.